Springer Series in Cognitive Development

Series Editor
Charles J. Brainerd

Springer Series in Cognitive Development

Series Editor: Charles J. Brainerd

Basic Processes in Memory Development
Progress in Cognitive Development Research

Edited by
Charles J. Brainerd and Michael Pressley

Springer-Verlag
New York Berlin Heidelberg Tokyo

Charles J. Brainerd
Department of Psychology
University of Alberta
Edmonton, Alberta
Canada T6G 2E9

Michael Pressley
Department of Psychology
University of Western Ontario
London, Ontario
Canada N6A 5C2

Series Editor: Charles J. Brainerd

With 12 Figures

Library of Congress Cataloging in Publication Data
Main entry under title:
Basic processes in memory development.
    (Springer series in cognitive development)
    Companion vol. to: Cognitive learning and memory in children.
    1. Memory in children—Addresses, essays, lectures. 2. Memory—Addresses, essays, lectures. I. Brainerd, Charles J. II. Pressley, Michael. III. Series.
BF723.M4B36   1985   155.4′13   84-24691

Typeset by Ampersand Publisher Services, Inc., Rutland, Vermont.
Printed and bound by R.R. Donnelley and Sons, Harrisonburg, Virginia.
Printed in the United States of America.

9 8 7 6 5 4 3 2 1

ISBN 0-387-96064-3 Springer-Verlag New York Berlin Heidelberg Tokyo
ISBN 3-540-96064-3 Springer-Verlag Berlin Heidelberg New York Tokyo

Series Preface

For some time now, the study of cognitive development has been far and away the most active discipline within developmental psychology. Although there would be much disagreement as to the exact proportion of papers published in developmental journals that could be considered cognitive, 50% seems like a conservative estimate. Hence, a series of scholarly books devoted to work in cognitive development is especially appropriate at this time.

The *Springer Series in Cognitive Development* contains two basic types of books, namely, edited collections of original chapters by several authors, and original volumes written by one author or a small group of authors. The flagship for the Springer Series is a serial publication of the "advances" type, carrying the subtitle *Progress in Cognitive Development Research*. Each volume in the *Progress* sequence is strongly thematic, in that it is limited to some well-defined domain of cognitive-developmental research (e.g., logical and mathematical development, development of learning). All *Progress* volumes will be edited collections. Editors of such collections, upon consultation with the Series Editor, may elect to have their books published either as contributions to the *Progress* sequence or as separate volumes. All books written by one author or a small group of authors are being published as separate volumes within the series.

A fairly broad definition of cognitive development is being used in the selection of books for this series. The classic topics of concept development, children's thinking and reasoning, the development of learning, language development, and memory development will, of course, be included. So, however, will newer areas such as social-cognitive development, educational applications, formal modeling, and philosophical implications of cognitive-developmental theory. Although it is anticipated that most books in the series will be empirical in orientation, theoretical and philosophical works are also welcome. With books of the latter sort, heterogeneity of theoretical perspective is encouraged, and no attempt will be made to foster some specific theoretical perspective at the expense of others (e.g., Piagetian versus behavioral or behavioral versus information processing).

C.J. Brainerd

Preface

This is the seventh volume in the *Progress in Cognitive Development* sequence. It is part of a two-volume treatment of research on memory development. Its companion volume is *Cognitive Learning and Memory in Children*.

The study of memory or, as it used to be called, verbal learning has been one of the cornerstones of experimental psychology since Ebbinhaus' time. The systematic study of memory development, however, is a contemporary phenomenon, with most studies having appeared within the present decade. It is true, of course, that certain child-memory measures, such as digit span, have always been incorporated in Binet-type intelligence tests. But as recently as 1964, Keppel drew attention to the scarcity of memory-development research in a review article that was published in *Psychological Bulletin*. In fact, Keppel's first sentence contained the statement that "subjects in experiments on verbal learning have been preponderantly the college sophomore, with only an occasional experiment reported in which younger or older subjects were employed." Keppel went on to observe that during the period covered by his review (1940–1964), virtually no developmental research had been reported with such redoubtable memory paradigms as serial learning, free recall, and long-term retention. Subsequent reviews of the early literature appeared in a 1968 article in the *Bulletin* by Goulet and in Reese and Lipsitt's classic textbook *Experimental Child Psychology* (1970). Although these reviewers painted a more rosy picture of memory-development research, they agreed that the extant data on most standard paradigms were very thin.

It seems, at least in retrospect, that the major reason for the lack of interest in memory development was the widespread opinion that such studies were of marginal theoretical significance. In those days, general learning theory was popular. Workers were inclined to assume that the laws of memory must be the same for all ages and that, consequently, developmental studies were of little more than descriptive value. This prevailing view was summarized as early as 1952 in Deese's textbook *Psychology of Learning*: "Certainly there is very little novel or new information which comes out of this research." Keppel stated a similar opinion in his review: "The developmental study, per se, is probably of little value to the verbal-learning theorist unless differential results are to be expected by theory." This opinion was, however, more a consequence of the fact that then-current theories (e.g., general learning theory) made no provision for developmental variables than it was a consequence of the intrinsic triviality of developmental research. Indeed, investigators were exhorted to formulate uniquely developmental theories in Keppel's review.

During the 1970s, an extensive literature on memory development in infants, children, and the aged began to accumulate. To many of us, this trend first became unmistakable at the 1975 meetings of the Society for Research in Child Development in Denver. Whereas reports of memory research had previously been limited to occasional papers and symposia, such reports occupied a solid chunk of the 1975 program. By 1977, the first "advances" volume in the area, Kail and Hagen's *Perspectives on the Development of Memory and Cognition,* had been published. Today, memory-development articles are a routine feature of most issues of developmental journals. Importantly, developmental articles now appear regularly in the mainstream adult-memory journals. Judging from its cumulative impact, we doubt that very many contemporary researchers, whether experimentalist or developmentalist, would claim that "very little novel or new information" accrues from such work or that the findings of developmental studies are "probably of little value" to memory theorists.

The literature has now become so extensive as to pose serious problems of selection and organization for reviewers and editors. As we surveyed this literature, we concluded that a case can be made to the effect that most current work tends to fall into one or the other of two broad categories: research on basic memory-development processes and research on the more cognitive aspects of memory development. Roughly speaking, the first category includes studies that are designed to illuminate fundamental dimensions of memory development (e.g., encoding, retrieval), to formulate or test basic theoretical principles, and to deal with measurement questions. Research in the second category, on the other hand, focuses on such issues as the more complex forms of memory (e.g., consciously imposed strategies), the use of memory concepts to explicate cognitive development, and the use of memory concepts in applied contexts (e.g., the psychology of instruction). The coverage in this volume is restricted to the first category. Work in the second category forms the subject matter of the companion volume.

The "basic processes" on which contributions appear in this book are retrieval development, encoding development, the development of organization in long-term memory, the relative contributions of storage and retrieval factors to memory development, the measurement of processing time in memory development, the development of short-term memory, and methodological issues in the study of memory changes within aged populations. In Chapter 1, Ackerman examines theory and

research concerned with the presumed retrieval deficits that children show on traditional long-term memory tasks. He also reviews findings from a program of
research that seeks to test various theories of retrieval deficit. Ackerman argues that
some influential adult models of retrieval (encoding specificity and generate–recognize) are inadequate to account for developmental data, and he proposes a new
interpretation based on the notion of the ability of a cue to "describe" information
that is stored in memory. In Chapter 2, Anooshian and Siegel consider current work
on children's encoding of spatial information, especially the sort of naturalistic
spatial encoding that is usually called cognitive mapping. They discuss a variety
of ways in which the representation of cognitive maps might properly be said to
develop. They formulate eight propositions that are intended to describe both the
state of the art in cognitive mapping research and the nature of development in this
area.

Age change in measures of organization in long-term memory is one of the most
extensively researched topics in the memory-development literature. That such
organization increases with age seems obvious enough from the fact that scores on
measures of so-called secondary organization (e.g., subjective organization in free
recall of unrelated items, category clustering in free recall of categorized lists)
increase during childhood and adolescence. The most common explanation has been
that the development of deliberate, effortful organizational strategies, especially
strategies that are imposed at the time of encoding, is responsible. However, Bjorklund argues in Chapter 3 that organization is largely an automatic process and,
consequently, that the development of organization is the result of age changes in
automatic rather than strategic processes. In particular, Bjorklund maintains that
developmental differences in the structure of semantic memory are more important
than developmental differences in the use of organizational strategies. In Chapter
4, Brainerd discusses the problem of how to factor the relative contributions to
memory development of variables that are responsible for getting traces into memory
(storage) and variables that are responsible for getting them out again (retrieval).
It is suggested that previous failures to resolve this problem are consequences of
the fact that it has been treated as a problem in experimental design when, actually,
it is a problem in measurement theory that requires the formulation of explicit
mathematical models of storage and retrieval. Recent model-based techniques for
disentangling storage and retrieval development are reviewed along with their respective data bases. Among other things, experimental applications of these models
point to an early "storage sensitive" period of development during the preschool
and early elementary school years, followed by a "retrieval sensitive" period during
later elementary school and adolescence.

In Chapter 5, Dempster surveys the state of our knowledge about the development
of short-term memory. Current substantive issues in this literature are summarized
with special reference to influential theories of short-term memory and to paradigms
that purport to measure short-term memory. Attention is also given to the currently
controversial question of whether the development of short-term memory is inti-
mately involved in the development of higher cognition. In Chapter 6, Kail analyzes
some of the uses of temporal measures of memory in the study of memory devel-

opment. Historically, investigators have studied memory tasks on which children show high rates of error (e.g., recall of unrelated lists of words). There are many other tasks, however, on which virtually errorless performance can be expected from even very young children, the most familiar examples being paradigms that focus narrowly on the retrieval of some simple fact or procedure from long-term memory (e.g., numeral comparison, sentence verification). Kail points out that, relatively speaking, such tasks have been neglected in memory-development re-search, and he discusses ways in which response time measures can be used to elucidate development in these situations. Kail also reviews evidence bearing on life-span curves for response-time data.

Finally, in Chapter 7, Salthouse and Kausler probe a literature that has been fraught with methodological and measurement problems, the literature on memory development during late adulthood. Their analysis is organized around questions of the internal and external validity of memory research with aged subjects. Salthouse and Kausler focus on specific dilemmas in such research (e.g., control and iden-tification of subject characteristics), and they present possible paths to solution. They conclude that while a variety of methodological problems threatens the internal validity of most gerontological memory research, there are grounds for optimism when it comes to the generalizability of such research to everyday remembering (external validity).

Charles J. Brainerd
Michael Pressley

Contents

Contributors

Brian P. Ackerman   Department of Psychology, University of Delaware, Newark, Delaware 19711, U.S.A.

Linda J. Anooshian   Department of Psychology, Trinity University, San Antonio, Texas 78284, U.S.A.

David F. Bjorklund   Department of Psychology, Florida Atlantic University, Boca Raton, Florida 33431, U.S.A.

Charles J. Brainerd   Department of Psychology, University of Alberta, Edmonton, Alberta T6G 2E9, Canada

Frank N. Dempster   College of Education, University of Nevada—Las Vegas, Nevada 89154, U.S.A.

Robert Kail   Department of Psychological Sciences, Purdue University, West Lafayette, Indiana 47907, U.S.A.

Donald H. Kausler   Department of Psychology, University of Missouri, Columbia, Missouri 65211, U.S.A.

Timothy A. Salthouse   Department of Psychology, University of Missouri, Columbia, Missouri 65211, U.S.A.

Alexander W. Siegel   Department of Psychology, University of Houston, Houston, Texas 77004, U.S.A.

1. Children's Retrieval Deficit

Brian P. Ackerman

How is episodic information retrieved from memory? According to Tulving (1976) and others (cf. Reddy & Bellezza, 1983; Watkins, 1979), the retrieval process involves the contact of a cue with event information in memory. All successful retrieval is cued. The problem for young children is that they may not use retrieval cues effectively, and so many suffer from a retrieval deficit (cf. Brainerd, Howe, Kingma, & Brainerd, 1984; Chechile & Richman, 1982; Emmerich & Ackerman, 1978). In the present chapter, I explore the nature of children's retrieval deficit. The focus is generally on retrieval from permanent memory rather the short-term memory retrieval discussed by Dempster in Chapter 6.

I begin by describing the generate-recognize and encoding specificity explanations of children's retrieval failures. The limitations of these models motivate the presentation of a third view of the deficit in the second section. In this view retrieval failures are attributed to deficiencies in the power of cues to "describe" information in memory (cf. Norman & Bobrow, 1979). The third section concerns research that supports the "Descriptions" framework; while the fourth section concerns constraints on children's use of cues. I conclude the chapter with a general discussion of children's retrieval deficit.

Current Accounts of Children's Retrieval Deficit

Although many theorists agree that children differ from adults in retrieval processes (cf. Brainerd et al., 1984; Kobasigawa, 1977; Perlmutter & Lange,

1978; Sophian & Hagen, 1978), relatively little is known about the nature of children's retrieval deficit. Most theorists have settled for general descriptions of developmental memory differences attributed, loosely, to retrieval processes, in lieu of finding encoding differences. The focus of only a few studies has been on retrieval processes per se (cf., Ackerman, 1982; 1983; Emmerich & Ackerman, 1978; Hall, Murphy, Humphreys, & Wilson, 1979; Kobasigawa, 1974). Further, explanations of the deficit vary with the theoretical model of retrieval processes. I describe two major models below, along with their developmental limitations.

The Generate-Recognize Theory

The generate-recognize two-stage theory of recall underlies most of the major recent reviews of children's retrieval deficits (cf. Kobasigawa, 1977; Perlmutter & Lange, 1978; Myers & Perlmutter, 1978), and, to this extent, dominates developmental approaches to retrieval processes. The theory and its origins are described first below, followed by a brief discussion of the supporting and conflicting evidence and an extended discussion of the limitations of the theory for conceptualizing children's retrieval deficit.

The generate-recognize theory is based on the distinction between generation and recognition as two independent stages of recall (cf. Watkins & Gardiner, 1979). Generation concerns the access to and search of a structural or associative network in memory. The network represents the associative relations among stimuli, or the organizational structure imposed on stimuli, at acquisition encoding. Access to this network concerns the use of cues at retrieval that represent the organizational structure in some way, such as a superordinate term for retrieval of category members, and so ensure contact with that structure in memory. Search concerns the use of the structure to generate candidates for retrieval output. Recognition concerns the decision made about these candidates.

The generate-recognize theory evolved from the two process theory of recognition and free recall (cf. Kintsch, 1970a, 1970b). In this theory recognition and free recall represent different retention processes, each with unique features. In recognition, an item is presented for a recognition decision that is a sensory copy of the item stored in memory. Call the latter a "trace." How the item is stored in memory is a matter of some dispute (cf. Anderson & Bower, 1972, 1974; Martin, 1975), but most theorists conceptualize the trace as a "tagged" or activated node in an associative network. The decision involves an automatic match of the copy with its trace representation in memory and a judgment about the "familiarity," "newness," or "response strength" (cf. Kintsch, 1970b; Mandler, 1979; Tulving & Bower, 1974) of the trace. If the strength satisfies some criterion, the copy is recognized. In contrast, in free recall, a sensory copy is not presented to the memory system and so the item trace must be generated or "retrieved" from memory. Retrieval involves searching from one trace to another by means of interitem associative relations.

The generate-recognize theory of recall represents a combination of these two processes, plus one additional assumption—that the retrieval search mechanism sometimes generates candidates for recall that are not the desired target item, and these candidates have to be edited in some way. That is, generation may occur without recall output. If so, some decision mechanism must operate in free recall that evaluates the familiarity or strength of the candidate. Since the same decision process occurs in recognition, recognitory processes must be part of free recall.

Supporting Evidence. Tests of the generate-recognize theory have concerned five key assumptions of the theory (cf. Watkins & Gardiner, 1979). The first is that the information in a stimulus item is encoded in an all-or-none unitary fashion, and, the resulting memory trace in a copy of the input stimulus. Second, recognition involves decisions about nominal re-presentations of the stimulus item. As a consequence, recognition tasks do not require active retrieval or search processes, and recognition performance can serve as a measure of the availability (cf. Tulving & Pearlstone, 1966) of the item in memory. Third, generation concerns the search of interitem relations or associative structures in memory, available preexperimentally or formed during acquisition.

Fourth, since recall presupposes successful recognition, recognition should always exceed recall memory, and items should never be recalled but not recognized. Fifth, if recall and recognition are different in some way (i.e., retrieval), recall and recognition task performance also should differ, for at least some variables.

Supporting evidence for the theory in the adult literature is discussed extensively elsewhere (cf. Brown, 1976; Kintsch, 1970b; Tulving, 1976; Watkins & Gardiner, 1979), and so it is described only briefly here. The bulk of the evidence concerns the last three assumptions. For example, concerning the third assumption, organizational theorists (cf. Bower, 1970; Mandler, 1967; Tulving, 1962) have shown repeatedly that associating stimuli at input affects free recall. Concerning the fourth assumption, the superiority of recognition over recall is one of the most consistent findings in the memory literature (cf. Kintsch, 1970a, 1970b). Finally, concerning the fifth assumption, Kintsch (1970a, 1970b) and Tulving (1976) review evidence that recognition and recall task performance vary differently with the relatedness (cf. Bruce & Fagan, 1970) and familiarity (cf. Dale, 1966) of word input stimuli and with other factors as well.

Similar support for assumptions three and four in the developmental literature has been reviewed by Brown (1975), Kobasigawa (1977), Lange (1978), Moely (1977), and others. In addition, a developmental implication of assumptions two and three combined concerning retrieval also has been tested. The implication is that recognition and recall patterns should vary developmentally. That is, age should interact with kind of memory test. Given that a stimulus is known and identified, recognition performance should be age-invariant. The same nominal information is encoded by all, and is re-presented to all at test. Recall, however, should vary developmentally. The variation could occur either because young children do not search memory structures effectively, or do not employ the active, strategic encoding processes that relate or organize stimuli in acquisition (cf. Brown, 1975), or because of changes in automatic memory processes (see Chapter 3 by Bjorklund).

The results of many studies are consistent with the predicted age × memory test interaction. For example, Perlmutter and Lange (1978) marshal evidence that developmental changes are minimal in recognition tasks. They argue that the few exceptions to this trend may have occurred either because the children were not as familiar with the stimulus events as the adults, or because children used different recognition decision criteria. In contrast, abundant evidence exists that recall varies developmentally (cf. Brown, 1975; Lange, 1978; Moely, 1977).

Conflicting Evidence. The conflicting evidence in the adult literature addresses each of the five assumptions. The first and second assumptions are vulnerable to demonstrations of stimulus sampling (cf. Bower, 1967; Estes, 1959) and sampling variability (cf. Melton, 1970) at encoding. For example, Estes and Bower and others have suggested that only selected aspects of the information in a nominal stimulus item may be encoded, for any one context, and this sampling may vary over repeated encodings of the same nominal item in different contexts. Similarly, Craik and Jacoby (1979; Jacoby & Craik, 1979; Jacoby, Craik, & Begg, 1979) have shown that the information in a stimulus item may be elaborated to various extents at encoding depending on the encoding context, affecting both recall and recognition. These findings indicate that the encoding of stimulus information is not unitary, or all-or-none, and the memory trace is not a copy (i.e., "tagged node") of the nominal item—the first assumption. Instead, the trace represents the *functional* "event" (cf. Thomson & Tulving, 1970; Tulving, 1983). In addition, if only selected aspects of event information are sampled in a particular encoding context, nominal re-presentation of the item may not be a sufficient basis for a recognition decision—the second assumption. Instead, as shown by Tulving (cf. Thomson & Tulving, 1970; Tulving & Thomson, 1973; Watkins & Tulving, 1975), recognition may vary with the context of the re-presentation of the item. Recognition, too, may require retrieval processes (cf. Mandler, 1979; Tulving, 1982) and also may show the effects of interitem organizational processes (cf. Neely & Balota, 1981), primarily in attempts to retrieve the encoding context.

The third, fourth, and fifth assumptions are vitiated by the same evidence, but in a slightly different way. For example, the finding of retrieval effects in recognition shows that generative search processes are not restricted to recall, weakening the argument for two independent, and different, stages in recall. Tulving (1976) also makes the argument against a two-stage recall model that there is little logical or empirical evidence that incorrect recall candidates are generated but not recalled. If the recognition stage indeed performs no recall editing function, there is little need to postulate the stage.

Even more to the point of the third assumption, Tulving (1976; Watkins & Tulving, 1975) argues that context effects in recognition and recall show that remembering involves more that activation of preexperimental interitem relations in memory, and indeed that the trace of the stimulus event episode is retained independent of these associative relations. The reason is that the encoding context may bias aspects of the stimulus item that do not reflect preexperimental interitem associations and so cannot be retrieved by means of a search of such associations. Context effects thus partly motivate Tulving's (1972; Watkins & Tulving, 1975) distinction between episodic and semantic memory.

Context effects also are evidence that successful recall often may occur without retrieval search of interitem associations. Cued recall may be a prototypical example. The generate-recognize theory fails to account for many cueing effects, primarily because the theory was developed to account for performance differences in free recall and "standard" recognition tasks (cf. Tulving & Bower, 1974). Tulving (1983), in particular, argues that the concept of "search" is empty because it presupposes a searcher knows what he wants, or can identify what he wants, before he finds the "desired" information. This begs the issue of retrieval, since in some real sense, the desired item is retrieved before the retrieval operation takes place.

Similarly, context effects are useful in showing that a stimulus event can be recalled in some task contexts, but not recognized. This is not possible according to the fourth assumption. Tulving and his associates (cf. Flexser & Tulving, 1978) have provided a lot of evidence documenting the phenomenon of recognition failure of recallable words. Finally, the demonstrations of dissociated recognition and recall effects, the fifth assumption, also can be explained by context effects at acquisition and test (cf. Tulving, 1976), at least in part.

Recent work in the developmental literature also supports the idea that stimulus information is sampled at acquisition, in conflict with the first assumption. For example, Ackerman (1981, 1984a; Ackerman & Rust-Kahl, 1982), Ghatala, Carbonari, and Wylie (1980) and other investigators using orienting tasks (cf. Geis & Hall, 1976, 1978; Owings & Baumeister, 1979) have shown that attribute sampling of stimulus information may vary developmentally, and Waters and Waters (1976, 1979) have shown that sampling variability across repeated exposures to the same nominal stimulus item may be greater in children than in adults. Similarly, Ackerman (1984a; Ackerman & Rust-Kahl, 1982) has shown that the encoding context, including orienting constraint, affects both recall and recognition. This finding conflicts with the second assumption that the nominal re-presentation of the item is sufficient for a recognition judgment. In addition, this finding, and others by Nelson and Kosslyn (1975) and Sophian and Stigler (1981) of developmental differences in recognition memory conflict with the predicted age × task interaction reflecting the combination of assumptions two and three. If both recall and recognition require search for functional contextually biased representations of event information in memory, both should be developmentally sensitive if children search inefficiently relative to adults. The results of Ackerman and Sophian and Stigler are especially important because they cannot be explained by familiarity or criterion differences across age (cf. Perlmutter & Lange, 1978).

In general, generate-recognize theory has had some success explaining organizational effects in memory and effects related to search of associative networks (cf. Anderson & Bower, 1974), though even here most of the recent theoretical descriptions downplay or exclude recognition as the second stage of associative recall (cf. Raaijmakers & Shiffrin, 1981; Roediger & Neely, 1982). Generate-recognize also may be useful as an optional retrieval strategy in some circumstances (cf. Rabinowitz, Mandler, & Barsalou, 1979; Tulving, 1983). However, in general, the strong conflicting evidence suggests recognition and recall usually require similar search and retrieval processes for functional representations of events stored in memory, and that contextual information plays some role in retrieval success.

Developmental Limitations. Regardless of its empirical success in describing possible sources of memory deficit, the generate-recognize theory has not been informative about the nature of children's retrieval deficit. First, the theory has induced developmentalists to focus on *encoding* deficits, and not *retrieval* deficits per se, as the primary contributor to developmental differences, an emphasis that is shared by classic studies of organization in memory (see Chapter 3 by Bjorklund). The reason is that encoding constrains retrieval. Associative structure that is not perceived or encoded in acquisition cannot be searched in retrieval.

Second, it has proven difficult to attribute developmental recall differences unambiguously to retrieval processes, though recent advances in mathematical models of retrieval have aleviated this problem (see Chapter 4 by Bramerd). As noted by Kobasigawa (1977) and others (Emmerich & Ackerman, 1978; Hall et al., 1979; Sophian & Hagen, 1978) recall deficits cannot be attributed to problems of retrieving stimulus information until the availability of the information in memory is ensured. Establishing equivalent availability is difficult. In many studies investigators have failed to manipulate encoding and retrieval simultaneously, and hence to show that differences in encoding, or in stimulus availability, can be eliminated. In other studies children and adults have sorted stimuli into categories until some criterion of sorting stability is reached (cf. Ceci & Howe, 1978; Emmerich & Ackerman, 1978; Sophian & Hagen, 1978). On the assumption that a stable sort ensures item availability in memory, performance differences have been attributed to various deficits in retrieval search. However stable stimulus sorts may not reflect stable categorical structure or information in memory (cf. Whitney & Kunen, 1983), and so may be an unreliable measure of item availability. When item availability cannot be ensured, attributing a recall deficit to encoding or retrieval is only possible under certain assumptions about the measurement scale that relates encoding and retrieval, as pointed out by Brainerd in Chapter 4. These assumptions have been articulated only rarely.

Third, the yield from the studies in which investigators attempted to equate stimulus availability has been small. For example, in several studies young children have not used category cues effectively to search memory (cf. Ceci & Howe, 1978; Emmerich & Ackerman, 1978; Melkman, Tversky, & Baratz, 1981; Sophian & Hagen, 1978). However, the reason for the deficit is not known. These studies were designed to *describe* but not *explain* the deficit. Similarly, with the exception of one study by Huttenlocher and Lui (1979), who suggest that developmental limitations on categorical activation in memory limit categorical search, little is known about deficits in the retrieval of associative information in memory. However, Bjorklund introduces a potentially promising theoretical perspective in his chapter. One reason is that because the focus of generate-recognize theory is on free recall, developmental investigators have made little use of cued recall tasks. Retrieval deficiencies can be specified more easily in cued recall than in most other kinds of tasks because variations in the use of the cue provide a direct measure of problems of retrieval access to trace information.

The Encoding Specificity Hypothesis

The organization of the discussion of the encoding specificity hypothesis is similar to that for generate-recognize theory. The hypothesis is described first, followed by brief discussion of supporting and conflicting evidence, and then a discussion of the limitations of the hypothesis as a developmental theory.

In contrast to generate-recognize theory, the encoding specificity hypothesis (cf. Tulving, 1979; Tulving & Thomson, 1973) focuses on the variable sampling of stimulus information. In brief, the hypothesis is based on the idea that a stimulus event may be represented as a collection of features or elements. The encoding context biases the sampling of a set of those features. That is, that which is encoded is "specific" to a particular context or situation. The memory trace represents that specific feature set. In order to retrieve the event information from memory, the contextual bias must be reinstated at retrieval, at least to some extent. That is, the retrieval environment must be compatible with the acquisition encoding context, in the sense that the features sampled in the act of retrieval overlap with those sampled at encoding. Compatibility is achieved through the use of a cue at retrieval that represents the encoding context.

The retrieval process, according to the encoding specificity hypothesis, is analogous to the use of a lock and key (cf. Tulving, 1976). The lock represents the memory trace, whch reflects a particular sampling of episodic event information. The key represents a retrieval cue. The critical notion is that a specific key (cue) that has features that match lock features, will open a particular lock (trace). Since the trace feature set is determined by the encoding context, the best cue is one that represents that context.

The underlying logic of the hypothesis differs from that of generate-recognize theory. Several key assumptions differ in particular. The first is that the nominal (or perceptual pattern) information in a stimulus may play a relatively minor role in memory for event information. Instead, the functional stimulus is primary. Through context-sensitive selective sampling, stimulus events are classified at acquisition (cf. Spyropoulous & Ceraso, 1977). Tulving's (Thomson & Tulving, 1970; Tulving, 1983; Tulving & Thomson, 1971) use of the term "event" to refer to an encoding episode is strategic in this regard in that it presupposes that the "what" of encoding is different from the nominal stimulus "item." Instead, encoding concerns the item-in-context.

Second, since the functional representation of a specific stimulus episode differs from the nominal stimulus, it must be stored independently of the nominal stimulus representation in permanent memory, in some way. Thus, though stimulus sampling in a specific encoding context depends on knowledge available in permanent memory, it results in a trace representation of the encoding episode that is independent of that knowledge (cf. Watkins & Tulving, 1975).

Third, since remembering depends on "locating" or gaining access to the functional trace, all remembering requires retrieval, and is cued, A cue represents both the question asked of memory that initiates a retrieval attempt, and also a constraint on the potentially infinite set of paths of access to the trace in memory. Cues can be internal or provided externally, and the effectiveness of a cue in retrieval varies to the extent that it represents the functional bias. In addition, because the memory trace is represented by a feature set that combines in different ways, the access to trace information can occur in multiple ways (cf. Jones, 1976; Tulving & Watkins, 1975), through the use of different cues. Cue-trace compatibility is defined in terms of the "overlap" (cf. Tulving & Watkins, 1975), of information in the cue and trace, not necessarily in terms of a point-for-point feature match.

Fourth, given the general lock and key conception, search processes play only a small role in event retrieval, especially search of associative structures in memory. Though there may be limited search *for* an appropriate key (i.e., repeated samplings of cue information, or the generation of different cues), there is minimal search *from* a key. The unlocking process may be mechanical and automatic, much like the description of how organizational processes operate in Chapter 3 by Bjorklund.

Fifth, recognition and recall are similar processes in that both represent a relation between a question addressed to memory and trace information (cf. Tulving & Bower, 1974). Traces are defined in terms of question-output relations (Tulving & Bower, 1974; Tulving & Watkins, 1975). Recognition and recall differ only in the kind of information provided in the question, or the basis for the functional match of cue and trace information in retrieval. Most recognition cues provide a stronger basis than recall because recognition provides a perceptual "copy" of the nominal event (cf. Jacoby & Dallas, 1981; Jacoby & Witherspoon, 1982; Tulving, 1976). In some situations at least, the nominal copy provides a sufficient basis for a functional cue-trace match.

Supporting Evidence. Much of the evidence in the adult literature cited earlier against generate-recognize theory provides general support for the encoding specificity hypothesis, at least in terms of the idea that stimulus sampling varies in specific encoding contexts (cf. Roediger & Adelson, 1980). In addition, Tulving and his associates (Flexser & Tulving, 1978; Tulving & Thomson, 1973; Watkins & Tulving, 1975) and others have provided much evidence that recognition and recall are similar in many respects, differing primarily in the basis provided for a functional match of cue and trace information.

However, perhaps the most direct support is provided by many demonstrations of study-test, or encoding-retrieval, interactions in recall and recognition (cf., Craik, 1979, 1981; Tulving, 1976, 1979). These demonstations suggest that memory success depends on using a cue at retrieval to reinstate the functional encoding context, and hence on the compatibility of cue and trace information. As Tulving (1979) puts it, the "goodness" of an encoding operation for item memory depends on the retrieval environment provided by cues, and the "goodness" of a cue for retrieval depends on the environment in which the item was encoded. Other support for the dependence of memory on specific cue/trace relations is provided by Morris, Bransford, and Franks (1977).

The encoding specificity hypothesis also has some success explaining developmental memory differences attributed to retrieval processes. For example, given variable sampling of event information, one potential source of retrieval deficit is that children and adults attend to different functional aspects of an event. In particular, the focus of childrens' encoding appears to shift from perceptual to conceptual information in the early school years (cf. Ackerman, 1981; Cramer, 1973; Melkman & Deutsch, 1977; Melkman, Tversky, & Baratz, 1981). The shift may broaden the basis for retrieval. Given a perceptual focus, a memory trace may be predominately represented by information specific to a particular perceptual modality. Successful retrieval then may occur only if cue information matches that modality, limiting the effectiveness of cross-model cues (i.e., pictures for words, and vice versa). This modality specificity effect (cf. Ackerman, 1981) is reduced when conceptual information, which may be similar across perceptual modalities, is the basis for retrieval.

Another source is that the sampling variability may be greater in children than in adults (cf. Waters & Waters, 1976, 1979). Since retrieval cue information also must be encoded (cf. Ackerman, 1982; Craik, 1979; Jacoby & Craik, 1979), sampling variability between acquisition and retrieval may reduce the compatibility of children's sampling of cue information, and hence the cue-trace feature overlap at retrieval. The difficulty of achieving compatibility may limit children's use of cues (cf. Ackerman, 1982; Ackerman & Hess, 1982; Pressley & McFadyen, 1983).

A final source arises from the idea that episodic trace information can be accessed in multiple ways, depending on the overlap of cue and trace features. Multiple access depends on flexibility in sampling retrieval cue information. Ceci and Howe (1978) and Hasher and Clifton (1974) suggest that adults may be more flexible in their use of cues than children.

Conflicting Evidence. Most of the conflicting evidence is useful primarily in setting boundary conditions on the encoding specificity hypothesis. Only evidence in the adult literature is discussed, since relevant developmental research is described in the next section.

One issue concerns limitations on stimulus sampling at encoding—the first assumption. Craik (1979) and Barsalou (1982), for example, have suggested that core generic properties of concept information might be sampled in all situations in which the concept is identified. If so, there might indeed be some basis for the "transsituational identity" of words and other stimulus events, in opposition to the claim of Watkins and Tulving (1975). The variable sampling of concept information might concern more peripheral features or attributes of information. Findings supporting the generic-specific hypothesis of Durso and Johnson (1979, 1980) are also consistent with this idea.

A second related issue concerns limitations on the influence of the encoding context on stimulus sampling, and the need to reinstate that context to retrieve the stimulus event—the first and third assumptions, respectively. In an important review, Baddeley (1982) marshals evidence for a distinction between context interactive and context independent encoding. The distinction is important because Baddeley suggests the different kinds of encoding may affect recognition and recall differently—against the fifth assumption—and also the use of cues. Neither recognition nor cue effectiveness may be affected much by variations in context independent encoding. Encoding specificity effects may follow predicted forms only in interactive situations where the context biases the sampling of episodic information (cf. Gardiner & Tulving, 1980).

A third issue concerns episodic memory. A review of the controversy concerning the episodic-semantic distinction is well beyond the scope of this chapter. However, Anderson (1983) has maintained consistently that the distinction has little merit. The issue is important because if episodic activation can be mapped onto an associative network in permanent memory in some way, the associative network and interitem associations may play a larger role in retrieval than allowed by Tulving (cf. 1979) and the encoding specificity hypothesis.

Finally, a fourth issue, related to the third, concerns the role of active search processes in retrieval—the fourth assumption. Although indeed cues may "unlock" memory traces directly in an automatic mechanical manner, Raaij- makers and Shiffrin (1981), Roediger and Neely (1982), Nelson, McEvoy, and Friedrich (1982), and others have shown that active associative search may mediate the effective use of a cue to retrieve event information in some circumstances. It may be that these mediational effects reduce simply to the operation of reinstating the encoding environment, or sampling compatible cue information (cf. Reddy & Bellezza, 1983). However, the idea of active associative search seems inconsistent with the thrust of the encoding specificity hypothesis that retrieval occurs automatically through the use of appropriate cues in episodic memory (cf. Baddeley, 1982). Other mediational effects that may occur in matching cue and trace information have been suggested by Jones (1976) and Levoi, Ayton, Jonckheere, McClelland, and Rawles (1983).

Developmental Limitations. The encoding specificity hypothesis also provides only a limited explanation of developmental retrieval deficits. Primarily, the limitation concerns the emphasis on cue-trace compatibility as the exclusive determinant of retrieval success. Thus, qualitative differences in either encoding or retrieval cues have no intrinsic "goodness" (Tulving, 1979). Children may retrieve less successfully than adults simply because children have more problems achieving cue-trace compatibility.

The problem with this view is that it is insensitive to developmental changes in the content, organization, and use of knowledge that affect the likelihood of achieving compatibility and the sufficiency of compatibility once achieved, for retrieval success. That is, it is insensitive to development. Simply put, because the knowledge system is developing, qualitative differences in encoding may vary in intrinsic "goodness," for children, as may different retrieval cues. Concerning the former, evidence in the adult literature suggests that the uniqueness or distinctiveness of cue-trace feature overlap may matter (cf., Craik, 1979, 1981; Jacoby & Craik, 1979; Stein, 1977) independently of cue compatibility at retrieval, and, as discussed earlier, the contextual interactiveness of encoding may have some intrinsic effects on the use of context cues at retrieval (cf. Baddeley, 1982). Both of these aspects of encoding are developmentally sensitive. Children seem to differ from adults both in the distinctiveness (cf. Ackerman, 1984a; Ackerman & Rust-Kahl, 1982; Ghatala, Carbonari, & Bobele, 1980) and contextual interactiveness (cf. Pressley, 1982) of their encodings.

Concerning qualitative differences in retrieval cues, the findings of Melkman and Deutsch (1977), Melkman, Tversky, and Baratz (1981), and Sophian and Hagan (1978) seem to be inconsistent with the encoding specificity principle in that perceptual cues that were compatible with the acquisition encoding focus were less effective than conceptual cues that were not focal in acquisition. These findings suggest that for children cue effectiveness may vary with qualitative differences in encoding, quite independently of cue-trace compatibility. Further, if the effective use of retrieval cues depends on the support or search of associative structure in permanent memory at all, differences in associative structure may result in differences in the effectiveness of cues in children and adults.

Conclusion

This selective overview of retrieval theories illustrates my main contention that retrieval development has been characterized inadequately. The generate-recognize theory is inadequate because it focuses on intrinsic differences in encoding that may contribute to developmental retrieval deficiencies, but fails to characterize the contributions of the retrieval environment, like retrieval cues, to those deficiencies. The encoding specificity hypothesis is inadequate because it addresses the latter, but ignores or discounts the contributions of intrinsic qualitative differences in encoding, and the support of associative structure in retrieval search. A more complete developmental theory is needed that can account for the contributions of both encoding and retrieval deficiencies to children's ineffective use of cues. Such an account is possible within the "Descriptions" framework (cf. Craik, 1979; Norman & Bobrow, 1979), which is presented next.

Descriptions: A Model of Memory Retrieval

The Framework

Like the encoding specificity hypothesis, in the "Descriptions" model Norman and Bobrow (1979) assume that the encoding of stimulus information varies with the episodic context. What is stored in memory, then, is a functional representation of the episodic event. Also like the encoding specificity hypothesis, retrieval cues are used to gain access to these representations. The difference is that in the Descriptions model, retrieval cues are used to delimit a search *set* of candidates for retrieval, not just one specific candidate, and so to initiate and guide active retrieval *search*. Search consists of the continual modification and updating of retrieval cue information so that it more nearly specifies one unique member in the search set, or the set size shrinks to one.

In essence, a "description" represents the relation between the information in the retrieval cue and in the memory trace for the episodic event. That is, the cue information is used to "describe" the event information in memory. The adequacy of the description depends on two factors: the power of the cue to delimit a search set containing the target event and to specify a unique event within the set. Norman and Bobrow refer to the first factor as the problem of constructing a sampling of cue information compatible with the functional event representation in memory, or the "constructability" component of descriptive adequacy. This component is derived from the encoding specificity hypothesis. They refer to the second factor as the problem of using cue information to discriminate a specific member within the search set, or the "discriminability" component of descriptive adequacy. This component is derived, in part, from demonstrations that encoding distinctiveness affects memory performance (cf. Craik, 1979; Jacoby & Craik, 1979).

The hypothesis that two factors influence retrieval success is important here because it gives rise to the possibility that cue-trace compatibility may be necessary but insufficient on occasion for successful retrieval. This possibility represents an important difference between the descriptions model and the encoding specificity hypothesis. Cue-trace compatibility ensures that the correct search set is delimited in using a retrieval cue. However, identification of the target event within the set requires further specification, achieved through some active sampling or search process.

Perhaps an analogy might be useful here to illustrate the descriptions model and distinguish it from the encoding specificity hypothesis. Tulving (1976) considers a retrieval cue to be like a key that opens a lock and hence a memory vault. A key is all that is necessary, and the right key is always sufficient to reveal the contents of the vault. In contrast, for Norman and Bobrow, a retrieval cue is like the address of a house. That is, it "describes" the location of the house. The address is more or less adequate on two counts: it must describe the town, street, or general location of the house (i.e., search set), and in addition, it must describe the specific house within the general area, either by house number or some list of unique attributes (e.g., second house on right with charteuse picket fence). Description of the general area is necessary, but only a narrower focus on the specific location is sufficient to find the house. A nonspecific description may force the traveler to "search" for the house in some way. The degree or difficulty of search varies with the specificity of the description (i.e., house by house if only the block is specified, block by block and then by house if only the town is specified, etc.).

Developmental Implications

The model incorporates the effects of intrinsic variations in the sampling of event information at encoding, and of cue information at retrieval. In addition, retrieval is considered an active search process in which the cue information, or retrieval description, is continually modified. In these respects, the model may address the different aspects of children's retrieval deficiency identified by generate-recognize theory and the encoding specificity hypothesis. For example, insofar as encoding specificity is concerned, the model can, in principle, capture developmental differences in sampling biases and in sampling variability. Children's greater sampling variability might increase the difficulty children have in "constructing" retrieval cue encodings that are compatible with the acquisition environment, while the less distinctive encodings might influence the "discriminability" of compatible cue information. The latter especially may affect children's recognition performance (cf. Jacoby & Craik, 1979; Jacoby, Craik, & Begg, 1979), while the former primarily affects recall. Similarly, the categorical encoding and search emphasis of the generate-recognize theory may concern either children's failure to gain access to categorical structures at retrieval (i.e., "construct" the appropriate categorical sampling), or to use the categorical information and structure to identify (i.e., "discriminate") a particular desired category member. Research on these deficiencies, interpreted within the Descriptions framework, is presented next.

The Research Program

Overview of the Program

Research on children's deficiency in using retrieval cues is described in the next two sections. The present section has two goals. The first is to outline the general nature of children's deficiency by establishing that encoding and retrieval processes contribute independently to developmental differences in cued recall. The second is to show that these contributions can be cast as affecting the "discriminability" and "constructability" of cue information, and that these components of descriptive power are empirically separable. The section concludes with a general summary of the strength and weaknesses of the "Descriptions" approach. In the end, the research will suggest that children's retrieval deficit in using cues may occur because (a) children have more difficulty than adults do in constructing interpretations of cue information that are compatible with acquisition samplings, (b) children have more difficulty than adults do in using compatible cues to discriminate target information in memory, and (c) young children do not use cues effectively to "search" memory. The first source of deficit is attributed to retrieval processes per se, and the second to encoding specification.

Retrieval Variability

My research on "retrieval variability" (cf. Ackerman, 1982) is described in detail, since it introduced the method used in many of the other studies in the research program. The goal of the research was to show that children have more difficulty than do adults in sampling cue information at retrieval compatible with the acquisition encoding environment.

Method. In general, the task was designed so that I could manipulate the compatibility of the cue-trace information at retrieval, in order to determine if second and fourth graders and college adults can recall desired target information in incompatible situations. To control, or fix, the nature of the trace representation in memory, cue-target words were paired in acquisition that shared some preexperimental association, and encoding of the associative information was ensured through the use of acquisition orienting questions. Compatibility at retrieval was manipulated through the use of orienting questions at retrieval that biased the sampling of cue information the "same" as or "different" from the acquisition bias. The logic of the task was based on the idea that the information in cues at retrieval must be encoded, and so could be sampled variably. When the sampling of event information at acquisition and cue information at retrieval differs, the cue information must be resampled to achieve cue-trace compatibility and recall success.

The stimulus set consisted of 34 cue-target word pairs (like *Knife-Axe*). The members of each pair were chosen carefully so that both the cue and target words were in the reading vocabulary of second-grade children, and the cue items had conceptual attributes both in common with the target items, and unique to themselves. The cue item could, for example, possess some secondary function, or membership in a secondary category (i.e., kitchen utensil for *Knife*) not shared by the target item. Table 1-1 contains examples. Of the pairs, 28 were experimental stimuli, and 6 were buffers used to control for primacy and recency effects. The members of each pair, and cue alone, were printed on index cards.

Orienting questions for both acquisition and retrieval were prepared for each pair. Examples are shown in Table 1-1. For acquisition, 21 of the experimental pairs and 3 of the buffer pairs were associated with *Congruent* questions that were supposed to be answered affirmatively. The Congruent questions were focused on the conceptual information that was common to both pair members (like "Are these weapons?" for *Knife-Axe*). The remaining pairs were associated with *Incongruent* questions that were focused on information contained in neither pair member (e.g., "Are these tools?" for *Bear-Camel*), and so should have been answered negatively. The Incongruent questions were used to ensure the subjects processed the information in the pairs associated with the Congruent questions, and did not just answer these questions affirmatively automatically. Only memory for the latter pairs will be considered further in this chapter.

The critical manipulation concerned the retrieval questions, which were asked about the *cues* only. For the 24 pairs (21 experimental + 3 buffers) receiving Congruent questions at acquisition, the retrieval questions were either the "*Same*" as those asked at acquisition (e.g., "Is this a weapon?" for *Knife*), "*Different*" in that the question addressed cue attribute information that was not shared with the target (e.g., "Does this go beside a dinner plate?"), or "*Negative*" in that the question did not address information in either the cue or target item (e.g., "Does this grow in a field?"). Three different lists of retrieval questions were prepared to counterbalance for kind of question. There were eight of each kind of question in each list. The *Same* questions were used to ensure the compatibility of cue-trace feature sampling.[1] The *Different* questions were used to determine if subjects can resample cue attribute information and achieve compatibility when incompatible cue attributes are sampled initially.

---

[1]Please note that *Same* retrieval questions can ensure that acquisition and retrieval encoding is reasonably *similar* but never *identical*. Change in the presentation position of the stimuli and other aspects of the temporal and physical context, as well as just simple random fluctuation in sampling, probably result in some variability in encoding between acquisition and retrieval.

Table 1-1. Sample Congruent Cue-Target Pairs and Orienting Questions Asked About the Pairs at Acquisition and Cues at Retrieval

Cue-Target Pairs	Acquisition Questions	Retrieval Questions		
		Same	Different	Negative
Window-Lamp[a]	Are these used for light?	Is this used for light?	Can this get dirty on a car?	Does this have feathers?
Apple Leaf[a]	Do these grow on trees?	Does this grow on a tree?	Can this go in a pie?	Does this have legs?
Specific Orienting[b]				
Knife-Axe	Might a prince use these to slash his enemies?	Might a prince use this to slash his enemies?	Does this go beside a plate at dinner?	Does this grow in a field?
Nail-Saw	Can these get rusty and cut you?	Can this get rusty and cut you?	Can this blow out a tire?	Is this made of paper?
Categorical Orienting				
Knife-Axe	Are these weapons?	Is this a weapon?	Does this go beside a plate at dinner?	Does this grow in a field?
Nail-Saw	Are these tools?	Is this a tool?	Can this blow out a tire?	Is this made of paper?

[a]These pairs were used in Ackerman (1982), where the specificity of the orienting questions was uncontrolled.
[b]The Item Specific and Categorical questions are examples of questions used in succeeding studies in which kind of acquisition question was manipulated.

The *Negative* questions were used to assess sampling difficulty when no specific cue attributes are sampled at all.

All subjects were informed about the cued recall procedure. The acquisition orienting questions were asked prior to pair presentation, and the pairs were presented in a flashcard kind of procedure for 5 seconds each. Similarly, the retrieval questions were asked prior to cue presentation. The subjects were instructed strictly to answer the questions out loud as soon as possible, before attempting written recall of the target word. This overt question answer then written recall sequence was emphasized because it was critical that the sampling of cue information was biased prior to a recall attempt. The procedure was illustrated carefully with the six buffer cues, which were presented before presentation of the experimental cues. All cues were presented for 10 seconds each, and the subjects were encouraged to guess if they could not recall a target item.

Results and Discussion. The mean percent recalled for the pairs receiving Congruent questions is shown in Table 1-2. In all the studies using this general method, there are three important results: the absolute recall level for the *Same* questions; the absolute recall level for the *Different* questions; and the recall difference between these levels. The difference is termed the "Encoding Shift Penalty," because subjects have to shift from an incompatible "different" encoding to a compatible "same" encoding of cue information, and the shift usually incurs a recall penalty.

The patterns in Table 1-2 are typical of those that I have consistently obtained. First, *Different* question recall was inferior to *Same* question recall. The inferiority shows that the compatibility of the cue attribute sampling at acquisition and retrieval encoding affects target recall. This finding supports the encoding specificity hypothesis.

Second, the children did particularly poorly in the *Different* question situation and the Encoding Shift Penalty decreased significantly with increasing grade.[2] So children's recall is inhibited more by an initially incompatible sample of cue information than is the recall of adults. Adults seem more able than children to resample successfully and ensure cue-trace compatibility.

---

[2] A ceiling on the college adults *Same* question recall could have contributed to the relatively small Encoding Shift Penalty in adults. The fact that the recall level of the *Same* question could go no higher than unity could have resulted in an artificially small difference between *Same* and *Different* question recall. Interpretation of several other results reported in this chapter also suffers from the same problem. However, the overwhelming bulk of the other evidence cited in the chapter suggests that the claim for a significantly larger Encoding Shift Penalty in children than adults is well-founded. For example, the penalties are greater in children when adults' *Same* question recall is around 70.0% (see Table 3), or well below ceiling, and when child recall approaches 90.0% (Table 3). In addition, in experiments designed to explore the limits of the "retrieval variability" phenomenon, not described in this chapter, the adults' penalties were significantly smaller than the children's even when adults' *Same* question recall was between 50.0% and 80.0% due to increases in list length and decreases in cue-target and cue presentation durations.

Table 1-2. Mean Percent Targets Recalled Under Orienting
Constraint at Both Acquisition and Retrieval Encoding

	Retrieval Question			Encoding Shift Penalty[a]
Grade	Same	Different	Negative	
Second	50.8	19.0	23.8	31.8
Fourth	50.8	28.6	30.6	22.2
College	96.8	88.9	82.5	7.9

[a] *Same* minus *Different* question totals.

Third, recall was similar for the *Negative* and *Different* questions. The similarity suggests that *sampling* retrieval cue information in the absence of any particular encoding bias (i.e., *Negative* questions) is functionally similar to *resampling* in the *Different* situation. The *Negative/Different* question comparison has been included in all of the experiments sharing this methodology, partly to gauge sampling-resampling similarity, and partly to equalize the number of positive and negative orienting questions asked at retrieval. No systematic differences have ever emerged for the two kinds of questions, supporting the similarity. Thus children seem less able than adults both to sample and resample compatible cue attribute information at retrieval.

The fourth result was the significant developmental increase in recall for the *Same* questions. Since cue compatibility was ensured by the *Same* questions, the increase indicates that something other than differences in matching cue and trace information at retrieval contributes to developmental differences in cued recall. Reinstating the acquisition encoding environment at retrieval may be necessary, but clearly it is not sufficient for retrieval success in children. What else could be responsible for the developmental differences? One possibility is that acquisition encoding also contributes independently of the compatibility of retrieval sampling and in some way not predicted by the encoding specificity hypothesis.

Acquisition Encoding Contributions

The encoding specificity hypothesis is based on the notion that the acquisition encoding context biases the sampling of episodic event information. The kind of bias is unspecified and is assumed to be unimportant. However, Hunt and Einstein (1981) distinguish between the biasing of specific and relational information in episodic events. The specific attributes of a stimulus event represent information that is unique to the event, and serve to isolate the event from other events. The relational attributes represent general categorical or associative information that relates the event to other similar events. The term "event" here refers to the stimulus-in-context, or stimulus target + context cue

+ encoding focus (i.e., orienting question). Hunt and Einstein found that the different sampling biases had independent effects on event memory in adults, and Ackerman (cf. Ackerman, 1984a; Ackerman & Rust-Kahl, 1982) has found the same for children. Ackerman also found that young children make particularly ineffective use of relational aspects of event meaning.

The specific/relational distinction is important here because most of the orienting questions in Ackerman (1982) focused on categorical (i.e., relational) information. This emphasis could have contributed to the developmental differences in *Same* question recall. Perhaps young children either cannot make efficient use of categorical attribute information, or perhaps adults spontaneously elaborate this information more than children do, making it more specific or distinctive at retrieval (cf. Jacoby & Craik, 1979). Either way, qualitative differences in attribute sampling at acquisition may contribute to the effective use of retrieval cues.

In order to test this hypothesis, in several experiments (Ackerman & Hess, 1982, Experiment 2; Ackerman, 1983, Experiment 1; Ackerman and Rathburn, 1984, Experiment 1), the specificity of acquisition encoding was manipulated by asking Categorical or Specific orienting questions. The Categorical questions were concerned with superordinate categorical membership or relations. The Specific questions were more distinctive in that they were concerned with unique or evocative event information. Examples of the questions are shown in Table 1-1.

In addition, *Specific* and *Categorical* orienting questions were asked at retrieval, as well as the *Different* and *Negative* questions. That is, acquisition orienting was fully crossed factorially with retrieval orienting. The purpose was to see if gradations in the conceptual compatibility of cue sampling (i.e., *Specific* retrieval questions for Categorical acquisition orienting and vice versa) affect recall relative to formally compatible (*Same* question) and incompatible (*Different* question) samplings.

The important results averaged across the three experiments are shown in Table 1-3. The Categorical acquisition recall patterns are similar to those shown in Table 1-2 in several ways. In particular, the children's recall is poor in the *Different* question conditions, the Encoding Shift Penalties decline with increasing age, and there are large developmental recall differences in the *Same* question conditions. In contrast, in the Specific acquisition condition, the children's recall again is poor in the *Different* question conditions, and again the Encoding Shift Penalties decline with grade. However, there are only small differences for *Same* question recall. Indeed, in two out of the three experiments that contributed to Table 1-3, there were no developmental recall differences at all for the *Same* questions. In addition, *Same* question recall for the Specific acquisition condition was superior to *Same* question Categorical recall.

The *Different* question and Encoding Shift Penalty results again indicate that children have more difficulty than adults in resampling cue information at retrieval to ensure cue compatibility. However, the *Same* question recall differences indicate that qualitative differences in acquisition encoding also

Table 1-3. Mean Percent Targets Recalled Averaged Across Experiments[a]

Grade	Same[b]	Different	Encoding Shift Penalty[c]	Constructability Estimate[d]
Second				
Specific	85.6	29.4	56.2	34.3
Categorical	39.4	12.5	26.9	31.7
Fourth/Fifth				
Specific	89.1	45.8	43.3	51.4
Categorical	51.2	35.2	16.0	68.8
College				
Specific	92.8	61.6	31.2	66.7
Categorical	68.6	53.7	14.9	78.3
Mean				
Specific	89.2	45.6	43.6	51.1
Categorical	53.1	33.8	19.3	63.7

[a]From Ackerman and Hess (1982, Experiment 2), Ackerman (1983, Experiment 1), and Ackerman and Rathbun (1984, Experiment 1).
[b]"*Same*" question refers to the Item Specific retrieval question for Item Specific acquisition, and Categorical retrieval question for Categorical acquisition.
[c]*Same* minus *Different* question recall.
[d]*Different* ÷ *Same* question recall.

affect the use of cues, independent of retrieval sampling compatibility. The results suggest, first, that cue effectiveness may vary directly with the specificity of encoding. Second, young children in particular make ineffective use of categorical samplings. However, when the encoding of event information is specific and distinctive and compatible cue attributes are sampled at acquisition and retrieval, young children make excellent use of retrieval cues. Note that the developmental similarity in *Same* question/Specific condition recall could have been due in part to ceiling effects in adults recall. Regardless, the above conclusions stand—intrinsic differences in encoding in particular affect children's use of retrieval cues. In opposition to Tulving (1979), the "goodness" of encoding does seem to matter for young children.

Another question that can be asked about the results concerns the similarity of unconstrained *sampling* of cue information at retrieval and *resampling* under conditions of orienting constraint. Although the logic of the retrieval variability demonstration is based on a functional analogy between unconstrained and constrained retrieval sampling, the analogy has received only indirect empirical support so far. Additional evidence is available from Ackerman (1983, Experiment 1). Categorical and Specific acquisition orienting constraint occurred only at acquisition (i.e., Orient-No Orient) for some subjects, as well as at both acquisition and retrieval (i.e., Orient-Orient manipulations) for others. The purpose of the Orient-No Orient manipulation was to determine if subjects could reinstate particular acquisition samplings at retrieval on their own. For the second graders, recall in both the Specific (mean percent = 41.1) and Categorical (18.2%) Orient-No Orient conditions was significantly lower than recall in the appropriate *Same* retrieval question Orient-Orient conditions, represented in Table 1-3 (85.6% and 39.4%, respectively), and only slightly greater than recall in the *Different* retrieval question conditions (29.4% and 12.5%). Similar patterns occurred for the fourth graders. For the adults, however, the recall levels in the Orient-No Orient conditions approached *Same* question recall in the Orient-Orient condition. These findings suggest children have similar levels of difficulty in sampling compatible cue information at retrieval on their own and in constrained encoding situations, and more difficulty than do adults.

Constructability and Discriminability

The previously cited research shows that a lack of acquisition encoding specification and sampling problems at retrieval contribute to children's inefficient use of retrieval cues. According to the "Descriptions" framework, the acquisition encoding problem concerns the use of a compatible sample to discriminate a particular event in memory, and the retrieval problem concerns constructing compatible cue samplings. Tables 1-2 and 1-3 document children's deficits in both discriminability and constructability in the following way. The poor *Same* question recall for Categorical acquisition is evidence of failures to use categorical samplings to discriminate or specify event information in memory. The Encoding Shift Penalties and the poor recall for the *Different* questions show that children have difficulty constructing compatible samples of cue information.

Unfortunately, the tables also suggest that acquisition encoding specification affects both discriminability (i.e., *Same* question recall) and constructability (i.e., *Different* question recall). These effects are shown in Table 1-3, in that the recall levels for both the *Same* and *Different* retrieval questions were higher for the Specific than for the Categorical acquisition conditions. The similar effects raise a parsimony question: Are the effects of encoding discriminability and retrieval constructability dissociable and independent at some level? If not, then the two components of descriptive power may be functionally equivalent.

The effects can be dissociated. The problem with the recall evidence is that the *Different* question levels may reflect contributions from both processes. Once a compatible resampling has been achieved for the *Different* sampling, the compatible cue information must be used to discriminate an event in memory. Since we already know that Specific acquisition encoding enhances discrimination (the *Same* question advantage), the advantage must be partialled out of the *Different* question recall to determine whether or not Specific acquisition also affects the probability of sampling compatible cue information at retrieval. This can be done in the following way. Assume that *Different* question recall equals the product of the probability of constructing a compatible sampling, and the probability of using the compatible sample to discriminate wanted event information in memory. Assume also that *Same* question recall is a reasonable estimate of the latter, since sampling compatibility is ensured. Given these assumptions, the construction probability equals *Different* question recall divided by *Same* question recall.

The mean constructability estimates for Specific and Categorical acquisition encoding derived from the above equation are shown in the last column in Table 1-3. The table shows that children differ from adults in constructability and also that encoding specification does not enhance constructability. In anything, specification reduces constructability, though there are usually no reliable differences. Since the primary factor that enhances discriminability (i.e., encoding specification) has no effect on constructability, it can be concluded that discriminability and constructability are separable empirically and may contribute independently to the successful use of retrieval cues.

Summary: Strengths and Weaknesses

One strength of the present approach to children's retrieval deficit is that developmental recall differences can be attributed precisely to problems of gaining access to, or retrieving, event information and not to the differential availability of event information in memory. Recall that problems of establishing availability vitiated many of the claims about children's retrieval arising from the generate-recognize theory of recall. Event availability in the "Descriptions" approach is ensured through the use of orienting questions that constrain the encoding of event information. Evidence that the constraint is effective comes from several sources. First, correct answers to the orienting questions have occurred uniformly for all grades at rates exceeding 90%. Second, the recall levels have approached unity in certain retrieval situations, and not in others, arguing that the variation is attributable to the differences in the retrieval situations. Third, assuming recognition performance can be used as a rough measure of availability, the retrieval manipulations have not affected item recognition in several experiments (cf. Ackerman, 1982).

All this is not to say that encoding differences have no effects on retrieval deficits. The converse is demonstrated above. However, assuming event information is available in memory, the "goodness" of encoding may affect retrieval primarily by limiting the sufficiency of cue-trace compatibility for achieving event recall. The idea that encoding differences have specific and measurable effects on retrieval processes is important because it provides a way to escape the ubiquitous problem in developmental research discussed by Brainerd (see Chapter 4) that attributions of developmental recall deficits to encoding *or* retrieval depend on the function assumed to relate encoding and retrieval. This problem pertains specifically to "design-based methods of separating storage and retrieval" (Brainerd, Chapter 4, page 146). Instead of describing "separate" deficits, the goal of the present approach is to describe the effects of encoding on retrieval, or the limits of study-test *interactions* in accounting for developmental variance in recall success.

Another problem raised by Brainerd is not escaped through this approach, however. The problem concerns the scaling assumptions underlying the constructability estimate measure. The use of the division procedure is valid only under the assumption that *Same* and *Different* question recall index the "amount" or "strength" of event memory according to a ratio, or at least an interval, scale. The justification for this assumption is weak. For example, the idea that cue-trace compatibility varies in equal increments, or ranges from an absolute zero, seems untenable, at least in a simple way (but see Tulving & Watkins, 1975). Thus the constructability estimate is weak and should be applied cautiously, pending the creation of some better index. The estimate is credible only to the extent that the estimates have been constant across the three experiments cited previously. The constancy provides support that the estimate indexes some stable aspect of the difficulty in achieving recall for the *Different* questions.

A second problem of the constructability estimates is that they may be distorted by ceiling effects for the *Same* question recall, for the Specific acquisition conditions. However if recall in these situations reached or exceeded 100%, the effect would be to *depress* the constructability estimates further for Specific orienting. Although such a finding might warrant the novel conclusion that constructability is more of a problem for Specific than for Categorical orienting, the finding in no way weakens the conclusion that discriminability and constructability are dissociable. More evidence on the separability of these factors and on some reasons why young children might be deficient in both is presented next.

Constraints on Descriptive Power

This section describes research on factors that affect the use of retrieval cues. Discriminability constraints are discussed first, followed by a discussion of the constraints on constructability, and then the general constraints on both. An

Table 1-4. Summary of the Factors Found to Affect Children's Use of Retrieval Cues

Discriminability	Constructability	General Constraints[a]
Encoding specification	Retrieval sampling	Trace mutability
Stimulus modality (pictures or words)	Delay	Contextual interactiveness of encoding
Event repetitions	Resampling set	Cohesiveness of associative structures
Cue associations		Multiple access
Event set size		

[a]The general constraints concern both discriminability and constructability.

overview and summary of the factors limiting acquisition encoding discriminability and retrieval constructability is presented in Table 1-4. Much of the evidence presented relies on *Same* retrieval question recall as the measure of discriminability and *Different* question recall divided by *Same* question recall as the measure of constructability. However, conceptually, evidence for constraints on discriminability comes from findings of variation in *Same* question recall, while evidence for constraints on constructability comes from findings of variation in *Different* question recall and the size of the Encoding Shift Penalties, with relative invariance in *Same* question recall. This conceptual evidence is important because of the logical weaknesses of the constructability estimate.

Discriminability Constraints

Stimulus Modality. Several theorists have suggested conceptual information is more specified and detailed in pictures than in words (cf. Durso & Johnson, 1979, 1980; Friedman & Bourne, 1976; Nelson, 1979). If so, picture cues may be more discriminable on average than word cues. Supporting evidence is presented in Ackerman and Hess (1982, Experiment 1). In this experiment, the cue-target pairs were either pictures or words, the cues were always in the same modality as at acquisition, and encoding was constrained at acquisition and retrieval by mostly Categorical orienting questions. Recall patterns similar to those for Specific and Categorical acquisition in Table 1-3 were found, supporting an analogy between Specific acquisition encoding and the encoding of pictorial information. That is, *Same* retrieval question recall was greater for the pictures (mean percent = 74.1) than for the words (64%), the picture facilitation was greater for the second (mean picture/word difference = +22.3%) and fourth (+11.2%) graders, than for the adults (−3.1%), but there were no picture/word differences in constructability estimates. In addition, the recall levels for *Same* question/picture condition were 79.4% for the adults and 74.6% for the fourth graders, which suggests that neither the extent of the picture facilitation, nor the constructability estimates were influenced by ceiling effects.

These results have two implications. First, stimulus factors that are theoretically likely to affect encoding specification should affect the power of retrieval cues to discriminate event information in memory, but not the probability of sampling compatible cue information. Second, these factors may have stronger effects on the use of cues by children than by adults. Adults seem to provide more specification in encoding than children do when the specification is not provided by the stimulus or encoding context.

Event Repetitions. In Ackerman and Rathburn (1984, Experiment 3) children were given two trials of constrained acquisition encoding prior to retrieval, featuring the factorial crossing of Specific and Categorical orienting on Trial 1 and Trial 2. The manipulation provided an excellent demonstration of the effects of stimulus sampling on recall in that recall varied substantially with nonidentical acquisition samplings of repeated presentations of cue-target information. However, one particular finding for the children was that discriminability (i.e., *Same* question recall) but not constructability was facilitated by specification (i.e., Specific Trial 2 encoding) of an original Categorical encoding (i.e., Trial 1 encoding). The reverse was not true. Broadening (i.e., Categorical Trial 2 encoding) an original specific encoding did not enhance children's recall. Neither did repetitive Categorical samplings. These results suggest that repeated exposure to nominal event information may aid children's use of cues, but only if specific aspects of event information are sampled.

Strength of Cue Associations. Several studies in the adult literature (cf. Nelson, McEvoy, & Friedrich, 1980; Raaijmakers & Shiffrin, 1981) suggest that search success in retrieval varies with the strength of association between the cue and the desired event information in memory. Strength of association may affect the discriminability of cue information, since the probability of sampling compatible cue features (i.e., constructability) and the strength of the associations of nominal cue information seem independent. Indeed, Tulving (1979) claims that the encoding specificity hypothesis was originally motivated by a need to demonstrate the independent effects on recall of feature samplings and the preexperimental associative values of cues.

Only one recent developmental study, by Hall, Murphy, Humphreys, and Wilson (1979), has examined the relation between cue association values and recall. Hall et al. found that second graders' cued recall correlated well with nominal cue-target associative values whereas the fifth graders' recall did not. Hall et al. concluded that the older children made more active attempts at retrieval search. An alternative account, suggested by Bjorklund and Thompson's (1983) recent work, is that the nominal cue-target associative values differed systematically for these groups of children. In any event, it seems likely that differences in cue associative values affect the discriminative power of children's cues, though little research has examined this point yet.

Set Size. Target discriminability in memory is a relative concept. Target salience must be evaluated relative to the number of similar events in memory whose features overlap with cue features. The smaller the set of events, the greater the discriminability of the cue and target overlap information. So set size in memory may affect discriminability.

Evidence for set size effects is provided for adults by Nelson et al. (1982), and for children by Ackerman and Rathburn (1984, Experiment 2). In the latter experiment, second and fourth graders and college adults were given orienting questions at acquisition and retrieval that stressed superordinate categorical information (termed "Large Category questions"), like the Categorical questions shown in Table 1-1, or stressed smaller subcategorical information. The contrast for *Chicken-Cow*, for example, was "Are these animals?" versus "Are these farm animals?," and for *Knife-Axe* was "Are these weapons?" versus "Are these small hand weapons?." The results showed that the *Same* retrieval question recall averaged 77.8% for the children in the Small subordinate Categorical condition, and 47.2% in the Large superordinate Categorical condition. Set size seems to affect the discriminability of cue information.

Constructability Constraints

Delay. Ackerman (1983, Experiment 1) used a 20-minute delay between acquisition and retrieval to determine how delay affects retrieval variability and the Encoding Shift Penalty. It turned out there was an interaction between grade, delay, and encoding specification. Delay only affected recall for the *Different* retrieval questions for Specific acquisition, and mostly for the adults. In the delay conditions, the Encoding Shift Penalty of the adults approached those of the child groups. Recall in the Categorical acquisition condition was not affected, nor was *Same* retrieval Question/Specific acquisition recall. These effects should be interpreted cautiously, since the delay was small and the effects have not been replicated. However, they suggest that delay affects constructability for cue attributes that are highly specified.

Sampling Versus Resampling. Earlier it was suggested that both sampling compatible cue attributes at retrieval, and resampling these attributes given an incorrect initial sample, are difficult for children. But are sampling and resampling difficulty equivalent? The evidence in Ackerman (1983) suggests not.

In Experiment 2 in this study, second and fifth graders and college adults were given Specific acquisition encoding questions, and two retrieval trials. On Trial 1, the important retrieval questions were *Same* (Specific) and *Different*. Trial 1 recall for these questions was similar to that presented in Table 1-3 for Specific acquisition. On Trial 2, the important retrieval questions were *Same* (Specific), *Different*, and *None*. These questions were crossed with kind of Trial 1 retrieval question. In the None condition, no questions were asked. The focal results are shown in Table 1-5, for three kinds of recall outcomes: Target items recalled on both trials $(T_1 T_2)$, on Trial 1 but not on Trial 2 $(T_1 \bar{T}_2)$, and on Trial 2, but not on Trial 1 $(\bar{T}_1 T_2)$.

The important findings are these. First, children may have difficulty sampling compatible cue attributes on their own even for events already sampled and recalled successfully. On 20.8% of the occasions of successful Trial 1 *Same* question recall, the second graders could not recall the targets on Trial 2 $(T_1 \bar{T}_2)$ in the *None* condition. The $T_1 \bar{T}_2$ *None* result represents 38.4% of the total successful Trial 1 recall (20.8% ÷ 54.1%) in the Specific/*None* condition. The corresponding percentages for the fifth graders and adults were 23.6 and 18.2, respectively. Thus, the constructability of an initial sample is a problem for children.

Table 1-5 Mean Percentages of Targets Recalled for the Specific Acquisition Question Condition for the Specific and Different Trial 1 Retrieval Questions and the Same, Different, and None Trial 2 Retrieval Questions

| | Trial 2 Questions | | | | | | | | |
| | Same | | | Different | | | None | | |
Grade	$T_1T_{2_a}$	$T_1\bar{T_2}$	$\bar{T_1}T_2$	T_1T_2	$T_1\bar{T_2}$	$\bar{T_1}T_2$	T_1T_2	$T_1\bar{T_2}$	$\bar{T_1}T_2$
Second									
Specific	83.3	0.0	4.2	16.7	62.5	0.0	33.3	20.8	0.0
Different	4.2	0.0	37.5	50.0	0.0	0.0	45.8	0.0	0.0
Fifth									
Specific	100.0	0.0	0.0	29.2	50.0	0.0	54.2	16.7	0.0
Different	12.5	0.0	62.5	8.3	16.7	0.0	70.8	0.0	0.0
College									
Specific	95.8	0.0	4.2	45.8	45.8	0.0	75.0	16.7	0.0
Different	62.5	0.0	25.0	45.8	4.2	8.3	79.2	0.0	0.0

[a] T_1T_2 represents successful recall on both trials; $T_1\bar{T_2}$ represents recall on Trial 1 but not Trial 2; and $\bar{T_1}T_2$ represents recall on Trial 2 but not Trial 1.

Second, resampling from an incompatible sampling also remains a problem, again despite successful Specific Trial 1 sampling and recall. The problem is shown in the high percentage (62.5%) of instances of Trial $T_1\bar{T_2}$ recall for the *Different* Trial 2 question.

Third and most important, the probability of successfully constructing a compatible sample differs for sampling and resampling in children. Essentially, *Same* question recall differed as a function of whether the question was Trial 1, or was Trial 2 and occurred after *Different* Trial 1 question recall. For example, the Trial 1 recall for the Specific/*Same* retrieval questions for the second graders was 76% (not shown in Table 1-5). The corresponding figure in Table 1-3 is even higher (85.6%). But, as shown Table 1-5, the *Same* question Trial 2 recall, after a *Different* Trial 1 question was only 41.7% ($T_1T_2 + \bar{T_1}T_2$). The corresponding figures for the older children were 85.4% for Trial 1 *Same* question recall, and 75.0% for *Same* question Trial 2 recall after a *Different* Trial 1 question. For adults, there was no difference.

Interpretation of these results depends on the assumption already mentioned that even *Same* question retrieval sampling only approximates the acquisition sampling and encoding environment. This assumption is supported by the fact that *Same* question recall is excellent, but imperfect. So there must be some sampling variability. Given sampling variability, the probability of successfully sampling compatible cue attributes (constructability) seems to differ for children for initially sampling and for resampling cue information. By hypothesis, an incorrect initial sample introduces an encoding set for young children, which is difficult to break. The set affects the probability of a successful resampling. Thus children may be doubly penalized relative to adults. Because of greater sampling variability, children may be less likely than adults to sample compatible cue information initially, and the incompatible initial sample may adversely affect the probability of resampling correctly.

General Constraints on Descriptive Power

Trace Mutability. So far, variations in retrieval cue effectiveness have been concerned with the specificity and compatibility of *cue* information. This account assumes that the trace *event* information in memory is constantly available. Only the key varies, never the lock. However, in some situations, and for some subjects, the assumption of constant availability may be incorrect. The memory trace itself may change with further experience with event information (cf. Baddeley, 1982; Loftus, Miller, & Burns, 1978). Thus, trace mutability may affect the power of cues to describe event information.

In particular, mutability may affect children's use of cues. Some weak empirical support for this claim can be found in Liben's (1977, 1981) demonstration that operative changes in cognition may affect children's representations of event information in memory. However, the claim also seems reasonable on the assumption that children have less experience with events, and may encode events in less stereotypical and more variable ways than adults. This assumption has received some confirmation from Waters and Waters (1976, 1979) and many other experiments described in the present chapter.

Direct empirical support is presented in Ackerman and Rathburn (in press). Second and fourth graders and college adults were presented with cue-target pairs at acquisition in a cued recall task. Specific and Categorical acquisition orienting were varied between subjects along with a control No Orient acquisition condition. Retrieval cue encoding was unconstrained (i.e., no orienting questions). However, a recognition test intervened between the acquisition and recall phases. In Experiment 1, the subjects were required to circle the target words (e.g., *Knife* of *Axe-Knife*) appearing on the recognition test. In Experiment 2, the subjects were instructed to circle the cue words (e.g., *Knife* of *Knife-Axe*) on the recognition test. Thus, the pairs were reversed in the experiments, but the recognition tests were identical. The critical manipulation was the recognition test context for each word. Each of the critical words (cue or target) was placed in a row of five context words. The context words were either of the *Same* category as the cue-target pair members, and as biased by the acquisition orienting questions (e.g., other weapons), a *Different* category appropriate for the critical word but not its paired associate (e.g., Kitchen utensils like *spoon*, *glass*, and *plate*, for the *Knife* member of *Knife-Axe*), or the words were categorically *Unrelated* to the critical word. In addition, one-fourth of the critical words were not included on the recognition test (*None* condition). The goal was to determine the effects of the recognition experience on cued recall.

The results, averaged across target and cue recognition context experience, are shown in Table 1-6. The logic underlying the design was that the *None* and *Unrelated* contexts serve as baselines for detecting the effects of *any* further recognition experience (*Unrelated* vs. *None* comparison) and any associatively related experience (*Same* or *Different* vs. *Unrelated* comparisons). Recall increments for the *Same* contexts and recall decrements for the *Different* contexts provide measures of the sensitivity of event representations in memory to experiences compatible and incompatible with the episodic associative information.

The *Mean* rows in Table 1-6 show that neutral intervening experience did not affect recall in general (i.e., *Unrelated* context recall = *None* context recall). However *Same* experience facilitated recall, and *Different* experience inhibited recall, relative to *Unrelated* experience, and these effects were larger in the children than in the adults. The difference between the two experiments was that the recall levels were roughly 25% higher in Experiment 1 than in Experiment 2.

The important implication of the results is that traces seem more mutable in children than in adults and the mutability may contribute to children's deficit in using cues. A retrieval deficit may occur not only because of inherent weaknesses in cue information, but also because the event representation may have changed slightly and the cue description has become slightly incompatible. The key may not fit well for children because the lock has changed.

Table 1-6. Mean Percent Recalled for Each Acquisition Orienting Condition and Recognition Experience

	Recognition Experience				
Grade	Same	Different	Unrelated	None	Mean
Second					
Specific	86.5	55.2	66.7	53.2	65.4
Categorical	47.9	18.8	31.3	25.6	30.9
No questions	28.7	16.7	18.2	11.0	18.7
Fourth					
Specific	88.6	65.1	74.5	56.8	71.3
Categorical	56.8	34.5	43.2	45.3	45.0
No questions	48.5	28.9	36.0	41.2	38.7
College					
Specific	89.1	69.8	78.7	72.4	77.5
Categorical	70.3	65.6	68.2	62.0	66.5
No questions	82.3	74.0	77.5	79.7	78.4
Mean					
Specific	88.1	63.4	73.3	60.8	
Categorical	58.3	39.6	47.6	44.3	
No questions	53.2	39.9	43.9	44.0	

Note that trace mutability does not imply that all attributes are mutable, or that any attribute is mutable in all situations. There may be core features of every concept that do not vary (cf. Barsalou, 1982; Jacoby & Craik, 1979). The claim here is only that some aspects of concept meaning may be more mutable for children than for adults.

The Contextual-Interactiveness of Encoding. Abundant evidence is available that young children often do not encode context and event information in interactive ways, and that noninteractive (i.e., context independent) encoding affects the use of context cues in recall. For example, Pressley (1982) and Reese (1977) reviewed many studies showing that young children do not spontaneously elaborate (i.e., encode interactively) the cue and target information in paired associates. Similarly, Ackerman (1981) has shown that young children's failure to encode conceptual information in cue-target events affects the use of the cue in recall. Finally, many of the studies described previously in this chapter have contained conditions in which encoding is unconstrained at acquisition (No Orient-No Orient or No Orient-Orient conditions). In all these studies, cued recall is poor for second graders. An example is the No Question recall in Table 1-6.

The contextual interactiveness of encodings may affect the use of cues in several ways. One way is that the power of a context cue to "describe" events in memory may depend on the degree to which the context biases event attribute sampling at acquisition (cf. Baddeley, 1982; Gardiner & Tulving, 1980). However, a complete explanation of the effects seems more complex because, as Baddeley (1982) points out, contexts can sometimes act as retrieval cues even in context independent encoding situations.

An alternative hypothesis is that discriminability varies directly while constructability varies inversely with the contextual interactiveness of encoding. The more the context specifies a particular encoding of event information, the more a context cue can be used to discriminate that information in memory, but the harder it is to construct or reinstate the specific contextual bias during retrieval. In context-independent situations virtually all samplings of cue information may be compatible, since no specific feature set was biased. So there is no construction difficulty. However, for the same reason, the cue may be ineffective in discriminating any particular event in memory.

Some direct evidence for the alternative hypothesis, and for the idea that deficits in contextual interactiveness constrain children's use of cues, is provided in Ackerman and Rathburn (1984, Experiment 4) and Ackerman (in press, a). In the former study, young children and adults were instructed at acquisition either to image the cue and target pair members separately side by side (context independent condition) or in interaction (context interactive condition). The encoding of cue information at retrieval was constrained by *Specific, Categorical, Different,* and *Negative* orienting questions.

In the Separate Imagery conditions, retrieval constraint did not influence target recall. There was no Encoding Shift Penalty for any group (i.e., poorer recall for the *Different* questions), and so constructability was not a problem. On the other hand, recall was relatively poor, especially for the second graders (mean percent = 21.9 overall). The fourth graders and adults had recall levels consistently around 60%.

In the Interactive Imagery conditions, *Same* question recall (*Specific* retrieval questions as it turned out) exceeded *Different* question recall, and there were large Encoding Shift Penalties. Thus, constructability was a problem in the Interactive Imagery situations. However, *Same* question recall was excellent (63.9%, 79.2%, and 93.1% for the second graders, fourth graders, and college adults, respectively). In the Interactive Imagery condition then, the context cue gained in discriminability, but lost in constructability. The reverse occurred in the Separate Imagery (i.e., context independent) condition.

In Ackerman (in press, a), the context cue members of each cue-target pair were either Interactive adjectives (e.g., *Bloody Sword*, *Clumsy Bear*) or Noninteractive adjectives (*Straight Sword*, *Big Bear*). The idea was that the former interacted with and modified the target event information more than the latter, as determined by adult ratings. The Noninteractive adjective information was somewhat redundant with the target information. Acquisition encoding was constrained by Specific or Categorical orienting questions, and the context adjectives were used as retrieval cues. There was no retrieval orienting constraint.

The important results, shown in the Specific columns of Table 1-7, were that recall was greater for the Interactive than the Noninteractive adjective cues, even for identical acquisition orienting questions, and the children in particular did poorly in the Noninteractive cue situations. These results support the ideas that context cue effectiveness varies with the contextual modification of event information, and that children's encoding may usually be less contextually interactive than is that of adults.

Other evidence for the trade-off between constructability and discriminability for context interactive encodings concerns Specific and Categorical acquisition orienting. While the discriminability estimate (i.e., *Same* question recall) has

Table 1-7. Mean Percent Cued Recall for the Interactive (Int) and Noninteractive (Non) Adjectives for the Congruent Specific and Categorical Acquisition Orienting Questions

Grade	Specific		Categorical	
	Int	Non	Int	Non
Second	77.1	40.6	50.0	31.3
Fourth	83.3	40.6	58.3	54.2
College	75.0	57.3	77.1	52.1
Mean	78.5	46.2	61.8	45.9

always been greater for Specific than for Categorical orienting in the present research program, the constructability estimate usually has been ten or more percent higher for Categorical orienting, at least for the older children and adults. As noted previously, this difference would be even greater if ceiling effects limit *Same* question recall for the older groups.

Structural Constraints. One of the most consistent results found in the research program is that developmental recall differences are largest, and the recall of second graders poorest, when retrieval is based on categorical information (see also Chapter 3 by Bjorklund). Young children do not make effective use of categorical information in cues during retrieval. Note that this deficit occurs even when categorical sampling is constrained and the "Same" at acquisition and retrieval, so the issue is not just sampling. One concrete example is found in Ackerman and Rathburn (in-press a, Experiment 3) where second-grade children failed to profit even from two repeated acquisition encoding trials of Categorical orienting. Other studies, too, have found that young children do not use categorical cues effectively, compared to adults, even when a stable categorical sort is achieved in acquisition encoding and category cues are provided at retrieval (cf. Emmerich & Ackerman, 1978; Melkman & Deutsch, 1977; Melkman et al., 1981; Whitney & Kunen, 1983).

The reason for the deficiency may be the structure of categorical information in memory. Norman and Bobrow (1979), for example, suggest that the power to describe event information may vary depending on the structure and amount of what is known. Structured knowledge may constrain the retrieval effectiveness of cues because some form of associative interitem structure may be the medium of retrieval "search" within the set of recall candidates delimited by the retrieval cue. The problem of young children, then, may be due to a lack of well-articulated and organized (cf. Bjorklund & Thompson, 1983) or easily activated (cf. Bjorklund & de Marchena, 1984) categorical associative networks. A fuller discussion of the nature of children's categorical memory appears in Chapter 3 by Bjorklund.

Direct evidence for structural constraints on children's use of categorical information in cues is provided by Ackerman and Rathburn (in press-a, Experiment 2), Ackerman (1984, b; in press, a, Experiment 2) and Ackerman (in press, b). Some aspects of the Ackerman and Rathburn research have been described already. Small subordinate (Are these zoo animals?) and large superordinate Categorical (Are these animals?) orienting questions were asked at acquisition, and *Same* and *Different* questions were asked again at retrieval. The results are shown in Table 1-8. Not only did Small Category acquisition aid discriminability, as shown in the *Same* question recall, it also strongly aided the children's constructability, as shown in the Constructability Estimates, relative to Large Category acquisition. Note also that the absolute recall for the second graders for Large Category acquisition is poor, in contrast to the good Small Category recall.

Table 1-8. Mean Percent Recalled for Each Kind of Acquisition and Retrieval Question

Grade	Retrieval Question		
	Same	Different	Constructability Estimate
Second			
Small Category	77.8	50.0	64.3
Large Category	47.2	13.8	29.2
Fourth			
Small Category	77.8	61.1	78.5
Large Category	47.2	19.4	41.1
College			
Small Category	91.7	69.4	75.7
Large Category	66.7	41.7	62.5
Mean			
Small Category	82.4	60.2	73.1
Large Category	53.7	25.0	46.6

Note: The Categorical questions were appropriate for the acquisition orienting (i.e., Small Category questions for Small Category acquisition).

These results indicate that young children can use subordinate but not superordinate categorical sampling effectively as a basis for cued recall. In line with the other evidence, the results suggest that deficits in superordinate structure may constrain children's use of cues.

Ackerman (1984, b; in press, a) employed standard cue-target cued recall tasks, with Specific and superordinate Categorical orienting constraint at acquisition, but no orienting constraint at retrieval. The acquisition orienting questions were either Congruent (i.e., affirmative) or Incongruent (negative). In Ackerman (in press, a), the retrieval cues were either the cue members of each cue-target pair ("Context" Cues), or the names of the appropriate superordinate category ("Category" Cues). Ackerman (1984, b) featured only the former kind of cue.

Table 1-9 documents three important results for Ackerman (in press, a, Experiment 2) collapsed across adjective type for the Adjective-Noun pairs (see page 31). First, for both kinds of cues superordinate Categorical orienting led to poor recall for the second graders, but not necessarily for the older subjects. Developmental recall differences were large in the Categorical conditions, but small in the Specific acquisition conditions. These results are similar to others reported earlier. Second, the second graders' use of the Category Cues was particularly poor relative to the adults' and relative to developmental differences in using the Context Cues. The children had difficulty using the Category Cues even for Categorical acquisition orienting.

Table 1-9. Mean Percent Recalled for Each Kind of Cue
and the Congruent (Cong) and Incongruent (Inc) Specific
and Categorical Acquisition Orienting Questions

	Category Cue		Context Cue	
Grade	Cong	Inc	Cong	Inc
Second				
Specific	51.6	31.8	58.9	27.1
Categorical	45.4	23.0	40.7	21.4
Fourth				
Specific	62.5	39.6	62.0	43.3
Categorical	62.5	37.0	56.3	27.1
College				
Specific	71.9	46.4	66.2	43.8
Categorical	87.5	58.9	64.6	57.3

The third result provides the most direct evidence for structural deficits underlying children's ineffective use of categorical information in cues. It is concerned with encoding congruency. Congruency effects refer to the recall advantage of Congruent over Incongruent acquisition orienting questions. These effects are usually attributed to elaborative encoding (cf. Craik & Jacoby, 1979; Craik & Tulving, 1975) occurring along some structured associative network in memory (cf. Ghatala et al., 1980). Hence, congruency effects may be used as direct, albeit weak, evidence for the presence of such a network. As shown in both Table 1-9 and in Ackerman (1984, b), young children show significantly smaller congruency effects than do older children and adults for Categorical information, but reasonably similar effects for Specific information. For example, in Table 1-9 the second graders' average congruency effect was about 20% in the three conditions involving Category Cues or Categorical acquisition, and about 32% in the Specific/Context Cue situation. The fourth graders' average effect in the three categorical conditions was about 26%, and about 29% in the Specific/Context situation. In Ackerman (1984, b), in two experiments, the mean congruency effect for second graders was 14.9% for Categorical acquisition orienting, and 46.5% for Specific acquisition orienting. For adults, the mean congruency effect was 32% for Categorical orienting, and 47.6% for Specific orienting. These effects provide additional evidence for structural constraints on children's use of categorical information during retrieval.

The goal of Ackerman (in press, b) was to determine directly how associative structure in permanent memory limits children's ability to search for episodic event information from a context or category cue. Second and fifth graders were presented with noun triplets in which the last target word (e.g., Lily) was related to either the preceding two context words (Related-Related-Target triplets, or

Table 1-10. Mean Percent Recalled for the High Category
Condition for Each Kind of Triplet and Retrieval Cue

Grade	Triplet Type		
	R-R-T	*R-U-T*	*U-U-T*
Second			
Noun-noun cue	75.0	36.1	22.2
Noun cue	38.9	25.0	18.1
Category cue	50.0	44.4	43.6
Fifth			
Noun-noun cue	76.4	66.7	29.2
Noun cue	65.3	58.3	16.7
Category cue	76.4	65.3	68.1
College			
Noun-noun cue	77.8	76.4	12.5
Noun cue	75.0	73.6	18.1
Category cue	87.5	70.8	62.5

R-R-T, as in Rose-Tulip-*Lily*), the first but not the second context word
(Related-Unrelated-Target triplets, or *R-U-T*, as in Rose-Brick-*Lily*), or none
of the context words (*U-U-T* triplets, as in Wood-Brick-*Lily*). In one condition,
the subjects were oriented to the associative information by means of questions
preceding triplet presentation (like "How many are flowers?"), and target recall
was cued by means of the two context nouns (*N-N* cue), the first context noun
(*N* cue) or the name of the target's superordinate category.

There were four important results shown in Table 1-10. First, for all groups
the effectiveness of the *N-N* and *N* context cues were more dependent on the
associative relatedness of the triplet members than were the Category cues. This
is shown in the *Mean* rows in the table in that the "triplet" effect (i.e., *R-R-T* >
U-U-T recall) was larger for the Context than for the Category cues. One
explanation of the interaction is that Category cues gained access to the targets
by means of "vertical" class-name to class-member interitem associations (cf.
Mandler, 1983; Rabinowitz & Mandler, 1983) in permanent memory that are
activated by category instantiation. Activation and instantiation was ensured by
the orienting questions. In contrast, the Context cues gained access by means of
"horizontal" interitem associations among class members that could only be
activated through associative structure in the encoding episode. The finding of
differential dependency supports the point made earlier, and made by many
others (cf. Pressley, 1982), that Context cues are strongly affected by the
interactiveness of encoding.

Second, the second graders recalled fewer targets for the Category cues than
did the other groups. This finding suggests that weak "vertical" interitem
associations limit children's "search" from cues representing an event's
superordinate category. This suggests that class names may have less

discriminability for children than adults, and shows how retrieval search is dependent on associative structure in memory.

Third, the children were more dependent on the episodic associative structure than the adults. The evidence shown in Table 1-10 was that the second graders showed little profit from the associative information in the R-U-T triplets (i.e., R-U-T = U-U-T recall), in contrast to the other groups. In Ackerman (in press, b) I argue this effect reflects the fact that interitem associative structures necessarily mediates (i.e., guides, or constrains) retrieval search from a cue. Such structures are more likely to be made available for adults than children through simple instantiation of an associative relation (i.e., R-U-T triplets) because the extant structure in memory is more cohesive or articulated for adults than children. Thus the use of associative information as a retrieval medium for children may be more dependent on episodic activation.

Fourth, the children were more dependent on full support of the context cues than the adults and made less effective use of the partial context cues. This is shown most clearly in Table 1-10 for the R-R-T triplets where recall was better for the N-N than for the N cues for the children, but there was no difference for the adults. Assuming constructability requires reinstatement of the full encoding context, the finding indicates that children are less able than adults to retrieve context information from a partial context cue, perhaps due in part to children's inability to use interitem associative structure as a retrieval medium. This finding is especially important because it provides the first solid illustration of a "search" deficit. Here the "continual modification and updating" of cue information operationally describes the complete retrieval of elements of the encoding context.

All these results suggest that the effective use of a retrieval cue is dependent in some circumstances on interitem associative information or structure in permanent memory. Of course, the best test of the idea that deficits in structure contribute to children's retrieval deficit would be to show that the developmental effects vary in some way with a direct manipulation of the associative structure. In Ackerman (in press, b), I conducted such a test by varying whether the related context words were high associates of the target's superordinate category (cf. Rose-Tulip-*Lily* or Robin-Sparrow-*Canary*), according to the Battig and Montague (1969) norms, relatively low associates (e.g., Lilic-Sunflower-*Lily* or Swan-Goose-*Canary*), subject to the reading limitations of the second graders, or related to the targets by co-occurrence in typical events or situations (e.g., like Easter for Bunny-Jelly Beans-*Lily* and a Pet Store for Cage-Perch-*Canary*). The purpose of the Co-Occurrence condition was to determine if similar cueing patterns occur for categorical and noncategorical associative information. The means for the High Category condition are shown in Table 1-10, and the means for the Low Category condition and Event Co-Occurrence condition are shown in Table 1-11, for the orienting groups.

The tables show that each of the four results discussed earlier for the High Category condition vary in predictable ways from the other conditions. Two findings in particular are noteworthy, and serve to illustrate my point here.

Table 1-11. Mean Percent Recalled for the Low Category and Event Co-Occurrence Condition for Each Kind of Triplet and Retrieval Cue

Grade	Low Category			Event Co-Occurrence		
	R-R-T	*R-U-T*	*U-U-T*	*R-R-T*	*R-U-T*	*U-U-T*
Second						
Noun-noun	41.7	30.6	11.1	87.5	27.8	9.7
Noun	16.7	15.3	9.7	45.8	18.1	13.9
Category	33.3	36.1	29.2	19.4	18.1	12.5
Fifth						
Noun-noun	77.8	45.8	16.7	94.4	54.2	6.9
Noun	33.3	19.4	0.0	66.7	44.4	15.3
Category	75.0	66.7	66.7	36.1	43.1	27.8
College						
Noun-noun	75.0	72.2	20.8	93.1	79.2	19.4
Noun	61.1	41.7	5.6	73.6	59.7	27.8
Category	73.6	65.3	62.5	34.7	47.2	16.7

First, Bjorklund and Thompson (1983) and others (cf. Whitney & Kunen, 1983) suggest that the links between low nonprototypical categorical associates to categorical structures in memory are weaker for children than adults. If so, and if these structures affect the use of retrieval cues in the ways discussed above, developmental differences in the effects cited above should be more extreme for the Low Category (Table 1-11) than for the High Category conditions (Table 1-10). The patterns for the fifth graders and adults agree with this prediction, as does the general finding of poor recall for the second graders, even in the most advantageous recall situation (i.e., *N-N* cue for *R-R-T* triplets). Floor effects obscure other trends in the second-grade data. Note there were no differences in answering the orienting questions, so the children judged that the low associates were category members. They just could not use the associative information to support search in retrieval.

Second, concerning the third result discussed earlier, if the dependency on episodic associative structure varies inversely with the "strength" of associative structure in permanent memory, recall in the Event Co-Occurrence condition (Table 1-11) should be more dependent on episodic structure than recall in the High Category condition (Table 1-10). After all, the events reflect fairly unique episodes that are unlikely to be represented by a "structure" in permanent memory. If so, the differences between *R-R-T* and *R-U-T* recall should be greater for the Event Co-Occurrence condition. The results support this prediction.

Multiple Access of Trace Information. Tulving (1982) argues that access to event information in memory can be gained in multiple ways. The only requirement is that the cue feature information at retrieval overlap with the trace feature information in memory. In this way, cues not present in the encoding context (i.e., "extra-list" cues) can be used to retrieve trace information (cf. Roediger & Adelson, 1980).

One constraint on children's use of cues may be a limitation on multiple access. The limitation may occur because children's retrieval search is inflexible (cf. Ceci & Howe, 1978) and is restricted to the primary use of episodic context cues and particular samplings of cue or event information. It also may occur because structural constraints limit children's effective use of extra-list category cues. Finally, it may occur simply because adults encode more attribute information than children do. The greater the number of features sampled, the greater the probability of overlap between any particular cue and trace information (cf. Tulving, 1982).

Direct evidence for the constraint comes from several experiments in the research program. In all the studies featuring retrieval constraint, retrieval questions were asked that emphasized feature information that overlapped with, but was not the "Same" as, the acquisition sampling. For example, Specific retrieval questions were asked for Categorical acquisition orienting and vice versa. The idea was that cue-trace overlap in these retrieval situations should be greater than for the *Different* and *Negative* retrieval questions, and so should lead to higher recall levels. The results met these expectations only for adults and generally only for the combination of Specific acquisition and Categorical retrieval questions. These results suggest that adults but not children can access event information in multiple ways in at least some situations.

General Discussion

Summary of Results

The goal of the present chapter was to develop a new conception of children's retrieval deficit. The research reported concerned limitations on the use of retrieval cues to describe (cf. Norman & Bobrow, 1979) episodic information in memory. The basis for the description may be relational information that links events, like categorical information, or more specific information that isolates a particular event. The kind or amount of specification required for event retrieval may vary with task situations and the goals underlying the retrieval attempt.

Normal and Bobrow (1979) identify constructability and discriminability as two primary determinants of descriptive power. The research suggests these determinants are independent at some level. First, conceptually, construct-ability focuses on the *retrieval* sampling of cue information in order to achieve cue-trace compatibility. Discriminability focuses on the specification of *acquisition* sampling. Specification affects event identification in memory once a compatible retrieval sampling is achieved. Second, constructability and discriminability may be dissociated empirically. The dissociation was shown in that the specification of acquisition encoding affected "Same" retrieval question recall (i.e., discriminability) but not the constructability estimates, and several of the experimental manipulations affected either discriminability or constructability uniquely.

Children may differ from adults in both components of descriptive power. The differences compose children's retrieval deficit. Concerning discriminability, the research suggests several sources of deficit. In general, discriminability may concern the identification of a target event in memory within a search set of related events. Discriminability then may vary with the salience of the event or the size of the search set. Concerning saliance, children may not encode context and target information in interactive ways, or in highly specified ways. So there may be little basis for using cue information to identify one privileged event in memory among other similar events. The search set, in this sense, is undifferentiated vis-à-vis the cue. Concerning the size of the search set, because of differences in psychological cohesiveness, some sets that are functional for adults may not be functional for children, like superordinate categories. The set is essentially undefined.

Concerning constructability, because of greater sampling variability children may have more difficulty than do adults in sampling compatible cue information at retrieval. Children are more likely than adults to incur an Encoding Shift Penalty (initial sampling probability) and children's penalties are likely to be larger than are those of adults (resampling probability). The larger penalties may occur because of an encoding set: Children seem less able than adults to escape an incompatible initial sample. Another contribution to constructability differences is that differences in set cohesiveness may bias the probability of sampling particular attributes either favorably (i.e., subordinate) or unfavorably (superordinate). In addition, because of differences in the number and variety of sampled episodic features, the basis for sampling compatibility may be greater in adults than in children. So constructability is less of a problem for adults than for children because the adults can access trace information in multiple ways.

General constraints on children's use of cues to describe events in memory seem to concern at least the following. First, because of knowledge or activity differences, children may encode context and event information less interactively than do adults. Second, deficits in associative structure in memory may constrain children's use of superordinate categorical information to describe events, or the use of interitem associations to retrieve and reinstate aspects of the episodic context. Third, trace mutability may limit children's use of cues more than that of adults, perhaps because concept representations are less stable or solidifed in children than in adults. Fourth, for the same reason, children may encode cue information between acquisition and retrieval more variably than do adults.

Implications and Extensions

Why Descriptions? The "Descriptions" framework has been adopted here for several reasons. First, in accord with much research in the adult literature, the framework focuses on differences in the sampling of attributes of episodic event information. Event encoding is not unitary and all-or-none. Second, the sampling differences may concern attribute information that specifies the "event" and isolates it from other similar events or relates it to other similar events. This focus on qualitative sampling differences advances developmental theory, which has attributed memory variation mainly to deficits in encoding relational organizational information. Third, the framework incorporates both acquisition encoding and retrieval differences in the final account of children's retrieval deficit. In this respect the model is more powerful than either generate-recognize theory, which focuses on encoding, or the encoding specificity hypothesis, which focuses on retrieval sampling and discounts any intrinsic effects of the "goodness" of encoding.

Extensions. The "descriptions" view of children's retrieval deficit focuses on differences in retrieval sampling and so accounts for encoding specificity phenomena. However, I have only begun to extend the model to problems of retrieval search, the traditional, though largely unexamined, source of developmental deficit in the generate-recognize model. My account of search deficits at present is simply that retrieval search involves the continual updating and sampling of cue information to more precisely describe particular events in memory. Search is constrained by the associative structures of memory, which may limit the possibility or utility of any particular sampling, and search may concern specific or relational aspects of an event, or of several related events (i.e., categorized lists at acquisition). The success of this approach remains to be demonstrated.

Limitations. Research on developmental differences in the use of cues to describe events in memory has just begun, but several limitations can be identified. The first is implicit in the last paragraph above. Though constructive sampling seems an active process, and Norman and Bobrow (1979) character-ize retrieval as effortful and guided, retrieval in the present account seems somewhat passive, and unguided.

The second is that the mechanics of attribute sampling are relatively unspecified. What exactly gets sampled, and what is contextual bias? Does the context bias all aspects of concept information, or is the conceptual core stable and constant across episodic variations (cf. Barsalou, 1982; Jacoby & Craik, 1979)? These are important issues because the nature and stability of core features may change with age, contributing to differences in the use of cue information at retrieval.

Finally, the present account of developmental differences in using retrieval cues seems paradoxical. Children's attribute samplings have been described as more variable than are adults' at retrieval, but usually less contextually biased, specified, or interactive than adults' at acquisition. This seems contradictory. Children's samplings are more and less variable and both contribute to their retrieval deficit.

The resolution of the paradox is central to the issue of using cues to describe and gain access to event information in memory. Simply, there may be two kinds of attribute variability. One concerns the variable sampling of conceptual information in any particular target or cue item. This kind of sampling variability may be greater in children than in adults because of the relative lack of a stable meaning core in children. The second concerns contextual bias, or the interactive sampling of the *relation* between context and item information. This kind may be greater in adults because adults employ more active and elaborative acquisition encoding processes. The former contributes to problems of constructing an appropriate encoding of *cue* information, and thus accounts for children's greater retrieval variability. The latter contributes to the descriptive power of the cue *relation*, and thus accounts for children's deficiency in using cues to discriminate target *events* in memory.

Acknowledgments. I thank Akira Kobasigawa for comments on the research, and Fergus Craik, Doug Herrmann, and the editors of this volume for comments on the manuscript. I also thank Gus Craik especially for the discussions and insight which led to the research program.

References

Ackerman, B. P. (1981). Encoding specificity in the recall of pictures and words in children and adults. *Journal of Experimental Child Psychology*, *31*, 193–211.

Ackerman, B. P. (1982). Retrieval variability: The inefficient use of retrieval cues by young children. *Journal of Experimental Child Psychology*, *33*, 413–428.

Ackerman, B. P. (1983). Encoding distinctiveness and the encoding shift penalty in children and adults. *Journal of Experimental Child Psychology*, *36*, 257–283.

Ackerman, B. P. (1984,a). Item specific and relational encoding effects in children's recall and recognition memory for words. *Journal of Experimental Child Psychology*, *37*, 426–450.

Ackerman, B. P. (1984,b). Constraints on children's use of cues to retrieve episodic information from memory. Manuscript submitted for publication.

Ackerman, B. P. (in press,a). The effects of item specific and categorical orienting on children's incidental and intentional memory for pictures and words. *Journal of Experimental Child Psychology*.

Ackerman, B. P. (in press,b). Constraints on retrieval search for episodic information in children and adults. *Journal of Experimental Child Psychology*.

Ackerman, B. P., & Hess, L. (1982). The effects of encoding distinctiveness on retrieval variability in children and adults. *Journal of Experimental Child Psychology*, *33*, 465–474.

Ackerman, B. P., & Rathburn, J. (1984). Developmental differences in the use of retrieval cues to describe episodic information in memory. *Journal of Experimental Child Psychology*, *38*, 147–173.

Ackerman, B. P., & Rathburn, J. (in press). The effect of recognition experience on cued recall in children and adults. *Child Development*.

Ackerman, B. P., & Rust-Kahl, E. (1982). The effects of contrastive encoding of semantic information on children's memory for words. *Journal of Experimental Child Psychology*, *34*, 414–434.

Anderson, J. R. (1983). A spreading activation theory of memory. *Journal of Verbal Learning and Verbal Behavior*, *22*, 201–295.

Anderson, J. R., & Bower, G. H. (1972). Recognition and retrieval processes in free recall. *Psychological Review*, *79*, 97–123.

Anderson, J. R., & Bower, G. H. (1974). A propositional theory of recognition memory. *Memory and Cognition*, *2*, 406–412.

Baddeley, A. D. (1982). Domains of recollection. *Psychological Review*, *89*, 708–729.

Barsalou, L. W. (1982). Context-independent and context-dependent information in concepts. *Memory and Cognition*, *10*, 82–93.

Battig, W. F., & Montague, W. E. (1969). Category norms for verbal items in 56 categories: A replication and extension of the Connecticut category norms. *Journal of Experimental Psychology Monographs*, *80*, 3.

Bjorklund, D. F., & de Marchena, M. R. (1984). Developmental shifts in the basis of organization in memory: The role of associative versus categorical relatedness in children's free-recall. *Child Development*, *55*, 952–962.

Bjorklund, D. F., & Thompson, B. E. (1983). Category typicality effects in children's memory performance: Qualitative and quantitative differences in the processing of category information. *Journal of Experimental Child Psychology*, *35*, 329–344.

Bower, G. H. (1967). A multicomponent theory of the memory trace. In K. W. Spence & J. T. Spence (Eds.), *The psychology of learning and motivation: Advance in research and theory* (Vol. 1) New York. Academic Press.

Bower, G. H. (1970). Organizational factors in memory. *Cognitive Psychology*, *1*, 18–46.

Brainerd, C. J., Howe, M. L., Kingma, J., & Brainerd, S. H. (1984). On the measurement of storage and retrieval contributions to memory development. *Journal of Experimental Child Psychology*, *37*, 478–499.

Brown, A. L. (1975). The development of memory: Knowing, knowing about knowing, and knowing how to know. In H. W. Reese (Ed.), *Advances in child development and behavior* (Vol. 10). New York: Academic Press.

Brown, J. (1976). *Recall and recognition*. London: Wiley.

Bruce, D., & Fagan, R. L. (1970). More on the recognition and free recall of organized lists. *Journal of Experimental Psychology*, *85*, 153–154.

Ceci, S. J., & Howe, M. J. A. (1978). Age-related differences in free recall as a function of retrieval flexibility. *Journal of Experimental Child Psychology*, *26*, 432–442.

Chechile, R. A., & Richman, C. L. (1982). The interaction of semantic memory with storage and retrieval development. *Developmental Review*, *2*, 239–250.

Craik, F. I. M. (1979). Human memory. *Annual Review of Psychology*, *30*, 63–102.

Craik, F. I. M. (1981). Encoding and retrieval effects in human memory: A partial review. In J. Long & A. Baddeley (Eds.), *Attention and performance IX*. Hillsdale, NJ: Lawrence Erlbaum Associates.

Craik, F. I. M., & Jacoby, L. L. (1979). Elaboration and distinctiveness in episodic memory. In L. G. Nilsson (Ed.), *Perspectives on memory research*. Hillsdale, NJ: Lawrence Erlbaum Associates.

Craik, F. I. M., & Tulving, E. (1975). Depth of processing and the retention of words in episodic memory. *Journal of Experimental Psychology: General, 104,* 268–294.

Cramer, P. (1973). Evidence for a developmental shift in the basis of memory organization. *Journal of Experimental Child Psychology, 16,* 12–22.

Dale, H. C. A. (1966). When recognition is no better than recall. *Nature, 211,* 324.

Durso, F. T., & Johnson, M. K. (1979). Facilitation in naming and categorizing repeated pictures and words. *Journal of Experimental Psychology: Human Learning and Memory, 5,* 449–459.

Durso, F. T., & Johnson, M. K. (1980). The effects of orienting tasks on recognition, recall, and modality confusion of pictures and words. *Journal of Verbal Learning and Verbal Behavior, 19,* 416–429.

Emmerich, H. J., & Ackerman, B. P. (1978). Developmental differences in recall: Encoding or retrieval? *Journal of Experimental Child Psychology, 25,* 514–525.

Estes, W. K. (1959). The statistical approach to learning theory. In S. Koch (Ed.). *Psychology: A study of a science* (Vol. II). New York: McGraw-Hill.

Flexser, A. J., & Tulving, E. (1978). Retrieval independence in recognition and recall. *Psychological Review, 55,* 153–171.

Friedman, A., & Bourne, L. E. (1976). Encoding the levels of information in pictures and words. *Journal of Experimental Psychology: General, 105,* 169–190.

Gardiner, J. M., & Tulving, E. (1980). Exceptions to recognition failure of recallable words. *Journal of Verbal Learning and Verbal Behavior, 19,* 194–209.

Geis, M. F., & Hall, D. M. (1976). Encoding and incidental memory in children. *Journal of Experimental Child Psychology, 22,* 58–66.

Geis, M. F., & Hall, D. M. (1978). Encoding and congruity in children's incidental memory. *Child Development, 49,* 857–861.

Ghatala, E. S., Carbonari, J. P., & Bobele, L. Z. (1980). Developmental changes in incidental memory as a function of processing level, congruity, and repetition. *Journal of Experimental Child Psychology, 29,* 74–87.

Ghatala, E. S., Carbonari, J. F., & Wylie, H. L. (1980). Attribute structure and incidental memory for words: Test of a developmental hypothesis. *Child Developmental, 51,* 685–690.

Hall, J. W., Murphy, J., Humphreys, M. S., & Wilson, K. P. (1979). Children's cued recall: Developmental differences in retrieval operations. *Journal of Experimental Child Psychology, 21,* 501–511.

Hasher, L., & Clifton, D. A. (1974). A developmental study of attribute encoding in free recall. *Journal of Experimental Child Psychology, 17,* 332–346.

Hunt, R. R., & Einstein, G. O. (1981). Relational and item-specific information in memory. *Journal of Verbal Learning and Verbal Behavior, 20,* 497–514.

Huttenlocher, J., & Lui, F. (1979). The semantic organization of some simple nouns and verbs. *Journal of Verbal Learning and Verbal Behavior, 18,* 141–162.

Jacoby, L. L., & Craik, F. I. M. (1979). Effects of elaboration of processing at encoding and retrieval: Trace distinctiveness and recovery of initial context. In L. S. Cermak & F. I. W. Craik (Eds.), *Levels of processing and human memory*. Hillsdale, NJ: Lawrence Erlbaum Associates.

Jacoby, L. L., Craik, F. I. M., & Begg, I. (1979). Effects of decision difficulty on recognition and recall. *Journal of Verbal Learning and Verbal Behavior, 18,* 585–600.

Jacoby, L. L., & Dallas, M. (1981). On the relationship between autobiographical memory and perceptual learning. *Journal of Experimental Psychology: General*, *3*, 306–340.

Jacoby, L. L., & Witherspoon, D. (1982). Remembering without awareness. *Canadian Journal of Psychology*, *36*, 300–324.

Jones, G. V. (1976). A fragmentation hypothesis of memory: Cued recall of pictures and of sequential position. *Journal of Experimental Psychology: General*, *105*, 277–293.

Kintsch, W. (1970a). *Learning, memory and conceptual processes*. New York: Wiley.

Kintsch, W. (1970b). Models for free recall and recognition. In D. A. Norman (Ed.), *Models of human memory*. New York: Academic Press.

Kobasigawa, A. (1974). Utilization of retrieval cues by children in recall. *Child Development*, *45*, 127–134.

Kobasigawa, A. (1977). Retrieval strategies in the development of memory. In R. V. Kail & J. W. Hagen (Eds.), *Perspectives on the development of memory and cognition*. Hillsdale, NJ: Lawrence Erlbaum Associates.

Lange, G. (1978). Organization-related processes in children's recall. In P. A. Ornstein (Ed.), *Memory development in children*. Hillsdale, NJ: Lawrence Erlbaum Associates.

Levoi, M. E., Ayton, P. J., Jonckheer, A. R., McClelland, A. G. R., & Rawles, R. E. (1983). Unidimensional memory traces: On the analysis of multiple cued recall. *Journal of Verbal Learning and Verbal Behavior*, *22*, 560–576.

Liben, L. S. (1977). Memory in the context of cognitive development: The Piagetian approach. In R. V. Kail, & J. W. Hagen (Eds.), *Perspectives on the development of memory and cognition*. Hillsdale, NJ: Lawrence Erlbaum Associates.

Liben, L. S. (1981). Copying and remembering pictures in relation to subjects' operative levels. *Developmental Psychology*, *17*, 357–365.

Loftus, E., Miller, D., & Burns, H. (1978). Semantic integration of verbal information into a visual memory. *Journal of Experimental Psychology*: *Human Learning and Memory*, *4*, 19–31.

Mandler, G. (1967). Organization and memory. In K. W. Spence & J. J. Spence (Eds.), *The psychology of learning and motivation: Advances in research and theory* (Vol. 1). New York: Academic Press.

Mandler, G. (1979). Organization and repetition: Organizational principles with special reference to rote learning. In L. G. Nilsson (Ed.), *Perspectives on memory research*. Hillsdale, NJ: Lawrence Erlbaum Associates.

Mandler, J. M. (1983). Representation. In J. H. Flavell & E. M. Markman (Eds.), *Handbook of child psychology: Cognitive development*. New York: Wiley.

Martin, E. (1975). Generation-recognition theory and the encoding specificity principle. *Psychological Review*, *82*, 150–153.

Melkman, R., & Deutsch, C. (1977). Memory functioning as related to developmental changes in bases of organization. *Journal of Experimental Child Psychology*, *23*, 84–97.

Melkman, R., Tversky, B., & Baratz, D. (1981). Developmental trends in the use of perceptual and conceptual attributes in grouping, clustering, and retrieval. *Journal of Experimental Child Psychology*, *31*, 470–486.

Melton, A. W. (1970). The situation with respect to the spacing of repetitions in memory. *Journal of Verbal Learning and Verbal Behavior*, *9*, 546–606.

Moely, B. E. (1977). Organizational factors in the development of memory. In R. V. Kail & J. W. Hagen (Eds.), *Perspectives on the development of memory and cognition.* Hillsdale, NJ: Lawrence Erlbaum Associates, 1977.

Morris, C. D., Bransford, J. D., & Franks, J. J. (1977). Levels of processing versus transfer appropriate processing. *Journal of Verbal Learning and Verbal Behavior, 16,* 519-533.

Myers, N. A., & Perlmutter, M. (1978). Memory in the years from two to five. In P. A. Ornstein (Ed.), *Memory development in children.* Hillsdale, NJ: Lawrence Erlbaum.

Neely, J. H., & Balota, D. A. (1981). Test-expectancy and semantic organization effects in recall and recognition. *Memory and Cognition, 9,* 283-300.

Nelson, D. L. (1979). Remembering pictures and words: Appearance, significance, and name. In L. S. Cermak & F. I. M. Craik (Eds.), *Levels of processing and human memory.* Hillsdale, NJ: Lawrence Erlbaum Associates.

Nelson, D. L., McEvoy, C. L., & Friedrich, M. A. (1982). Extralist cueing and retrieval inhibition. *Journal of Experimental Psychology: Learning, Memory and Cognition, 8,* 89-105.

Nelson, K. E., & Kosslyn, S. (1975). Semantic retrieval in children and adults. *Developmental Psychology, 11,* 807-813.

Norman, D. A., & Bobrow, D. G. (1979). Descriptions: An intermediate stage in memory retrieval. *Cognitive Psychology, 11,* 107-123.

Owings, R. A., & Baumeister, A. A. (1979). Levels of processing, encoding strategies and memory development. *Journal of Experimental Child Psychology, 28,* 100-118.

Perlmutter, M., & Lange, G. (1978). A developmental analysis of recall-recognition distinctions. In P. A. Ornstein (Ed.), *Memory development in children.* Hillsdale, NJ: Lawrence Erlbaum Associates.

Pressley, M. (1982). Elaboration and memory development. *Child Development, 53,* 296-309.

Pressley, M., & MacFadyen, J. (1983). Mnemonic mediator retrieval testing by preschool and kindergarten children. *Child Development, 54,* 474-479.

Raaijmakers, J. G. W., & Shiffrin, R. M. (1981). Search of associative memory. *Psychological Review, 88,* 93-134.

Rabinowitz, M. & Mandler, J. M. (1983). Organization and information retrieval. *Journal of Experimental Psychology: Learning, Memory and Cognition, 9,* 430-439.

Rabinowitz, J. C., Mandler, G., & Barsalou, L. W. (1979). Generation-recognition as an auxiliary retrieval strategy. *Journal of Verbal Learning and Verbal Behavior, 18,* 57-72.

Reddy, B., & Bellezza, F. S. (1983). Encoding specificity in free recall. *Journal of Experimental Psychology: Learning, Memory, and Cognition, 9,* 167-174.

Reese, H. W. (1977). Imagery and associative memory. In R. V. Kail & J. W. Hagen (Eds.), *Perspectives on the development of memory and cognition.* Hillsdale, NJ: Lawrence Erlbaum Associates.

Roediger, H. L., & Adelson, B. (1980). Semantic specificity in cued recall. *Memory and Cognition, 8,* 65-74.

Roediger, H. L., & Neely, J. H. (1982). Retrieval blocks in episodic and semantic memory. *Canadian Journal of Psychology, 36,* 213-242.

Sophian, C., & Hagen, J. W. (1978). Involuntary memory and the development of retrieval skills in young children. *Journal of Experimental Child Psychology*, *26*, 458–471.

Sophian, C., & Stigler, J. W. (1981). Does recognition memory improve with age? *Journal of Experimental Child Psychology*, *32*, 343–353.

Spyropoulos, T., & Ceraso, J. (1977). Categorized and uncategorized attributes as recall cues: The phenomenon of limited access. *Cognitive Psychology*, *9*, 384–402.

Stein, B. S. (1977). The effects of cue-target uniqueness on cued-recall performance. *Memory and Cognition*, *5*, 319–322.

Thomson, D. M., & Tulving, E. (1970). Associative encoding and retrieval: Weak and strong cues. *Journal of Experimental Psychology*, *86*, 255–262.

Tulving, E. (1962). Subjective organization in free recall of unrelated words. *Psychological Review*, *69*, 344–354.

Tulving, E. (1972). Episodic and semantic memory. In E. Tulving & W. Donaldson (Eds.), *Organization of memory*. New York: Academic Press.

Tulving, E. (1976). Ecphoric processes in recall and recognition. In J. Brown (Ed.), *Recall and recognition*. London: Wiley.

Tulving, E. (1979). Relation between encoding specificity and levels of processing. In L. S. Cermak & F. I. M. Craik (Eds.), *Levels of processing and human memory*. Hillsdale, NJ: Lawrence Erlbaum Associates.

Tulving, E. (1982). Synergistic energy in recall and recognition. *Canadian Journal of Psychology*, *36*, 130–147.

Tulving, E. (1983). Elements of episodic memory. Oxford: Oxford University Press.

Tulving, E., & Bower, G. H. (1974). The logic of memory representations. In G. H. Bower (Ed.), *The psychology of learning and motivation: Advances in research and theory* (Vol. 8). New York: Academic Press.

Tulving, E., & Pearlstone, A. (1966). Availability versus accessibility of information in memory for words. *Journal of Verbal Learning and Verbal Behavior*, *5*, 381–391.

Tulving, E., & Thomson, D. M. (1971). Retrieval processes in recognition memory: Effects of associative context. *Journal of Experimental Psychology*, *87*, 116–124.

Tulving, E., & Thomson, D. M. (1973). Encoding specificity and retrieval processes in episodic memory. *Psychological Review*, *80*, 352–373.

Tulving, E., & Watkins, M. J. (1975). Structure of memory traces. *Psychological Review*, *82*, 261–275.

Waters, H. S., & Waters, E. (1976). Semantic processing in children's free recall: Evidence for the importance of attentional factors and encoding variability. *Journal of Experimental Psychology: Human Learning and Memory*, *2*, 370–380.

Waters, H. S., & Waters, E. (1979). Semantic processing in children's free recall: The effects of context and meaningfulness on encoding variability. *Child Development*, *50*, 735–746.

Watkins, M. J. (1979). Engrams as cuegrams and forgetting as cue overload: A cueing approach to the structure of memory. In C. R. Puff (Ed.), *Memory structure and organization*. New York: Academic Press.

Watkins, M. J., & Gardiner, J. M. (1979). An appreciation of generate-recognize theory of recall. *Journal of Verbal Learning and Verbal Behavior*, *18*, 687–704.

Watkins, M. J., & Tulving, E. (1975). Episodic memory: When recognition fails. *Journal of Experimental Psychology: General*, *104*, 25–29.

Whitney, P., & Kunen, S. (1983). Development of hierarchical conceptual relationships in children's semantic memories. *Journal of Experimental Child Psychology*, *35*, 278–293.

2. From Cognitive to Procedural Mapping

Linda J. Anooshian and Alexander W. Siegel

Cognitive maps are typically defined as internal representations of spatial information that permit individuals to maintain orientation or find their way in large-scale spaces (Acredolo, 1981; Downs & Stea, 1973; Siegel, Kirasic, & Kail, 1978). Rather than attempt to review the literature on cognitive mapping, we will take a broad and integrative approach in examining literature as it is relevant to the *development* of cognitive mapping. By development, we mean change in the direction of differentiation and hierarchical integration in any organized system over various spans of time—for example, microgenesis, ontogenesis, phylogenesis, and so forth (see Siegel, Bisanz, & Bisanz, 1983).

We will also consider a variety of ways of knowing or cognizing about environments. What does it mean, for example, to say that one has come to *know* a neighborhood? It usually means that one does not get lost and that one knows where particular landmarks are located. But it also means that one has at least bits and pieces of information about social systems (e.g., information about neighborhood cliques and patterns of social interaction). And there is affective or emotional knowing; we know if we like or dislike the layout of the neighborhood or the family down the street. Thus, the processes involved in encoding and/or retrieving information about a neighborhood are more complex and diverse than may be apparent from research examining *children's* knowledge of purely *spatial* information (e.g., distances and directions) about a large-scale environment (e.g., Anooshian & Young, 1981; Cousins, Siegel, & Maxwell, 1983; Curtis, Siegel, & Furlong, 1981).

In trying to establish a broad and integrative perspective for the developmental study of cognitive mapping, we will review relevant literature as it supports eight basic arguments or propositions. The first two propositions relate to traditional research and theory that has been generated from the restrictive definition of cognitive mapping discussed previously:

Proposition 1. The study of cognitive mapping is now an active pluralistic enterprise.

Proposition 2. The cognitive mapping enterprise has tended to operate on its own, in relative isolation from other relevant research domains.

From here, our propositions will focus on relations between cognitive mapping and the broader domains of cognition and cognitive development:

Proposition 3. The study of cognition and cognitive development is more mature than the study of cognitive mapping.

Proposition 4. Spatial representation is paradigmatic of nonspatial thought.

There are sufficient similarities between spatial and nonspatial processing to indicate that the isolationist stance of the study of cognitive mapping is no longer theoretically or empirically viable. In fact,

Proposition 5. The cognitive mapping enterprise can profit from the activities of cognitive psychology.

Any thorough examination of the possibilities for borrowing from the activities of the larger cognitive industry will necessarily lead to the discovery that neither spatial nor nonspatial processing is entirely "cognitive:"

Proposition 6. Emotions play a significant role in both spatial and nonspatial thought.

Our last two propositions relate to the interplay between cognitions and emotions or between "cold" and "hot" cognitions (e.g., Zajonc, 1980) across the course of development:

Proposition 7. Cognitive processing has a heavier emotional component in early development.

Proposition 8. Emotional agenda have greater priority than cognitive agenda early in development.

The result of following this sequence of propositions should be the development of an integrated approach for examining diverse aspects of cognitive processing about environments—an approach we call "procedural mapping." At some future date, this sequence of propositions may provide a useful historical summary of research on cognitive mapping. That is, if cognitive mapping research moves in the directions recommended in this chapter, it will be following a natural course of development, characterized by increasing differentiation and integration of diverse research domains.

Proposition 1: The Study of Cognitive Mapping Is Now an Active Pluralistic Enterprise

Less than a decade ago, a new production emerged on the stage of developmental psychology—the development of cognitive mapping of large-scale environments. In a sense, the production was not new. There had been a few early papers by Trowbridge (1913) and Lord (1941) on the spatial orientation systems used by children; Maier (1936) had examined children's learning in a large maze; Tolman had written his classic paper and coined the term "cognitive map" (Tolman, 1948). Two theoretical papers by Hart and Moore (1973) and Siegel and White (1975) and two empirical studies by Kosslyn, Pick, and Fariello (1974) and Acredolo, Pick, and Olsen (1975) initiated current work in this area. Articles appeared increasingly in the journals over the next several years; by 1980, the study of cognitive mapping of large-scale environments had become an industry.

Working primarily from a Piagetian perspective, Hart and Moore (1973) argued that stages in the development of cognitive mapping reflected the acquisition of egocentric, fixed, and finally, coordinated frames of reference for maintaining one's orientation in the environment. During the first two stages, a child's position and movement in space are defined in terms of the child's current position or in terms of the position of a fixed element in that space. From a somewhat broader perspective, Siegel and White (1975) proposed a "main sequence" for both ontogenetic and microgenetic change in cognitive mapping. This sequence starts with the recognition of landmarks and is followed by route learning. Landmarks and routes are then organized by clusters. Finally, cluster and route knowledge (e.g., information about temporal sequences and scaled distances) are integrated in a "survey" or configurational representation. Configurations are map-like in the sense that landmark locations (and their interrelations) are no longer tied to particular routes.

Subsequent studies have yielded results which have been interpreted as support for the general sequence proposed by Siegel and White—landmark to route to configurational knowledge (Allen, Kirasic, Siegel, & Herman, 1979; Anooshian, Pascal, & McCreath, in press, Cohen & Schuepfer, 1980; Cousins et al., 1983; Curtis et al., 1981; Hazen, Lockman, & Pick, 1978). For example, Curtis et al. (1981) found that fifth and eighth graders obtained similar scores on measures of route knowledge, but eighth graders achieved higher scores for measures of configurational knowledge. Cousins et al. (1983) distinguished two levels of route knowledge and assessed relative performance across landmark, route ordering, route scaling, and configurational knowledge tasks for children in the first, fourth, and seventh grades. On each task, children were asked to provide specific information about their school campus. For the landmark task, children selected photographs of landmarks that they would encounter when walking a particular route on the campus. For the route-ordering task, children were required to place five photographs of landmarks to correspond to the order of the landmarks along those same routes. The route-scaling task required that children space the photographs to represent the actual distances between the five landmarks on the school campus. Finally, measures of configurational knowledge reflected the accuracy of both distance and bearing estimates to different landmarks from four different siting locations on the school campus. Using measures derived from these tasks, Cousins et al. applied Guttman scaling to establish whether relative performance across tasks was consistent with the order proposed by Siegel and White (1975)—that is, landmark before route ordering before route scaling before configurational knowledge. Guttman scaling confirmed the hypothesized developmental sequence; a pattern of passes and failures consistent with that order was observed for 37 of 40 children tested.

A similar strategy was recently used by Anooshian et al. (in press) to examine landmark, route ordering, and route scaling knowledge among preschool children. The three tasks were similar to those designed by Cousins et al. (1983). Children selected photographs of the landmarks that would be seen in walking familiar routes through the preschool campus (e.g., the route they followed to get to their classroom each morning), sequentially ordered photographs of the landmarks, and finally spread the photographs out to represent the interlandmark distances. Using Guttman scaling, Anooshian et al. confirmed the same developmental order: landmark recognition, route ordering, route scaling.

Methodological Issues

In the last decade, cognitive mapping research has changed from a limited enterprise hampered by the unavailability of methods for measuring externalized spatial representations to a pluralistic field with numerous methods for asking different questions about different types of spatial processing (see Liben, 1981, 1982). This is also true of other areas of memory development (e.g., see Chapter 5 by Dempster and Chapter 7 by Salthouse and Kausler). A listing of the major methods now used to study spatial representations is presented in Table 2-1. Debate over methodological issues has led to a new focus on theoretical issues relating to the complexity and variety of spatial processing.

The rapid growth of cognitive mapping research was closely tied to the development and refinement of acceptable methodologies for "externalizing" cognitive maps (Newcombe, 1984; Siegel, 1981). Before detailing some of these, it is essential to deal with two other related issues, namely the nature of the cognitive map and the competence/performance problem(s).

The term "cognitive map" is used extensively in this chapter and in the literature. A number of investigators (inadvertently) reify the term. Cognitive map is an inferred construct; it is, in effect, a state description of a process at a moment in time. Like other state descriptions—for example, the labels for various cognitive-developmental stages—it may be misleading. Cognitive maps are not static things-in-the-head, fixed in form or content. Like stages, cognitive

Table 2-1. Major Methods for Assessing Spatial Knowledge

Method	Subject's Task	Illustrative Study
Map drawing	Draw sketch map in different scale and perspective	Piaget, Inhelder, & Szeminska (1960)
Verbal report	Translate spatial knowledge to verbal description	Piaget & Inhelder (1967)
Model building	Arrange small-scale replicas using different scale and perspective	Siegel & Schadler (1977)
Reconstruction	Reconstruct space in same scale	Herman & Siegel (1978)
Distance estimation	Estimate relative distance, absolute distance or travel time between landmarks	Cohen, Weatherford, & Byrd (1980)
Bearing estimation	Estimate directional relations between landmarks	Anooshian & Young (1981)
Multidimensional scaling	Rank order distances between landmarks	Kosslyn et al. (1974)
Triangulation	Estimate bearings to landmarks	Hardwick, McIntyre, & Pick (1976)
Projective convergence	Estimate bearings and distances to landmarks	Curtis et al. (1981)

maps are abstractions that we use to understand the sequence and development of the dynamic activity of cognitive mapping (Downs & Stea, 1977). In this sense, cognitive maps are convenient fictions.

We have the same problem with the concept of "competence"—whether in cognitive mapping or in other domains. Competence is not a thing-in-the-head either. Competence is performance in a medium. Further, competencies are wobbly and wander as a function of subtle differences in task procedures, instructions, and other load factors (Stone & Day, 1980). That is, there is a danger in leaping to inferences about competencies (which have the flavor of universality) from performances in different contexts. Nonetheless, in the early cognitive mapping studies—driven more by an organismic than a contextual root metaphor (Overton & Reese, 1973)—attempts were made to unconfound spatial abilities and verbal and praxic abilities so that the "real" cognitive map could be externalized and measured.

Techniques were developed that could, it was hoped, assess children's changing knowledge of large-scale spaces independently of changes in other skills required in verbal reports, map drawing, and model building (see Table 2-1). For example, Kosslyn et al. (1974) used multidimensional scaling procedures (Kruskal, Young, & Seery, 1978) to derive a spatial configuration of landmarks from children's rank ordering of distances among them. The resulting configuration seemed less influenced by nonspatial task demands than was the case for map drawing or model construction tasks (Siegel, 1981). Consequently, many subsequent studies have used scaling procedures (Allen et al., 1979; Anooshian & Kromer, 1984; Kirasic, Siegel, Allen, Curtis, & Furlong, as cited by Siegel, 1981; Newcombe & Liben, 1982; Siegel, Allen, & Kirasic, 1979).

Other techniques were also designed to assess spatial knowledge from a somewhat more functional view. The question was, How do children know where they are in relation to other landmarks? Hardwick et al. (1976) proposed a triangulation procedure through which the location of a landmark in a cognitive map could be inferred from the intersections of bearing estimates made from different siting locations. Curtis et al. (1981) used both bearing and distance estimates to derive a spatial configuration using a procedure called projective convergence (see Siegel, 1981).

It is now apparent that different procedures tap different types of specific processes involved in cognitive mapping (Liben, 1981, 1982; Newcombe, 1984; Newcombe & Liben, 1982). As researchers in other domains have realized for some time, the selection of a particular methodology or procedure can have substantial theoretical implications (see related discussion in Chapter 5 by Dempster and Chapter 6 by Kail). Newcombe (1984) argues, for example, that map drawing—previously rejected as an inappropriate method for externalizing cognitive maps (e.g., Hardwick et al., 1976; Siegel, 1981)—is a legitimate method for assessing spatial processing that is different from that demanded by ranking distances.

A recent study by Anooshian and Kromer (1984) on children's knowledge of their school campus exemplifies the interrelations among some of these methodological and theoretical issues in cognitive mapping. Children were asked (1) to make bearing and distance estimates (from different siting locations) to nine campus buildings, and (2) to rank order distances among these landmarks (see Siegel, 1981). Results indicated little difference in the developmental trends associated with the different measures. However, correlational analyses suggested that the bearing and distance measures tapped different types of spatial processing. While direct distance estimates and congruence scores (derived from rank orderings of distances) were strongly related, neither distance measure was related to the bearing estimates; the spatial processing involved in estimating directions seems different from that required in processing distances. These results were interpreted as being consistent with theoretical approaches which postulate that cognitive maps consist of separate codes for different types of information about a space (Hintzman, O'Dell, & Arndt, 1981; Kuipers, 1982; Thorndyke, 1981; Tversky, 1981). Thus, different methodologies seem to be appropriate and necessary to study different aspects of cognitive mapping.

Cognitive Mapping Is Pluralistic

While theories point to different sets of components or processes, our examination of the literature indicates that research has focused on four variables: landmark encoding; spatial inferences; clusters and subdivisions; and distortions.

Landmark Encoding. According to Siegel and White (1975), landmarks are "unique configurations of perceptual events" that "identify a specific geographical location" (p. 23). Research has made considerable progress in distinguishing between types of landmark encoding that emerge early versus late in development. For example, young children appear to encode the spatial locations that are associated with particular events. In contrast, landmark encoding that requires more effortful processing emerges considerably later in development.

On balance, the literature confirms the suggestion of Siegel and his colleagues (Kail & Siegel, 1977; Siegel et al., 1978) that landmark recognition emerges early in the development of cognitive mapping. Acredolo et al. (1975) found that 3-year-olds were as adept as 8-year-olds at recognizing the location of a specific event (dropping keys), as long as the space was differentiated (i.e., the location was distinctive). DeLoache (1980) has studied young preschoolers' abilities to find and recognize the locations of hidden objects. Kail and Siegel (1977) concluded that, in contrast to semantic features, place information is encoded at an early age. They further suggested that this encoding is fairly automatic, a conclusion based on evidence that place encoding does not interfere with the effortful encoding of other features (e.g., semantic features). Of course, these arguments are consistent with Hasher and Zacks' (1979) distinction between automatic and effortful processing and their suggestion that the spatial locations of events are encoded automatically (see also Chapter 3 by Bjorklund). If place information is encoded automatically, the accuracy of encoding should not be affected by such factors as the motivation, intentions, or developmental level of the encoder.

If landmarks are encoded automatically, one should also find that places are effective retrieval cues for information about events that occurred at those places (Tulving & Thomson, 1973). Results of a number of studies have confirmed this prediction (Smith, 1979, 1982; Smith, Glenberg, & Bjork, 1978). Such effects should also be apparent for young children. For example, if Acredolo et al. (1975) had taken children back to where the keys were dropped, they should have found that even the 3-year-olds could recall the details of the event. Hazen and Volk-Hudson (1984) found that giving 3- and 4-year-olds the opportunity to return to distinctive places facilitated their recall of objects that they had previously seen. If spatial context effects are a function of automatic encoding, remembering for young children may be closely tied to their movement in physical environments.

The continuum of automatic to effortful processing provides a useful framework for differentiating types of landmark knowledge. Automatic encoding does not imply an ability to recognize a place in an undifferentiated environment. If the physical characteristics of a landmark are not distinctive, encoding would depend on elaborate processing (Eysenck, 1979b). Recognition is aided by distinctiveness, and elaborative processing is clearly effortful (Eysenck & Eysenck, 1979; Hasher & Zacks, 1979). Consistent with this perspective, Acredolo et al. (1975) found age differences when the environment was undifferentiated (i.e., the older children performed more accurately). Microgenetic increases in landmark encoding are also clearly affected by landmark distinctiveness (Allen et al., 1979; Lynch, 1960).

Recognition-in-context (e.g., Kirasic, Siegel, & Allen, 1980; Siegel et al., 1978) should also require effortful processing because encoding that involves integrating basic landmark information with the surrounding context is elaborative and effortful. Kirasic et al. confirmed that kindergarteners had more difficulty than fourth graders in recognizing landmarks in context. This difficulty could not be attributed simply to a tendency to focus on landmarks to the exclusion of contexts. The encoding of landmark-context relations may be critical for the temporal integration of landmark knowledge required for route mapping (Kirasic et al., 1980; Allen, Siegel, & Rosinski, 1978).

While some landmark information may be automatically encoded, there are developmental changes in the richness of that encoding. Developmental differences should also be apparent when individuals *recall* place information (see Light & Zelinski, 1983) or *represent* landmarks in route or configurational maps. Being at a distinctive place may support recognition as well as provide an effective retrieval cue for recalling events that previously occurred at that place. The encoding of distinctive information about a place may be useful for recognition, but recall seems to depend on the encoding of relations (Einstein & Hunt, 1980; Eysenck, 1979b). In general, recalling place information requires a good retrieval cue—for example, detailed information about an event associated with the place. Just as places can be retrieval cues for event information, the recall of place information is affected by the availability of cues that were associated with the original learning of the places (Cohen et al., 1980; Cohen, Weatherford, Lomenick, & Koeller, 1979; Herman, Roth, Miranda, & Getz, 1982; Siegel, Herman, Allen, & Kirasic, 1979).

Similarly, representing a space obviously involves more than recognizing distinctive landmarks. A representation of a space consists of a limited number of *selected* landmarks that are connected by linear pathways/routes through undifferentiated space (Allen, 1981; Allen et al., 1978; Kaplan, 1976; Lynch, 1960; Siegel et al., 1978). Hence, an important component of route learning involves the selection and use of good landmarks for representing distances between landmarks along a route (Allen et al., 1979; Siegel et al., 1978). Allen et al. found that second and fourth graders did less well than adults in judging the potential of particular landmarks to serve as way-finding aids. However, the ability to *use* landmarks in route learning (i.e., to make more accurate interlandmark distance judgments) emerged earlier.

Spatial Inferences. Research in this area indicates that some inferencing abilities emerge early in development. As is the case for landmark encoding, spatial inferences that emerge later seem to require effortful processing.

We depend on spatial inferences for many of our way-finding decisions and other spatial judgments (e.g., telling someone the approximate distance to a shopping center). These inferences occur so frequently (see Chase & Chi, 1981) and are made with such apparent ease, that we often are unaware of the distinction between spatial judgments that do or do not require inferences. For example, suppose you travel frequently between your home and a grocery store and between your home and a friend's house. It may be equally easy for you to estimate the direction and distance of the store from the friend's house (that is, make a spatial inference) as to make those estimates from your own home. Spatial inferences may seem simple because, as adults, we use configurational or survey maps which represent the spatial relations and distances among the three landmarks rather than representations that are tied to specific routes that we have experienced previously. However, this association between spatial inferences and configurational mapping suggests that the ability to make spatial inferences is acquired fairly late (see Curtis et al., 1981).

Anooshian and Nelson (1984) attempted to simulate the grocery store example with 10- and 12-year-old children in their own neighborhood. Children were familiarized with direct routes by walking several times between a central point (the neighborhood pool) and several outlying locations with which they were initially unfamiliar. Children never walked from one outlying location to another. Later, children were asked to make a number of different bearing estimates, pointing a "telescope" to specified but nonvisible targets. Age differences were found in the accuracy of bearing estimates made from one outlying location to another, but not for noninference estimates from the pool to an outlying location (or vice versa). Anooshian and Nelson also found age group differences for "reversal" estimates which required inferences about directions that did not correspond with their past experience. Children were familiarized with a route that connected four locations, but this familiarization involved walking the route in only one direction. Age differences were observed for bearing estimates from one landmark back to another that had been passed on the route of travel, but not for forward estimates. Anooshian and Nelson interpreted these results in terms of demands for effortful processing. They argued that bearing estimates that correspond with past experience should require less effortful processing than estimates based on inferences or mental reversals. This interpretation is consistent with the view that inferences require configurational representations (e.g. Curtis et al., 1981; Siegel & White, 1975); if appropriate configurations cannot be retrieved, they must be constructed in working memory. That construction would require effortful processing (Johnson-Laird & Bethell-Fox, 1978).

Other studies of inferencing have attempted to determine what *types* of spatial inferences can be made by young children. Hazen et al. (1978) found that older preschoolers could make spatial inferences similar to those described above in a small configuration of rooms in a laboratory. Infants can make such spatial inferences in small reaching spaces (Pick, 1976; Pick & Lockman, 1981). Pick has suggested that there is developmental change in the extensiveness of the space across which inferences can be made. From this perspective, it makes sense that infants make inferences in a small reaching space, older preschoolers make inferences in a configuration of small rooms, and only 12-year-olds make inferences in a large neighborhood area. Consistent with Anooshian and Nelson's focus on effortful processing, it may be that the larger the space, the greater the processing demands for spatial inferences. If cognitive maps consist largely of partial information about past experiences with an environment (Kuipers, 1982; Tversky, 1981), then inferences would usually be based on configurational maps constructed in working memory. Since this construction is effortful, it seems reasonable that a continuum of effort might be associated with the relative size of the mapped space. For inferences requiring greater effort, one should also expect a later emergence (Hasher & Zacks, 1979).

There is evidence that inferences based on hierarchical relations also appear early. This type of inference is best understood in the context of Stevens and Coupe's (1978) proposal that location information is encoded in terms of propositional hierarchical models (see also Chase & Chi, 1981; Downs & Stea, 1973; Kaplan, 1976). The spatial location of a city is encoded as part of a state which in turn is encoded as part of the United States. Thus, when asked about the spatial relation between two cities in different states, individuals infer the relation between the cities from information about the relation between the two states. This hierarchical system is economical in the amount of information that must be stored. In support of this model, Stevens and Coupe found that adults often incorrectly inferred that Reno was West of San Diego. Acredolo and Boulter (1983) translated Stevens and Coupe's city and state problem into a laboratory task in which objects were located in two different subdivisions of a board separated by a wavy line. The results indicated that first and third graders were more likely than adults to use subdivision membership in encoding object location. For example, the younger children were more likely to remember an object in the left subdivision as being to the left of an object in the right subdivision.

While young children make inferences based on simple hierarchical relations, it is likely that development is associated with increasingly hierarchical systems. It is also likely that different frameworks for encoding spatial location are organized in such hierarchical systems. Thus, making inferences across more extensive spaces (e.g., Pick, 1976) may involve the use of higher levels in a hierarchical system. Consistent with our earlier arguments, the construction of a mental model with information from different hierarchical levels would appear to be an effortful task.

Clusters and Subdivisions. In being simpler and less effortful than the encoding of exact location, cluster-based processing should predominate in early development. Research, which substantiates this assertion, also suggests that more attention should be given to developmental differences in the number and type of clusters that are typically encoded (see Chapter 5 by Dempster).

Cognitive mapping seems to consist of a divide-and-conquer strategy that starts with the encoding of information about cluster or subdivision membership, and ends with the acquisition of more specific information about the spatial relations within individual clusters (Allen, 1981; Hart & Moore, 1973; Siegel et al., 1978). Siegel et al. suggested that these two processes may be analogous to part versus whole learning. Developmentally, young children may have access to information about specific locations (part) or information about clusters (whole), but are unable to integrate them into an overall spatial representation. (Note that, at a more global level, a cluster could well be an element, i.e., there are nested levels of representation [Mandler, 1962]).

We focus here on evidence that the encoding of simple hierarchical information emerges fairly early in development. In addition to directional inferences, children and adults also base distance judgments on hierarchical relations or subdivision membership. Further, young children are more likely than older children and adults to judge distances as shorter if two objects/landmarks are in the same rather than different subdivisions (Acredolo & Boulter, 1983; Allen, 1981). Allen suggests a specific ontogenetic order for two methods for making proximity judgments. The first involves judging simply whether one location belongs to a particular spatial subdivision. Later on, these judgments are supplemented by metric estimates (Laurendau & Pinard, 1970; Piaget & Inhelder, 1967). Further, Allen suggests the same microgenetic order for older children and adults who have access to these two methods, namely, subdivision membership prior to metric distance.

Siegel and Schadler (1977) also obtained evidence that early development is characterized by the encoding of cluster membership (see the related discussion in Chapter 3 by Bjorklund). Kindergarten children who were tested near the end of the school year constructed more accurate models of their classroom when the models were scored in terms of *absolute* metric accuracy. In contrast, children tested at the beginning of the year were fairly accurate at reproducing the *relative* spatial relations among *clusters* of objects in the classroom; these accuracy measures were not affected by familiarity.

In many cases, measures of the relational accuracy of bearing and distance estimates may reflect the accuracy of the child's encoding of cluster membership and relations between clusters. Specifically, if a child considers only cluster information in making these estimates, that child's inaccuracy will be more apparent in absolute than relational accuracy measures. Researchers have consistently observed that relational accuracy emerges early and undergoes considerably less improvement than does absolute accuracy (Anooshian & Kromer, 1984; Anooshian & Young, 1981; Curtis et al., 1981; Hardwick et al., 1976; Siegel & Schadler, 1977). While Hardwick et al. distinguished between general- and specific-level representations, the more important distinction may be between cluster-based versus more specific processing of location information. The literature seems to suggest that spatial processing is dominated by the encoding of cluster information in early development.

Of course, evidence of divide-and-conquer strategies or cluster-based processing can be found at all levels of development (Allen, 1981; Stevens & Coupe, 1978). Anooshian and Nelson (1984) suggested that when 10- and 12-year-old children estimated the location of a target outside of the neighborhood cluster, they defined their current position in terms of the location of the cluster they occupied. While the accuracy of bearing estimates to neighborhood targets varied considerably across different siting locations within the neighborhood, no such effects were obtained for bearing estimates to their schools. A similar conclusion is suggested by Cousins et al.'s (1983) analysis of familiarity effects. Children made more accurate bearing estimates from an unfamiliar cluster to a target in a familiar cluster than vice versa. It appears that bearing estimates are minimally affected by children's previous exposure to their current position in an unfamiliar cluster.

If cluster-based processing plays a significant role in cognitive mapping, any explanation of developmental change must focus on differences in the nature, number, and types of clusters that children encode. The earliest forms of cluster encoding may be restricted to information about whether a landmark is within or outside the home cluster. Both Siegel (1982) and Hart (1981) have suggested that children initially represent the locations of landmarks within a home cluster. In fact, Siegel has suggested further that a child may represent the home cluster at a configurational level while being limited to landmark recognition for areas outside that cluster. But what defines the home or neighborhood cluster? In addition to developmental changes in the number and types of clusters that might be encoded, it is likely that there are developmental differences in the criteria used for defining cluster boundaries. For example, a young child would be more likely to define the home cluster in terms of social activities (e.g., play) than would an adult. A cluster boundary might be designated by a barrier (e.g., a major highway) or other physical dividing line (Acredolo & Boulter, 1983; Allen, 1981; Newcombe & Liben, 1982) or by social and geographical conventions (Stevens & Coupe, 1978). There are almost certainly a variety of other factors that determine how individuals designate smaller and less obvious clusters.

Finally, it is important to recognize that the extent to which individuals use a divide-and-conquer strategy is probably context-specific. For example, Newcombe and Liben (1982) found more evidence of errors associated with clustering landmarks (e.g., overestimating distances between landmarks separated by a barrier) when children were asked to rank order distances than when they made direct distance estimates; the former was considered to be the more difficult task. Cluster-based processing may be most dominant when one's limited processing capacity is challenged, as it is when young children (Hasher & Zacks, 1979) or adults attempt to navigate in unfamiliar environments.

Distortions in Cognitive Maps. Some implicit, but critical assumptions underlying most cognitive mapping research are that (a) accuracy is the most appropriate measure of cognitive representations, (b) the standard against which these externalized cognitive maps should be assessed is the "world according to Rand-McNally" (i.e., a model of the world based on Euclidean geometry), and (c) discrepancies between externalized maps and the Rand-McNally model represent errors, or distortions, or, in young children, deficits or egocentricity. There are serious problems with these assumptions (Downs & Siegel, 1981; Downs & Stea, 1973; Kaplan, 1976; Siegel, 1982). Regarding (a), the issue is not accuracy, but rather accuracy-for-what-purpose. A casual visitor to a city and a potential home buyer will probably have different purposes, and hence, will have different accuracies in their cognitive maps. Regarding (b), the world according to Rand-McNally (with its axes of latitude and longitude) is but one possible model of the world. Less sophisticated models of the world have been shown to have enormous adaptive value, and navigational systems based on these models are extremely effective (e.g., Gladwin, 1970). Regarding (c), it is difficult, if not impossible, to define a "distortion" in the absence of knowing what model of the world is being used by the mapper. The geometry is in the head of the researcher, not necessarily in the head of the child. What follows must be interpreted in light of these considerations.

Issues related to distortions and accuracy are closely related to externalization issues. The production of accurate renditions of environments may necessarily require the production of distortions. Maps on pieces of paper must lie about some things in order to be accurate about others. For example, we use Mercator projections because we care about truth in directionality more than we care about truth in distances. Multidimensional scaling procedures seem to underestimate knowledge of directional relations, possibly because subjects rank order distances and are never asked about directions (see Newcombe, 1984). Any single method for assessing spatial knowledge must emphasize the significance of some types of information over others (see Table 2-1). It follows that what is most or least correct in a cognitive map is a function of the method used to derive that map.

Numerous researchers have documented specific types of distortions in cognitive maps (e.g., Allen, 1981; Anooshian & Wilson, 1977; Briggs, 1973; Canter & Tagg, 1975; Cohen, Baldwin, & Sherman, 1978; Holahan, 1978; Holahan & Dobrowolny, 1978; Kosslyn et al., 1974; Lee, 1970, 1973; Lowrey, 1970; Maurer & Baxter, 1972; Moar & Bower, 1983; Newcombe & Liben, 1982; Tversky, 1981). For example, individuals judge the distances to and from city centers as asymmetrical (Briggs, 1973; Lee, 1970); the same asymmetry has been observed for estimates of the distances between reference points and nonreference points (Sadalla, Burroughs, & Staplin, 1980). The distance between two landmarks seems shorter if the landmarks are located in the same rather than different subdivisions (Allen, 1981), when individuals report emotional involvement with the destination for travel (Ekman & Bratfisch, 1965), or when there are no barriers to direct travel (Kosslyn et al., 1974). When considered in the context of our review so far, it becomes clear that such distortions do not represent isolated peculiarities or deficiencies. Rather, distortions provide evidence that modes of processing complex information about environments are quite adaptive in the context of limited processing capacity. Constructing an organized representation of a space requires landmark selection; distance distortions seem to be a function of which landmarks are selected (Allen et al., 1978; Sadalla et al., 1980). Hierarchical or cluster-based processing allows for economy in the amount and specificity of information that must be encoded, but specific inference errors occur as a consequence. It now appears that distance distortions associated with barriers (e.g., Cohen et al., 1978; Kosslyn et al., 1974) may not reflect the improper encoding of the distance required to walk around barriers. Rather, young children seem to use barriers to define clusters (see Acredolo & Boulter, 1983; Newcombe & Liben, 1982).

We have seen that distortions confirm the adaptiveness and efficiency of cognitive mapping. We have also seen how the study of cognitive mapping has become a pluralistic area composed of related research programs. Spatial inferences may be based on the encoding of cluster information; both inferences and cluster-based processing emerge early developmentally and are relevant in accounting for specific distortions. We have seen that developmental trends for both landmark encoding and spatial inferences are best understood in the context of the continuum of automatic to effortful processing. Likewise, it is essential to consider mental effort in accounting for specific distortions. That is, it "costs" to do veridical mapping. The cost in mental effort outweighs the benefits; there is usually little need to map one's surroundings precisely. Further, because the demands of mapping all details of an environment will usually exceed our limited processing capacity, some things must be sacrificed in order to be accurate about others. In some cases, it may be more important to highlight emotions and to construct a map in which all the hot spots are correct than to have a map in which all the inches, feet, and yards are correct.

Proposition 2: The Cognitive Mapping Enterprise Has Tended to Operate on Its Own, in Relative Isolation from Other Relevant Research Domains

We have previously described the syntheses of both Hart and Moore (1973) and Siegel and White (1975) as theoretical approaches to the development of cognitive mapping derived from literature in other domains. In addition to careful attention to the theories of Werner (1957) and Piaget (e.g., Piaget & Inhelder, 1967; Piaget, Inhelder, & Szeminska, 1960), Siegel and White searched for parallels outside of the organismic tradition. However, recent cognitive mapping research has failed to use parallels from other areas to guide theory development, tending instead to leave such possibilities as points for discussion sections of research reports. The argument that researchers have failed to recognize analogies receives support from Newcombe (1982). Newcombe initially claimed that,

> the study of spatial cognition has diverged from the mainstream of cognitive development and has become established as a separate subfield with its own concerns and methods of inquiry. (pp. 65–66)

but then concluded that

> researchers in spatial cognition are more part of the mainstream of cognitive development research than it has sometimes seemed in the past. (p. 78)

A more nonisolationist stance would involve using similarities across areas to develop new approaches to theory and research (Teitelbaum, 1977). Cognitive mapping research has, for the most part, ignored or not taken seriously "synthesis by parallel" which, according to Teitelbaum:

> says that something new is like something else that is already familiar. A parallel is a similarity, and the more detailed it is the more confidence we have that the similarity is not mere coincidence. One uses this method from the conviction that nature is parsimonious: if a given phenomenon works in a particular fashion, it is likely that the same method is used to produce other phenomena which up to now we have not recognized as being the same. Therefore, look for a parallel. (p. 11)

Researchers in the cognitive mapping area have not taken full advantage of the strategy of looking for parallels, as emphasized by Siegel et al. (1983):

> Thus, a thorough understanding of one system (and development within that system) may be useful in gaining an understanding of a second, less familiar system that is similar to the first in structure or function . . . the establishment and use of parallels as a heuristic (a) provides the investigator of an unfamiliar domain with suggestions for initial hypotheses, and (b) leads the investigator to diverse literatures where similar problems may have been explored (and perhaps successfully resolved). (pp. 64–67)

While developmentalists involved in cognitive mapping have considered points of overlap with organismic approaches to cognitive development, they have not systematically looked for parallels in other literatures (see Cousins, 1984). Obviously, it would be unreasonable to recommend "looking for parallels" if there were reason to suppose that spatial encoding is fundamentally different from other forms of encoding. Paradoxically, it is the previously discussed evidence for parallels that reinforces our argument that cognitive mapping research is operating in relative isolation. To emphasize the heuristic value of pursuing these largely unexplored similarities across areas, we briefly mention a few of them here.

The *levels-of-processing* approach to memory postulates that deep, elaborate encoding leads to greater memorability (see Craik & Lockhart, 1972; Einstein

& Hunt, 1980; Eysenck, 1977, 1979b; Eysenck & Eysenck, 1979). The importance of the distinctiveness of landmarks has similarly been stressed in the spatial representation literature (Acredolo et al., 1975; Siegel & White, 1975). Further, one could argue that more advanced configurational representations necessarily involve more elaborative encodings and, thus, greater memorability than route representations. Configurational representations are derived from elaborative encodings of multiple associations based on a variety of routes of travel.

Chunking and *clustering* are important organizational strategies for verbal memory (Hagen, Jongeward, & Kail, 1975; Lange, 1978), and developmental change in these strategies can account for a significant amount of improvement on memory tasks (data are reviewed in Chapter 5 by Dempster). Similarly, we have argued that developmental changes in cognitive mapping cannot be understood without considering changes in the number and type of clusters that are encoded. On a more general level, references to elaboration and the use of organizational strategies (see Chapter 3 by Bjorklund) suggest that individuals construct memories by filling in gaps and making inferences (Barclay & Reid, 1974; Bartlett, 1932/1973; Paris, 1978). Such a view has been essential in conceptualizing developmental change in representations of large-scale environments, where many of the distances and directional relations between landmarks cannot be viewed but must be inferred (see Hazen et al., 1978; Moore, 1974; Pick & Lockman, 1981; Siegel & White, 1975).

Finally, we have suggested that developmental sequences for both spatial and nonspatial tasks are related to *effortful processing* and that age differences should be greatest for tasks requiring such processing. Further, attention to processing requirements may be essential in understanding similar developmental sequences for microgenetic and ontogenetic change. Such sequences should show that both young children and new learners first demonstrate those encoding operations that require the least amount of effortful processing.

Our review of cognitive mapping suggests that the area may now be experiencing an identity crisis. That is, there are an increasing number of recent developmental studies that are progressing beyond the isolationist stance (see Acredolo & Boulter, 1983; Allen, 1981; Hazen & Volk-Hudson, 1984; Herman et al., 1982). These studies emphasize the value of generating experimental hypotheses (a) through exploring parallels between spatial and nonspatial processing, and (b) within the framework of contextualism, rather than organicism (Cousins, 1984).

Proposition 3: The Study of Cognition and Cognitive Development Is More Mature Than the Study of Cognitive Mapping

Looking for parallels should be most productive if there are other research traditions that are more well-developed than one's own (Siegel et al., 1983). Since psychologists have studied cognition and cognitive development for many years, it is not surprising that the domains are considerably more advanced than the study of cognitive mapping. The greater maturity of the field of cognition is most apparent in research on representational issues. While most cognitive mapping researchers recognize that spatial representations are not map-like, they have been overly preoccupied with map-like metaphors (see Cousins, 1984). This preoccupation has been most apparent in attempts to develop techniques for externalizing *the* cognitive map. As discussed earlier, multi-dimensional scaling procedures were used to assess children's cognitive representations of a specific large-scale space. Researchers have tended to assume that there is a single type of representation involved in cognitive mapping. For example, we have seen the emergence of a confusing and conflicting set of studies designed to determine whether propositional or analogical models of representation are most appropriate in describing *the* cognitive map (see Evans, 1980; Hintzman et al., 1981; Levine, Jankovic, & Palij, 1982). Both the preoccupation with the holistic metaphor and the recent controversy over the format of the representation fail to recognize the complexity and diversity of the processes involved in cognitive mapping. As discussed earlier, research has clearly shown that there are different types of representations and processes associated with cognitive mapping.

In contrast, cognitive psychology has long recognized the complexity and diversity of different types of representations and associated processing (see Anderson, 1978). Although there may be disagreement regarding the viability of particular models of long-term memory, cognitive psychologists agree that different levels and types of representation can coexist in long-term memory; one can have both specific and holistic representations of the same information. For example, Hayes-Roth has distinguished between component representations and unitized assemblies or configurations (1977). Similarly, Wickelgren (1979) has distinguished between horizontal and vertical associative memory; for the latter, a complex idea could be represented by a single node in semantic memory.

Further, for some time, cognitive psychologists have assumed that the representation that individuals may use on particular tasks may be different from the long-term memory representation from which it is derived. This assumption is embodied in the distinction between long-term memory and the working representations contained in a short-term working memory (see Chapter 5 by Dempster). Considerable reconstruction and transformation may intervene between the retrieval of information from long-term memory and the information as it exists in immediate working memory.

The literature indicates that a variety of cognitive tasks may involve constructing a representation or mental model in working memory. It now appears that both children and adults solve comprehension and reasoning tasks by constructing a mental model in working memory, rather than, for example, applying logic directly to the information contained in the premises (e.g., Huttenlocher, 1968; Inhelder & Piaget, 1964; Piaget, 1928). In syllogistic reasoning tasks, for example, one may start with premise information in the form of statements that "John is taller than Tom," and "Dick is taller than John." From this information, individuals construct a mental model which, in this case, may be a spatial image consistent with the information contained in the premises. Decisions about the relationship between Tom and Dick are made directly from the mental model rather than from inferences based on the propositional information in the premises. This explanation of syllogistic reasoning has received considerable empirical support (Bryant & Trabasso, 1971; DeSoto, London, & Handel, 1965; Handel, DeSoto, & London, 1968; Huttenlocher, 1968; Johnson-Laird, 1975, 1982; Riley, 1976; Riley & Trabasso, 1974; Scribner, 1975; Trabasso, 1975; Trabasso & Riley, 1975; Trabasso, Riley, & Wilson, 1975). One developmental implication is that success in solving such problems is dependent on a child's ability to construct an appropriate mental model. The acceptance of this approach has emphasized how developmental change in the structure or logic of thought can account for the different types of mental models constructed by children of different ages (see Falmagne, 1975).

Other research has demonstrated the viability of this approach for tasks other than syllogistic reasoning. For example, Johnson-Laird (1975, 1982) has suggested that there are two stages in the interpretation or comprehension of sentences, an initial propositional representation, and a more articulated and integrated mental model. What he calls "procedural semantics" are involved in constructing the mental model from the propositional representation. An emphasis on the nature of representation can also be found in the literature on problem solving (Anooshian, Hartman, & Scharf, 1982; Eisenstadt & Kareev, 1975; Newell & Simon, 1972). Siegel, Goldsmith, and Madson (1981) have argued that estimates of extent and number (e.g., "How many beans are in this jar?") are derived from such mental models. Finally, how an individual constructs a mental model may be the best predictor of success on mathematics and science problems:

> It is clear from research on children's arithmetic (Groen & Resnick, 1977), children's solution of word problems (Heller & Greeno, 1979), and expert physicists solving mechanics problems (Larkin & Reif, 1976) that both children and adults construct cognitive representations of the terms, numbers, and operations involved, and subsequently re-transform this "qualitative" representation into a mathematical expression (Larkin, 1977). That is, both children and adults "solve" the problem from the constructed representation rather than from printed words. (Siegel et al., 1981, p. 6).

While the cognitive mapping enterprise was still preoccupied with an holistic, map-like metaphor, cognitive psychology had long recognized the coexistence of different types of representations, as well as the importance of specific processes and procedures as they were required to construct representations for particular tasks.

Proposition 4: Spatial Representation Is Paradigmatic of Nonspatial Thought

A theoretical approach that is viable for a variety of cognitive domains should be seriously considered in any explanation of the development of cognitive mapping (Siegel et al., 1983). We suggested this possibility earlier in discussing spatial inferences. Specifically, we suggested that the mental effort required to construct a configuration in working memory varied with the size of the space being represented. Siegel and White (1975) first implicated such a common theoretical approach in their discussion of "spatial thinking on nonspatial matters." Their argument was based on Huttenlocher's (1968) demonstration that syllogisms are solved by constructing a spatial image (mental model) that is consistent with the premise information.

If the mental models constructed for comprehension and reasoning tasks are often spatial images, then it follows that study of the development of spatial representation provides information about nonspatial thought (see Johnson-Laird, 1982). Knowing how a child represents environments should be relevant in determining the kinds of spatial images that a child could construct in making spatial inferences or solving reasoning problems. Similarly, Luria (1966) referred to a general deficit in "spatial synthesis"; patients with parieto-occipital lesions have difficulty comprehending terms that describe comparative and tempoal relations, logical-grammatical constructions such as "father's brother," and passive sentences requiring mental reversal of action. They also have difficulty in telling time from the hands on a clock and with basic arithmetic operations.

Some recent research by Anooshian et al. (1982; in press) has been concerned with relations between cognitive mapping and general problem solving. These authors selected logical search tasks as good prototypes for problem solving (see Wellman & Somerville, 1982). Anooshian et al. (1982) first suggested that a child who is not at least at the level of route mapping should have difficulty with any problem solving task that requires inferences based on temporal sequences. They found that only preschool children who represented landmarks sequentially were likely to make a logical inference about the location of a missing object. In this case, the inference was that a missing object was likely to be found somewhere between the last place the child had used the object and the first place it was discovered missing (see also Haake, Somerville, & Wellman, 1980; Wellman, Somerville, & Haake, 1979).

Route mapping may be critical in determining when individuals first construct mental models (e.g., Johnson-Laird, 1982). If the knowledge of landmark mappers is restricted to fragmented information about landmarks (Siegel & White, 1975; Siegel et al., 1978), there is simply no information about relations between landmarks that could be represented in a mental model. This reasoning suggests a more general relationship between level of spatial representation and problem solving than had been originally suggested by Anooshian et al. (1982). Landmark mappers should have difficulty with a variety of tasks because they do not construct mental models of the problem space. In a further study by Anooshian et al. (in press), children visited locations in a search environment. Activities were contrived so that they would search for a missing object at several locations. At a later time, the children were asked to go back and look for the missing object. Search was evaluated in terms of whether children restricted their planned search to locations that had not already been searched in their initial exposure to the environment. Children who obtained higher scores for separate route knowledge tasks were most likely to restrict their searches in such a fashion.

The Paradigm for Development

We have been assuming that the differences between landmark, route, and configurational representations are descriptive of the mental model constructed by children of different ages or by adults with varying degrees of familiarity with an environment. Given this assumption, the developmental sequence for cognitive mapping is paradigmatic for the development of nonspatial knowledge. Route mapping is the core of cognitive mapping (Allen, 1982; Kaplan, 1976; Siegel et al., 1978) and is acquired on two developmental levels. Children can construct mental models that represent the temporal sequence of landmarks before they scale the distances between those landmarks (Cousins et al., 1983), and this sequence may also hold for nonspatial thought.

Route Ordering. Anooshian et al. (in press) suggested that the first mental models constructed by children are representations of temporal sequences of landmarks. The acquisition of route ordering is significant for two reasons. First, the existence of route ordering is the first real evidence that children are using some organizational strategies in encoding and/or retrieving spatial information. Linear orders provide an organizational tool for remembering events and objects (Foellinger & Trabasso, 1977; Johnson, Perlmutter, & Trabasso, 1979; Myers & Perlmutter, 1978) as well as places (Siegel, Allik, & Herman, 1976). Hence, how a child orders landmarks along a route may be relevant to the more general use of organizational strategies. Such strategies are, of course, critical for verbal memory (Hudson & Fivush, 1983; Lange, 1978; Mandler & Pearlstone, 1966; Townsend, 1983).

Second, we have seen that spatial images of linear order are used in solving a variety of nonspatial tasks. Bower's (1971) work emphasizes the significance of route ordering for cognitive development. He suggests that "the generalized internal representation of linear ordering is a cognitive structure or scaffold that is applied to the arrangement of a number of stimulus domains" (p. 194). How a child represents landmark order should reflect how that child represents such dimensions as brightness, size, distance, weight, and semantic attributes of objects. From this perspective, it is not surprising that children as young as 6 years of age solve transitive inference problems *by constructing spatial images of ordered relations* (Trabasso et al., 1975). Route ordering may be essentially the logic of ordinal scaling, dominance hierarchies, ordered sets (e.g., days of the week, months of the year)—the logic of Piagetian concrete operations.

Route Scaling. It is also likely that the transition to route scaling (Cousins et al., 1983) is critical for nonspatial thought. Certainly, syllogistic reasoning may sometimes require the representation of interobject distances. For example, if one is given the information that "John is 10 inches taller than Tom," and "Dick is 5 inches taller than Tom," inferences about the relation between John and Dick require a mental model in which the distances between individual heights are scaled correctly. Certainly, the mental models required for many mathematical and scientific problems involve scaling distances between objects. In fact, symbolic distance effects were documented for such nonspatial dimensions as size and height (see review by Moyer & Dumais, 1978) long before such effects were generalized to physical distances (Evans & Pezdek, 1980; Maki, Maki, & Marsh, 1977). Individuals take less time to evaluate relations between objects (e.g., that one animal is larger than another) if the distance between these objects along the evaluated dimension is large (e.g., one is comparing a sparrow and an elephant). Of course, symbolic distance effects are consistent with the notion that individuals make relational decisions by "reading" mental models in which distances are scaled along the appropriate dimension.

As discussed earlier, route scaling depends on the selection of landmarks that provide good distance information. Johnson et al. (1979) have suggested that children select the head and legs as distinctive body landmarks. Distances among other body parts would presumably be scaled in terms of these selected landmarks. Loftus and Marburger (1983) have recently emphasized the significance of landmark selection for scaling the temporal distances between events. In reporting when particular events had occurred, their subjects were more accurate if they estimated time of occurrence relative to a significant and distinctive event (e.g., the eruption of Mt. St. Helens). In fact, people use landmarks in memory all the time. If someone asks what you were doing on June 2, 1978, there is little possibility of cashing in the question for a memory. To succeed in answering the question, you must identify a particular event that occurred that June (e.g., someone's birthday or wedding, the beginning of a vacation, etc.). Retrieving information about that event will often trigger associated memories about other events. Hence, you can cash in a metric question for a landmark-oriented one.

Physical Environments as Memory Aids

If there are similarities between the ways individuals represent relations between landmarks and relations between nonspatial objects, then it makes sense to suppose that nonspatial information may sometimes be organized and remembered in terms of relations with physical environments. We have suggested that physical locations can serve as contextual retrieval cues for a variety of nonspatial information—for example, the names of people met at a particular place, the content of a lecture heard in a particular room, and so on. Further, one's knowledge of a specific physical environment may be used as an organizational aid to recall. Neisser (1976) has noted that, since cognitive maps are relatively long lasting and yet easily modifiable, they are useful for mnemonic purposes—for example, the Method of Loci. Consistent with this perspective, Johnson et al. (1979) found that children cluster their recall of activities in terms of the spatial location of the relevant body part (top, middle, bottom). Smith (1982) interpreted the advantage of learning lists in multiple rooms, rather than in a single room, in terms of organizational strategies in recall. Since young children have a limited number of alternative organizational structures or strategies for recall (see Hudson & Fivush, 1983; Kobasigawa, 1977), their recall of everyday events is probably more dependent on cognitive maps of their physical environments than is the case for older children and adults. In summary, one is struck with the extent to which spaces and spatial representations are involved in nonspatial cognition.

Proposition 5: The Cognitive Mapping Enterprise Can Profit From the Activities of Cognitive Psychology

There should, of course, be reciprocal borrowing between cognitive mapping and cognitive psychology. If cognitive mapping is indeed paradigmatic of nonspatial thought, then those interested in cognition and cognitive development should borrow extensively from the cognitive mapping literature. This direction of borrowing is also suggested by Neisser's (1976) argument that "cognitive psychologists must make a greater effort to understand cognition as it occurs in the ordinary environment and in the context of natural purposeful activity" (p. 7). Yet, similarities between spatial and nonspatial processing also suggest that the cognitive mapping enterprise can profit from the selective borrowing of well-developed theoretical approaches from cognitive psychology and cognitive development. We have argued for a theoretical approach to cognitive mapping that recognizes the processes that intervene between the retrieval of spatial information from long-term memory and the construction of a mental model for particular tasks.

We propose an approach to cognitive mapping based on Johnson-Laird's (1982) analysis of procedural semantics. Procedural semantics is an approach to the psychology of meaning that emphasizes the *processes* of interpretation. One does not represent the meaning of a word or sentence as a procedure. But, to understand a word, one must be able to enter the semantic representation of the word into diverse mental processes/procedures. To illustrate this, Johnson-Laird developed a procedural semantics for spatial relations. Understanding assertions about spatial relations (e.g., premises in a syllogistic reasoning problem) requires the use of "a number of general procedures for responding to sentences by constructing, manipulating, or interrogating, spatial arrays" (p. 116).

We suggest a new perspective on cognitive mapping which we call procedural mapping. Procedural maps are cognitive maps or, more generally, mental models that are constructed in working memory. They are the products of general procedures or production systems. Hence, the content of these maps reflects the application of procedures more than the accuracy or nature of an individual's long-term representation(s) of a large-scale space (e.g., Anderson, 1978). Individuals have a number of available production systems for constructing procedural maps. This being the case, one cannot discuss an individual's knowledge of space without also discussing the activities and procedures by which they "externalize" or "produce evidence of" their spatial knowledge.

Our approach is quite consistent with the thrust of Siegel and White's (1975) model; cognitive maps are mental constructions based on temporal integration. This theory of procedural mapping can help integrate cognitive mapping research within a broader cognitive perspective. Other benefits of borrowing from cognitive psychology will be discussed in the context of procedural mapping.

Representational Issues

We propose that individuals make spatial decisions of many types on the basis of procedural maps. Rather than discuss how different researchers define spatial representation (e.g., Liben, 1981), it may be more useful to consider differences in the nature of the procedural map that is required for different tasks. The important issue may be whether a particular task requires an integrated and articulated procedural map (see Johnson-Laird, 1982). In accord with Liben, we would agree that the level of sophistication required to construct a procedural map for way-finding is less than that required to draw a Euclidian map. Yet we think it prudent to emphasize the similarities in the processes involved in both types of tasks.

Procedural mapping provides a systematic way of accounting for why researchers have sometimes concluded that cognitive maps are propositional and sometimes that they are holistic or analogical. Adults who are capable of constructing procedural maps may fail to do so, especially if the task requires only the representation of a single direction to a particular landmark. Spatial representations may appear more analogical or holistic when investigators choose tasks that are more readily solved by constructing a holistic procedural map (e.g., Levine et al., 1982). In contrast, when children or adults are asked to consider only their present position and a single other landmark, as is the case for direct estimates of bearing or distance, the construction of such a procedural map seems unlikely because it would provide no useful information over that contained in the representation of a single direction or distance between a reference site and landmark. The important methodological implication is that, in addition to other types of task demands (Liben, 1981; Siegel, 1981), researchers should pay close attention to the type of information requested.

A closer examination of the work of Johnson-Laird (1975, 1982) on procedural semantics helps one identify those situations in which individuals are most likely to construct procedural maps. Johnson-Laird suggests that individuals construct mental models in comprehension and reasoning tasks when information is unambiguous as to a particular configuration of objects. Also, the mental model must contain either more information or a more parsimonious representation of information than would otherwise be available. With these guidelines in mind, it appears that the distance ranking tasks associated with the multidimensional-scaling methodology call for a procedural map. Consistent with Johnson-Laird's suggestion, Newcombe and Liben (1982) have suggested that ranking tasks require more integrative processing capacity than do direct distance estimates (see also Newcombe, 1984).

Way-finding experiences also differ in terms of whether individuals rely on specific representations or construct procedural maps. In unfamiliar environments, there are usually several configurations that are consistent with our directional and distance information. Thus, we may keep track of the direction and distance to a salient landmark. In contrast, greater familiarity permits construction of an unambiguous procedural map. An individual is most likely to construct such a map when the way-finding demands are such that specific representations are insufficient; procedural maps allow for spatial inferences and for finding shortcuts or detours. When individuals plan ahead or attempt to rehearse the sequence of steps involved in a complex route, we suggest that they also construct such maps and that these efforts should lead to greater memorability (Johnson-Laird, 1982; Johnson-Laird & Bethell-Fox, 1978). Individual differences in way-finding strategies can be discussed in a similar fashion. One might speculate that "spatial idiots," probably known to all of us, are individuals who, because way-finding is not their major purpose at the time, depend primarily on specific representations rather than procedural maps. Individuals in such contexts, like many young children, can be successful in a variety of way-finding tasks by retrieving bearing and distance information associated with their current position and the upcoming landmark on a particular route. "Spatial idiocy" usually becomes apparent when one asks for the relative direction of travel (e.g., north vs. south), about the directional relation between the start- and end-point of travel, or requests a configurational map. The relation between effortful processing and memorability further suggests a vicious circle set up by the failure to construct procedural maps.

In general, we maintain that individuals construct different procedural maps for different purposes. Because of different agenda associated with different places, an individual may act like a spatial idiot in one environment and a configurational mapper in another. Further, the procedural map an individual constructs in order to describe what areas of a city are unsafe may be quite different than the procedural maps constructed for the purpose of way-finding (Cousins, 1984). Procedural maps do not represent universal competencies, but rather the results of specific task demands and contexts (see Siegel, 1982). The procedural mapping approach strongly emphasizes contextual determinants of behavior (e.g., Pepper, 1961; Rogoff, 1981; Vygotsky, 1962).

Inferences

As suggested by Johnson-Laird, a major reason that individuals construct mental models is that they permit inference making. The usefulness of mental models or procedural maps is apparent whether one is talking about transitive inferences or spatial inferences; such maps allow us to go beyond the information available in representations of specific past experiences.

It is not surprising that inferences that depend on the construction of holistic procedural maps emerge fairly late in ontogeny (Anooshian & Nelson, 1984). Paris (1978) has noted fairly late developmental differences in inferences about verbal material. Inferences about the causes of particular affective states also seem to emerge fairly late (e.g., Weiner, Graham, Stern, & Lawson, 1982). Yet, there is evidence from both the cognitive (e.g., Fajardo & Schaeffer, 1982; Trabasso et al., 1975) and spatial domains (e.g., Hazen et al., 1978; Pick & Lockman, 1981) that young children have some inferential abilities. Another parallel between spatial and nonspatial inferences is apparent in Johnson and Smith's (1981) finding that third graders can and do make inferences in text comprehension, but fail to make such inferences when the relevant information is contained in separate scenes of a story.

Attention to inference processes can lead to new interpretations of past research on spatial representation. For example, one might argue that active exploration of large-scale spaces produces better spatial representations than passive exploration because it encourages children to make inferences that would not otherwise be made. Here, we are referring to active exploration that requires some anticipation or advance planning on the part of the explorer (e.g., Feldman & Acredolo, 1979; Herman, 1980; Poag, Cohen, & Weatherford, 1983). Mental models are required for inferences, and constructing mental models leads to greater memorability. Johnson-Laird has demonstrated greater recall when premises are designed to lead to the construction of a mental model; recall is better when premises are unambiguous than when ambiguous with regard to the appropriate mental model. In the latter case, subjects should not construct a mental model. Current cognitive research has also emphasized the distinction between externally versus internally generated information (see Johnson & Raye, 1981; McFarland, Frey, & Rhodes, 1980). Research on word recall (e.g., Raye, Johnson, & Taylor, 1980) would suggest that the products of inferences (internally generated) should be better remembered than information obtained from direct observation (externally generated).

As children grow older and explore a larger set of environments more actively (Barker & Wright, 1954), their inferences should lead to further improvements in procedural mapping (Hazen, 1982). This perspective on active versus passive exploration is consistent with other findings that the act of constructing a model of a space leads to improved accuracy without further exposure to the environment itself (Hart, 1981; Herman & Siegel, 1978). Both model-building and way-finding tasks with an active planning component require the construction of procedural maps.

Proposition 6: Emotions Play a Significant Role in Both Spatial and Nonspatial Thought

It is an opportune time for a symposium on the psychology of feeling and emotion. These aspects of mental processes have not been investigated so thoroughly as those of cognition, but already sufficient experimental work has been done in their regard to warrant the bringing together of psychologists to discuss them. (p. 49)

Readers familiar with recent developments in the area of cognition and affect might infer that the above quote came from the recent Carnegie Symposium on Cognition and Affect (Clark & Fiske, 1982). Actually, these remarks were made by Aveling in 1928 at the Wittenberg Symposium on Feelings and Emotions. Since cognition researchers are now re-recognizing the significance of emotions in cognitive processing (e.g., Bower, 1981), it is time for students of cognitive mapping to do so as well. We have already argued that cognitive mapping research should seek closer ties with cognition and cognitive development. In our discussion of procedural mapping, we have emphasized the viability of a common theory for reasoning, comprehension, and spatial representation. However, logical decisions in reasoning tasks are affected by values and prior emotional biases (Isen, Means, Patrick, & Nowicki, 1982; McGuire, 1960; Revlin, Leirer, Yopp, & Yopp, 1980; Thistlethwaite, 1950). Revlin et al. (1980) concluded that such errors reflect the role of values in determining how subjects interpret premise information. In other words, values determined how the information in the premises was represented in the mental model or "personalized representation from whence rational decisions are made" (p. 591). Tyler and Voss (1982) interpreted the effects of attitude on prose comprehension in terms of a network-like structure for long-term memory in which knowledge and feelings are components of the same system (e.g., Bower, 1981). We have stressed that procedural mapping reflects constructive aspects of memory; when remembering, we construct details to fit our overall attitude or feeling about the remembered event (Bartlett, 1932/1973; Buckhout, 1974; Holahan, 1978). Once we recognize the parallels between procedural mapping and performance on nonspatial tasks such as syllogistic reasoning and comprehension, it becomes apparent that emotions are also involved in constructing procedural maps.

The Cognitive Mapping Literature

References to the impact of emotions on cognitive mapping have a long history. As early as 1897, G. Stanley Hall noted reports of fear and terror associated with being lost or losing one's sense of orientation (Hall, 1897). Various authors have noted the intensity of such terror (Acredolo, 1982; Lynch, 1960; Siegel, 1982). If we get lost in an environment, it is likely that we will reexperience the original fear with every new encounter or mental reconstruction of that place (see Bower, 1981).

Even if we do not get lost, we still react to and parse environments in terms of a few basic connotative dimensions (Horayangkura, 1978; Mehrabian, 1976). Ittelson (1978) notes that emotional reactions such as whether certain places are safe or dangerous are made early and quickly; individuals maintain these early assessments despite subsequent evidence to the contrary. Thus, emotions become part of our memory for an environment and are likely to shape the way in which we construct procedural maps.

Although there are certainly numerous ways in which emotions could affect a particular procedural map (see Downs & Stea, 1973; Kaplan, 1973, 1976; Siegel, 1982), emotions clearly affect how we represent size and distance. We know that subjects judge the distance to the center of a city as different from the reverse distance in traveling away from the center of the city (Briggs, 1973; Lee, 1970). Rapoport (1976) has suggested that this asymmetry (e.g., which distance is remembered as longer) reflects whether one generally likes or dislikes downtown areas; traveling to a pleasant destination is remembered as shorter than traveling to an unpleasant destination. Similarly, Ekman and Bratfisch (1965) found that subjects judged the distance to a particular city as shorter if they reported greater emotional involvement with events happening in that city. Positive emotional involvement also seems to lead to larger sizes for landmarks in procedural maps. Holahan and Dobrowolny (1978) reported such effects in the campus maps drawn by college students. Similarly, Maurer and Baxter (1972) suggested that black children draw their homes as quite large in sketch maps because they perceive the outside world as threatening.

These examples all suggest that spatial and emotional information are integrated in long-term memory (Bower, 1981; Bower & Cohen, 1982). When we attempt to retrieve information about size and distance, we also retrieve information about our emotional reactions to the represented space, an idea that is consistent with the theories of retrieval discussed in Chapter 1 by Ackerman. The same can be said for procedural maps of nonspatial information; the intensity of one's values and needs affect subjective size (Bruner & Goodman, 1947; Levine, Chein, & Murphy, 1942).

Evidence that emotions are involved in procedural mapping is not restricted to literature on representations of distances and sizes (Acredolo, 1982; Newcombe, 1982; Siegel, 1982). Presson and Ihrig (1982) found that infants encoded the locations of specific events in relation to the position of the mother (obviously an emotional landmark). Acredolo (1979, 1982) has observed that egocentric behavior was less likely in infants when they were tested in the home than when they were tested in an emotionally neutral laboratory situation. Hazen and Durrett (1982) found significant relations between 2-year-olds' security of attachment to their mothers and the extent and mode of their exploration in a large-scale space. These studies suggest not just that emotions are important, but that emotions are involved in cognitive development and procedural mapping from the beginning (Biber, 1981; Franklin, 1981).

Implications for a Theory of Procedural Mapping

Alfred Binet, as early as 1911, addressed the inseparability of thoughts and emotions in intellectual functioning:

> Binet's attempted resolution of this problem, for which he did not claim originality but only acknowledgment for particularizing it, lay in "attitudes" as an organizational hierarchy. "Attitudes" represented the inseparable union of emotions and intellect that combined to tend toward, or to effect, action. (Wolf, 1973, p. 214)

A theory of procedural mapping is necessarily incomplete unless we consider the nature of the memory system from which information is retrieved to construct maps. Every time we experience an emotion, that emotion becomes associated with other information that we have already encoded. If one takes a developmental perspective, one cannot ignore the extent to which emotions have a cumulative effect in shaping the nature of both future procedural maps and the further acquisition of knowledge. Neisser (1963) emphasizes this point in discussing the complexities of simulating human thought; he argues that, by one year of age, the child

> will necessarily interpret his own explorations in terms of experience that he already has: of losing love or gaining it, of encountering potential disaster, joy, or indifference. These preconceptions must affect the kind of explorations he makes, as well as the results of his ventures; and these consequences in turn help to shape the conceptual schemes with which the next developmental problem is met. (p. 195)

Similarly, Bruner (1983) has noted that, as soon as a child uses language and participates in a culture, emotions become inseparable from that child's knowledge of language. If cognitive development involves internalizing representations of interpersonal interactions (Vygotsky, 1962), then emotions are necessarily a part of any cognitive representation.

The notion that cold and hot information are encoded and associated in the same memory system is not new. In 1928, Washburn noted that, "it is a well-known fact that emotional states may function as the associative links between ideas, thus forming what in Freudian terminology are called complexes" (p. 109). Just as we have borrowed our model of procedural mapping from cognitive psychology, it appears that further borrowing is necessary to account for cognitive-emotional processing. Bower (1981) has proposed that

> Human memory can be modeled in terms of an associative network of semantic concepts and schemata that are used to describe events. An event is represented in

memory by a cluster of descriptive propositions. These are recorded in memory by describing the event. The basic unit of thought is the proposition; the basic process of thought is activation of a proposition and its concepts. . . . Activation presumably spreads from one concept to another, or from one proposition to another, by associative linkages between them. . . . The semantic-network approach supposes that each distinct emotion such as joy, depression, or fear has a specific node or unit in memory that collects together many other aspects of the emotion that are connected to it by associative pointers. (pp. 134–135)

Procedural maps are derived from associative networks of spatial, nonspatial, and emotional information (see also Kaplan, 1976). While we can never know the exact format of the long-term memory representation (Anderson, 1978), the cognitive-emotional processing that seems to be involved in procedural mapping strongly suggests that "hot" and "cold" information about environments is encoded within the same long-term memory systems. The approach of procedural mapping, together with Bower's semantic network model, can provide a good theoretical base for cognitive mapping research. The procedural map constructed for the purpose of avoiding unpleasant areas of a city is likely to be considerably different from a procedural map constructed to communicate way-finding information to an out-of-town visitor. Each procedural map would be based on different types of information retrieved from a complex and diverse set of nodes and associations in long-term memory.

The Activation of Emotions

Procedural mapping will be affected by emotions whenever emotion nodes are activated. There are a variety of ways in which this activation could occur. Bower (1981) has argued that emotion nodes are activated by mood states. If one is happy when traveling through a space or when making specific spatial judgments, emotion nodes are necessarily activated. Associations then become established between a node for "happiness" and specific physical features of that environment. Future encounters with the same environment should also be pleasant (i.e., lead to activation of the same node). Of course, various authors have suggested that at least some activation pathways for emotional responses are canalized. Tomkins (1970, 1981), working from the perspective of personality theory, has argued that emotions are activated automatically, through innately determined pathways. He argues that affect is triggered by the frequency of neuronal firing or, more generally, by changes in the level of stimulation. For example, a sudden decrease in stimulation leads to enjoyment while a sudden increase in stimulation leads to fear. More gradual changes would activate different emotions. The theory stresses the commonality of emotional responses across development, postulating a similar mechanism for hard-wired and learned emotional responses (e.g., the enjoyment triggered by the decrease in stimulation upon solving a mystery). Tomkin's theory can account for the enjoyment upon hearing the punchline of jokes (Mindess, 1971; Wicker, Thorelli, Barron, & Ponder, 1981) as well as for emotional fluctuations occurring in daydreaming (Singer, 1975). The theory may have something to do with why we become interested in environments that are never completely knowable and fear environments that are confusing and unknowable.

Like Tomkins, various authors have stressed the extent to which emotional reactions or judgments are fast and automatic (e.g., Clark, 1982; Sherer & Rogers, 1980; Zajonc, 1980, 1981). Automaticity suggests that emotional reactions are minimally affected by other processing demands or limitations in processing capacity and, further, that they are not readily controlled by thought. The literature on nonverbal communication is based on the assumption that mental effort has no effect on emotions (Sherer & Rogers, 1980). One can consciously control verbal behavior, but not the nonverbal expression of emotion (Waxer, 1978). It is for these reasons that clinical and counseling psychologists have emphasized the importance of nonverbal behavior in inferring emotion and attitude (Hill, Siegelman, Gronsky, Sturniolo, & Fretz, 1981; Waxer, 1978).

Biological determinants of emotional responses have also been stressed from an evolutionary perspective (Baldwin, 1895/1906; Fishbein, 1976; Hall, 1898; Livingston, 1967; MacLean, 1980; Romanes, 1889; Stanley-Jones, 1970). MacLean has argued that the emotional system has a system of intelligence and memory that is different than systems that were added in later evolutionary history. The more primitive the system in an evolutionary sense, the more automatic and highly organized it should be (see also Jackson, 1958). Of course, an evolutionary perspective does not require that emotions be restricted to their own separate system (Izard & Buechler, 1980; Langer, 1967; Lazarus, Averill, & Opton, 1970; Plutchik, 1980).

We contend that the existence of a separate system may be useful in accounting for the automaticity of some emotional reactions, but that any conscious experience of emotion can only be understood and appreciated in the context of an integrated cognitive-emotional system such as Bower's (1981; Bower & Cohen, 1982). However, Tomkins (1981) has vehemently argued that single-system or "cognitive" theories of emotions that stress the priority of cognitive appraisal or interpretation (e.g., Lazarus et al., 1970; Schachter, 1970) are as ludicrous as:

> a theory of pain and pleasure which argued that the difference between the pain of a toothache and the pleasure of an orgasm is not in the stimulation of different sensory receptors, but in the fact that since one experience occurs in a bedroom, the other in a dentist's office, one interprets the undifferentiated arousal state differently. (p. 311)

But an integrated knowledge or memory system can also emphasize the extent to which cognitive processing is affected by emotions (see also Drucker, 1981; Escalona, 1981). Lazarus (1982) has stressed that emotions can only give meaning to thought if they are fused in the same system:

> Such meaning exists not merely in the environmental display, but inheres in the cognitive structures and commitments developed over a lifetime that determine the personal and hence emotional significance of any person-environment encounter. (p. 1022)

In summary, we postulate that procedural mapping can only be understood from the perspective of a long-term memory system in which "hot" and "cold" information about environments are integrated in a complex network of associations. While some emotions may be activated automatically, any conscious experience must involve a cognitive-emotional system.

Proposition 7: Cognitive Processing Has a Heavier Emotional Component in Early Development

Are emotions more dominant during certain periods of development? Do emotions have a greater effect on procedural maps early in development? Authors who have argued for a separate emotional system have tended to emphasize the developmental priority of emotions (e.g., Tomkins, 1981; Zajonc, 1980). Romanes (1889) referred to the early emotional reactions of children, as well as emotional reactions across species, as being proof for the relation between ontogeny and phylogeny. These questions have also been addressed in discussions of microgenetic change in intelligence. For example, Binet noted the special significance of emotions in undeveloped thoughts and suggested that,

> The greater the organization [of a directed act], other things being equal, the more it will be intellectual in character; the weaker the organization, the more we shall have a phenomenon of pure emotion. (Wolf, 1973, p. 215)

In contrast, cognitive approaches to emotions imply that emotions should play a greater role in processing as development progresses. Clearly, the complex evaluative decisions involved in aesthetic judgments require advanced development. For example, Mandler and Shebo (1983) have shown that evaluative judgments of liking a painting take longer than decisions about familiarity. If an older child can experience a greater number of differentiated emotions than a younger child (Piaget, 1981; Werner, 1957), there should be a greater potential for these emotional experiences to impact cognitive processing.

Our interest here is in exploring ways in which one might account for the significance of emotions in early development from a cognitive perspective. While not denying that emotions develop, and may do so in ways consistent with principles of cognitive development, we think that it is also important to recognize ways in which processing can be more dominated by emotions in early development.

Associative Versus Cognitive Levels

The role of emotions in early cognitive processing can be understood in the context of White's (1965) distinction between associative and cognitive levels of functioning. According to this perspective, the associative level is laid down early in childhood and the cognitive level is added later:

> Adults may have available an "associative level," laid down early in development, relatively fast acting, following conventional associative principles, and in the normal adult relatively often existing as a potential, but inhibited, determinant of behavior. The "cognitive layer," laid down after the associative mode of response, is taken to be relatively slower in action and to process information in ways which are only beginning to be understood. (White, 1965, pp. 215–216)

Once experienced, emotion nodes are activated and associations are established with other information represented in long-term memory (Bower, 1981). At the associative level, information is remembered solely through activated associations in semantic memory. At the cognitive level, the organism may impose an alternative structure on memory (or inhibit associative responding). For example, free associations to "New York" are more likely to lead to the activation of emotion nodes than a cognitive analysis of city size or composition. The notion that associative responding is more emotion based than cognitive responding is consistent with White's analysis. Bower (1981) has noted powerful effects of mood states on subjects' free associations to neutral words. In accounting for a decrease in children's susceptibility to conditioning at around 6 years of age, White suggests the possibility of a transition associated with a decline in emotionality. White and Pillemer (1979) have noted that memories of childhood events—memories that are often affectively laden—are most easily retrieved through free associations. Emotions seem to emerge in situations where attention is diverted from normal modes of effortful cognitive processing. For example, the emotional content of meditation experiences and the content of dream images may reflect the activation of emotion nodes in associative responding. Deikman (1966) has described meditation in terms of the "deautomatization" of routine cognitive processing. Foulkes (1978) has noted the extent to which dream images have a structure similar to that found in free associations. Finally, common references to the emergence of emotion-based responding can be found in reports of pathology and brain damage (Schilder, 1965; Werner, 1957). In these cases, one would expect difficulties with effortful processing and hence reversion to an associative level of functioning.

A Matter of Alternatives

A second perspective for understanding the early dominance of emotions in cognitive processing involves assessing alternative structures for encoding and organization. For example, Hudson and Fivush (1983) discuss the young child's retrieval strategies in terms of the lack of available alternatives for organization. The number of alternative organizations that are available depends on the child's world knowledge (Mandler, 1978; Townsend, 1983). Only if children know that a couch, TV, and chair are pieces of furniture are they likely to cluster the retrieval of word lists in terms of that taxonomic category. Certainly, associations to emotion nodes for good versus bad are established in long-term memory long before similar associations are established to such concept nodes as furniture and animal. On a more general level, it is probably the case that a larger proportion of the nodes and associations in semantic networks involve emotions for young than older children or adults. While the world knowledge of 2-year-olds may be limited, they have a "keen sense of good vs. bad" (Escalona, 1981).

The choice of reference sites or landmarks for direction and distance judgments may also be a matter of alternatives. Infants may use the mother as a reference point for spatial location (Presson & Ihrig, 1982) because there are few alternative reference systems available (see Pick, 1976). Young children also use the mother as a reference site for estimating physical distance; the close-distant dimension is defined in terms of feelings about self and mother (Escalona, 1981). It is not necessary to speculate that the mother has less emotional significance for older children. There are simply more nonemotional alternatives.

Adults may have a variety of alternative ways to encode information or organize recall, but few are likely to be simpler or less effortful than those based on emotional distinctions. Thus, emotions should be dominant in our first exposures to new and complex environments that challenge our limited processing capacity. The tendency to cluster landmarks or environmental areas in terms of emotional or connotative distinctions may relate to the common observation that emotions consist of a limited number of bipolar pairs (Baldwin, 1895/1906; Beebe-Center, 1932/1965; Darwin, 1965; Eliade, 1958; Osgood, Suci, & Tannenbaum, 1957; Plutchik, 1980). As such, emotions are conducive to simple black-white distinctions like good versus bad or joyful versus sad. Our early categorizations of environments may not be all that different from the distinctions between "sacred" and "profane" places observed in nonwestern, nonliterate societies (see Eliade, 1959).

Cognitive Development

We have argued that there are many similarities between the development of procedural mapping and cognitive development. The literature on cognitive development presents a convincing case that emotions are most dominant in cognitive processing in the early stages of development. For almost any aspect of early cognitive development that one might choose to explore, one can find evidence that emotions play their greatest role in early development.

Objects and Words. Objects are first known and defined in terms of affect (Osgood et al., 1957; Zajonc, 1980). Infants come to know objects through sensory-motor interactions that necessarily involve affective interchanges (see Escalona, 1981). According to Werner and Kaplan (1963):

> The early objects, even on the human level, are probably much like "things-of-action" characteristic of the infra-human level, that is, they are things of

momentary affective striving and of biologically directed action . . . early objects are defined almost exclusively through the changing affective-sensory-motor patterns of the individual. (p. 44)

In terms of Bower's (1981) model, associations between object and emotion nodes must be among the first to be established in long-term memory. The predominance of emotions in early world knowledge systems is most apparent in noting the consequences of pathology where objects are evaluated entirely in terms of affective drives: "this occurs not in the sense that the world of things becomes invested with an especially strong overtone of emotion, but rather in the sense that affect actually forms the world itself" (Werner, 1957, p. 81).

The child's first words are also closely tied to emotional experiences. Bruner (1983) has emphasized that much of language learning is motivated by the desire to communicate emotional responses or feelings. Similarly, Werner and Kaplan (1963) discuss development in terms of decontextualization—words gradually take on general meaning outside of the specific context in which they were first used. When decontextualized, words are also deemotionalized. For example, the child's first use of the word "hot" is not descriptive, but an "expression of an experience in which perceptual elements and affective-motor reactions are indissolubly fused" (p. 167).

Imagery and Memory. Objects with emotional significance are likely to be drawn as larger than other objects (Werner, 1957). This association between emotions and the memory images is most obvious in early development:

> The drawings of Bushmen in which they represent themselves as giants and their enemies as dwarfs are well known. The objective representation is determined to a large degree by an affective evaluation. We speak here of "emotional perspective," a common feature, as we shall see, of children's drawings. It is a generally recognized fact that the *child's* memory is often radically transformed under the influence of affect. (p. 148)

These observations are consistent with our earlier suggestions that, since emotions are necessarily associated with information retrieved from long-term memory, they are likely to affect the representation of size in procedural maps. Schilder's (1965) observations of thought patterns associated with pathology have revealed distortions in memory images similar to those described by Werner.

Literature on the retrieval of early childhood memories confirms that these memories are largely based on associations with emotion nodes (but cf. Chapter 1 by Ackerman). White and Pillemer (1979) make a general distinction between learning from experience and learning based on conscious mental effort (e.g., the intentional coordination of schemes). The "experience-based" memories characterizing early childhood are retrievable through situational and affective cues associated with the original learning experiences, but not through intentional strategies. White and Pillemer note that "early memories may be activated by affective or contextual cues, although these images may not be recognized as memories" (p. 66). Consistent with this perspective, Neisser

(1962) also discusses childhood amnesia in terms of discontinuities in cognitive functioning. There seems to be converging evidence that, when childhood memories are retrieved, emotions are usually evoked. For example, Salaman (1982) summarizes literary work in terms of references to the emotions associated with any integrated retrieval of childhood memories. Tomkins (1970) refers to the creation of childhood affective states as a tool for retrieving childhood memories. Brewer, Doughtie, and Lubin (1980) demonstrated that mood induction was more effective with methods based on autobiographical recollection than with methods in which subjects were exposed to structured sets of mood statements. Hertel and Anooshian (1983) found better recall for words that subjects rated as being emotionally intense; however, such effects were restricted to the first-learned language for bilinguals who had learned their second language after early childhood.

Classification. We have suggested that few nonemotional alternatives are available for classification or organizational strategies in early development. The classification of objects according to emotional valence seems to be a characteristic of nonwestern, nonliterate thought (Werner, 1957):

> For the Cora Indians, flowers and stars are the same, not because of any similarity in their brightness, but rather because they are both experienced as life-creating ... because they are *felt* as identical. (p. 302)

When children appear illogical in grouping objects, it may be that they are simply using different characteristics to define group membership. Further, classifications based on concrete characteristics of objects may, in some cases, really be emotional classifications: "The 'smallness' and 'largeness' of objects or persons are not merely concrete, factual qualifications; they also represent affective evaluations" (Werner, 1957, p. 233).

Time and Distance Concepts. In early development, time is perceived as being filled with emotional qualities (Werner, 1957):

> Concrete time-of-action, embedded in a continuum of activity, naturally exhibits an altogether different structure from the quantitatively continuous ordering schema of the intellectual man. Time may be thought of as filled with certain emotional qualities. (pp. 183–184)

Similarly, Neisser (1963) has noted that the child's "first accommodations to such basic features of the world as time, distance, and causality are interwoven with strongly emotional experiences" (p. 196). The child's first concept of distance is derived from emotional distancing from significant adults (Escalona, 1981).

Magical Versus Rational Thought. It seems that the strong involvement of emotions in defining objects, remembering events, classifying objects, and time and distance concepts, provides the basis for the magical thought so commonly observed in young children and nonwestern, nonliterate societies. Magical thought may be limited primarily to thoughts about objects and events that have some emotional significance. Magical thought means emotion-based thought:

> The world becomes constituted of magic entities that are the reflections of the interplay of human fears and desires. Therefore, in any primitive society it is usually those activities that exhibit a dominance of emotion which evolve into magic practices. (Werner, 1957, p. 337)

Schilder (1965) has noted the same association between emotions and magical thought:

> Thinking gains its reality-orientation, its factual meaning, only in the last phase of its development. This, as we have seen, is preceded by a phase of affective transformations and symbolizations. . . . When wishes have such a direct effect of the development of thought it seems to the individual that every event is due to a wish and that nothing but wishes can bring about any event (the belief in magic). (p. 515)

The notion that emotions and magical thought characterize early development is also found in the philosophical literature on cultural evolution. Both Auguste Comte and Giambattista Vico postulated that the human intellect developed in successive stages (Bidney, 1953, 1969; Levy-Bruhl, 1973; White, 1983). The most primitive state of culture for Vico was the "Age of Gods" in which individuals attributed all causal action to divine and supernatural beings and were subject to strong feelings of imagination. The final stage for Vico was the "Age of Peoples"—the state of rationality and civilization. For Comte, it was the scientific or positive state.

Procedural Mapping

The preceding review emphasizes the extent to which developmental theories of procedural mapping must recognize not only that emotions are involved, but also that cognitive-emotional processing is *more* emotional at early stages of development. We will discuss the significance of emotions within the context of each of the four areas of cognitive mapping research discussed in Proposition 1.

Landmark Encoding. Our previous discussion of landmark knowledge focused on types of information about landmarks that were encoded automatically versus encoding that required effortful processing. Just as some place information may be automatically encoded in association with an experienced event, emotions may be automatically encoded and associated with places. As Siegel (1982) has noted, spatial areas are easily differentiated in terms of the social and emotional agenda associated with them. While the encoding of relations between a landmark and its physical context may require elaborative and effortful processing (Kirasic et al., 1980), it is likely that associations between places and their emotional contexts are established fairly automatically in early development. A significant component of landmark knowledge in early development must consist of knowledge about emotional valence (e.g., liking or disliking a place).

Distinctive emotions should be effective as contextual retrieval cues for the places with which they are associated. Since young children are limited in their ability to generate retrieval cues or strategies (Kobasigawa, 1977; Kobasigawa & Mason, 1982), they may be more dependent on emotional context in retrieving landmark information than older children. Again, it is a matter of alternatives. This suggestion is consistent with literature on both state- and mood-dependent learning (Bower, 1981; Eich, 1980). Such effects seem to be limited to situations in which there are no good retrieval cues for learned information. In general, the retrieval of landmark information, and hence the nature of the procedural map contructed by a young child, is likely to be dependent on the child's current mood state. The child is likely to remember different landmarks and environmental areas when sad than when happy (see Bower, 1981). If children perform better on cognitive mapping tasks when they are tested in a familiar environment (e.g., Acredolo, 1979), it may be because their moods (e.g., happy and comfortable) are generally consistent with the emotions normally associated with that environment.

In addition to contextual or mood-dependency effects, emotional involvement is likely to affect one's accuracy in recalling landmark information. The literature is now fairly clear in establishing the relation between emotional intensity and memorability. That is, memorability is greatest when the emotional intensity of the to-be-remembered information is high and when subjects are emotionally involved in the learning situation (see Dutta, 1975; Rapaport, 1959). Bower (1981) has interpreted this evidence in terms of the greater elaboration and/or distinctiveness that would occur in encoding emotionally significant events. Regardless of how one interprets the effects of emotional intensity, it is clear that landmarks that are recalled and selected for representation in procedural maps are likely to be those that have some emotional significance for the individual.

Particular environmental features are selected as landmarks for scaling distances along routes (see Allen et al., 1979). Distance judgments vary as a function of the particular landmarks that are selected (Holyoak & Mah, 1982; Sadalla et al., 1980). If places with some emotional significance are generally recalled first, they are the most likely candidates for landmarks or reference sites in procedural maps. Various authors have discussed the relation between emotional significance and benchmark memories (Neisser, 1982), snapshots (Siegel & White, 1975; White & Pillemer, 1979), or flashbulb memories (Brown & Kulik, 1977; Colgrove, 1982; Livingston, 1967). For example, Livingston (1967) postulated that the accuracy and detail of memory for the places in which individuals first heard about significant events (e.g., the assassination of John Kennedy), was due to a "Now print!" mechanism: When any event of novelty or biological meaningfulness occurs, the organism takes a snaphot of the event. Encoded in the snapshot are details of place, time, and persons, as well as the organism's own emotional state. While there is controversy about the actual accuracy of these memories and about whether a physiological mechanism is implicated (see Neisser, 1982), it is likely that the landmarks that are selected as benchmarks for the scaling of time (Loftus & Marburger, 1983) or distance have some special emotional significance.

The earlier discussion points to the utility of a contextual metaphor for procedural mapping (see Rogoff, 1981). There is no "natural" set of testing conditions for determining children's competencies. While accuracy may be maximized when children construct procedural maps of happy places when they are in a happy mood, this is not necessarily any more natural than other possible circumstances. In contrast to the concern about how to best measure context-free competencies, our theoretical approach focuses on variations in procedural maps as a function of different social and emotional contexts.

Spatial Inferences. Early inferences based on emotions appear to be quite long-lasting and resistant to change (Bower, 1981; Ittelson, 1978). These characteristics are most likely to be observed for pragmatic inferences based on past experiences and world knowledge (see Acredolo & Boulter, 1983; Paris, 1978). These inferences may be derived from past experiences with similar places. As Bower notes, one's current mood can also have a significant effect on the inference that is selected. If one is in a positive mood state, there is a bias toward inferences that environments are safe rather than unsafe. Since one interprets as well as retrieves further information in accordance with one's prevailing mood, such inferences should be resistant to change.

As discussed earlier, spatial inferences about interlandmark distances or landmark locations are often based on cluster membership or the encoding of hierarchical relations (e.g., Stevens & Coupe, 1978). It is likely that emotions play a significant role in defining landmark clusters, especially in early development. Thus, one may be more likely to judge two landmarks as being in close physical proximity if they belong to the same emotional subdivision—for example, if they are both happy places. In terms of Bower's (1981) model, activation of knowledge about one happy place is more likely to lead to retrieval of information about another happy place, rather than a sad place.

Clusters and Subdivisions. We have suggested that the classification of objects, as well as organizational strategies, are based on emotional distinctions in early development (see Chapter 3 by Bjorklund for other possibilities). It follows that procedural maps in early development reflect clusters and subdivisions that are defined in terms of emotional valence. Our conclusion that cluster-based processing is more dominant in early development reinforces the role of emotions in cognitive-emotional processing. The early task of dividing landmarks and areas into emotional clusters (e.g., safe vs. unsafe, sacred vs. profane) serves to simplify processing demands as well as to reduce uncertainty for adults in complex and confusing environments (Deal & Kennedy, 1982; Eliade, 1959; Holahan, 1978).

We also concluded earlier that future research should focus on the characteristics of physical environments that define cluster boundaries at different developmental levels. It now appears likely that boundaries are first defined in terms of emotions. The home cluster or neighborhood for young children may consist of those landmarks to which the positive emotional valence of the home is generalized. The neighborhood boundary is most likely to reflect the point at which there is a clear change in emotional valence—for example, the point at which children no longer feel safe. Because of inhibitory connections between bipolar emotions (Bower, 1981; Plutchik, 1970), the physical distance between landmarks on either side of this boundary is likely to be exaggerated in procedural maps.

Distortions in Procedural Maps. If decisions about safety or about whether particular places are good versus bad are made early in development, it seems that the primary elements of procedural maps must be emotional reactions to places. In fact, one could argue that we have cognitions—or construct procedural maps—in order to understand and organize our emotional experiences. For example, exaggerations of size in procedural maps may help individuals account for their feelings that some landmarks are more significant than others. If so, it would be surprising if procedural maps resembled those of Rand-McNally. It is likely that the general procedures or production systems for constructing these two types of maps are quite different.

Consistent with our earlier discussion of distortions, we will argue that the presence of the emotions in procedural maps reflects normal and adaptive modes of cognitive-emotional processing. It makes sense that emotionally significant landmarks should be emphasized in procedural maps; exaggerations of size serve this function. It is probably adaptive to avoid unpleasant or unsafe places. Such avoidance is most likely if one exaggerates the physical distance to such places in procedural maps. If one generally selects emotionally significant features as landmarks for scaling distances or defining locations, it is likely that the derived distance and direction information will be retrievable for future attempts to map the same environment. Finally, emotional clustering provides one of the simplest and least effortful means of imposing structure on complex and confusing environments.

Proposition 8: Emotional Agenda Have Greater Priority Than Cognitive Agenda Early in Development

For the preceding proposition, our focus was on the cognitive-emotional processing involved in meeting *cognitive* agenda. We concluded that emotions were most dominant in early development. Another reasonable conclusion is that more attention is given to meeting emotional than cognitive agenda in early development. This possibility is implicated by the need to be comfortable with a place before one is likely to begin mapping it (Acredolo, 1982; Lee, 1973). Emotional agenda must be met before cognitive agenda can be tackled. This may also be a reasonable interpretation of Acredolo's (1979) finding that infants are less egocentric when tested in the home as well as Hazen and

Durrett's (1982) observation that 2-year-olds with secure attachments to the mother are likely to explore environments actively. Although Piaget (1981) has been careful to exclude the possibility that emotions shape the course of cognitive structural change, he recognized the importance of emotions as motivating forces:

> The affective side of assimilation is interest . . . the cognitive aspect is understanding. Accommodation in its affective aspect is interest in the object in as much as it is new. In its cognitive aspect, accommodation is the adjustment of schemes of thought to phenomena. . . . It would be like gasoline, which activates the motor of an automobile but does not modify its structure. (p. 5)

Obviously, cars cannot run without gasoline. In general, if emotional agenda are not met, the fuel for cognitive development will not be available.

This perspective on development is consistent with White and Fishbein's (1971) proposal that there are at least three separate and competing adaptational systems involved in goal-directed behavior:

> We assume (1) that the child's multiple regulation agenda includes cognitive, social and mood-tension issues; (2) that the purposive behavior of the child is, effectively, a "one-channel" vehicle directed by one goal at a time; (3) that the selection of which goal is to direct behavior is a continuous issue. We do *not* assume any physiological or psychological separation of the three domains beyond the taxonomy of purposes. (p. 196)

Consistent with this viewpoint, we have argued that there is no physiological or psychological separation between the cognitive and emotional processing associated with meeting cognitive agenda. Meeting emotional agenda may involve the kind of mood-tension regulation described by White and Fishbein:

> There is a third great regulational issue in human learning, an issue having to do with the child's sense of ease and sense of moment-to-moment control over himself and the situation. . . . it may be rather important to see human tension states as independent regulational issues, presenting their own agenda that, in an important sense, competes with cognitive and social regulation for the child's behavior. . . . All children will try to circumvent, deny or avoid situations that arouse more stress than they can handle. (pp. 207–208)

We propose that emotional/mood-tension agenda have priority in early development; the consequent attention and mental effort allocated to these agenda prohibit individuals from simultaneously working on cognitive agenda.

Our current proposition is based on the assumption that adaptational or regulational agenda (White & Fishbein, 1971) compete for resources in a limited capacity system. Early development is characterized by priority rules that reserve the greatest proportion of mental effort for emotional or mood-tension issues. Although we have suggested that at least some emotional reactions are automatic, the psychological literature is replete with references to the recruitment of attention and consciousness to emotional processing. Spiller (1904) referred to the total recruitment of consciousness in strong emotional reactions. Similarly, Hall (1898) discussed anger in terms of the consequent loss of self-control and inability to meet other agenda. Various authors have described mood induction or mood control as involving the conscious redirection of mental activity (e.g., Bower, 1981; Brewer et al., 1980). Singer (1975), for example, suggests that individuals must work at positive-vivid daydreaming in order to use it effectively for mood control and adaptive self-distraction. It has been suggested that the enjoyment associated with both listening to music (Davies, 1980) and humor (Mindess, 1971; Wicker et al., 1981) results from the redirection of attention away from routine modes of processing. Leight and Ellis (1981) suggest that depressed mood states interfere with organizational processes in memory because effortful processing is directed almost exclusively to worry and other task-irrelevant activities:

> Perhaps cognitive interference from the negative self-statement associated with depressed mood competes for limited-capacity processing space. Thus the storage capacity of working memory may be reduced, as well as the capacity for effortful processing. (p. 262)

It seems reasonable to suggest that the memory deficits associated with depression, anxiety and emotional thought disorders (Beck, 1967; Eysenck, 1979a; Hasher & Zacks, 1979; Henry, Weingartner, & Murphy, 1973; Hiebert & Fox, 1981; Mueller, 1980) reflect the preferential allocation of effortful processing to emotional agenda.

There are a number of important implications of this proposition for procedural mapping. First, the developmental priority of emotional agenda may account for why associations to emotion nodes are established early in development (Proposition 7). Attention to these agenda is likely to bias the types of information encoded in long-term memory. Second, it is likely that different landmarks or environmental areas are associated with different adaptational agenda (see Siegel, 1982). We may reserve certain places for positive emotional reflection—for example, positive-vivid daydreaming (Singer, 1975)—and this may determine how emotional clusters or subdivisions are defined. Third, the association between spaces and emotional agenda may be relevant in accounting for why individuals often react negatively to (apparently) inconsequential physical changes in their surroundings (Kline, 1898; Lynch, 1960; Seaman, 1979). Such changes are likely to disrupt one's organization of the environment. In general, our preferences for familiar environments with good structure (Kaplan, 1976) may reflect that way-finding requires little mental effort. Such environments are thus likely candidates for effortful and positive emotional reflection.

Epilogue: Cognitive Development Among Cognitive Mappers

In the course of taking the reader through our extensive set of arguments concerning mapping, cognition, and emotion, we have implied that cognitive mapping is a myth. It is a myth in Donald Campbell's sense of the word (Campbell, 1979)—as a coherent story that guides thought and action in the face of uncertainty, and as a social force binding together the tribal society of cognitive mappers. Cognitive mapping is also a myth in the sense that a cognitive map is a convenient fiction, and that cognitive mapping is more than cognitive. We have suggested procedural mapping as a new way of looking at cognitive-emotional processing and development. We have tried to document the role of emotions in procedural mapping and have argued that learning, mapping, and adaptation have a heavier emotional component early in both ontogenetic and microgenetic development.

In developing this approach we have used a strategy of looking for parallels in diverse literatures that, on the surface, appear only tangentially related to mapping and its development. Our belief in a common process of development (see Siegel et al., 1983) has led us to find similarities between spatial and nonspatial knowledge, cognitive mapping and cognitive psychology, between microgenesis and ontogenesis. We have traveled symbolically to a variety of different behavior settings.

White and Siegel (1984) have argued that cognitive development in children consists, in large part, of traveling to an increasingly large and diverse and distal set of behavior settings. These settings require the child to learn a variety of different roles, personae, styles, and etiquettes involved in what is generically referred to as "socialization." Beyond this first-order travel to concrete and proximal behavior settings, some larger and later part of cognitive development requires that the child engage in a second-order kind of travel—symbolic travel—to behavior settings distant in time and space. We have tried to engage the reader in a form of symbolic travel similar to the child's—travel to a wider set of more distal behavior settings than cognitive mapping researchers have previously entered and inhabited.

Just like the young child, cognitive mapping researchers have, until now, restricted their symbolic travel to a relatively small set of behavior settings close to home—for example, the journals of developmental psychology. If we want to understand cognitive development in some full-blooded sense, restricting symbolic travel to the known behavior settings of cognitive mapping will simply not do. We use the term procedural mapping as a pointer to the importance of entering and inhabiting a wider set of more distant behavior settings—that is, different literatures—in order to gain this fuller understanding. As children cognitively develop, they need to enter and inhabit, through symbolic travel, distal behavior settings. No less is required of a domain of intellectual inquiry if it is to reach a level of operational maturity.

Acknowledgment. We express our deep appreciation to Shep White of Harvard University for a critical and helpful review of an earlier draft of the manuscript.

References

Acredolo, L. P. (1979). Laboratory versus home: The effect of environment on the 9-month-old infant's choice of a spatial reference system. *Developmental Psychology, 15,* 596–597.

Acredolo, L. P. (1981). Small- and large-scale spatial concepts in infancy and childhood. In L. S. Liben, A. H. Patterson, & N. Newcombe (Eds.), *Spatial representation and behavior across the lifespan* (pp. 63–81). New York: Academic Press.

Acredolo, L. P. (1982). The familiarity factor in spatial research. In R. Cohen (Ed.), *Children's conceptions of spatial relationships* (pp. 19–30). San Francisco, CA: Jossey-Bass.

Acredolo, L. P., & Boulter, L. (1983, April). Development of inference processes in making spatial judgments. In. N. Hazen & L. J. Anooshian (Chairs), *Thinking about space: The development of cognitive processes and spatial representation.* Symposium conducted at the meeting of the Society for Research in Child Development, Detroit, MI.

Acredolo, L. P., Pick, H. L., & Olsen, M. (1975). Environmental differentiation and familiarity as determinants of children's memory for spatial location. *Developmental Psychology, 11,* 495–501.

Allen, G. L. (1981). A developmental perspective on the effects of "subdividing" macrospatial experience. *Journal of Experimental Psychology: Human Learning and Memory, 7,* 120–132.

Allen, G. L. (1982). The organization of route knowledge. In R. Cohen (Ed.), *Children's conceptions of spatial relationships* (pp. 31–39). San Francisco: CA: Jossey-Bass.

Allen, G. L., Kirasic, K. C., Siegel, A. W., & Herman, J. F. (1979). Developmental issues in cognitive mapping: The selection and utilization of environmental landmarks. *Child Development, 50,* 1062–1070.

Allen, G. L., Siegel, A. W., & Rosinski, R. R. (1978). The role of perceptual context in structuring spatial knowledge. *Journal of Experimental Psychology: Human Learning and Memory, 4,* 617–630.

Anderson, J. R. (1978). Arguments concerning representations for mental imagery. *Psychological Review, 85,* 249–277.

Anooshian, L. J., Hartman, S. R., & Scharf, J. S. (1982). Determinants of young children's search strategies in a large-scale environment. *Developmental Psychology, 18,* 608–616.

Anooshian, L. J., & Kromer, M. K. (1984). *Children's processing of directions and distances.* Unpublished manuscript, Trinity University.

Anooshian, L. J., & Nelson, S. K. (1984). *Children's spatial knowledge of their neighborhood.* Unpublished manuscript, Trinity University.

Anooshian, L.J., Pascal, V.U., & McCreath, H. (in press). Problem mapping before problem solving: Young children's cognitive maps and search strategies in large-scale environments. *Child Development.*

Anooshian, L. J., & Wilson, K. L. (1977). Distance distortions in memory for spatial locations. *Child Development, 48,* 1704–1707.

Anooshian, L. J., & Young, D. (1981). Developmental changes in cognitive maps of a familiar neighborhood. *Child Development, 52,* 341–348.

Aveling, F. (1928). Emotion, conation, and will. In M. L. Reymert (Ed.), *Feelings and emotions: The Wittenberg Symposium* (pp. 49–57). Worcester, MA: Clark University Press.

Baldwin, J. M. (1906). *Mental development in the child and the race: Methods and processes.* New York: Macmillan. (Original work published 1895).

Barclay, J. R., & Reid M. (1974). Semantic integration in children's recall of discourse. *Developmental Psychology, 10,* 277–281.

Barker, R. G., & Wright, H. F. (1954). *Midwest and its children: The psychological ecology of an American town.* Evanston, IL: Row, Peterson.

Bartlett, F. C. (1973). *Remembering.* New York: Cambridge University Press. (Original work published 1932).

Beck, A. T. (1967). *Depression: Clinical, experimental and theoretical aspects.* New York: Harper and Row.

Beebe-Center, J. G. (1965). *The psychology of pleasantness and unpleasantness.* New York: Russell & Russell. (Original work published 1932).

Biber, B. (1981). The evolution of the developmental-interaction view. In E. K. Shapiro & E. Weber, *Cognitive and affective growth: Developmental interaction* (pp. 9–30). Hillsdale, NJ: Lawrence Erlbaum Associates.

Bidney, D. (1953). *Theoretical anthropology.* New York: Columbia University Press.

Bidney, D. (1969). Vico's new science of myth. In G. Tagliacozzo and H. V. White (Eds.), *Giambattista Vico: An international symposium* (pp. 259–277). Baltimore: The Johns Hopkins Press.

Bower, G. H. (1971). Adaptation-level coding of stimuli and serial position effects. In M. H. Appley (Ed.), *Adaptation-level theory: A symposium* (pp. 175–201). New York: Academic Press.

Bower, G. H. (1981). Mood and memory. *American Psychologist, 36,* 129–148.

Bower, G. H., & Cohen, P. R. (1982). Emotional influences in memory and thinking: Data and theory. In M. S. Clark & S. T. Fiske, *Affect and cognition: The seventeenth annual Carnegie symposium on cognition* (pp. 291–331). Hillsdale, NJ: Lawrence Erlbaum Associates.

Brewer, D., Doughtie, E. B., & Lubin, B. (1980). Induction of mood and mood shift. *Journal of Clinical Psychology, 36,* 215–226.

Briggs, R. (1973). Urban cognitive distance. In R. M. Downs and D. Stea (Eds.), *Image and environment: Cognitive mapping and spatial behavior* (pp. 361–388). Chicago: Aldine Publishing Company.

Brown, R., & Kulik, J. (1977). Flashbulb memories. *Cognition, 5,* 73–99.

Bruner, J. (1983, May). *Thought and emotion.* Presented at the meetings of the Jean Piaget Society, Philadelphia, PA.

Bruner, J. S., & Goodman, C. C. (1947). Value and needs as organizing factors in perception. *Journal of Abnormal and Social Psychology, 42,* 33–44.

Bryant, P. E., & Trabasso, T. (1971). Transitive inferences and memory in young children. *Nature, 232,* 456–458.

Buckhout, R. (1974). Eyewitness testimony. *Scientific American, 231,* 23–31.

Campbell, D. T. (1979). A tribal model of the social system vehicle carrying scientific knowledge. *Knowledge: Creation, Diffusion, Utilization, 1,* 181–201.

Canter, D., & Tagg, S. (1975). Distance estimation in cities. *Environment and Behavior, 7,* 59–80.

Chase, W. G., & Chi, M. T. H. (1981). Cognitive skill: Implications for spatial skill in large-scale environments. In J. H. Harvey (Ed.), *Cognition, social behavior, and the environment* (pp. 111–136). Hillsdale, NJ: Lawrence Erlbaum Associates.

Clark, M. S. (1982). A role for arousal in the link between feeling states, judgments, and behavior. In M. S. Clark & Susan T. Fiske, *Affect and cognition: The seventeenth annual Carnegie symposium on cognition* (pp. 263–289). Hillsdale, NJ: Lawrence Erlbaum Associates.

Clark, M. S., & Fiske, S. T. (Eds.). (1982). *Affect and cognition: The seventeenth annual Carnegie symposium on cognition*. Hillsdale, NJ: Lawrence Erlbaum Associates.

Cohen, R., Baldwin, L. M., & Sherman, R. C. (1978). Cognitive maps of a naturalistic setting. *Child Development, 49*, 1216–1218.

Cohen, R., & Schuepfer, T. (1980). The representation of landmarks and routes. *Child Development, 51*, 1065–1071.

Cohen, R., Weatherford, D. L., & Byrd, D. (1980). Distance estimates of children as a function of acquisition and response activities. *Journal of Experimental Child Psychology, 30*, 464–472.

Cohen, R., Weatherford, D. L., Lomenick, T., & Koeller, K. (1979). Development of spatial representations: Role of task demands and familiarity with the environment. *Child Development, 50*, 1257–1260.

Colgrove, F. W. (1982). The day they heard about Lincoln. In U. Neisser (Ed.), *Memory observed: Remembering in natural contexts* (pp. 41–42). San Francisco: W. H. Freeman and Company. (From Colgrove, F. W. [1899]. Individual memories. *American Journal of Psychology, 10*, 228–255)

Cousins, J. H. (1984). *Conceptual and methodological issues in cognitive mapping: On the varieties of environmental experience*. Unpublished manuscript, University of Houston.

Cousins, J. H., Siegel, A. W., & Maxwell, S. (1983). Way finding and cognitive mapping in large-scale environments: A test of a developmental model. *Journal of Experimental Child Psychology, 35*, 1–20.

Craik, F. I. M., & Lockhart, R. S. (1972). Levels of processing: A framework for memory research. *Journal of Verbal Learning and Verbal Behavior, 11*, 671–684.

Curtis, L. E., Siegel, A. W., & Furlong, N. E. (1981). Developmental differences in cognitive mapping: Configurational knowledge of familiar large-scale environments. *Journal of Experimental Child Psychology, 31*, 456–469.

Darwin, C. (1965). *The expression of the emotions in man and animals*. Chicago: Illinois: University of Chicago Press.

Davies, S. (1980). The expression of emotion in music. *Mind, LXXXIX*, 67–86.

Deal, T. E., & Kennedy, A. A. (1982). *Corporate cultures*. Menlo Park, CA: Addison-Wesley.

Deikman, A. J. (1966). De-automatization and the mystic experience. *Psychiatry, 29*, 324–338.

DeLoache, J. S. (1980). Naturalistic studies of memory for object location in very young children. In M. Perlmutter (Ed.), *Children's memory* (pp. 17–32). San Francisco, CA: Jossey-Bass.

DeSoto, C. B., London, M., & Handel, S. (1965). Social reasoning and spatial paralogic. *Journal of Personality and Social Psychology, 2*, 513–521.

Downs, R. M., & Siegel, A. W. (1981). On mapping researchers mapping children mapping space. In L. S. Liben, A. H. Patterson, & N. Newcombe (Eds.), *Spatial representation and behavior across the lifespan* (pp. 237–248). New York: Academic Press.

Downs, R. M., & Stea, D. (1973). Cognitive maps and spatial behavior: Process and products. In R. M. Downs & D. Stea (Eds.), *Image and Environment* (pp. 8–26). Chicago: Aldine.

Downs, R. M., & Stea, D. (1977). *Maps in minds*. New York: Harper & Row.

Drucker, J. (1981). Developmental concepts of cognition and affect. In E. K. Shapiro & E. Weber (Eds.), *Cognitive and affective growth: Developmental interaction* (pp. 33–46). Hillsdale, NJ: Lawrence Erlbaum Associates.

Dutta, S. (1975). *Affect and memory: A reformulation*. Oxford: Pergamon Press.

Eich, J. E. (1980). The cue-dependent nature of state-dependent retrieval. *Memory and Cognition, 8*, 157–173.

Einstein, G. O., & Hunt, R. R. (1980). Levels of processing and organization: Additive effects of individual-item and relational processing. *Journal of Experimental Psychology: Human Learning and Memory, 6*, 588–598.

Eisenstadt, M., & Kareev, Y. (1975). Aspects of human problem solving: the use of internal representations. In D. Norman & D. Rumelhart (Eds.), *Explorations in cognition* (pp. 308–346). San Francisco: Freeman.

Ekman, G., & Bratfisch, O. (1965). Subjective distance and emotional involvement: A psychological mechanism. *Acta Psychologica, 24*, 430–437.

Eliade, M. (1958). *Rites and symbols of initiation*. New York: Harper and Row.

Eliade, M. (1959). *The sacred and the profane*. New York: Harper and Row.

Escalona, S. K. (1981). The reciprocal role of social and emotional developmental advances and cognitive development during the second and third years of life. In E. K. Shapiro & E. Weber (Eds.), *Cognitive and affective growth: Developmental interaction* (pp. 87–95). Hillsdale, NJ: Lawrence Erlbaum Associates.

Evans, G. W. (1980). Environmental cognition. *Psychological Bulletin, 88*, 259–287.

Evans, G. W., & Pezdek, K. (1980). Cognitive mapping: Knowledge of real-world distance and location information. *Journal of Experimental Psychology: Human Learning and Memory, 6*, 13–24.

Eysenck, M. W. (1977). *Human memory: Theory, research and individual differences*. Oxford: Pergamon Press.

Eysenck, M. W. (1979a). Anxiety, learning and memory: A reconceptualization. *Journal of Research in Personality, 13*, 363–385.

Eysenck, M. W. (1979b). Depth, elaboration, and distinctiveness. In L. S. Cermak & F. I. M. Craik (Eds.), *Levels of processing in human memory* (pp. 89–118). Hillsdale, NJ: Lawrence Erlbaum Associates.

Eysenck, M. W., & Eysenck, M. C. (1979). Processing depth, elaboration of encoding, memory stores, and expended processing capacity. *Journal of Experimental Psychology: Human Learning and Memory, 5*, 472–484.

Fajardo, D. M., & Schaeffer, B. (1982). Temporal inferences by young children. *Developmental Psychology, 18*, 600–607.

Falmagne, R. J. (1975). Overview: Reasoning, representation, process, and related issues. In R. J. Falmagne (Ed.), *Reasoning: Representation and process* (pp. 247–264). Hillsdale, NJ: Lawrence Erlbaum Associates.

Feldman, A. L., & Acredolo, L. P. (1979). The effect of active versus passive exploration on memory for spatial location in children. *Child Development, 50*, 698–704.

Fishbein, H. D. (1976). *Evolution, development and children's learning*. Santa Monica, CA: Goodyear Publishing.

Foellinger, D. B., & Trabasso, T. (1977). Seeing, hearing, and doing: A developmental study of memory for actions. *Child Development, 48*, 1482–1489.

Foulkes, D. (1978). *A grammar of dreams*. New York: Basic Books.

Franklin, M. B. (1981). Perspectives on theory: Another look at the developmental-interaction point of view. In E. K. Shapiro & E. Weber (Eds.), *Cognitive and affective growth: Developmental interaction* (pp. 65–84). Hillsdale, NJ: Lawrence Erlbaum Associates.

Gladwin, T. (1970). *East is a big bird*. Cambridge, MA: Harvard University Press.

Haake, R. J., Somerville, S. C., & Wellman, H. M. (1980). Logical ability of young children in searching a large-scale environment. *Child Development, 51*, 1299–1302.

Hagen, J. W., Jongeward, R. H., & Kail, R. V. (1975). Cognitive perspectives on the development of memory. In H. W. Reese (Ed.), *Advances in child development and behavior* (Vol. 10, pp. 57–101). New York: Academic Press.

Hall, G. S. (1897). A study of fears. *American Journal of Psychology, 8*, 147–249.

Hall, G. S. (1898). A study of anger. *American Journal of Psychology, 10*, 516–591.

Handel, S., DeSoto, C., & London, M. (1968). Reasoning and spatial representations. *Journal of Verbal Learning and Verbal Behavior, 7*, 351–357.

Hardwick, D. A., McIntyre, C. W., & Pick, H. L., Jr. (1976). The content and manipulation of cognitive maps in children and adults. *Monographs of the Society for Research in Child Development, 41* (4, Serial No. 166).

Hart, R. A. (1981). Children's spatial representation of the landscape: Lessons and questions from a field study. In L. S. Liben, A. H. Patterson, & N. Newcombe (Eds.), *Spatial representation and behavior across the lifespan* (pp. 195–233). New York: Academic Press.

Hart, R. A., & Moore, G. T. (1973). The development of spatial cognition: A review. In R. M. Downs & D. Stea (Eds.), *Image and environment* (pp. 246–288). Chicago: Aldine.

Hasher, L., & Zacks, R. T. (1979). Automatic and effortful processes in memory. *Journal of Experimental Psychology: General, 108*, 356–388.

Hayes-Roth, B. (1977). Evolution of cognitive structures and processes. *Psychological Review, 84*, 260–278.

Hazen, N. L. (1982). Spatial exploration and spatial knowledge: Individual and developmental differences in very young children. *Child Development, 53*, 826–833.

Hazen, N. L., & Durrett, M. E. (1982). Relationship of security of attachment to exploration and cognitive mapping abilities in 2-year-olds. *Developmental Psychology, 18*, 751–759.

Hazen, N. L., Lockman, J. J., & Pick, H. L. (1978). The development of children's representations of large-scale environments. *Child Development, 49*, 623–636.

Hazen, N. L., & Volk-Hudson, S. (1984). *Young children's use of spatial context in memory*. Manuscript submitted for publication.

Henry, D. M., Weingartner, H., & Murphy, D. L. (1973). Influence of affective states and psychoactive drugs on verbal learning and memory. *American Journal of Psychiatry, 130*, 966–971.

Herman, J. F. (1980). Children's cognitive maps of large-scale spaces: Effects of exploration, direction, and repeated experience. *Journal of Experimental Child Psychology, 29*, 126–143.

Herman, J. F., Roth, S. F., Miranda, C., & Getz, M. (1982). Children's memory for spatial locations: The influence of recall perspective and type of environment. *Journal of Experimental Child Psychology, 34*, 257–273.

Herman, J. F., & Siegel, A. W. (1978). The development of cognitive mapping of the large-scale environment. *Journal of Experimental Child Psychology, 26*, 389–406.

Hertel, P., & Anooshian, L. (1983, November). *Emotion in bilingual memory*. Paper presented at the meeting of the Psychonomic Society, San Diego, CA.

Hiebert, B., & Fox, E. E. (1981). Reactive effects of self-monitoring anxiety. *Journal of Counseling Psychology, 28*, 187–193.

Hill, C. E., Siegelman, L., Gronsky, B. R., Sturniolo, F., & Fretz, B. R. (1981). Nonverbal communication and counseling outcome. *Journal of Counseling Psychology, 28*, 203–212.

Hintzman, D. L., O'Dell, C. S., & Arndt, D. R. (1981). Orientation in cognitive maps. *Cognitive Psychology, 13*, 149–206.

Holahan, C. J. (1978). *Environment and behavior*. New York: Plenum Press.

Holahan, C. J., & Dobrowolny, M. B. (1978). Cognitive and behavioral correlates of spatial behavior: An interactional analysis. *Environment and Behavior, 10*, 317–333.

Holyoak, K. J., & Mah, W. A. (1982). Cognitive reference points in judgments of symbolic magnitude. *Cognitive Psychology, 14*, 328–352.

Horayangkura, V. (1978). Semantic dimensional structures: A methodological approach. *Environment and Behavior, 10*, 555–584.

Hudson, J., & Fivush, R. (1983). Categorical and schematic organization and the development of retrieval strategies. *Journal of Experimental Child Psychology, 36*, 32–42.

Huttenlocher, J. (1968). Constructing spatial images: A strategy in reasoning. *Psychological Review, 75*, 550–560.

Inhelder, B., & Piaget, J. (1964). *The early growth of logic in the child*. London: Routledge & Kegan Paul.

Isen, A. M., Means, B., Patrick, R., & Nowicki, G. (1982). Some factors influencing decision-making strategy and risk taking. In M. S. Clark & Susan T. Fiske, *Affect and cognition: The seventeenth annual Carnegie symposium on cognition* (pp. 243–261). Hillsdale, NJ: Lawrence Erlbaum Associates.

Ittelson, W. H. (1978). Environmental perception and urban experience. *Environment and behavior, 10*, 193–213.

Izard, C. E., & Buechler, S. (1980). Aspects of consciousness and personality in terms of differential emotions theory. In R. Plutchik & H. Kellerman (Eds.), *Emotion: Theory, research, and experience* (Vol. 1, pp. 165–187). New York: Academic Press.

Jackson, J. H. (1958). Evolution and dissolution of the nervous system. In J. Taylor (Ed.), *The selecting writings of John Hughlings Jackson* (Vol. 2, pp. 45–75). New York: Basic Books.

Johnson, H., & Smith, L. B. (1981). Children's inferential abilities in the context of reading to understand. *Child Development, 52*, 1216–1223.

Johnson, L. R., Perlmutter, M., & Trabasso, T. (1979). The leg bone is connected to the knee bone: Children's representation of body parts in memory, drawing, and language. *Child Development, 50*, 1192–1202.

Johnson, M. K., & Raye, C. L. (1981). Reality monitoring. *Psychological Review, 88*, 67–85.

Johnson-Laird, P. N. (1975). Models of deduction. In R. J. Falmagne (Ed.), *Reasoning: Representation and process in children and adults* (pp. 7–54). Hillsdale, NJ: Lawrence Erlbaum Associates.

Johnson-Laird, P. N. (1982). Propositional representations, procedural semantics, and mental models. In J. Mehler, E. C. T. Walker, & M. Garrett (Eds.), *Perspectives on mental representation* (pp. 111–131). Hillsdale, NJ: Lawrence Erlbaum Associates.

Johnson-Laird, P. N., & Bethell-Fox, C. E. (1978). Memory for questions and amount of processing. *Memory and Cognition, 6*, 496–501.

Kail, R. V., & Siegel, A. W. (1977). The development of mnemonic encoding in children: From perception to abstraction. In R. V. Kail & J. W. Hagen (Eds.), *Perspectives on the development of memory and cognition* (pp. 61–88). Hillsdale, NJ: Lawrence Erlbaum Associates.

Kaplan, S. (1973). Cognitive maps in perception and thought. In R. M. Downs and D. Stea (Eds.), *Image and environment: Cognitive mapping and spatial behavior* (pp. 63–78). Chicago: Aldine Publishing Company.

Kaplan, S. (1976). Adaptation, structure, and knowledge. In G. T. Moore & R. G. Golledge (Eds.), *Environmental knowing* (pp. 32–45). Stroudsberg, PA: Dowden, Hutchinson, & Ross.

Kirasic, K. C., Siegel, A. W., & Allen, G. L. (1980). Developmental changes in recognition-in-context memory. *Child Development, 51*, 302–305.

Kline, L. W. (1898). The migratory impulse vs. love of home. *American Journal of Psychology, 10*, 1–81.

Kobasigawa, A. (1977). Retrieval strategies in the development of memory, In R. V. Kail & J. W. Hagen (Eds.), *Perspectives on the development of memory and cognition* (pp. 177–201). Hillsdale, NJ: Lawrence Erlbaum Associates.

Kobasigawa, A., & Mason, P. L. (1982). Use of multiple retrieval cues by children in memory retrieval situations. *Journal of General Psychology, 107*, 195–201.

Kosslyn, S. M., Pick, H. L., & Fariello, G. R. (1974). Cognitive maps in children and men. *Child Development, 45*, 707–716.

Kruskal, J. B., Young, F. W., & Seery, J. B. (1978). *How to use Kyst-2a, a very flexible program to do multidimensional scaling and unfolding*. Murray Hill, NJ: Bell Telephone Laboratories.

Kuipers, B. (1982). The "map in the head" metaphor. *Environment and Behavior, 14*, 202–220.

Lange, G. (1978). Organization-related processes in children's recall. In P. A. Ornstein (Ed.), *Memory development in children* (pp. 101–128). Hillsdale, NJ: Lawrence Erlbaum Associates.

Langer, S. K. (1967). *Mind: An essay on human feeling* (Vol. 1). Baltimore: The Johns Hopkins Press.

Laurendeau, M., & Pinard, A. (1979). *The development of the concept of space in the child*. New York: International Universities Press.

Lazarus, R. S. (1982). Thoughts on the relations between emotion and cognition. *American Psychologist, 37*, 1019–1024.

Lazarus, R. S., Averill, J. R., & Opton, E. M. (1970). Towards a cognitive theory of emotion. In M. B. Arnold (Ed.), *Feelings and emotions* (pp. 207–232). New York: Academic Press.

Lee, T. R. (1970). Perceived distance as a function of direction in the city. *Environment and Behavior, 2*, 40–51.

Lee, T. R. (1973). Psychology and living space. In R. M. Downs & D. Stea (Eds.), *Images and environment: Cognitive mapping and spatial behavior* (pp. 87–108). Chicago: Aldine.

Leight, K. A., & Ellis, H. C. (1981). Emotional mood states, strategies, and state-dependency in memory. *Journal of Verbal Learning and Verbal Behavior, 20*, 251–266.

Levine, M., Jankovic, I. N., & Palij, M. (1982). Principles of spatial problem solving. *Journal of Experimental Psychology: General, 111*, 157–175.

Levine, R., Chein, I., & Murphy, G. (1942). The relation of the intensity of the need to the amount of perceptual distortion: Preliminary report. *Journal of Psychology, 13*, 283–293.

Levy-Bruhl, L. (1973). *The philosophy of Auguste Comte*. Clifton, NJ: Augustus M. Kelley Publishers.

Liben, L. S. (1981). Spatial representation and behavior: Multiple perspectives. In L. S. Liben, A. H. Patterson & N. Newcombe (Eds.), *Spatial representation and behavior across the lifespan* (pp. 3–36). New York: Academic Press.

Liben, L. S. (1982). Children's large-scale spatial cognition: Is the measure the message? In R. Cohen (Ed.), *Children's conceptions of spatial relationships* (pp. 51–64). San Francisco: CA: Jossey-Bass.

Light, L. L., & Zelinski, E. M. (1983). Memory for spatial information in young and old adults. *Developmental Psychology, 19*, 901–906.

Livingston, R. B. (1967). Reinforcement. In G. C. Quarton, T. Melnechuk, & F. O. Schmitt (Eds.), *The neurosciences: A study program* (pp. 568–577). New York: Rockefeller University Press.

Loftus, E. F., & Marburger, W. (1983). Since the eruption of Mt. St. Helens, has anyone beaten you up? Improving the accuracy of retrospective reports with landmark events. *Memory and Cognition, 11*, 114–120.

Lord, F. E. (1941). A study of spatial orientation of children. *Journal of Educational Research, 34*, 481–505.

Lowrey, R. A. (1970). Distance concepts of urban residents. *Environment and Behavior, 2*, 52–73.

Luria, A. R. (1966). *Higher cortical functions of man*. New York: Basic Books.

Lynch, K. (1960). *The image of the city*. Cambridge, MA: MIT and Harvard University Press.

MacLean, P. D. (1980). Sensory and perceptive factors in emotional functions of the triune brain. In A. O. Rorty (Ed.), *Explaining emotions* (pp. 9–36). Berkeley: University of California Press.

Maier, N. R. F. (1936). Reasoning in children. *Journal of Comparative Psychology, 21*, 357–366.

Maki, R. H., Maki, W. S., Jr., & Marsh, L. B. (1977). Processing locational and orientational information. *Memory and Cognition, 5*, 602–612.

Mandler, G. (1962). From association to structure. *Psychological Review, 69*, 415–427.

Mandler, J. (1978). Categorical and schematic organization in memory. In C. R. Puff (Ed.), *Memory, organization, and structure* (pp. 259–299). New York: Academic Press.

Mandler, G., & Pearlstone, Z. (1966). Free and constrained concept learning and subsequent recall. *Journal of Verbal Learning and Verbal Behavior, 5*, 126–131.

Mandler, G., & Shebo, B. J. (1983). Knowing and liking. *Motivation and Emotion, 7,* 125–144.

Maurer, R., & Baxter, J. C. (1972). Images of the neighborhood and city among black-, anglo-, and Mexican-American children. *Environment and Behavior, 4,* 351–388.

McFarland, C. E., Jr., Frey, T. J., & Rhodes, D. D. (1980). Retrieval of internally versus externally generated words in episodic memory. *Journal of Verbal Learning and Verbal Behavior, 19,* 210–225.

McGuire, W. (1960). A syllogistic analysis of cognitive relationships. In C. I. Hovland & M. J. Rosenberg & (Eds.), *Attitude organization and change* (pp. 65–111). New Haven: Yale University Press.

Mehrabian, A. (1976). *Public places and private spaces.* New York: Basic Books.

Mindess, H. (1971). *Laughter and liberation.* Los Angeles, CA: Nash.

Moar, I., & Bower, G. H. (1983). Inconsistency in spatial knowledge. *Memory and Cognition, 11,* 107–113.

Moyer, R. S., & Dumais, S. T. (1978). Mental comparisons. In G. H. Bower (Ed.), *The psychology of learning and motivation* (Vol. 12, pp. 117–155). New York: Academic Press.

Mueller, J. H. (1980). Test anxiety and the encoding and retrieval of information. In I. G. Sarason (Ed.), *Test anxiety: Theory, research, and applications* (pp. 63–86). Hillsdale, NJ: Lawrence Erlbaum Associates.

Myers, N. A., & Perlmutter, M. (1978). Memory in the years from two to five. In P. A. Ornstein (Ed.), *Memory development in children* (pp. 191–218). Hillsdale, NJ: Lawrence Erlbaum Associates.

Neisser, U. (1962). Cultural and cognitive discontinuity. In T. E. Gladwin & W. Sturtevant (Eds.), *Anthropology and human behavior.* Washington, DC: Anthropological Society of Washington.

Neisser, U. (1963). The imitation of man by machine. *Science, 139,* 193–197.

Neisser, U. (1976). *Cognition and reality.* San Francisco, CA: W. H. Freeman.

Neisser, U. (1982). Snapshots or benchmarks? In U. Neisser (Ed.), *Memory observed: Remembering in natural contexts* (pp. 43–48). San Francisco: W. H. Freeman.

Newcombe, N. (1982). Development of spatial cognition and cognition development. In R. Cohen (Ed.), *Children's conceptions of spatial relationships* (pp. 65–81). San Francisco, CA: Jossey-Bass.

Newcombe, N. (1984). Methods for the study of spatial cognition. In R. Cohen (Ed.), *The development of spatial cognition.* Hillsdale, NJ: Lawrence Erlbaum Associates.

Newcombe, N. & Liben, L. S. (1982). Barrier effects in the cognitive maps of children and adults. *Journal of Experimental Child Psychology, 34,* 46–58.

Newell, A., & Simon, H. A. (1972). *Human problem solving.* Englewood Cliffs, NJ: Prentice-Hall.

Osgood, C. W., Suci, J. G., & Tannenbaum, P. H. (1957). *The measurement of meaning.* Urbana: University of Illinois Press.

Overton, W. F., & Reese, H. W. (1973). Models of development: Methodological implications. In J. R. Nesselroade & H. W. Reese (Eds.), *Life-span developmental psychology: Methodological issues* (pp. 65–86). New York: Academic Press.

Paris, S. (1978). The development of inference and transformation as memory operations. In P. A. Ornstein (Ed.), *Memory development in children* (pp. 129–156). Hillsdale, NJ: Lawrence Erlbaum Associates.

Pepper, S. C. (1961). *World hypotheses.* Berkeley: University of California Press.

Piaget, J. (1928). *Judgment and reasoning in the child*. London: Routledge & Kegan Paul.

Piaget, J. (1981). In T. A. Brown & C. E. Kaegi, (Eds. and Trans.), *Intelligence and affectivity: Their relationship during child development*. Palo Alto, CA: Annual Reviews.

Piaget, J., & Inhelder, B. (1967). *The child's conception of space*. New York: W. W. Norton.

Piaget, J., Inhelder, B., & Szeminska, A. (1960). *The child's conception of geometry*. New York: Harper & Row.

Pick, H. (1976). Transactional-constructivist approach to environmental knowing. In G. T. Moore & R. G. Golledge (Eds.), *Environmental knowing* (pp. 185–188). Stroudsberg, PA: Dowden, Hutchinson, & Ross.

Pick, H. L., Jr., & Lockman, J. J. (1981). From frames of reference to spatial representations. In L. S. Liben, A. H. Patterson & N. Newcombe (Eds.), *Spatial representation and behavior across the lifespan* (pp. 39–61). New York: Academic Press.

Plutchik, R. (1970). Emotions, evolution, and adaptive processes. In M. B. Arnold (Ed.), *Feeling and emotions* (pp. 3–24). New York: Academic Press.

Plutchik, R. (1980). A general psychoevolutionary theory of emotion. In R. Plutchik & H. Kellerman (Eds.), *Emotion: Theory, research, and experience* (Vol. 1, pp. 3–33). New York: Academic Press.

Poag, C. K., Cohen, R., & Weatherford, D. L. (1983). Spatial representations of young children: The role of self- versus adult-directed movement and viewing. *Journal of Experimental Child Psychology, 35*, 172–179.

Presson, C. C., & Ihrig, L. H. (1982). Using mother as a spatial landmark: evidence against egocentric coding in infancy. *Developmental Psychology, 18*, 699–703.

Rapaport, D. (1959). *Emotions and memory*. New York: International Universities Press.

Rapoport, A. (1976). Environmental cognition in cross-cultural perspective. In G. T. Moore & R. G. Golledge (Eds.), *Environmental knowing* (pp. 220–234). Stroudsberg, PA: Dowden, Hutchinson, & Ross.

Raye, C. L., Johnson, M. K., & Taylor, T. H. (1980). Is there something special about memory for internally generated information? *Memory and Cognition, 8*, 141–148.

Revlin, R., Leirer, V., Yopp, H., & Yopp, R. (1980). The belief-bias effect in formal reasoning: The influence of knowledge on logic. *Memory and Cognition, 8*, 584–592.

Riley, C. A. (1976). The representation of comparative relations and the transitive inference task. *Journal of Experimental Child Psychology, 22*, 1–22.

Riley, C. A., & Trabasso, T. (1974). Comparatives, logical structures, and encoding in a transitive inference task. *Journal of Experimental Child Psychology, 17*, 187–203.

Rogoff, B. (1981). Approaches to integrating context and cognitive development. In M. E. Lamb & A. L. Brown (Eds.), *Advances in Developmental Psychology* (Vol. 2, pp. 125–170). Hillsdale, NJ: Lawrence Erlbaum Associates.

Romanes, G. J. (1889). *Mental evolution in man*. New York: D. Appleton.

Sadalla, E. K., Burroughs, W. J., & Staplin, L. J. (1980). Reference points in spatial cognition. *Journal of Experimental Psychology: Human Learning and Memory, 6*, 516–528.

Salaman, E. (1982). A collection of moments. In U. Neisser (Ed.), *Memory observed:*

Remembering in natural contexts (pp. 49–63). San Francisco, CA: W. H. Freeman.

Schachter, S. (1970). The assumption of identity and peripheralist-centralist controversies in motivation and emotion. In M. B. Arnold (Ed.), *Feeling and emotions* (pp. 111–121). New York: Academic Press.

Schilder, P. (1965). On the development of thoughts. In D. Rapaport (trans.), *Organization and pathology of thought: Selected sources* (pp. 497–518). New York: Columbia University Press.

Scribner, S. (1975). Recall of classical syllogisms: a cross-cultural investigation of error on logical problems. In R. J. Falmagne (Ed.), *Reasoning: Representation and process* (pp. 153–173). Hillsdale, NJ: Lawrence Erlbaum Associates.

Seamon, D. (1979). *A geography of the lifeworld*. New York: St. Martin's Press.

Sherer, M., & Rogers, R. W. (1980). Effects of therapist's nonverbal communication on rated skill and effectiveness. *Journal of Clinical Psychology, 36*, 696–700.

Siegel, A. W. (1981). The externalization of cognitive maps by children and adults: In search of ways to ask better questions. In L. S. Liben, A. H. Patterson & N. Newcombe (Eds.), *Spatial representation and behavior across the lifespan* (pp. 167–194). New York: Academic Press.

Siegel, A. W. (1982). Toward a social ecology of cognitive mapping. In R. Cohen (Ed.), *Children's conceptions of spatial relationships* (pp. 83–94). San Francisco, CA: Jossey-Bass.

Siegel, A. W., Allen, G. L., & Kirasic, K. C. (1979). Children's ability to make bidirectional distance comparisons: The advantage of thinking ahead. *Developmental Psychology, 15*, 656–657.

Siegel, A. W., Allik, J. P., & Herman, J. F. (1976). The primacy effect in young children: Verbal fact or spatial artifact? *Child Development, 47*, 242–247.

Siegel, A. W., Bisanz, J., & Bisanz, G. L. (1983). Developmental analysis: A strategy for the study of psychological change. *Contributions to Human Development, 8*, 53–80.

Siegel, A. W., Goldsmith, L. T., & Madson, C. R. (1981). *The development of skills in estimation problems of extent and numerosity*. Newton, MA: Education Development Center.

Siegel, A. W., Herman, J. F., Allen, G. L., & Kirasic, K. C. (1979). The development of cognitive maps of large- and small-scale spaces. *Child Development, 50*, 582–585.

Siegel, A. W., Kirasic, K. C., & Kail, R. V. (1978). Stalking the elusive cognitive map. In I. Altman and J. F. Wohlwill (Eds.), *Human behavior and environment* (Vol. 3, pp. 223–258). New York: Plenum.

Siegel, A. W., & Schadler, M. (1977). The development of young children's spatial representations of their classrooms. *Child Development, 48*, 388–394.

Siegel, A. W., & White, S. H. (1975). The development of spatial representations of large-scale environments. In H. W. Reese (Ed.), *Advances in child development and behavior* (Vol. 10, pp. 9–55). New York: Academic Press.

Singer, J. L. (1975). *The inner world of daydreaming*. New York: Harper and Row.

Smith, S. M. (1979). Remembering in and out of context. *Journal of Experimental Psychology: Human Learning and Memory, 5*, 460–471.

Smith, S. M. (1982). Enhancement of recall using multiple environmental contexts during learning. *Memory and Cognition, 10*, 405–412.

Smith, S. M., Glenberg, A. M., & Bjork, R. A. (1978). Environmental context and human memory. *Memory and Cognition, 6*, 342–353.

Spiller, G. (1904). The problem of the emotions. *American Journal of Psychology, 15*, 569–580.

Stanley-Jones, D. (1970). The biological origin of love and hate. In M. B. Arnold (Ed.), *Feeling and emotions* (pp. 25–37). New York: Academic Press.

Stevens, A., & Coupe, P. (1978). Distortions in judged spatial relations. *Cognitive Psychology, 10*, 422–437.

Stone, C. A., & Day, M. C. (1980). Competence and performance models and the characterization of formal operational skills. *Human Development, 23*, 323–353.

Teitelbaum, P. (1977). Levels of integration of the operant. In W. K. Honig & J. E. R. Staddon (Eds.), *Handbook of Operant Behavior* (pp. 7–27). Englewood Cliffs, NJ: Prentice-Hall.

Thistlethwaite, D. (1950). Attitude and structure as factors in the distortion of reasoning. *Journal of Abnormal and Social Psychology, 45*, 442–458.

Thorndyke, P. W. (1981). Spatial cognition and reasoning. In J. H. Harvey (Ed.), *Cognition, social behavior, and the environment* (pp. 137–149). Hillsdale, NJ: Lawrence Erlbaum Associates.

Tolman, E. C. (1948). Cognitive maps in rats and men. *Psychological Review, 55*, 189–208.

Tomkins, S. S. (1970). A theory of memory. In J. S. Antrobus (Ed.), *Cognition and affect* (pp. 59–130). Boston: Little, Brown and Company.

Tomkins, S. S. (1981). The quest for primary motives: Biography and autobiography of an idea. *Journal of Personality and Social Psychology, 41*, 306–329.

Townsend, M. A. R. (1983). Schema shifting: Children's cognitive monitoring of the prose-schema interaction in comprehension. *Journal of Experimental Child Psychology, 36*, 139–149.

Trabasso, T. (1975). Representation, memory and reasoning: How do we make transitive inferences? In A. D. Pick (Ed.), *Minnesota Symposium on child psychology* (Vol. 9, pp. 135–172). Minneapolis: University of Minnesota Press.

Trabasso, T., & Riley, C. A. (1975). The construction and use of representations involving linear order. In R. L. Solso (Ed.), *Information processing and cognition: The Loyola Symposium* (pp. 381–410). Hillsdale, NJ: Lawrence Erlbaum Associates.

Trabasso, T., Riley, C. A., & Wilson, E. G. (1975). The representation of linear order and spatial strategies in reasoning: a developmental study. In R. J. Falmagne (Ed.), *Reasoning: Representation and process* (pp. 201–229). Hillsdale, NJ: Lawrence Erlbaum Associates.

Trowbridge, C. C. (1913). On fundamental methods of orientation and "imaginary maps." *Science, 38*, 888–897.

Tulving, E., & Thomson, D. M. (1973). Encoding specificity and retrieval processes in episodic memory. *Psychological Review, 80*, 352–373.

Tversky, B. (1981). Distortions in memory for maps. *Cognitive Psychology, 13*, 407–433.

Tyler, S. W., & Voss, J. F. (1982). Attitude and knowledge effects in prose processing. *Journal of Verbal Learning and Verbal Behavior, 21*, 524–538.

Vygotsky, L. A. (1962). *Thought and language*. Cambridge, MA: MIT Press.

Washburn, M. F. (1928). Emotion and thought: a motor theory of their relations. In M. L. Reymert (Ed.), *Feelings and emotions: The Wittenberg Symposium* (pp. 104–115). Worcester, MA: Clark University Press.

Waxer, P. H. (1978). *Nonverbal aspects of psychotherapy*. New York: Praeger.

Weiner, B., Graham, S., Stern, P., & Lawson, M. E. (1982). Using affective cues to infer causal thoughts. *Developmental Psychology, 18*, 278–286.

Wellman, H. M., & Somerville, S. C. (1982). The development of human search ability. In M. E. Lamb and A. L. Brown (Eds.), *Advances in developmental psychology* (Vol. 2, pp. 41–84). Hillsdale, NJ: Lawrence Erlbaum Associates.

Wellman, H. M., Somerville, S. C., & Haake, R. J. (1979). Development of search procedures in real-life spatial environments. *Developmental Psychology, 15*, 530–542.

Werner, H. (1957). *Comparative psychology of mental development.* New York: International Universities Press.

Werner, H., & Kaplan, B. (1963). *Symbol formation.* New York: John Wiley & Sons.

White, S. H. (1965). Evidence for a hierarchical arrangement of learning processes. In H. W. Reese & C. C. Spiker (Eds.), *Advances in child development and behavior* (Vol. 2, pp. 187–220). New York: Academic Press.

White, S. H. (1983). The idea of development in developmental psychology. In R. M. Lerner (Ed.), *Developmental psychology: Historical and philosophical perspectives* (pp. 55–77). Hillsdale, NJ: Lawrence Erlbaum Associates.

White, S. H., & Fishbein, H. D. (1971). Children's learning. In N. Talbot, J. Kagan, & L. Eisenberg (Eds.), *Behavioral Sciences and Pediatric Medicine* (pp. 188–227). Philadelphia, PA: Saunders.

White, S. H., & Pillemer, D. B. (1979). Childhood amnesia and the development of a socially accessible memory system. In J. F. Kihlstrom & F. J. Evans (Eds.), *Functional disorders of memory* (pp. 29–73). Hillsdale, NJ: Lawrence Erlbaum Associates.

White, S. H., & Siegel, A. W. (1984). Cognitive development in time and space. In B. Rogoff & J. Lave (Eds.), *Social cognition: Its development in everyday contexts* (pp. 238–287). Cambridge, MA: Harvard University Press.

Wickelgren, W. A. (1979). Chunking and consolidation: A theoretical synthesis of semantic networks, configuring in conditioning, S-R versus cognitive learning, normal forgetting, the amnesic syndrome, and the hippocampal arousal system. *Psychological Review, 86*, 44–60.

Wicker, F. W., Thorelli, I. M., Barron, W. L., & Ponder, M. R. (1981). Relationships among affective and cognitive factors in humor. *Journal of Research in Personality, 15*, 359–370.

Wolf, T. H. (1973). *Alfred Binet.* Chicago, IL: The University of Chicago Press.

Zajonc, R. B. (1980). Feeling and thinking: Preferences need no inferences. *American Psychologist, 35*, 151–175.

Zajonc, R. B. (1981). A one-factor mind about mind and emotion. *American Psychologist, 36*, 102–103.

3. The Role of Conceptual Knowledge in the Development of Organization in Children's Memory

David F. Bjorklund

The development of organization in children's memory has received substantial research attention over the past 10 years (for reviews see Lange, 1978; Mandler, 1979; Moely, 1977; Ornstein & Corsale, 1979). Organization is customarily defined as the structure discovered or imposed upon a set of items by a learner, with this structure facilitating retrieval of items from memory (see Chapter 1 by Ackerman for a discussion of factors affecting retrieval from children's memory). Organization has generally been thought of as a strategic process (i.e., deliberate and effortful), with age changes in the use of organization being attributed to age differences in strategic functioning. Such a conclusion is supported by the results of numerous studies demonstrating that young children, who show little evidence of spontaneous organization, can be trained to cluster their recall according to adult categorizations (e.g., Bjorklund, Ornstein, & Haig, 1977; Moely & Jeffrey, 1974; Moely, Olson, Halwes, & Flavell, 1969). In this chapter, I dispute this position, arguing instead that most of the age changes in the organization of children's recall are not strategic, but rather can be attributed to developmental changes in the structure and content of children's conceptual representations. Organization in memory does become strategic, I believe, sometime during adolescence, resulting in a qualitatively different type of memory functioning. However, I argue that the regular improvements observed in memory organization over the course of the preschool and elementary school years can most parsimoniously be attributed to developmental differences in the structure of semantic memory and the ease with which certain types of semantic relationships can be activated.

The extent of a child's knowledge about a particular content area will certainly affect how he or she will process information pertinent to that domain. For example, when children have a more detailed knowledge for a particular content area than adults, their levels of memory performance are often elevated beyond those of adults (e.g., Chi, 1978; Lindberg, 1980); and age differences in memory span (e.g., Chi, 1976; Dempster, 1978, and Chapter 5 in this volume) and recall of unrelated words (e.g., Chechile & Richman, 1982; Richman, Nida, & Pittman, 1976) have been attributed to age differences in familiarity with the to-be-remembered materials rather than to age differences in memory capacity or strategic intervention. With respect to organization in recall, which features or relations children use to represent familiar word concepts, as well as the extent of children's knowledge of category relations, will influence the degree to which children's retrieval is organized. As category relations become better established in a child's semantic memory, they are apt to be activated in a wider range of contexts, resulting in increased incidences of organization in a child's recall of categorizable material.

In the sections to follow, I will first review studies demonstrating age changes in semantic memory, emphasizing developmental differences in children's understanding of natural language concepts. Children's use of conceptual knowledge will next be reviewed, and I will present data from a variety of memory paradigms consistent with the interpretation that most age changes in organization in memory are due to developmental changes in concept knowledge. Then I will argue that when elevated levels of clustering are first seen in development, they are mediated by the relatively automatic activation of semantic memory relations, which may in turn lead children to identify an organizational strategy. Thus, early mnemonic strategies may result from children clustering highly associated items together in their recall, identifying categorical relations in their output *after they are generated*, and only then implementing a deliberate categorical search. In other words, intentional organizational strategies may have their genesis in the relatively automatic clustering children observe in their own recall. This viewpoint suggests that metamnemonic awareness develops as a result of a child demonstrating competent memory behavior. That children may learn strategy knowledge through strategy use has been shown recently in memory training studies by Pressely and his colleagues for elaboration strategies (e.g., Pressely, Borkowski, & O'Sullivan, 1984; Pressely, Levin, & Ghatala, 1984), although they claim that strategy knowledge is more easily acquired by children when the benefits of a strategy are explained explicitly to subjects.

The Development of Conceptual Knowledge

One thing that becomes apparent when examining the semantic memory literature is that estimates of the sophistication of children's conceptual knowledge are highly task dependent. For example, in some tasks super-ordination appears to be well within the cognitive repetoire of 4- and 5-year-olds (e.g., Smith, 1979; Steinberg & Anderson, 1975), whereas in other tasks which appear to tap similar knowledge, "true" superordination is not achieved until early adolescence (e.g., Winer, 1980). What can be said generally is that in development, the number of situations in which children demonstrate knowl-edge of categorical relations broadens with age. Although 2- and 3-year-olds may be aware of the category membership of a set of items, they will display this knowledge only under optimal conditions.

In this section, I will review studies on the development of children's conceptual knowledge, concentrating on the development of taxonomic cate-gorization which, I believe, is most pertinent to understanding the development of organization in memory as it has been studied over the last decade. However, an examination will also be made of other forms of representation which contribute to children's concepts, specifically children's use of functional/complementary relations.[1]

From Functional/Complementary to Taxonomic/Similarity Relationships

There is a substantial literature indicating that children's early semantic concepts are based on functional/thematic/complementary relationships rather than similarity/taxonomic category relationships. For example, Nelson (1973; 1974a) has claimed that children's early word concepts are based on perceptual-motor experiences, with functional characteristics being the core of the developing concept. More recently, Nelson and her colleagues (1983; Nelson, Fivush, Hudson, & Lucariello, 1983; Nelson & Gruendel, 1981) have argued that event representations or *scripts* are a basic form of conceptual representation for young children. Scripts can be thought of as a form of schematic organization, with real-world events "organized in terms of temporal and causal relations between component acts" (Nelson, 1983, p. 55). Related to this is work by Mandler (1983), who argued that young children's knowledge is organized schematically rather than categorically. Schematic organization

---

[1]Age differences in the use of perceptual versus conceptual criteria in forming concepts have also been reported. This perceptual to conceptual shift has been noted in studies of classification (e.g., Naron, 1978; Reichard et al., 1944), recognition memory (e.g., Felzen & Anisfeld, 1970), semantic generalization (Riess, 1946), and paired-associate learning (Rice & Di Vesta, 1965). However, despite this natural bias of encoding items in terms of perceptual features, young children's performance on cognitive tasks is usually hindered when they are oriented toward perceptual rather than semantic stimulus properties (e.g., Bjorklund et al., 1978; Geis & Hall, 1976, 1978; Ghatala, Carbonari, & Bobele, 1980; Murphy & Brown, 1975). Although there is some evidence that young children will use perceptual stimulus features as an organizational guide in recall (Hasher & Clifton, 1974; Naron, 1978; Perlmutter & Ricks, 1979), the concern of the present chapter is with the development of meaning-based relations in children's concepts and their relationship to subsequent organization in memory. Accordingly, the role of perceptual encoding and organization in children's concept development and memory performance will not be examined.

typifies the relationships found in real-world scenes, stories, and events. Scripts and schemes, then, rely on functional relationships among items to serve as a basis for conceptual structures in semantic memory.

Denney (1974) has similarly emphasized the role of functional or complementary relationships in young children's concepts. Denney suggested that preschool children generally form concepts on the basis of complementary relations and that somewhere between the ages of 6 and 9 years there is a shift to the use of similarity criteria. Categories based on complementary relationships are defined as those "composed of items that are different but share some interrelationship either in the subject's past experience or in the experimental situation" (Denney,1974, p. 41). Categories based on similarity, according to Denney, emphasize the perceptual or functional "sameness" among items and include common taxonomic categories (e.g., animals, clothes, transportation, etc.).

Evidence for this shift from reliance on functional/complementary to taxonomic/similarity relations comes from a variety of experimental sources. The most direct evidence for a complementary to taxonomic shift in organizational styles comes from classification studies where children are asked to sort familiar items into meaning-based groups. Although organizational preferences of children may vary as a function of the particular stimulus list (e.g., Olver & Hornsby, 1966), the evidence for a developmental change in classification criteria from complementary-based groupings to those based on taxonomic category properties is impressive (e.g., Anglin, 1970; Annett, 1959; Inhelder & Piaget, 1964; Reichard, Schneider, & Rappaport, 1944; Sigel, 1953; Strand, 1983; Szeminska, 1965; Thompson, 1941). Results consistent with the above findings have also been obtained from a variety of nonclassification studies, including those assessing conceptual styles (e.g., Kagan, Moss, & Sigel, 1963), recognition memory (Heidenhiemer, 1978; Scott, Serchuk, & Mundy, 1982), children's specification of relations existing among a series of items (e.g., Anglin, 1970; Olver & Hornsby, 1966), word associations (e.g., Emerson & Gekowski, 1976; Entwisle, 1966), and word definitions (see Denney, 1974).

However, although preschool children tend to use complementary criteria in forming categories, they are familiar with alternative ways of grouping items (i.e., by taxonomic similarity) and will vary their classification schemes as a function of changes in sorting procedure (e.g., Markman, Cox, & Marchida, 1981) and instructions (see Flavell, 1970). Perhaps the clearest example of young children's classification flexibility is a study by Smiley and Brown (1979). In their study, subjects were to choose which of two alternative pictures "went best" with a standard picture. One of the two alternatives was related to the standard on the basis of taxonomic category relations (e.g., for *needle*-PIN), whereas the other picture was related to the standard on the basis of thematic (complementary) relations (e.g., for *needle*-THREAD). The vast majority of the selections of preschool and first-grade children were for the thematically related pictures. The reverse was true for fifth-grade and college subjects. In a second experiment, Smiley and Brown trained one group of kindergarten children to make selections based on taxonomic relationships. They reported that these 5-year-olds were easily able to learn a taxonomic style, and claimed that "although conceptual preferences are quite pronounced, they are easily overcome by a brief period of training" (p. 256). However, the day after training when subjects were tested again, this strong bias toward taxonomic responding was greatly reduced. Smiley and Brown concluded that although taxonomic training can be easily realized, "there is a tendency for trainees to revert to the preferred mode when free to do so" (p. 256).

In summary, the research literature indicates that complementary or functional categorization represents an early form of interitem organization which developmentally precedes organization on the basis of taxonomic category relations. Sometime between the ages of 6 and 9 years, complementary organization decreases in use and is replaced by organization based on categorical similarity (Denney, 1974). Such a shift cannot be attributed to young children's ignorance of category relations, however, as demonstrated by preschoolers' ability to form taxonomic groupings under certain instructional or procedural conditions (e.g., Markman et al., 1981; Smiley & Brown, 1979). In a similar vein, the advent of taxonomic categorization does not eliminate the use of complementary relations. Such organizational schemes continue to be used by older children and adults when the task demands call for them (e.g., Inhelder & Piaget, 1964; Rabinowitz & Mandler, 1983). Thus, subjects over a broad age range have available to them both taxonomic and complementary semantic relationships. What changes in development is the tendency with which these two forms of categorization are used, with taxonomic category relations being used in a wider range of contexts with increasing age.

The Development of Superordinate Categories

As the Smiley and Brown (1979) study so clearly demonstrated, preschool children are well aware of the taxonomic relations existing among familiar items, even though they show a consistent bias toward nontaxonomic modes of representation. Preschool children's encoding of familiar items in terms of category features has been inferred in studies of recognition memory (e.g., Hall & Halperin, 1972; Mansfield, 1977), cued recall (e.g., Bjorklund, 1976; Eysenck & Baron, 1974; Williams & Goulet, 1975), release from proactive interference (e.g., Esrov, Hall, & LaFaver, 1974; Hoeman, DeRosa, & Andrews, 1974), and habituation (Faulkender, Wright, & Waldron, 1974). However, although there is compelling evidence that young children encode individual items in terms of category features, substantial development in terms of category knowledge occurs through the elementary school years. For example, in a study where children were required to label pictures and to categorize them (i.e., name a group to which the pictured object belonged), Winters and Brzoska (1976) reported regular increases in the number of items reliably categorized by children from 5 to 14 years of age. Similar findings have been reported in studies in which children are to select appropriate exemplars from sets of words or pictures from designated categories (e.g., Bjorklund, Thompson, & Ornstein, 1983; Saltz, Soller, & Sigel, 1972), and where children are to generate category instances to a superordinate label (e.g., Nelson, 1974b; Posnansky, 1978). These results are consistent with the position that children's category boundaries broaden with age.

When do children first acquire taxonomic categories? Using habituation/ dishabituation techniques, evidence is accumulating indicating concept formation in preverbal infants for categories in which exemplars are perceptually similar (see Cohen & Younger, 1983; Reznick & Kagan, 1983). Rosch and her colleagues (Mervis & Crisafi, 1982; Rosch, Mervis, Gray, Johnson, & Boyes-Braem, 1976) postulate that children's first taxonomies are not for superordinate concepts but, as with infants, are for groupings of objects having similar overall configurations (e.g., chairs and cars but not furniture and vehicles). Rosch et al. (1976) have referred to such groupings as basic level categories. Using a matching procedure (e.g., "Which two of these three pictures are the same type of thing?") and a sorting task (e.g, "Group together pictures that are alike or go together in some way"), Rosch et al. (1976) demonstrated that preschool children could group basic level objects taxonomically before they could categorize at the superordinate level. Related to this is work by Mervis and Crisafi (1982). Using artificial concepts, they reported that visual categories at the basic level were learned more easily by children than either subordinate or superordinate categories.

Other work examining the origins of children's taxonomic concepts has been done by Anglin (1977). Anglin suggests that language concepts develop from children's experiences with specific exemplars, with children generating category prototypes based upon their interactions with members of a concept. Accordingly, young children often attribute to a category features that may characterize only some of its members (e.g., flowers are yellow; dogs have spots). With development, these characteristic features—attributes that are associated with a concept but are not necessary for its definition—are given less emphasis as children are exposed to increasing numbers of concept instances. More recent research provides some support for this position. For example, Keil and Batterman (1984) reported that, with age, children give less weight to characteristic features (e.g., a robber uses a gun and is mean) and more weight to defining features (e.g., a robber steals things, regardless of what his/her personality characteristics might be). Similarly, Schwanenflugel, Bjorklund, Guth, Willenborg, and Boardman (1984), using a rating task with 5-, 7- and 10-year-olds, reported improvements with age in children's ability to discriminate among features that are critical in defining a word (e.g., *sailor*: is found on ships), features that are characteristic of many members of a concept (e.g., *sailor*: wears a uniform), and features that are only occasionally associated with the concept (e.g., *sailor*: wears a hat).

One area where substantial controversy exists concerning children's category knowledge is the age at which class-inclusion relations are available. Class inclusion, as defined by Inhelder and Piaget (1964), refers to the knowledge that a class must always be smaller than any more inclusive class in which it is contained. In a typical class-inclusion problem, children are presented with several examples from two subordinate categories of a single superordinate class (e.g., seven pictures of ducks and three pictures of robins). When asked whether there are more ducks or more birds, a child lacking class inclusion would respond that there are more ducks. Most researchers using Inhelder and Piaget's method report that class inclusion is not reliably found until early adolescence (see Winer, 1980), although there is considerable controversy concerning what type of cognitive processing is tapped by such tests (e.g., Klahr & Wallace, 1972). For example, McCabe, Siegel, Spence, and Wilkinson (1982) found qualitative changes in how children of different ages solved class-inclusion problems. In their study, children 3 through 8 years of age were given a series of standard class-inclusion tasks. They reported that mean number of correct solutions varied curvilinearly with age, with 5- and 6-year-olds solving the fewest number of problems. Based on their data, they proposed a three-stage model of how children approach class-inclusion problems. The youngest children (3- and 4-year-olds) fail to discern any rule governing task completion but rather respond randomly and thus sometimes correctly. For slightly older children (5- and 6-year-olds), task performance is guided by a consistently applied rule of comparing the size of the subsets and selecting the larger of the two, which produces wrong answers. Finally, children recognize that the task requires a comparison between a subordinate and superordinate class and respond accordingly.

Although most researchers claim that standard class-inclusion problems are not mastered until early adolescence, others claim that school-age and even preschool children possess inclusion relations for natural language categories. For example, several researchers have shown that 3- and 4-year-old children can be trained to solve class-inclusion tasks and generalize them to similar problems (e.g., Brainerd, 1974; Siegel, McCabe, Brand, & Mathews, 1978; Wilkinson, 1976). Other researchers have inferred class-inclusion relations in preschoolers using a variety of nonstandard tasks. For example, Steinberg and Anderson (1975) working with 5- and 6-year-old children, found that retrieval cues that were superordinately related to target items were more effective in mediating recall than were cues that were similar in some way to the target word. For instance, for the target word *dog*, PET, a close superordinate, and ANIMAL, a remote superordinate, were more effective retrieval cues than was CAT, a member of the same superordinate class. Mansfield (1977), using a false recognition paradigm, similarly reported that for preschool and early school-age children, superordinate-subordinate category relations were more effective in influencing recognition memory performance than were concrete part-whole relations. Smith (1979) presented nursery school, kindergarten, and first-grade children with a series of questions concerning their knowledge of superordination. Included were questions assessing children's knowledge of subordinate and superordinate relations (e.g., "Are all dogs animals?" or "Are all animals dogs?"), and questions requiring class inferences (e.g., "A pug is a kind of a dog. Does a pug have to be an animal?" or "A pug is a kind of animal. Does a pug have to be a kind of dog?"). Based on children's responses to these and other questions, Smith concluded that young children do indeed represent inclusion relations. Following the interpretations of Steinberg and Anderson (1975) and Mansfield (1977), Smith suggested that "young children and adults share the same basic representation format, but differ in their ability to derive certain consequences of that representation" (p. 454).

In summary, it is difficult to make a single, sweeping statement concerning young children's category knowledge. Preschool children most certainly know many of the category relations known by older children and adults (e.g., Mansfield, 1977; Smiley & Brown, 1979). However, compared to older subjects, they apparently use different features or give different weight to features in defining common language terms (e.g., Keil & Batterman, 1984; Schwanenflugel et al., 1984), and have more limited boundaries for category membership (e.g., Bjorklund et al., 1983, Nelson, 1974b; Winters & Brzoska, 1976). There is also no single answer to the question, "When do children acquire class-inclusion relations?," with some investigators claiming it is an accomplishment of late childhood (e.g., Inhelder & Piaget, 1964; Winer, 1980) and others claiming that it is well within the ability of preschool children (e.g., Smith, 1979; Steinberg & Anderson, 1975). Children's demonstration of category knowledge is highly task dependent. Young children appear to possess basic categorical and inclusion relations for certain sets of stimuli, but will use such relations only under optimal instructional and procedural conditions. Generally, the number of situations in which children will demonstrate category knowledge broadens with age.

Category Typicality. One reason for the discrepancy in findings concerning young children's knowledge of superordination can be attributed to the specific category exemplars used in the various studies. According to contemporary cognitive theory, natural categories cannot be viewed as having a set of critical features that determines absolutely category membership. Rather, natural categories are viewed as consisting of a core meaning (i.e., best examples or prototype), with the judged typicality of category items decreasing as the similarity between the examplar and the prototype diminishes (e.g., Mervis & Rosch, 1981; Rosch, 1973; 1975; Smith, Shoben, & Rips, 1974). In other words, not all category items are created equal, with some items judged to be more representative of their categories than others. Adults show high inter-subject agreement in their ratings of category items in terms of goodness of example or typicality (Bjorklund et al., 1983; Rosch, 1973, 1975; Uyeda & Mandler, 1980), and are influenced by differences in judged typicality in a variety of cognitive tasks, including category verification (Rips, Shoben, & Smith, 1973; Rosch, 1973; Smith et al., 1974), same-different judgements (Rosch, 1975), and free recall (Greenberg & Bjorklund, 1981; Keller & Kellas, 1978; Whitney, Cocklin, Juola, & Kellas, 1983).

With respect to development, Rosch (1973) hypothesized that children first learn prototypic examples of semantic categories and only later learn the category membership of less typical exemplars. Rosch's theory has received support from a variety of sources. For example, Anglin (1977) and White (1982) each reported that preschool children, given sets of pictures from which to choose category exemplars, generally selected as appropriate category members that adults judged to be highly typical or central of their concept (e.g., *horse* for ANIMAL). However, these children tended to deny category membership to many atypical items, regardless of their familiarity with them (e.g., *butterfly* for ANIMAL). In a similar study, Saltz et al. (1972) asked kindergarten, third-, and sixth-grade children to select from a large set of pictures examples of specified categories. They reported that most of the age differences in inclusion rates were attributed to younger children's reluctance to include as category members atypical exemplars (e.g., *gloves, hat*, and *shoes* for CLOTHES). Fewer developmental differences in inclusion rates were found for more typical items (e.g., *dress, sweater*, and *shirt* for CLOTHES). Comparable findings were reported by Nelson (1974b), who used a category production task (i.e., "List all the examples of [CATEGORY NAME] that you can."). She found few developmental differences in children's listing of typical category exemplars; greater age differences were found in children's mention of less typical category instances, with older children being more apt to list peripheral category exemplars than younger children.

In a recent study by Bjorklund et al. (1983), children's category-selection decisions were supplemented with actual judgments of typicality. Children in kindergarten, third and sixth grades were presented with sets of spoken words from 12 natural language categories. Included in each set were category items that varied in adult-judged typicality, as well as several noncategory items. Children first decided whether each word was a member of the designated category and later were re-presented with each selected word and asked to rate it on a 3-point scale in terms of goodness of example (i.e., being a "very good," "OK," or "poor" example of its category). A group of college students also rated the words on a 3-point scale and were tested using a procedure similar to that of Rosch (1975).

Figure 3-1 presents the percentage of appropriate category items included as a function of age and level of adult-defined typicality. As can be seen, age differences were minimal for the most typical exemplars (level I), and increased as adult-typicality scores declined. An examination of the typicality judgments indicated that despite the generally significant correlations among the ratings for all groups of subjects, the correspondence between the ratings of each child group and of the adults increased with age (median correlation between ratings of children and adults = .72, .84, and .92 for kindergarten, third, and sixth graders, respectively). Thus, in addition to age differences in which items were included, age differences were also apparent in the judged typicality of items selected as category exemplars. That is, not only were there quantitative age

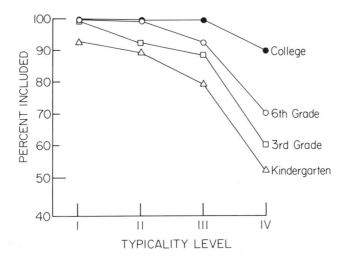

Figure 3-1. Percentage of category appropriate items included by grade as a function of level of adult-judged typicality (Level I = most typical; level IV = least typical). (From Bjorklund et al., 1983.)

differences concerning which items are considered to be appropriate category examples, but there were also qualitative age differences in the nature of children's prototypes (i.e., differences in how category items are represented).

Other evidence that children's natural language concepts change with age comes from studies examining differences in how children process typical and atypical category instances in cognitive tasks. For example, Rosch (1973), using a sentence verification task ("An [EXEMPLAR] is a [CATEGORY NAME]"), reported that the reaction times (RT) of 9- to 11-year-old children were similar to those of adults; for true statements, RTs were faster for adult-defined central than for adult-defined peripheral category members. However, unlike adults, children made significantly more errors when atypical items were presented in true sentences (22.8%) than when more prototypic items were used (5.6%). (Some other implications of these findings are discussed in Chapter 6 by Kail.) The fact that typical and atypical items were processed similarly by adults and children (as reflected by the RT data) suggested that children have the same type of conceptual representations as do adults (presumably prototypes). Yet children's reluctance to acknowledge category membership for many atypical items supports Rosch's (1973) view that children learn more prototypic examples of a concept before learning less typical members. This interpretation has been supported in studies of class inclusion (Carson & Abrahamson, 1976; Scholnick & Johnson, 1981) and cued recall (Bjorklund, Greenberg, Hurlburt, & Thompson, 1978), which provided evidence that performance differences between typical and atypical items were due to young children's lack of knowledge concerning the category membership of many atypical items.

In addition to quantitative age differences in which items are considered to be category members, qualitative age differences in how category items are represented also exist. A distinction between quantitative and qualitative differences in children's processing of category information was investigated in a cued-recall experiment by Bjorklund and Thompson (1983). Working with kindergarten, third-, and sixth-grade children, they gave half of the subjects at each grade level typical and atypical category items with item typicality determined on the basis of adult norms. The other half of the subjects received items evaluated in terms of typicality by age-mates, that is, based on age-appropriate norms for each grade level (from Bjorklund et al., 1983). Category labels served as both input and retrieval cues. Typical category exemplars were recalled to a greater extent than atypical ones by children of all ages, with recall being higher for the child-norm than for the adult-norm lists. The presence of a typicality effect with the child-norm lists demonstrated that, as with adults, typicality is a meaningful dimension for describing the category structures of children over a broad age range. However, the results also indicated several ways in which the structure of semantic categories vary between children and adults.

Based on the child-generated norms of Bjorklund et al. (1983), Bjorklund and Thompson (1983) were able to determine which atypical items in the adult-norm lists children at each grade level were likely to know were appropriate category members and which they did not. They reported that at each grade level, recall of atypical items in the adult-norm lists *not* considered to be category members by the children was significantly less than the recall of atypical items the children believed to be appropriate category exemplars. That is, the typicality effect found for children in this condition was due not so much to qualitative differences in perceived goodness of example between the typical and atypical exemplars, but to children's lack of knowledge concerning the category membership of many of the adult-defined atypical instances.

In addition to this evidence for a quantitative difference in children's category knowledge, there was also evidence for age differences in how specific category exemplars were understood (i.e., qualitative differences). Children's recall of adult-defined typical instances varied as a function of how typical they were judged to be by children in the Bjorklund et al. (1983) normative study. For example, typical exemplars included in both the child- and adult-norm lists which were viewed as reasonably typical by both children and adults were recalled to a greater extent (62%) than typical items found only in the adult-norm list (56%) which were viewed as reasonably typical only by adults. Children's recall was greatest, overall, for typical items found only in the child-norm lists (72%) which were viewed as highly typical by the children but not necessarily by the adults. The fact that children's ratings do differ from those of adults and that memory performance is related to these ratings, indicates a qualitative change in the nature of children's semantic memory representations which is still undergoing modification in 12-year-olds.

There are a number of other typicality effects that suggest qualitative changes in the nature of children's semantic concepts. For example, Duncan and Kellas (1978) using a same/different judgment task and Keller (1982) using a sentence verification task, interpreted age differences in children's processing of category information to be due to the fact that, with age, children re-organize their semantic concepts, realizing that some features are more critical than others for defining items. Similar conclusions were obtained from the results of a recent depth-of-processing experiment by Whitney and Kunen (1983). In an incidental cued-recall task, 5-, 7-, and 9-year-old children were oriented toward either semantic or acoustic word properties. Semantic orientation produced enhanced levels of recall performance for 7- and 9-year-old children regardless of whether category labels, prototypic category items, or moderately typical category items served as targets and/or retrieval cues. In contrast, no semantic facilitation was noted for 5-year-old children when moderately typical items were the target or the cue stimuli. Whitney and Kunen claimed that "moderate instances of semantic categories are not well represented in conceptual memories of 5-year-olds" (p. 287), and suggested that children's conceptual systems undergo substantial change between the ages of 5 and 9 years. The pattern of cued-recall data reported in this incidental memory experiment is similar to that reported by Bjorklund and his colleagues (Bjorklund et al., 1978; Bjorklund & Thompson, 1983) for intentional cued recall and suggests that the age changes observed in these tasks are probably not strategic, but can be attributed to underlying changes in children's semantic memory representations.

The research described in this section indicates both quantitative and qualitative changes in children's conceptual representations over the course of childhood. Although children may be familiar with a specific word concept, they are not always willing to include it as a member of its appropriate semantic category, particularly when the item is atypical of its category. Thus, quantitative changes in the contents of concepts constitute a major source of developmental variation in children's natural language categories, with more typical exemplars being incorporated into a child's category structure before less typical items (Rosch, 1973). Moreover, the manner in which children's word concepts are represented in semantic memory seems to correspond to the prototype model suggested for adults' concepts. Yet although young children's concepts may best be described via a prototype model, the nature of the prototype is not necessarily identical to that of adults. Rather, children appear to emphasize different features in defining natural language concepts than do adults (e.g., Duncan & Kellas, 1978; Keller, 1982; Schwanenflugel et al., 1984), resulting in prototypes that are similar but not congruent with adults' (e.g., Bjorklund et al., 1983). Thus, in addition to quantitative changes in the contents of children's concepts, substantial qualitative changes also occur, with children's semantic representations being re-organized to resemble those of adults by early adolescence. Differences in both the content and structure of natural language categories are greatly minimized by the time a child is approximately 9 or 10 years of age (e.g., Bjorklund & Thompson, 1983;

Bjorklund et al., 1983; Duncan & Kellas, 1978; Keller, 1982; Whitney & Kunen, 1983), although differences are still apparent in 11- and 12-year-old children (e.g., Bjorklund & Thompson, 1983; Bjorklund et al., 1983; Rosch, 1973; Saltz et al., 1972).

The Activation of Relations in Semantic Memory

I would like to propose that age differences in the types of relations children use to organize information (e.g., complementary versus categorical) and the likelihood of using taxonomic category relations to perform cognitive tasks are generally not related to age differences in conscious preferences for one mode of organization over another nor to age differences in deliberate strategy implementation. Rather, I propose that it is the ease with which semantic memory relations are activated that changes with age. Complementary relations among items are generally more easily activated by young children than are taxonomic category relations, accounting for young children's biases toward complementary organization. Which relations are activated can be easily manipulated however. Young children can be biased to attend to the taxonomic category properties of items. Once processing within a category begins, the threshold for activation of category relations decreases and processing is likely to continue on the basis of category features. However, when the taxonomic prompts are removed, young children's initial biases return (e.g., Smiley & Brown, 1979), presumably because these relations are better established and more easily activated than are category relations. Thus, young children's biases toward complementary organization is not due to an ignorance of category relations, nor is it due to a deliberate choice of one mode over another. Rather, this tendency can be interpreted as the result of the differential ease with which certain types of relations are activated in semantic memory.

As mentioned above, once a child enters a category and begins processing information in terms of category relations, the probability of continuing to do so increases. However, continued processing within a category will be influenced by the strength of relationships among category members. Very young children, for example, whose category structures are ill-defined, will be more apt to stray between categories or modes of organization than older children, whose category structures are better established. At the extreme, the category switching shown by young children for some forms of graphic collections (Inhelder & Piaget, 1964) may represent insufficient category knowledge rather than a lack of planfulness per se. In one type of graphic collection described by Inhelder and Piaget (1964), a child begins to organize information on one dimension (e.g., color) but switches sorting criteria throughout the task. It is possible that such switching is attributable to the fact that the stimulus dimensions are not yet well conceptualized. So for example, although a child may begin sorting objects by color, between-category relations among stimuli (e.g., shape) are as easily activated as are within-category relations. Thus, the 4- or 5-year-old child who organizes an entire array on the basis of a single dimension may not be more planful than the 3-year-old who continually switches criteria; rather, he/she may merely have a more highly developed conceptual memory for that category, with within-category relations being more easily activated once he/she is operating within that category than are between-category relations.

Let me provide an anecdote consistent with this position. My daughter, Heidi, at 3 years and 3 months of age, was examining a page in her *Sesame Street Magazine* consisting of eight colored balloons. At the time, she was capable of counting to 10, although not reliably getting past 6, and could identify colors as well as could her color-blind dad, which is to say not perfectly. She began pointing to the balloons and labeling each one in succession as follows: "1, 2, 3, red, blue, green, yellow, pink." She did this without a significant pause between "3" and "red," as though one always follows the other. Following the argument presented above, I suggest that her switching categories in this episode was due to the fact that neither her counting nor her color-naming categories were well established. As such, the level of activation for the number "4" was sufficiently low and the level of activation for the color features of the balloons was sufficiently high to enable her to switch categories without any apparent conflict.

Another shift in conceptual organization that is consistent with this hypothesis concerns changes from associative to categorical relations. Associative relations, based upon the frequent co-occurrence of items (words) in a child's experiences, have been hypothesized to be a primitive form of organization which change minimally with age (Lange, 1978). Support for this view comes from a recent study in which ratings of associative strength between pairs of words were assessed for children in grades 3, 4, 6, and 8 and for college students (Jacobs, 1984). Unlike studies examining age differences in estimates of category relatedness (e.g., Bjorklund al., 1983; Posnansky, 1978; Winters & Brzoska, 1976), no age differences were found in subjects' estimates of associative strength between word pairs. Further support for the stability of associative relations with age is provided by the results of a semantic priming study by McCauley, Weil, and Sperber (1976). In their experiment, facilitative effects of associative priming were found for both 5- and 7-year-old children, whereas category priming facilitated speed of identification only for the older subjects. McCauley et al. concluded that superordinate-subordinate relations are probably added to children's semantic memories with age but do not alter children's existing associative structures, which are operative early and presumably remain stable throughout development.

Additional support for an associative to categorical shift is found in a sorting study by Bjorklund and de Marchena (1984). They reported a change in children's groupings of items from a reliance on associative relations (first graders) to a predominant use of nonassociative category relations (seventh graders). This trend was found even when the categorical structure of the list was made distinctive by increasing the number of items per category. Bjorklund and de Marchena speculated that young children's predominant use of associative rather than categorical relations reflects age differences in children's conceptual memories, with some relationships (associative) being more easily activated than others (categorical). With age, children's categorical relations become re-organized, making their activation relatively automatic, as is presumably the case for associative relations in both younger and older children. The results of this and the previously cited studies are consistent with the position that associative relations change little during development and are easily activated by children of all ages. This stands in contrast to taxonomic category relations, which undergo substantial change through childhood and are more easily activated by older children.

The Development of Organization in Children's Memory

It is well documented that young children show minimal amounts of organization in recall when lists consist of exemplars from adult-defined natural language categories (for reviews see Lange, 1978; Mandler, 1979; Moely, 1977; Ornstein & Corsale, 1979). However, young children can easily be trained to cluster their recall on the basis of adult categorizations (although transfer is more tenuous), causing some researchers to conclude that the deficiency lies in children's tendencies to implement spontaneous organizational strategies and not in any deficit in their knowledge of the to-be-remembered information (e.g., Bjorklund et al., 1977; Moely et al., 1969). This position, I believe, is no longer tenable. Rather than assume that the gradual age increases customarily found in recall and organization are due to increases in the use of intentional, mnemonic strategies, I propose that these improvements are due to the increasing ease with which semantic relations are activated and used in memory tasks. This position does not obviate the role of deliberate strategies in memory performance. When children can intentionally store incoming information on the basis of conceptual relations and generate retrieval cues to guide recall, children's memory behavior changes qualitatively. Strategies become generalizable, not limited to a specific content in which a subject has a particular expertise. However, I propose that such development is not a result of children becoming gradually more strategic with age. Rather, children's organization in memory increases because of changes in their knowledge bases; with age, the interitem relations in memory tasks are more easily activated, increasing the probability that children will cluster their recall in terms of those relations. Once relations between two items from the same category are activated, the likelihood of subsequent category relations becoming activated increases, resulting in elevated levels of organization. In fact, with this spreading activation, children may come to identify the category features shared by several consecutively recalled items and use these features to guide subsequent retrieval. That is, the development of deliberate organizational strategies may have their origins in the clustering children notice in their own output (e.g., Bjorklund, 1980a; Bjorklund & Hock, 1982; Bjorklund & Zeman, 1982; 1983; Pressely, Levin, & Ghatala, 1984), with clustering being mediated by the relatively automatic activation of category relations.

I will now review some studies consistent with these views. Work germane to this issue includes (a) experiments examining young children's use of complementary or schematic relations (rather than taxonomic category relations) to organize list information; (b) recent research examining children's memory performance as a function of the perceived typicality of to-be-remembered exemplars; (c) research examining the role of associative relations in memory performance; and (d) studies examining how an elaborated knowledge base for a specific content influences children's memory behavior. However, before examining these studies, I will first review concepts of automatic cognitive processing, applying such concepts to issues of memory development.

Automaticity in Cognition

Psychologists have long believed that human information processing abilities are limited (e.g., Broadbent, 1958; James, 1890; Treisman, 1960). Contemporary cognitive theorists postulate a finite amount of energy or capacity that individuals can allocate to various cognitive processes, with different mental operations requiring different amounts of this limited capacity for their successful completion (e.g., Hasher & Zacks, 1979; Kahneman, 1973; LaBerge & Samuels, 1974; Posner & Snyder, 1975; Schneider & Shiffrin, 1977; Shiffrin & Schneider, 1977). Most theorists have proposed a continuum of processes, with automatic processes at one extreme and effortful or deliberate processes at the other. Definitions of automaticity vary somewhat across theories, but most assume that automatic processes (a) occur without intention, (b) do not necessarily give rise to awareness, (c) interfere minimally with other processing, (d) do not improve with practice, and, (e) do not require effort or attention. In addition, Hasher and Zacks (1979) proposed that, unlike most effortful operations, some automatic processes show little improvement with age and are relatively unaffected by differences in motivation, education, early experience, culture, or intelligence. At the opposite end of the information processing continuum are those mental activities that require the allocation of attention from the limited pool of resources, and have been referred to as *conscious* (Posner & Snyder, 1975), *controlled* (Schneider & Shiffrin, 1977), or *effortful* (Hasher & Zacks, 1979). These processes require effort and thus interfere with the execution of other effortful processes. Their use is voluntary, they may be available to consciousness, and they improve with practice.

One contemporary theory of particular interest to researchers concerned with memory development is that of Shiffrin and Schneider (Schneider & Shiffrin, 1977; Shiffrin & Schneider, 1977). Shiffrin and Schneider conceptualized the information processing system following Atkinson and Shiffrin's (1968) model of human memory, and specifically addressed the issue of the acquisition of automatic, long-term memory relationships. Information is viewed as being permanently stored in terms of collections of nodes that become increasingly interassociated through experience. Long-term memory represents the state of information that is currently inactive. Currently activated nodes constitute short-term memory. The passage of information through the memory system is influenced by controlled processes—techniques for handling information that are under the control of the individual. Allocation of limited attentional capacity is determined by a person's use of controlled processes, which are effortful and capacity limited by nature. However, not all mental activity is directed by controlled processes. Automatic processes represent activation of sequences of nodes without the necessity of active control on the part of the individual, thus requiring little or none of the system's limited capacity. Automatic processes can be learned. They are acquired by means of extensive practice or repeated exposure and, once learned, they are difficult to ignore, modify, or suppress. As automation for a particular task increases, more attentional capacity is freed for other cognitive purposes. The Shiffrin and Schneider model suggests that an individual's actual capacity for processing information at any point in time should vary as a function of how automated task performance has become. Two people may have the same amount of limited capacity to expend on a particular task, but because the processing of person A has become more highly automatic through extensive practice than that of person B, the amount of information that can be effectively handled by the two individuals in a secondary task will vary.

Capacity Limitations and Memory Development. Several developmental theorists have addressed the issue of capacity limitations and how such limitations may contribute to age differences in children's memory performance (e.g., Case, Kurland, & Goldberg, 1982; Chechile & Richman, 1982; Chi, 1976; Dempster, 1978). (This issue is also discussed in some detail by Dempster in Chapter 5 on short-term memory development.) For example, Case et al. (1982) proposed that short-term memory can be conceptualized in terms of *storage space* and *operating space*. Storage space refers to the hypothetical amount of space an individual has available for storing information. Operating space refers to the hypothetical amount of space an individual has available for performing mental operations. *Total processing space* is used to refer to the sum of storage and operating space or an individual's total central processing resources. Case et al. proposed that total processing space remains relatively constant in development. Age differences observed on tasks that purportedly assess memory capacity (e.g., short-term span) are attributed to developmental increases in available storage space, accompanied by developmental decreases in the amount of operating space necessary for successful task completion. In other words, with age, children's processing becomes more efficient, requiring less operating space. This, in turn, makes available more space for storing information, resulting in overall improvement in task performance.

In the present chapter, I propose that one reason information processing becomes more efficient throughout development is that the activation of semantic relations becomes increasingly automatic with age. I believe that the human nervous system is biased toward making associations among frequently co-occurring objects/events/words in one's environment. Which specific items become associated, and the likelihood that the activation of these relations will become relatively automatic, will, for the most part, be a function of experience. Following Shiffrin and Schneider (1977), I propose that in development, the activation of semantic memory relations becomes increasingly less effortful, freeing processing space which can be used for storage (e.g., Case et al., 1982) or for the execution of controlled processes. In fact, the use of organization as a deliberate strategy may be possible only when encoding and categorization processes are sufficiently automatic so that enough of the system's capacity is available for the execution of effortful operations.

This argument is similar to one made by Chechile and Richman (1982). They proposed that the

> hardware of the memory system is developmentally invariant (at least from age 5 on), but nevertheless, retention can increase with age as a consequence of the richer semantic memory system that develops. (p. 238)

They demonstrated that levels of recall for sets of unrelated words did not vary between kindergarten and second-grade children when controlling for the meaningfulness of the to-be-remembered items (see also Richman et al., 1976). They speculated that as children's semantic memory networks become more complex, rates of forgetting decrease for both storage and retrieval processes. Chechile and Richman's data address memory for relatively unrelated information, with meaningfulness affecting retention presumably by making individual memory traces more resistant to forgetting. However, their contention that age differences in content knowledge is responsible to a large extent for developmental differences in memory performance is similar to the position taken in the present chapter that age differences in conceptual knowledge influence organizational processes which in turn influence levels of memory performance.

Let me make one final comment on the degree of automaticity proposed to be involved in children's memory organization. By hypothesizing that much of the organization seen in the memory performance of young children is relatively automatic, I do not mean to imply that the process of children's recall is effortless. Young children most certainly exert effort as they try to retrieve a list of recently presented words, the gist of a story, a sequence of events, or the names of their classmates. What is nondeliberate is the organization inherent in a child's recall protocols, which is not subject to conscious evaluation but is mediated primarily by the relatively automatic activation of semantic relations. Furthermore, I am not proposing that the activation of semantic relations is always fully automated. Rather, when viewed on a continuum of effortful processing, the activation of semantic relations becomes less and less effortful with age, freeing more and more storage/operating space. Thus, the activation of semantic relations in certain tasks may be viewed not as absolutely automatic, but possibly as *veiled* controlled processes. Veiled controlled processes are described by Shiffrin and Schneider (1977) as operations that are difficult to perceive through introspection, are not easily modified through instructions, and take place quickly (p. 159). Such processing, I argue, is relatively efficient in the use of attentional capacity in comparison to controlled processes which are readily available to conscious evaluation (e.g., rehearsal). In this chapter I will use the terms "automatic" and "relatively automatic" to refer to operations that require relatively little processing capacity, thus not distinguishing among processes that are truly automatic and those unconscious, veiled controlled processes that require some minimal effort for their execution.

Alternatives to Categorical Organization

One explanation that has been suggested for young children's relatively poor memory performance on taxonomically related lists is that these lists do not correspond to how information is structured in their conceptual memories (e.g., Denney & Ziobrowski, 1972; Worden, 1976). If young children's conceptual knowledge is represented differently than that of older children and adults (e.g., Denney, 1974; Mandler, 1983; Nelson et al., 1983), memory organization should be enhnaced by the use of stimuli that match their conceptual representations. As noted above, there is evidence that young children's conceptual memories are schematically organized (e.g., Mandler, 1983; Nelson et al., 1983), and recent studies indicate that young children use schematic organization to aid in their memory for scenes (e.g., Kirasic, Siegel, & Allen, 1980; Mandler & Robinson, 1978; Saarnio & Bjorklund, 1984) and stories (e.g., Mandler, 1978; Paris & Mahoney, 1974). With respect to organization in free recall, a number of studies have contrasted children's use of taxonomic and complementary relations, and these studies will be discussed below.

There are several published studies in which children were given a single free-recall trial with sets of items that could be organized on the basis of either taxonomic-category or complementary relations. These studies have produced equivocal results. For example, Denney and Ziobrowski (1972) reported that first-grade children demonstrated better clustering on lists that could be organized on the basis of complementary relations (e.g., *chair, sit; examine, doctor*) than on lists that could be organized on the basis of taxonomic relations (e.g., *king, ruler; flower, blossom*). The reverse was true for college students. However, other investigators have failed to replicate Denney and Ziobrowski's findings and report greater levels of recall and clustering for 5- and 6-year-old children when lists are taxonomically organized (Bjorklund, 1980b; Galbraith & Day, 1978).

A technique that has proved useful in assessing children's organizational biases is that of sort/recall. Lists are constructed that afford both taxonomic and complementary organization. Children are instructed to sort items into meaning-based groups of their own choosing, thus imposing an input organizational strategy on them. Levels of performance in recall can then be evaluated in terms of children's self-professed organizational styles (as exemplified by how they formed groups during the sorting phase). Using this sort/recall procedure and requiring that subjects sort pictures to a criterion of two consecutive, identical sorts before recall, Lange and Jackson (1974) and Worden (1976) each reported high levels of recall and clustering for children (age range 6½ to 16 years) who formed self-generated, complementary groupings. Furthermore, in the Worden (1976) study, children who generated their own classifications of the to-be-remembered items (most of which were complementary in nature) showed better memory performance than children who were required to learn a taxonomic classification scheme. However, in these investigations, complementary organization was high relative to taxonomic organization, even for older subjects. For example, in Lange and Jackson's (1974) experiment, 62% of the groupings of their seventh graders and 49% of the groupings of their tenth graders were complementary; similarly, in Worden's (1976) study, 50% of an adult sample sorted the list items into complementary groupings. Given these data, it is not surprising that most of the elementary school students in these experiments formed groupings on the basis of complementary relations.

In an attempt to control for differences in the saliency of complementary and taxonomic relations, Bjorklund and Zaken-Greenberg (1981) constructed lists that preschool children would be equally likely to sort on the basis of complementary and taxonomic criteria. In their study, approximately 50% of all subjects who demonstrated a consistent sorting style organized list items according to taxonomic relations and 50% according to nontaxonomic relations, mostly complementary. Approximately one-half of the taxonomic and complementary sorters were permitted to sort pictures into groups only once prior to a recall test (Single Sort condition). The remaining subjects sorted items to a criterion of two identical sorts before recall (Criterion Sort condition), as was done in the Lange and Jackson (1974) and Worden (1976) studies. They reported that level of recall varied as a function of subjects' sorting styles (i.e., taxonomic vs. complementary), but not in a simple way. In the Single Sort condition, subjects whose groupings were mostly taxonomic recalled significantly more items than subjects whose groupings were based mostly on complementary relations. This effect was reversed for subjects who sorted items to a stable criterion, with complementary sorters recalling significantly more items than taxonomic sorters. Levels of clustering, based upon children's self-generated groupings, were high and did not vary between the taxonomic and complementary sorters.

Why should the influence of sorting style on levels of recall interact with whether or not subjects sorted items to a stable criterion? Bjorklund and Zaken-Greenberg speculated that the taxonomic categories used in this study were generally better represented in children's conceptual memories than were many of the self-generated complementary groupings. For example, in the Single Sort condition children were unable to provide a verbal description for only 1% of all taxonomic groupings. In contrast, nonscorable responses accounted for 18% of all complementary groupings for subjects in the Single Sort condition, suggesting that many of these groupings consisted of novel interitem arrangements that were created by children during the experiment. Thus, when subjects were *not* permitted to sort to a stable criterion, the taxonomic groupings, because they fit more closely with children's semantic memory organization than did the complementary groupings, enhanced performance. However, when stable sorting was achieved and the complementary relations represented plausible but somewhat unusual combinations of items, their novelty made them more resistant to forgetting than the more common taxonomic category relations (see Hock, Romanski, Galie, & Williams, 1978).

In the Bjorklund and Zaken-Greenberg study, novel interobject relations were inferred from children's failures to provide an explanation of their sorts. However, many of the explanations given by 4- and 5-year-olds for complementary groups in this and related experiments reveal the nonschematic basis of their sorts. For example, a 5-year-old subject seen in our laboratory arranged 11 of 16 pictures into mostly complementary groupings based on real-world contexts (e.g., "*Cat* and *milk* go together because a cat drinks milk"). Faced with five items left and not willing to re-sort the previously grouped items, the child placed the pictures *squirrel* and *banana* together and said, "A squirrel *might* eat a banana." He then arranged the final three pictures into a single group: *pants, shirt, pie*. When asked why these three pictures went together, the child paused for a few seconds and said, "Well, you've got to get dressed-up to eat dessert." We would not want to propose that *squirrel* and *banana* or *pants*, *shirt*, and *pie* correspond to stable semantic memory representations for this child, but rather that these relations were invented solely for the purpose of the sorting task.

Why should young children form novel arrangements of items when they could form categories from preexisting relations in their semantic memories? One possibility is that even though the children knew the taxonomic category relations, those relations were not so easily activated as were schematic relationships. In fact, for most complementary sorters, a majority of their groupings were schematically organized (i.e., corresponded to real-world schemes) and did *not* represent novel combinations of items. However, when no obvious schematic relations were evident, the children tended to continue to create complementary groupings despite the fact that these groupings did not correspond to preexisting relations (either categorical or schematic). That is, children's biases to organize information schematically prompted them to search for complementary relations among previously unrelated items. Thus, not all self-generated complementary groupings should be viewed equivalently. When these groupings are schematic and correspond to children's conceptual memory structures, they can be used to guide recall under most instructional conditions. However, when complementary groupings are generated because no other relations are obvious to a child, they are novel interitem combinations and will hinder recall unless they become well learned in the experimental setting.

The research cited above suggests that young children's conceptual memories are, to a large extent, schematically based and that sets of items that correspond to schematic structures will be remembered well. Although such relations are normally complementary, Lucariello and Nelson (in press) suggest that some taxonomic categories have their origins in real-world, schematically organized events. They suggest that children organize much information in terms of scripts, a form of schematic organization that represents events based on real-world experience. A breakfast script, for instance, may include eating toast, cereal, or pancakes and drinking cocoa, juice, or milk. Thus, in the representation of a script, several different items can be included, each of which could satisfy the conditions of the script. "Slot fillers" refer to these often perceptually different items that could successfully complete a portion of the script (e.g., toast and pancakes). Nelson (1983) has argued that children's early taxonomies may be derived from such scripts, and that slot-filler categories (e.g., breakfast foods) should be learned prior to more superordinate categories.

In the Lucariello and Nelson (in press) study, preschool children were given one of three sets of items for recall. One group received items from superordinate categories (animals, food, clothes). A second group received items from script-derived categories, that is, slot-filler categories (zoo animals, lunch foods, clothes you put on in the morning). A third group of subjects received complementary items. Children recalled significantly more items from the slot-filler lists than from either the superordinate category or complementary lists, with the latter two not differing from one another. Lucariello and Nelson interpreted these findings as showing that the slot-filler items have a more cohesive structure than context-free superordinate or complementary groupings.

To sum up, the research cited here and elsewhere (e.g., Mandler, 1983) indicates that much of young children's conceptual knowledge is schematically organized, with their memory performance being facilitated when lists can be organized on the basis of familiar event knowledge. The relations among items within an event representation can usually be considered to be complementary. However, taxonomic category relations are not absent. In fact, following Nelson and her colleagues, early taxonomies may have their origins in event representations. Such slot-filler categories are highly context dependent, with items often being highly associated with one another. These are likely to be the first superordinate categories that become well established in children's semantic memories, serving as the basis for broader, context-free superordinates.

Categorical Organization in Children's Recall

Category Typicality and Children's Organization in Memory. The great majority of studies investigating the development of organization in memory have used superordinate categories. As has been mentioned, preschool children know, at some level, the category membership of many common instances of familiar natural language categories and will use this information on cognitive tasks. However, young children's category knowledge changes substantially during childhood. Much recent work on the nature of children's natural language concepts has concentrated on the role of category typicality. To recapitulate, typical category exemplars are incorporated into children's category knowledge before less typical exemplars. Thus, many items judged to be appropriate category instances by older children and adults (albeit atypical ones) may not be viewed as category members by younger children. Furthermore, the nature of children's category prototypes changes with age, so that items judged to be typical by adults will not necessarily be so judged by children.

Relations among typical category instances are better established in semantic memory and are more easily activated by subjects of all ages than are relations among atypical items. This should result in greater levels of recall and organization for typical than for atypical items in free recall. However, because the category structures of young children are not as well developed as those of older children, age differences in the ease of processing typical and atypical category information should also be found, with younger children requiring more prompts before category relations are activated.

In a study investigating typicality effects on children's memory performance, Bjorklund and Ornstein (1976) presented kindergarten children with sets of pictures that were (a) highly typical of their categories, (b) atypical of their categories or, (c) relatively unrelated. One-half of the children received items in random orders, whereas the items were blocked by categories for the remaining children. (For the set of unrelated pictures, items were blocked by subjectively determined adult groupings.) No effect of the material manipulation was observed for either recall or clustering when items were presented randomly. Differences in performance emerged only when items were blocked by categories, with subjects having significantly higher levels of recall and clustering for the typical lists than for the atypical or unrelated lists, with these latter two lists not differing from one another. That is, performance improved only under the most optimal of stimulus and presentation conditions. Presumably, category relations are not activated by young children unless the category structure is made salient to them.

Related to this is a study by Corsale (1980) who gave kindergarten and third-grade children sets of typical and atypical items in a sort/recall task. Subjects were asked either to sort pictures into meaning-based groupings or to sort the pictures in preparation for a recall test. Corsale reported that the third-grade children generally organized the list items according to taxonomic category relations when highly typical items served as stimuli regardless of the instructional condition, or when instructed to sort by meaning for the atypical items. In contrast, kindergarten children organized the list items taxonomically only when highly typical category exemplars were used and subjects were instructed to sort by meaning. Levels of recall generally followed sorting. Thus, as in the Bjorklund and Ornstein (1976) experiment, kindergarten children made use of the categorical properties of stimuli only under optimal stimulus and instructional conditions. Fewer prompts were required for the older children, presumably because category relations were better established in their semantic memories and, thus, were more easily activated.

Recently, Rabinowitz (1984a) has presented evidence supportive of the automatic activation position on organization in children's memory. He presented second- and fifth-grade children with sets of items for free recall that were either highly typical or moderately typical of their categories. For both the second- and fifth-grade children, levels of recall and clustering were greater for the highly typical than for the moderately typical items. This was true even in a condition that minimized deliberate organization strategies by requiring children to repeat single words during the interstimulus intervals. Rabinowitz argued that the typical exemplars represented tightly structured, highly integrated conceptual schemes. Such structures, in comparison to less typical instances, may result in automatic organization, with recall being guided by the relatively automatic activation of category relations. Rabinowitz (1984b) has since developed a computer simulation of children's memory, using the strength of an item's relationship to its category label to predict levels of recall and organization. He reports that the customary age differences in levels of memory performance are obtained when these category-associative values are used as a basis for predicting recall, suggesting that strategies per se, may play a minor role in the development of organization in recall.

One factor that may influence the amount of organization in children's memory is whether children realize that to-be-remembered lists consist of exemplars from familiar categories. Although there is convincing evidence that even preschool children customarily encode individual items in terms of category features (e.g., Esrov et al., 1974; Mansfield, 1977), these studies did not examine the role of typicality in children's category encoding. In a recent release from proactive interference (PI) study (Bjorklund, Smith, & Ornstein, 1982), second-grade children were given sets of typical or atypical items from a familiar category (food or animals) for three trials. Following the third trial, children were shifted to exemplars from the second category, keeping the level of typicality constant. The customary pattern of a build-up (decrease in recall over trials 1 through 3) and release (increase in recall on trial 4) from PI, indicative of category encoding, was found only when subjects received typical instances. No release from PI was found for subjects given atypical exemplars to remember. These results indicate that unlike more typical items, young children may not spontaneously encode the category features of atypical items.

However, even in situations where children normally encode category features, they may not identify the category relations among sets of items when they are presented for memorization (Bjorklund, 1978; 1980b). Rather, because category relations are not easily activated, they often attempt to learn a list on an item-by-item basis (e.g., Tighe, Tighe, & Schechter, 1975). One factor that should influence children's tendencies to identify categories in a list is item typicality. This question is currently being investigated in our lab in collaboration with Larry Malcus. Although results are preliminary, young children are able to identify more list categories when highly typical items serve as category exemplars rather than moderately typical items. This difference cannot be attributed to children not realizing that the less typical instances are appropriate category members. Interviews following the memory task indicate that children can identify most of the list categories when asked to sort the pictures into groups. Consistent with the work cited above, I believe that these differences are not due to differences in the implementation of deliberate organizational strategies, but rather to age differences in the ease with which category relations can be activated.

The Role of Associativity in Mediating Organization in Children's Memory. As previously noted, associative relations have been viewed as an early form of semantic organization which, in contrast to categorical organization, undergo minimal change with age (e.g., Jacobs, 1984; Lange, 1973, 1978; McCauley et al., 1976). Lange (1973, 1978) has suggested that the above-chance levels of clustering often observed in preadolescents is due to children's use of associative relations to guide retrieval and not to categorical organization. Lange (1973) demonstrated that when the degree of associativity among categorically related items was reduced (e.g., *cat, rabbit* as opposed to *lion, tiger*), organization in recall was minimized for young children while remaining high for older subjects. One possible reason for the powerful impact that associativity has on organization is that associatively related items represent preestablished units in a child's semantic memory. That is, associative relations are readily activated (compared to categorical relations) by young children, with clustering in recall based on such relationships representing nonstrategic (i.e., relatively automatic) processing.

Some recent work that is consistent with this position was reported by Frankel and Rollins (1982, in press). In an initial study (1982), they examined the length and number of intracategory repetitions in the recall of kindergarten children and adults. They reported that unlike adults, who typically recalled as many items as they could from a single category before proceeding to the next, when 6-year-olds recalled items from the same category together, they usually did so in pairs, suggesting that organized retrieval for these children was mediated by associative rather than categorical relations. In a subsequent experiment, Frankel and Rollins (in press) manipulated high and low category relatedness and high and low interitem associations. They reported that fourth- and tenth-grade children performed best whenever associative strength or categorical relatedness was high. In contrast, only interitem associativity affected kindergarten children's performance (cf. McCauley et al., 1976).

In a recent study from our laboratory (Bjorklund & Jacobs, in press), the effects of associative versus categorical relatedness on recall and organization were examined in children from grades 3, 5, 7, and 9 and in college students. Lists were constructed so that some items within a category were highly associated with one another. For example, for the ANIMAL category, individual items included *cat*, *dog*, *tiger*, *lion*, and *cow*, with strong associations existing between two pairs of the items (*cat*, *dog*; *tiger*, *lion*). All other possible combinations of pairs of items had low interitem associative values. One finding of particular interest concerned developmental differences in patterns of interitem latencies (i.e., the number of seconds that transpired between the recall of two consecutive words). Each adjacent pair of words in a subject's recall protocol was classified into one of three categories: (a) between-category (e.g., *dog*, *apple*); (b) within-category, low-associates (e.g., *dog*, *tiger*); (c) or within-category, high-associates (e.g., *dog*, *cat*). For all grade levels, interitem latencies were shorter between high associates than between items from different categories. However, age differences were observed for the within-category, low-associative pairs. For the seventh and ninth graders, these latencies were shorter than the between-category latencies. In contrast, there was no difference between the within-category, low-associated interitem latencies and the between-category interitem latencies for the third and fifth graders. These findings indicate that, unlike older children, category processing for the younger subjects was limited to highly associated pairs of items. These children did not differentiate between unassociated category members (e.g., *dog*, *tiger*) and categorically unrelated items (e.g., *dog*, *apple*). In other words, consistent with the interpretation of Frankel and Rollins (in press), category relations are not easily activated by young children in a recall task in the absence of associative relations.

Bjorklund and Jacobs (in press) also made an examination of the contents of category clusters of three words or more. Although the number of these long intracategory word strings increased with age, the percentage of these strings that included associative pairs was comparable across ages, implying that associative relations were used equally by subjects of all age groups. However, the percentage of category clusters that were led by an associative pair (e.g., *cat*, *dog*, *cow* but not *cow*, *dog*, *cat*) was curvilinearly related to age, with the number of word strings beginning with an associative pair peaking at seventh grade. The proportion of intracategory word strings of three or more words beginning with an associative pair was .47, .51, .75, .68, and .51 for third graders through college students, respectively. These data suggest that categorical relations may have been discovered by some of the older children as a result of recalling associatively related category items. That is, a categorical search may have been implemented by the activation of associative links between categorically related items. The college students were less apt to begin category clusters with an associative pair presumably because they were sufficiently strategic that associative prompts were not necessary. In contrast, the third- and fifth-grade children were less apt to begin category clusters with associative pairs presumably because nonassociative relations were not readily activated for them, making associative prompts relatively inefficient in elicitng category clustering.

The results of these studies indicate that associative relations play a substantial role in children's memory organization. It seems unlikely that such associative organization is deliberate. Furthermore, the results of the Bjorklund and Jacobs study suggest that such automatic organization may be the basis for deliberate categorically based retrieval strategies.

The Effects of an Elaborated Knowledge Base on Organization in Memory

The major thesis of this chapter is that age differences in conceptual knowledge play an important role in development of the organization observed in children's recall memory. Most of the work cited earlier was concerned with children's recall of exemplars from natural language categories, with regular age improvements being observed for both conceptual knowledge and memory performance. However, the role of conceptual knowledge in the development of organization in memory can also be investigated for content domains in which children have some particular expertise. For example, it has been reported that the typical age difference in memory performance is reversed when children know more about the relations among the to-be-remembered items than do adults (e.g., Chi, 1978; Lindberg, 1980). Chi and her colleagues (1978, 1981, in press; Chi & Koeske, 1983) have speculated that the strategies observed when a subject is processing information related to an elaborated knowledge base are not necessarily generalizable but are domain specific. Presumably, processing is facilitated by the fact that information is highly integrated and easily activated, making the implementation of deliberate mnemonics unnecessary (see also Naus & Ornstein, 1983; Ornstein & Naus, in press; Roth, 1983).

Recent work from our laboratory has investigated the effects that an elaborated knowledge base have on children's memory organization. Using a class-recall task, Bjorklund and Zeman (1982, 1983) had first-, third-, and fifth-grade children recall the names of their current classmates. Organization in recall was evaluated in terms of structural dimensions of the classroom (e.g., seating arrangements, reading groups), physical characteristics of the children themselves (e.g., sex, race), and child-defined social groupings (in Bjorklund & Zeman, 1983, only), among others. Levels of recall and organization were high for children at all grades. However, despite high levels of performance, the majority of children at each grade level was unable to identify a strategy they had used in recalling their classmates' names (as reflected by clustering scores). Many children professed using a strategy not observed in their recall (e.g., professing alphabetic organization but having low levels of clustering for that mode), and levels of strategy identification did not improve when children were given a simplified strategy recognition task instead of being required to provide a verbal description of their strategy (Bjorklund & Zeman, 1982, Experiment 2). These results suggested that the recall of classmates' names was, in all likelihood, based on the relatively automatic activation of associative relations among the names. This conclusion was bolstered by Bjorklund and Zeman's (in press) evidence that children's levels of class recall were comparably high when they were requested to retrieve their classmates' names in a specified order (i.e., seating arrangement or sex) as when no special instructions were given (i.e., free recall). In other words, recall was the same regardless of whether subjects followed (often perfectly) a specified strategy or not, suggesting that the recall of a child's classmates has a strong nonstrategic component to it.

However, subjects in these experiments who accurately professed a strategy (i.e., those who claimed to be using a strategy observed in their recall protocols) showed higher levels of recall and clustering than subjects who did not, although the absolute level of performance for all subjects was high. Thus, despite the relatively automatic nature of organization, strategic processing appeared to be taking place for some subjects. But these strategic subjects did not necessarily enter the class-recall task with a preconceived plan. Rather, we believe that some children may have discovered a strategy while retrieving individual names. For example, several children from a single reading group may be recalled without the subject being aware that these children share anything particular in common. In recalling names of children from a reading group, two (or more) of these children may also sit adjacently, resulting in the child switching from reading groups to seating arrangement as the basis of organization. The child may or may not be aware of how he/she is organizing recall. However, children who do become aware of how they are organizing their retrieval show higher levels of recall and clustering than other children (Bjorklund & Zeman, 1982, 1983).

I believe that the mechanisms underlying children's processing of information from an elaborated knowledge base are similar to those involved in the processing of other, less familiar information. Relations among items in a well-established conceptual memory network are easily activated, resulting in high levels of organization in recall without the need for strategic intervention. Once in a category (e.g., recalling the names of children in the *Sun and Shadows* reading group or recalling ANIMAL names), the threshold for activating other members of that group is reduced, resulting in high levels of memory organization. It may well be that it is from such organized output that children identify conceptual relations among items and begin to implement strategic organization (e.g., Bjorklund, 1980a; Bjorklund & Jacobs, in press), Bjorklund & Hock, 1982; Pressley, Levin & Ghatala, 1984). In other words, the development of strategic organization may have its origin in the relatively automatic organization that results from the activation of relations in a well-established semantic memory structure.

What Develops?

Memory strategies have generally been viewed as deliberate plans that are adopted to enhance performance and are subject to conscious evaluation (e.g.,

Brown, 1975; Hasher & Zacks, 1979; Naus & Ornstein, 1983). Given this definition of memory strategies, age changes in children's organization in memory do not seem to be mediated by improvements in strategic functioning. Rather, organization in children's memory appears to be relatively automatic, unconscious, unplanned, and to require only minimal attentional demands. Automatic processes involved in memory encoding have been hypothesized to be relatively unaffected by practice, levels of motivation, intelligence, and to show relatively little change in development (Hasher & Zacks, 1979). With respect to organization, then, what develops?

The contention of the present chapter has been that children's knowledge base is what develops. Age changes in memory organization observed through the preadolescent years are primarily attributable to developmental differences in semantic memory. With increasing language experience, semantic categories become better established, increasing the ease with which relations among items within a category are activated. This increased efficiency in the processing of category information results in elevated levels of organization in memory, which are based on the relatively automatic activation of relations within a well-established conceptual system.

What of strategies? Our intuitions tell us that they exist, at least for the adolescent and adult. But what is their developmental history? Does the presence of deliberately implemented organizational strategies represent a drastic discontinuity in development, or are these strategies influenced by the nonstrategic memory functions that come before them? I have argued here and elsewhere (Bjorklund & Zeman, 1982, 1983) that deliberate organizational strategies emerge from unconscious and relatively automatic cognitive processes. The organization observed in a child's recall may be the result of the relatively automatic activation of associative or categorical relations within a well-established semantic memory structure. Yet children may first consciously identify category relations as a result of such automatic activation and subsequently use this category information as an intentional guide for retrieval. Children may identify category relations in this way either during input, while stimulus information is being presented, or during output, while stimulus information is being retrieved. The mechanism for such a discovery may be similar to Piaget's (1971) concept of reflective abstraction, in which children's perceptions of their own actions (here, category relations existing among items retrieved via automatic processes) result in their considering or reflecting upon the significance of these actions. Such analyses, in turn, result in changes in children's cognitive structures. In this case, awareness of the presence of categorical relations in a list of words leads to retrieval that is organized on the basis of these relations. This processing is effortful, involving the examination of the products of recent cognitive activities, but it is not planful in that the child does not enter the task with a preconceived notion about how to organize the to-be-remembered information.

In this developmental sequence, strategic organization does not arise de novo but has its genesis in earlier processes that are qualitatively different in form. As children's conceptual knowledge becomes better elaborated, the activation of categorical relations is more apt to occur, providing children with increased opportunities to observe organization in their own behavior. This, however, is not sufficient to produce spontaneously implemented organizational strategies, as illustrated by the results of numerous training studies in which children display sophisticated use of an organizational strategy during training, but fail to transfer that strategy to new sets of materials (e.g., Bjorklund et al., 1977; Hall, 1976). Children's failures to transfer a successfully trained memory strategy have also been demonstrated in studies of rehearsal (e.g., Keeney, Cannizzo, & Flavell, 1967), elaboration (e.g., Pressely, Levin, & Ghatala, 1984), and retrieval (e.g., Scribner & Cole, 1972). Thus, it is not sufficient that children merely observe memory competence in their own performance for them to adopt and generalize a memory strategy. Other aspects of development must also be involved. One aspect which I believe contributes to this transition is the amount of processing capacity that children have available for the execution of effortful memory activities. Consistent with Case et al. (1982), it is hypothesized that, with age, children process information more efficiently, leaving greater amounts of the limited processing capacity for encoding information for storage (but see Chapter 5 by Dempster for contrasting views). One reason for this increased efficiency is the greater ease with which semantic memory relations can be activated. The resulting improvement in processing efficiency frees sufficient attention so that subjects may engage in higher-order cognitive activities such as reflective abstraction and planful organizational strategies.

What of planful organizational strategies? How might they enhance memory behavior beyond the effects attributed to the activation of semantic relations and reflective abstraction? Planful organization at input can facilitate processing by accentuating semantic memory relations. Once a subject discerns categories in a list, he or she may take special effort to activate the category features of subsequent items (possibly to the exclusion of other word features), thus making highly salient the categorical structure of the list. This self-induced activation of categorical relations at input would be especially helpful for atypical items. This is because the category label is less apt to be activated for atypical than for typical instances. In fact, Greenberg and Bjorklund (1981) found that adults' greater memory performance for sets of typical relative to atypical items was eliminated when category cues were provided at input. They proposed that many atypical items were not spontaneously encoded in terms of category features, and the presentation of category cues at input served to activate category relations, resulting in higher levels of recall and clustering.

Organizational strategies also work at output, a fact that is consistent with the "descriptions" view of retrieval in Chapter 1 by Ackerman. Subjects can generate each category label and search memory for recently activated items from that category (see Kobasigawa, 1977). When category features are specifically activated at input and retrieval in terms of category relations is followed systematically, levels of recall will be high, with subjects no longer being dependent on the retrieval of one item to cue another. In fact, when categorical organization at input is emphasized, it may be difficult to retrieve individual items unless the category label is first generated. For example, Bjorklund and Hock (1982) biased fourth-grade children to organize information according to category cues at input. Some subjects were then given category cues at retrieval (Experiment 2), whereas other subjects were not (Experiment 3). Children were assessed on two lists: one where recall was tested immediately following list presentation and one where recall was tested after a 4-minute filled delay period. Subjects in both cuing conditions showed high levels of recall and organization in immediate testing. For delayed testing, subjects not given the category cues at output showed a drop in recall relative to immediate testing. This decrement, not found for subjects provided with both input and retrieval cues, was the result of some subjects forgetting the list categories. Children's clustering was nearly perfect, but if they could not generate the category label, all items stored under that label at input were forgotten. The identity of individual items was subjugated by the category label. Representations of items were so integrally associated with their category membership that they could be accessed only through this relationship.

Why should 9-year-old children forget, on the average, one of four category names following a brief delay period? One explanation consistent with the present framework is that the cognitive effort subjects expended to organize information at input and to plan for categorical retrieval limited the amount of capacity available for processing the category names (see also the normative findings on age differences in capacity in Chapter 5 by Dempster). Thus, children's recall was highly organized, but because of the limited efficiency of their strategy use, fewer specific pieces of information (category names) could be retained for delayed recall. This interpretation is consistent with the results of many training studies. Young children who are instructed to use an efficient mnemonic strategy can do so, although their levels of performance are rarely comparable to uninstructed adults or adolescents (e.g., Bjorklund et al., 1977; Ornstein, Naus, & Stone, 1977). One possible reason for this is that the children allocated substantial portions of their limited processing capacity to executing these trained strategies, leaving relatively little capacity for storage. Thus, the strategy is followed efficiently, but often with only small improvements in overall memory performance.

In conclusion, with age, the relations among items in children's semantic memories become more elaborated, making their activation relatively automatic. This automation frees processing capacity for other cognitive activities, among them reflective abstraction. Via this mechanism, children examine the products of their own processing and may identify an organizational scheme that they can use to guide subsequent processing. Although effortful, reflective abstraction is not planful. Planful organizational strategies require even more processing capacity for their efficient execution and occur spontaneously in development when other memory processes (e.g., the activation of categorical relations) have become sufficiently automatic so that they use little of this limited capacity. Thus, when spontaneous, planful organization is first seen in development (usually early adolescence) it does not replace the less effortful organization based on the activation of well-established semantic memory relationships but rather builds upon it. At this time in development, children's memory behavior continues to be influenced by the extent and nature of their conceptual knowledge, much as it is for younger children. In fact, even for the adolescent and adult, knowledge base effects may account for a major portion of memory organization. Nevertheless, such effects are supplemented by the imposition of deliberate organizational strategies. These strategies are based on children's existing conceptual knowledge and serve to transform to-be-remembered information both at time of input and retrieval, resulting in a system that is qualitatively different than that of the preadolescent child.

Acknowledgments. I would like to thank Barbara Zeman, Paula Schwanenflugel, Howard Hock, and Larry Malcus for helpful comments on earlier drafts of this chapter. I also wish to express my appreciation to Sylvia Friedman, Susan McDonough, Sherry Pontek, and Ruth Murray for their help in the preparation of the manuscript.

References

Anglin, J. M. (1970). *The growth of word meaning.* Cambridge, MA: MIT Press.

Anglin, J. M. (1977). *Word, object, and conceptual development.* New York: Norton.

Annett, M. (1959). The classification of instances of four common class concepts by children and adults. *British Journal of Psychology, 29,* 233–236.

Atkinson, R. C., & Shiffrin, R. M. (1968). Human memory: A proposed system and its control processes. In K. W. Spence & J. T. Spence (Eds.), *The psychology of learning and motivation: Advances in research and theory* (Vol. 2). New York: Academic Press.

Bjorklund, D. F. (1976). *Children's identification and encoding of category information for recall.* Unpublished doctoral dissertation, University of North Carolina at Chapel Hill.

Bjorklund, D. F. (1978). Negative transfer in children's recall of categorized materials. *Journal of Experimental Child Psychology, 26,* 299–307.

Bjorklund, D. F. (1980a). Developmental differences in the timing of children's awareness of category relations in free recall. *International Journal of Behavioral Development, 3,* 61–70.

Bjorklund, D. F. (1980b). Children's identification of category relations in lists presented for recall. *Journal of Genetic Psychology, 136,* 45–53.

Bjorklund, D. F., & de Marchena, M. R. (1984). Developmental shifts in the basis of organization in memory: The role of associative versus categorical relatedness in children's free-recall. *Child Development, 55,* 952–962.

Bjorklund, D. F., Greenberg, M. S., Hurlbert, B. E., & Thompson, B. E. (1978, April). *Children's cued retrieval and the structure of semantic memory.* Paper presented at meeting of Southeastern Conference on Human Development, Atlanta, GA.

Bjorklund, D. F., & Hock, H. S. (1982). Age differences in the temporal locus of memory organization in children's recall. *Journal of Experimental Child Pscyhology*, *32*, 347–362.

Bjorklund, D. F., & Jacobs, J. W. (in press). Associative and categorical processes in children's memory: The role of automaticity in the development of organization in free recall. *Journal of Experimental Child Psychology*.

Bjorklund, D. F., & Ornstein, P. A. (1976). *Young children's recall and organization of materials differing in list structure*. Unpublished manuscript, University of North Carolina at Chapel Hill.

Bjorklund, D. F., Ornstein, P. A., & Haig, J. R. (1977). Development of organization and recall: Training in the use of organizational techniques. *Developmental Psychology*, *13*, 175–183.

Bjorklund, D. F., Smith, S. C., & Ornstein, P. A. (1982). Young children's release from proactive interference: The effects of category typicality. *Bulletin of the Psychonomic Society*, *20*, 211–213.

Bjorklund, D. F., & Thompson, B. E. (1983). Category typicality effects in children's memory performance: Qualitative and quantitative differences in the processing of category information. *Journal of Experimental Child Psychology*, *35*, 329–344.

Bjorklund, D. F., Thompson, B. E., & Ornstein, P. A. (1983). Developmental trends in children's typicality judgements. *Behavior Research Methods & Instrumentation*, *15*, 350–356.

Bjorklund, D. F., & Zaken-Greenberg, F. (1981). The effects of differences in classification style on preschool children's memory. *Child Development*, *52*, 888–894.

Bjorklund, D. F., & Zeman, B. R. (1982). Children's organization and metamemory awareness in their recall of familiar information. *Child Development*, *53*, 799–810.

Bjorklund, D. F., & Zeman, B. R. (1983). The development of organizational strategies in children's recall of familiar information: Using social organization to recall the names of classmates. *International Journal of Behavioral Development*, *6*, 341–353.

Bjorklund, D. F., & Zeman, B. R. (in press). *Organization versus item effects of an elaborated knowledge base on children's memory*. Developmental Psychology.

Brainerd, C. J. (1974). Training and transfer of transitivity, conservation, and class inclusion of length. *Child Development*, *45*, 324–334.

Broadbent, D. E. (1958). *Perception and communication*. London: Pergamon Press.

Brown, A. L. (1975). The development of memory: Knowing, knowing about knowing, and knowing how to know. In H. W. Reese (Ed.), *Advances in child development and behavior* (Vol. 10). New York: Academic Press.

Carson, M. T., & Abrahamson, A. (1976). Some members are more equal than others: The effect of semantic typicality on class-inclusion performance. *Child Development*, *47*, 1186–1190.

Case, R., Kurland, M., & Goldberg, J. (1982). Operational efficiency and the growth of short-term memory span. *Journal of Experimental Child Psychology*, *33*, 386–404.

Chechile, R. A., & Richman, C. L. (1982). The interaction of semantic memory with storage and retrieval processes. *Developmental Review*, *2*, 237–250.

Chi, M. T. H. (1976). Short-term limitations in children: Capacity or processing deficits? *Memory and Cognition*, *4*, 559–572.

Chi, M. T. H. (1978). Knowledge structure and memory development. In R. Siegler (Ed.), *Children's thinking: What develops?* Thirteenth Annual Carnegie Symposium on Cognition. Hillsdale, NJ: Lawrence Erlbaum Associates.

Chi, M. T. H. (1981). Knowledge development and memory performance. In M. Friedman, J. P. Das, & N O'Connor (Eds.), *Intelligence and learning*. New York: Plenum Press.

Chi, M. T. H. (in press). Interactive roles of knowledge and strategies in development. In S. Chipman, J. Segal, & R. Glaser (Eds.), *Thinking and learning skills: Current research and open questions* (Vol. 2). Hillsdale, NJ: Lawrence Erlbaum Associates.

Chi, M. T. H., & Koeske, R. D. (1983). Network representation of a child's dinosaur knowledge. *Developmental Psychology, 19,* 29–39.

Cohen, L. B., & Younger, B. A. (1983). Perceptual categorization in the infant. In E. K. Scholnick (Ed.), *New trends in conceptual representation: Challenges to Piaget's theory?* Hillsdale, NJ: Lawrence Erlbaum Associates.

Corsale, K. (1980, April). *Children's knowledge and strategic use of organizational structure in recall.* Paper presented at meeting of the Society for Research in Child Development, Boston, MA.

Dempster, F. N. (1978). Memory span and short-term memory capacity: A developmental study. *Journal of Experimental Child Psychology, 26,* 419–431.

Denney, N. (1974). Evidence for developmental changes in categorization criteria for children and adults. *Human Development, 17,* 41–53.

Denney, N., & Ziobrowski, M. (1972). Developmental changes in clustering criteria. *Journal of Experimental Child Psychology, 13,* 275–282.

Duncan, E. M., & Kellas, G. (1978). Developmental changes in the internal structure of semantic categories. *Journal of Experimental Child Psychology, 26,* 328–340.

Emerson, H. F., & Gekowski, W. L. (1976). Interactive and categorical grouping strategies and the syntagmatic-paradigmatic shift. *Child Development, 47,* 1116–1121.

Entwisle, D. R. (1966). *Word associations of young children.* Baltimore: Johns Hopkins Press.

Esrov, L. V., Hall, J. W., & LaFaver, D. K. (1974). Preschoolers' conceptual and acoustic encoding as evidenced by release from PI. *Bulletin of the Psychonomic Society, 4,* 89–90.

Eysenck, M. W., & Baron, C. R. (1974). Effects of cuing on recall from categorized word lists. *Developmental Psychology, 10,* 665–666.

Faulkender, P. J., Wright, J. C., & Waldron, A. (1974). Generalized habituation of concept stimuli in toddlers. *Child Development, 45,* 1002–1010.

Felzen, E., & Anisfeld, M. (1970). Semantic and phonetic relations in the false recognition of words by third- and sixth-grade children. *Developmental Psychology, 3,* 163–168.

Flavell, J. H. (1970). Concept development. In P. Mussen (Ed.), *Carmichael's manual of child psychology.* New York: Wiley.

Frankel, M. T., & Rollins, H. A. (1982). Age-related differences in clustering: A new approach. *Journal of Experimental Child Psychology, 34,* 113–122.

Frankel, M. T., & Rollins, H. A. (in press). Associative and categorical hypotheses of organization in the free recall of adults and children. *Journal of Experimental Child Psychology.*

Galbraith, R. C., & Day, R. D. (1978). Developmental changes in clustering criteria? A closer look at Denney and Ziobrowski. *Child Development*, *49*, 889–891.

Geis, M. F., & Hall, D. M. (1976). Encoding and incidental memory in children. *Journal of Experimental Child Psychology*, *22*, 58–66.

Geis, M. F., & Hall, D. M. (1978). Encoding and congruity in children's incidental memory. *Child Development*, *49*, 857–861.

Ghatala, E. S., Carbonari, J. P., & Bobelo, L. Z. (1980). Developmental changes in incidental memory as a function of processing level, congruity and repetition. *Journal of Experimental Child Psychology*, *29*, 74–87.

Greenberg, M. S., & Bjorklund, D. F. (1981). Category tyicality in free recall: Effects of feature overlap or differential category encoding? *Journal of Experimental Psychology: Human Learning & Memory*, *7*, 145–147.

Hall, J. W. (1976). A reexamination of the effects of organization training on children's recall of category items. *Child Development*, *47*, 1211–1213.

Hall, J. W., & Halperin, M. S. (1972). The development of memory encoding processes in young children. *Developmental Psychology*, *6*, 181.

Hasher, L., & Clifton, D. A. (1974). A developmental study of attribute encoding in free recall. *Journal of Experimental Child Psychology*, *17*, 332–346.

Hasher, L., & Zacks, R. T. (1979). Automatic and effortful processes in memory. *Journal of Experimental Psychology: General*, *108*, 356–388.

Heidenheimer, P. (1978). A comparison of the roles of exemplar, action, coordinate, and superordinate relations in the semantic processing of 4- and 5-year old children. *Journal of Experimental Child Psychology*, *25*, 143–159.

Hock, H. S., Romanski, L., Galie, A., & Williams, C. S. (1978). Real-world schemata and scene recognition in adults and children. *Memory and Cognition*, *6*, 423–431.

Hoemann, H. W., DeRosa, D. V., & Andrews, C. E. (1974). Categorical encoding in short-term memory by 4- to 11-year old children. *Bulletin of the Psychonomic Society*, *3*, 63–65.

Inhelder, B., & Piaget, J. (1964). *The early growth of logic in the child*. New York: Norton.

Jacobs, J. W. (1984). *The role of associativity in the development of strategic organization in children's memory*. Unpublished masters thesis, Florida Atlantic University.

James, W. (1980). *Principles of psychology*. New York: Holt.

Kagan, J., Moss, H., & Sigel, I. E. (1963). Psychological significance of styles of conceptualization. *Monograph of the Society for Research in Child Development*, *28*(2), 73–112.

Kahneman, D. (1973). *Attention and effort*. Englewood Cliffs, NJ: Prentice-Hall.

Keeney, T. J., Cannizzo, S. R., & Flavell, J. H. (1967). Spontaneous and induced verbal rehearsal in a recall task. *Child Development*, *38*, 953–966.

Keil, F. C., & Batterman, N. (1984). A characteristic-to-defining shift in the development of word meaning. *Journal of Verbal Learning and Verbal Behavior*, *23*, 221–236.

Keller, D. (1982). Developmental effects of typicality and superordinate property dominance on sentence verification. *Journal of Experimental Child Psychology*, *33*, 288–297.

Keller, D., & Kellas, G. (1978). Typicality as a dimension of encoding. *Journal of Experimental Psychology: Human Learning and Memory*, *4*, 78–85.

Kirasic, K. C., Siegel, A. W., & Allen, G. L. (1980). Developmental changes in recognition-in-context memory. *Child Development*, *51*, 302–305.

Klahr, D., & Wallace, J. G. (1972). Class inclusion processes. In S. Farnham-Diggory (Ed.), *Information processing in children*. New York: Academic Press.

Kobasigawa, A. (1977). Retrieval strategies in the development of memory. In R. V. Kail, Jr., & J. W. Hagen (Eds.), *Perspectives on the development of memory and cognition*. Hillsdale, NJ: Lawrence Erlbaum Associates.

LaBerge, D., & Samuels, S. J. (1974). Toward a theory of automatic information processing in reading. *Cognitive Psychology*, *6*, 293–323.

Lange, G. W. (1973). The development of conceptual and rote recall skills among school age children. *Journal of Experimental Child Psychology*, *15*, 394–407.

Lange, G. W. (1978). Organization-related processes in children's recall. In P. A. Ornstein (Ed.), *Memory development in children*. Hillsdale, NJ: Lawrence Erlbaum Associates.

Lange, G., & Jackson, P. (1974). Personal organization in children's free recall. *Child Development*, *45*, 1060–1067.

Lindberg, M. (1980). The role of knowledge structures in the ontogeny of learning. *Journal of Experimental Child Psychology*, *30*, 401–410.

Lucariello, J., & Nelson, K. (in press). Slot-filler categories as memory organizers for young children. *Developmental Psychology*.

Mandler, J. M. (1978). A code in the node: The use of a story scheme in retrieval. *Discourse Processes*, *1*, 14–35.

Mandler, J. M. (1979). Categorical and schematic organization in memory. In C. R. Puff (Ed.), *Memory, organization, and structure*. New York: Academic Press.

Mandler, J. M. (1983). Representation. In J. H. Flavell & E. M. Markman (Eds.), *Cognitive development* (Vol. 3 of P. Mussen (Ed.), *Carmichael's manual of child psychology*). Wiley: New York.

Mandler, J. M., & Robinson, C. A. (1978). Developmental changes in picture recognition. *Journal of Experimental Child Psychology*, *26*, 122–136.

Mansfield, A. F. (1977). Semantic organization in the young child: Evidence for the development of semantic feature systems. *Journal of Experimental Child Psychology*, *23*, 57–77.

Markman, E. M., Cox, B., & Marchida, S. (1981). The standard object-sorting task as a measure of conceptual organization. *Developmental Psychology*, *17*, 115–117.

McCabe, A. E., Siegel, L. S., Spence, I., & Wilkinson, A. (1982). Class-inclusion reasoning: Patterns of performance from three to eight years. *Child Development*, *53*, 780–785.

McCauley, C., Weil, C. M., & Sperber, R. D. (1976). The development of memory structure as reflected by semantic-priming effects. *Journal of Experimental Child Psychology*, *22*, 511–518.

Mervis, C. B., & Crisafi, M. A. (1982). Order of acquisition of subordinate-, basic-, and superordinate-level categories. *Child Development*, *53*, 258–266.

Mervis, C. B., & Rosch, E. (1981). Categorization of natural objects. *Annual review of psychology*, *32*, 89–115.

Moely, B. E. (1977). Organizational factors in the development of memory. In R. V. Kail, Jr., & J. W. Hagen (Eds.), *Perspectives on the development of memory and cognition*. Hillsdale, NJ: Lawrence Erlbaum Associates.

Moely, B. E., & Jeffrey, W. E. (1974). The effect of organization training on children's free recall of category items. *Child Development*, *45*, 135–143.

Moely, B. E., Olson, F. A., Halwes, T. G., & Flavell, J. H. (1969). Production deficiency in young children's clustered recall. *Developmental Psychology*, *1*, 26–34.

Murphy, M. D., & Brown, A. L. (1975). Incidental learning in preschool children as a function of levels of cognitive analysis. *Journal of Experimental Child Psychology*, *19*, 509–523.

Naron, N. K. (1978). Developmental changes in word attribute utilization for organization and retrieval in free recall. *Journal of Experimental Child Psychology*, *25*, 279–297.

Naus, M. J., & Ornstein, P. A. (1983). Development of memory strategies: Analysis, questions and issues. In M. T. H. Chi (Ed.), *Contributions to human development*. Vol. 9. *Trends in memory development research*. Basel: S. Karger.

Nelson, K. (1973). Structure and strategy in learning to talk. *Monograph of the Society for Research in Child Development*, *38*, (No. 149).

Nelson, K. (1974a). Concept, word, and sentence: Inter-relations in acquisition and development. *Psychological Review*, *81*, 267–285.

Nelson, K. (1974b). Variations in children's concepts by age and category. *Child Development*, *45*, 577–584.

Nelson, K. (1983). The derivation of concepts and categories from event representation. In E. K. Scholnick (Ed.), *New trends in conceptual representation: Challenges to Piaget's theory?* Hillsdale, NJ: Lawrence Erlbaum Associates.

Nelson, K., Fivush, R., Hudson, J., & Lucariello, J. (1983). Scripts and the development of memory. In M. T. H. Chi (Ed.), *Contributions to human development*. Vol. 9. *Trends in memory development research*. Basel: S. Karger.

Nelson, K., & Gruendel, J. M. (1981). Generalized event representations: Basic building blocks of cognitive development. In A. Brown & M. Lamb (Eds.), *Advances in developmental psychology* (Vol. 1). Hillsdale, NJ: Lawrence Erlbaum Associates.

Olver, R. R., & Hornsby, J. R. (1966). On equivalence. In J. S. Bruner, R. R. Olver, & P. M. Greenfield (Eds.), *Studies in cognitive growth*. New York: Wiley.

Ornstein, P. A., & Corsale, K. (1979). Organizational factors in children's memory. In C. R. Puff (Ed.), *Organization, structure, & memory*. New York: Academic Press.

Ornstein, P. A., & Naus, M. J. (in press). Effects of the knowledge base on children's memory processing. In J. B. Sidowski (Ed.), *Conditioning, cognition, and methodology: Contemporary issues in experimental psychology*. Hillsdale, NJ: Lawrence Erlbaum Associates.

Ornstein, P. A., Naus, M. J., & Stone, B. P. (1977). Rehearsal training and developmental differences in memory. *Developmental Psychology*, *13*, 15–24.

Paris, S. G., & Mahoney, G. J. (1974). Cognitive integration in children's memory for sentences and pictures. *Child Development*, *45*, 633–642.

Perlmutter, M., & Ricks, M. (1979). Recall in preschool children. *Journal of Experimental Child Psychology*, *27*, 423–436.

Piaget, J. (1971). *Biology and knowledge*. (B. Walsh, Trans.), Chicago: University of Chicago Press.

Posnansky, C. J. (1978). Category norms for verbal items in 25 categories for children in grades 2–6. *Behavior Research Methods & Instrumentation*, *10*, 819–832.

Posner, M. I., & Snyder, C. R. P. (1975). Attention and cognitive control. In R. L. Solso (Ed.), *Information processing and cognition: The Loyola Symposium*. Hillsdale, NJ: Lawrence Erlbaum Associates.

Pressley, M., Borkowski, J. G., & O'Sullivan, J. T. (1984). Memory strategy instruction is made of this: Metamemory and durable strategy use. *Educational Psychologist, 19,* 94–107.

Pressley, M., Levin, J. R., & Ghatala, E. S. (1984). Memory strategy monitoring in adults and children. *Journal of Verbal Learning and Verbal Behavior, 23,* 270–288.

Rabinowitz, M. (1984a). The use of categorical organization: Not an all-or-none situation. *Journal of Experimental Child Psychology, 38,* 338–351.

Rabinowitz, M. (1984b). *Variations in knowledge and memory performance: Implications of a spreading activation network.* Manuscript in preparation, University of Pittsburgh.

Rabinowitz, M., & Mandler, J. M. (1983). Organization and information retrieval. *Journal of Experimental Psychology: Learning, Memory and Cognition, 9,* 430–439.

Reichard, S., Schneider, M., & Rappaport, D. (1944). The development of concept formation in children. *American Journal of Orthopsychiatry, 14,* 156–161.

Reznick, J. S., & Kagan, J. (1983). Category detection in infancy. In L. P. Lipsitt & C. K. Rovee-Collier (Eds.), *Advances in infancy research* (Vol. 2). Norwood, NJ: Ablex.

Rice, U. M., & DiVesta, F. J. (1965). A developmental study of semantic and phonetic generalization in paired-associate learning. *Child Development, 36,* 721–730.

Richman, C. L., Nida, S., & Pittman, L. (1976). Effects of meaningfulness on child free-recall learning. *Developmental Psychology, 12,* 460–465.

Riess, B. F. (1946). Genetic changes in semantic conditioning. *Journal of Experimental Psychology, 36,* 143–152.

Rips, L. J., Shoben, E. J., & Smith, E. E. (1973). Semantic distance and the verification of semantic relations. *Journal of Verbal Learning and Verbal Behavior, 12,* 1–20.

Rosch, E. (1973). On the internal structure of perceptual and semantic categories. In T. E. Moore (Ed.), *Cognitive development and the acquisition of language.* New York: Academic Press.

Rosch, E. (1975). Cognitive representations of semantic categories. *Journal of Experimental Psychology: General, 7,* 192–233.

Rosch, E., Mervis, C. B., Gray, W. D., Johnson, D. M., & Boyes-Braem, P. (1976). Basic objects in natural categories. *Cognitive Psychology, 8,* 382–439.

Roth, C. (1983). Factors affecting developmental changes in the speed of processing. *Journal of Experimental Child Psychology, 35,* 509–528.

Saarnio, D. A., & Bjorklund, D. F. (1984). Children's recall of objects from self-generated scenes. *Merrill Palmer Quarterly, 30,* 287–301.

Saltz, E., Soller, E., & Sigel, I. E. (1972). The development of natural language concepts. *Child Development, 43,* 1191–1202.

Schneider, W., & Shiffrin, R. M. (1977). Controlled and automatic human information processing: I. Detection, search, and attention. *Psychological Review, 84,* 1–66.

Scholnick, E. K., & Johnson, J. W. (1981, April). *Knowledge and conceptual structure in semantic memory.* Paper presented at meeting of the Society for Research in Child Development, Boston, MA.

Schwanenflugel, P. J., Bjorklund, D. F., Guth, M. E., Willenborg, M. F., & Boardman, J. L. (1984, April). *A developmental trend in the understanding of concept attribute importance.* Paper presented at the Meeting of the Southeastern Conferece on Human Development, Athens, GA.

Scott, M. S., Serchuk, R., & Mundy, P. (1982). Taxonomic and complementary picture pairs: Ability in two- to five-year olds. *International Journal of Behavioral Development*, 5, 243–256.

Scribner, S., & Cole, M. (1972). Effects of constrained recall training on children's performance in a verbal memory task. *Child Development*, 43, 845–857.

Shiffrin, R. M., & Schneider, W. (1977). Controlled and automatic human information processing: II. Perceptual learning, automatic attending, and a general theory. *Psychological Review*, 84, 127–190.

Siegel, L. S., McCabe, A. E., Brand, A. E., & Mathews, J. (1978). Evidence for the understanding of class inclusion in preschool children: Linguistic factors and training effects. *Child Development*, 49, 688–693.

Sigel, I. E. (1953). Developmental trends in the abstraction ability of children. *Child Development*, 24, 131–144.

Smiley, S. S., & Brown, A. L. (1979). Conceptual preference for thematic or taxonomic relations: A nonmonotonic age trend from preschool to old age. *Journal of Experimental Child Psychology*, 28, 249–257.

Smith, C. L. (1979). Children's understanding of natural language categories. *Journal of Experimental Child Psychology*, 30, 191–205.

Smith, E., Shoben, E., & Rips, L. (1974). Structure and process in semantic memory: A featural model for semantic decisions. *Psychological Review*, 81, 214–241.

Steinberg, E. R., & Anderson, R. C. (1975). Hierarchical semantic organization in 6-year olds. *Journal of Experimental Child Psychology*, 19, 544–553.

Strand, K. (1983, October). *The relation of metamemory to memory performance in language-impaired children*. Paper presented at meeting of the Boston University Conference on Language Development, Boston, MA.

Szeminska, A. (1965). The evolution of thought: Some applications of research findings to educational practice. In P. Mussen (Ed.), European research in cognitive development. *Monograph of the Society for Research in Child Development*, 30, (No. 100).

Tighe, T. J., Tighe, L. S., & Schechter, J. (1975). Memory for instances and categories in children and adults. *Journal of Experimental Child Psychology*, 20, 22–37.

Thompson, J. (1941). The ability of children of different grade levels to generalize on sorting tests. *The Journal of Psychology*, 11, 119–126.

Treisman, A. M. (1960). Contextual cues in selective listening. *Quarterly Journal of Experimental Psychology*, 12, 242–248.

Uyeda, K. M., & Mandler, G. (1980). Prototypicality norms for 28 semantic categories. *Behavior Research Methods & Instrumentation*, 12, 567–595.

White, T. (1982). Naming practices, typicality and underextension in child language. *Journal of Experimental Child Psychology*, 33, 324–346.

Whitney, P., Cocklin, T. G., Juola, J. F., & Kellas, G. (1983). A reassessment of typicality effects in free recall. *Bulletin of the Psychonomic Society*, 21, 321–323.

Whitney, P., & Kunen, S. (1983). Development of hierarchical conceptual relationships in children's semantic memories. *Journal of Experimental Child Psychology*, 35, 278–293.

Wilkinson, A. (1976). Counting strategies and semantic analysis as applied to class inclusion. *Cognitive Psychology*, 8, 64–85.

Williams, K. G., & Goulet, L. R. (1975). The effects of cueing and constraint instructions on children's free recall performance. *Journal of Experimental Child Psychology*, 19, 464–475.

Winer, G. A. (1980). Class-inclusion reasoning in children: A review of the empirical literature. *Child Development*, *51*, 309–328.

Winters, J. J., Jr., & Brzoska, M. A. (1976). Development of the formation of categories by normal and retarded persons. *Developmental Psychology*, *12*, 125–131.

Worden, P. E. (1976). The effects of classification structure on organized free recall in children. *Journal of Experimental Child Psychology*, *22*, 519–529.

4. Model-Based Approaches to Storage and Retrieval Development

Charles J. Brainerd

As everyone knows, the distinction between processes that lead to the formation of traces, commonly called storage, and processes that permit access to such traces, commonly called retrieval, is fundamental to modern theories of memory. Students of the memory literature usually credit Melton (1963) with being the first to focus attention on the storage-retrieval distinction. Melton remarked, "What, then, are the principal issues in a theory of memory? These are about either the storage or the retrieval of traces" (1963, p. 4). Although this observation appeared more than two decades ago, it was only during the past decade that concepts of storage and retrieval replaced older associative ideas as cornerstones of memory theories.

To a neutral observer, the centrality of the storage-retrieval distinction would be obvious enough from its repeated use in contemporary explanations of memory data. Importantly, such explanations are inclined to differ in the relative significance that they assign to storage and retrieval processes. This point may be illustrated by considering contrasting theoretical accounts of three familiar long-term memory effects—namely, the primacy effect in serial learning, the categorization effect in recall, and the concreteness effect in recall.

Concerning the primacy effect, it is possible to argue (e.g., see Skoff & Chechile, 1977) that the first few items on a list are easier to remember because they are more likely to be transferred from short-term memory to long-term memory on study trials, a storage explanation, or because traces of these items are easier to locate on test trials, a retrieval effect, or both. With respect to the categorization effect, it is normally easier to learn to recall a list when the items belong to a few familiar categories than when they are unrelated. One class of theories of how categorical information is represented in long-term memory (so-called prototype theories) implies that this effect occurs because categorized items are easier to store, whereas another class of theories (so-called relational coding theories) implies that categorized lists are simply easier to retrieve (cf. Bjorklund's Chapter in this volume). Last, the concreteness effect refers to the fact that, other things being equal, it becomes easier to memorize a list as the judged concreteness or imagability of the items increases. The traditional explanation of this result assumes that the chances of having more than one code available for an item increase as their judged concreteness increases (Kee, Stovall, Bell, & Davis, 1981; Paivio, 1971), which is a storage hypothesis. More recently, it has been argued that traces become progressively easier to locate in long-term memory as the judged concreteness of items increases (Brainerd, Desrochers, & Howe, 1981; Brainerd & Howe, 1982), which is a retrieval hypothesis.

These examples, and many others that could be mentioned, serve to illustrate a basic point about memory research: It is often difficult to make progress in testing contrasting theoretical proposals without effective procedures for disentangling the relative contributions of storage and retrieval factors to memory data. As this chapter unfolds, it will, I hope, become increasingly apparent that this is a more complex and challenging problem that the task of merely demonstrating that storage processes per se or retrieval processes per se are implicated in memory performance.

The empirical segregation of storage and retrieval factors is an equally important matter when it comes to the study of memory development. There are numerous research questions about children's memory that turn on the existence of satisfactory separation technologies. In the first place, there is what might be called the Big Question: Are the changes that we observe in memory performance as functions of chronological age more dependent on the development of storage processes or on the development of retrieval processes? This question, which is comparable in generality to nature-nurture and about as likely to ever be resolved through experimentation, decomposes into many little questions on which research is actually focused. Here are some well-worn examples. Are the changes in performance on some specific task (e.g., span of immediate recall, recognition memorizing, free recall) during some well-defined age range consequences of the development of specific storage and/or retrieval factors? Do two tasks that show different amounts of age change (e.g., recognition and recall) do so because the contribution of certain storage and/or retrieval factors is greater for one task than for the other? Does some manipulation that is known to increase or decrease performance on a variety of tasks during a given age range (e.g., familiarity, elaboration) do so by affecting some specific set of storage and/or retrieval factors? Does some manipulation that is known to produce Age $\times$ Treatment interactions during a given age range (e.g., degree of list organization, item concreteness) do so because its effects are localized within some particular set of storage and/or retrieval factors that are developing during that age range?

Lately, some investigators have taken the position that answers to these and similar questions require the formulation of general mathematical models of storage and retrieval. The main purposes of this chapter are to discuss some issues that motivate the adoption of this view and to review the nuts and bolts of some techniques that are applicable to a reasonably broad assortment of memory-development data.

The first theme, the conceptual background for mathematical models of storage and retrieval development, is considered in the first section of this chapter. Although the motivational issues that are reviewed are not utterly foreign to the memory-development literature, indeed some are widely acknowledged, their research implications do not seem to be generally understood. The remaining sections of the chapter are then devoted to the assumptions, experimental procedures, and associated data bases of three storage-retrieval models—a model for short-term memory tasks, a model for long-term memory tasks, and a model for retention tasks. These models were chosen for review both because of their breadth of potential application and because their statistical development phases are more or less complete. Thus, the sorts of experiments that one conducts to generate pertinent data and, crucially, the machinery that produces measurements of storage and retrieval from raw data, are well established. Relative to other, still evolving models, these three models provide the same advantage that tailor-made clothing provides over machine-produced garments; they are, so to speak, ready to wear without alteration.

Why Models?

Heretofore, many branches of psychology, most frankly, have not been hospitable environments for serious mathematical modeling. Research on developmental phenomena, in particular, has historically been almost wholly qualitative. For example, a survey of research trends in developmental psychology during the present century reveals that major advances in mathematical psychology have had essentially no impact on developmental work (Brainerd, 1982b).

This situation has begun to change, especially with regard to research on the development of cognition and memory. Just now, model-based work is one of our most productive sources of new theoretical ideas. However, the fact that such work has begun to appear only recently means that there is still considerable doubt as to why some investigators have adopted modeling aproaches. The aim of what follows in this section is to clarify this matter. Not surprisingly, the frame for the discussion will be the problem of how to separate the contributions of storage and retrieval factors to age changes in memory performance. But the principal issues that arise are not in any sense unique to the problem of discriminating storage and retrieval, similar considerations motivate most mathematical modeling work in psychology.

Design-Based Separation: Two Illustrations

As researchers, our natural inclination is to treat the job of separating different process variables as a problem in experimental design rather than recognizing it for what it is, a problem in measurement theory. The standard strategy is to institute various procedural manipulations, normally in the context of factorial designs, whose aim is to purge the data, to some degree, of the effects of certain processes. Conclusions about the respective contributions of these processes to data are then based on the relative levels of memory performance in conditions that differ in their respective degrees of purification. A key feature of this strategy is that it does not involve any explicit assumptions about the measurement scales that underlie performance on memory tasks.

Although this design-based approach predominates in the study of memory development, it is intrinsically flawed. Its specific shortcomings are consequences of the fact that the things that we seek to differentiate are theoretical constructs, not empirical variables. Rather than examine these matters in the abstract, it might be better to illustrate them with instances from the literature of design-driven attempts at separation. We begin, therefore, with an overview of two paradigms that will be familiar to most readers, and this will be followed by a more general discussion of the limitations of the designed-based approach. Two points should be stressed in connection with these illustrations, however. First, the literature contains several other examples of paradigms that could have been used for the same purpose; these two were selected merely because of their simplicity and familiarity. Second, in considering these paradigms it is not my intention to criticize the work of particular investigators. For this reason, specific studies in which these paradigms have been employed will not be cited. As these paradigms have been frequently used, readers will be able to fill in this detail for themselves.

The first paradigm, the *study-test technique*, is used in conjunction with most laboratory list learning tasks (e.g., recognition, paired-associate learning, free recall). It has been applied to the study of list manipulations that are known to increase or decrease the age differences that are typically observed on these tasks (e.g., elaborated vs. unelaborated items, abstract vs. concrete items, pictures vs. words). A general question about such variables is whether they maximize (or minimize) age differences because they affect ease of storage or ease of retrieval. Depending on how this question is answered, further inferences may be possible about the relative importance of storage and retrieval development during the target age range.

Suppose that children are administered some list-learning task and that a list variable of developmental interest is being manipulated. Suppose, further, that this variable can be *independently* manipulated on study trials and on test trials in an A (Study Trials) $\times B$ (Test Trials) factorial design. As a case in point, suppose that children are learning a list of paired associates via the study-test method, that the manipulation of interest is whether the cue member of each cue-target pair is a picture or a word, and that this manipulation is executed independently on study and test trials in a 2 (Study Trials: Picture Cues vs. Word Cues) $\times$ 2 (Test Trials: Picture Cues vs. Word Cues) design. In other words, when the cue-target pairs appear on test trials, the cues are either pictures of common objects or the names of those objects, and when the cues appear by themselves on test trials, they are either pictures or equivalent names.[1]

The study-test technique relies on the following logic to isolate storage effects from retrieval effects with such designs. To begin with, it is assumed, quite sensibly, that storage and retrieval vary in their impact on memory strength on study and test trials. Explicitly, it is assumed that storage factors make proportionately larger contributions to memory strength on study trials than on test trials or, conversely, that retrieval factors are more important to memory strength on test trials than on study trials. In an actual $A \times B$ experiment, these qualitative results are possible: (a) an A main effect only; (b) a B main effect only; (c) main effects for both A and B; (d) an A main effect and an $A \times B$ interaction; (e) a B main effect and an $A \times B$ interaction; (f) an A main effect, a B main effect, and an $A \times B$ interaction; (g) an $A \times B$ interaction only, and (h) no effects.

According to the logic of this methodology, certain of these results can be interpreted as showing that the locus of a variable's effects are primarily at storage or primarily at retrieval. In our hypothetical paired-associate experiment, finding (a) would prompt the conclusion that the effects of the picture-word manipulation are pure storage effects. Finding (b) would prompt the conclusion that the manipulation only affects retrieval. Finding (c) would prompt the conclusion that the manipulation affects both storage and retrieval. Finding (d) would prompt the conclusion that the manipulation affects storage more than retrieval. Finding (e) would prompt the conclusion that the manipulation affects retrieval more than storage. Depending on the nature of the interaction, finding (f) would prompt either the conclusion that the manipulation affects storage more than retrieval or that the manipulation affects retrieval more than storage. Finding (f) would prompt the conclusion that the *direction* of the manipulation's effects are different for storage and retrieval. Finally, each of these conclusions might then serve as a basis for further inferences as to the relative importance of storage and retrieval development to age changes in

---

[1]Many readers will have noticed that there are certain tasks and certain list variables to which this technique cannot readily be applied because the variables cannot be independently manipulated on study and test trials. Although this is an important limitation of the study-test technique, it will not concern us here because it is unrelated to the technique's inherent capacity to discriminate storage effects from retrieval effects.

paired-associate performance. Finding (a), for example, would probably be interpreted as showing that the development of storage factors is more important than the development of retrieval factors, at least insofar as age changes in paired-associate performance are concerned.

The second paradigm, the *different-task technique*, is also used with list-learning procedures. It relies on the presumed variability of storage and retrieval contributions to different methods of list memorization. Although our present concern is with its applications to storage-retrieval separation, this technique has also been used to study Age × Treatment interactions (see Wilkinson & Koestler, 1983a). Its key features are that children have to remember a single set of items but that the method of remembering them varies for different groups of children. The contrasting memorization methods, of course, are ones that are assumed to differ in the respective importance of storage and retrieval factors; memory strength is assumed to depend more on ease of storage with some tasks and to depend more on ease of retrieval with other tasks.

The rationale for the different-task technique is that if the strength of children's memory for a single set of items varies as a function of the memorization procedure, this tells us something about the relative contributions of storage and retrieval because the procedures are believed to vary on this factor. More important, if memory for a single set of items shows more pronounced age changes with one procedure than with another, this tells us something about the relative impact of storage and retrieval development during the target age range, especially if this discrepancy holds for most types of items.

In theory, the different-task technique could be used with any set of procedures whose members differ in the respective contributions of storage ease and retrieval ease to memory strength. In practice, however, the procedural manipulation in developmental experiments has traditionally been recognition versus recall. The selection of this manipulation is motivated by the fact that in the adult memory literature recognition has long been regarded as a task in which memory strength depends more on storage difficulty than on retrieval difficulty, whereas recall has long been regarded as a task for which the reverse is true. Estes and Dapolito (1967) were the first investigators to explore this hypothesis with adults.

When recognition and recall serve as contrasting memorization procedures for the same list, it is known that children of all ages find it more difficult to learn to recall the list than to learn to recognize it. This outcome is obtained for virtually all types of items, is highly pronounced in preschool children, and is also obtained when recognition performance is adjusted for guessing. If recognition performance is compared to recall performance across a fairly broad age spectrum, the amounts of age change are typically greater for recall than for recognition. Findings such as these have often been interpreted as showing, first, that storing an item is easier than retrieving it at all age levels and, second, that the development of retrieval skills plays a more central role in memory development than the development of storage processes.

Although the study-test and different-task techniques are procedurally distinct, they do share a critical assumption, an assumption that is implicit in all designed-based methods of discriminating storage and retrieval—that if it can be supposed, either for theoretical or empirical reasons, that storage and retrieval make proportionately different contributions to memory strength in different treatment combinations of an experiment, then this permits conclusions about the relative impact of storage and retrieval factors on performance in those conditions. But it is rather easy to show that response scaling considerations make this hypothesis untenable.

Some Scaling Issues

The reason that the assumption is untenable can be traced to a point to which passing mention was made earlier, namely, the design-based approach does not deliver an account of the measurement scales associated with memory tasks. To see why this point is significant, it is necessary to introduce two scaling concepts: (a) the notion of a *composition rule* (or an *integration rule*) and (b) the notion of an *output transformation* (or *response scale*). First, however, recall that three theoretical concepts have figured in the discussion so far: storage, retrieval, and memory strength. It is important to bear in mind that none of these concepts is a directly measurable empirical variable, and it is especially important to bear in mind that memory strength is not equivalent to performance on some memory task (see also Kail's Chapter in this volume).

With respect to the notion of a composition rule, suppose that we think of the concepts of storage, retrieval, and memory strength as numerical scales and that the scales are denoted S, R, and M, respectively. No assumptions are being made here about the theoretical meanings of these concepts. We are merely assuming that *whatever* they mean, numbers can be used to represent different amounts of the storage variable (Scale S), different amounts of the retrieval variable (Scale R), and different amounts of the memory strength variable (Scale M). The last variable, of course, is supposed to be a product of the first two—that is, an item's memory strength increases as its trace becomes more adequately stored and/or as its trace becomes more retrievable. A composition rule specifies the exact manner in which increments in the storage variable and increments in the retrieval variable produce increments in memory strength; it tells us how S numbers and R numbers combine to produce M numbers.

If, for the sake of simplicity, we restrict attention to arithmetical composition rules, it is clear that various modes of combination are possible. For example, rules such as $S + R = M$, $SR = M$, $aS + bR = M$ (where a and b are constants), $S + R - c = M$ (where c is a constant, $S(R - b) = M$, and $R(S - a) = M$ are all possibilities. As we know, the designed-based strategy makes no scaling assumptions about these three variables. In circumstances of this sort, the strongest assumption that can normally be justified is monotonicity (e.g., cf. Krantz, Luce, Suppes, & Tversky, 1971; Krantz & Tversky, 1971). That is, M values become larger as either S numbers or R numbers become larger. Obviously, the monotonicity assumption does not tell us which of the preceding composition rules is correct, or even if the composition rule is arithmetical, because all of these rules are strongly monotonic. About all that the assumption does is to eliminate nonmonotonic rules of combination. For example, if we say that the three scales can only take on values that are real numbers greater than one, such rules as $S - R = M$, $R - S = M$, $S + 1/R = M$, $1/S + R = M$, $1/S + 1/R = M$, and the like are all elminated because M increases as S and/or R decreases in each case.

Concerning output transformations, there is a fourth variable that must also be considered, namely, subjects' performance on memory tasks. Let us introduce another scale, P, whose numbers represent different levels of performance on such tasks. Since these are memory tasks, performance presumably depends on memory strength; scale values of P are derived in some manner from scale values of M. An output transformation is simply a numerical rule that describes how P values are generated from M values. Some candidate rules are $P = bM$ (where B is a constant), $P = a + bM$ (where a and b are constants), $P = \log M$, and $P = am^b$. As before, the fact that the designed-based approach makes no scaling assumptions means that the precise output transformation for a given experiment is always unknown. Also as before, the strongest assumption that would normally be justified in such an experiment is that P is a monotonic transformation of M:

> The strongest assumption which does seem warranted about the relation between performance scores and memory strength is that the relation is monotonic. . . . That is, the measurement of memory strength via current performance situations can be valid only up to some (unknown) order-preserving transformation. (Nelson, 1978, pp. 453–454)

Technically speaking, the notion of memory strength can now be dispensed with. Since scale values of P are derived from scale values of M, which are in turn derived from scale values of S and R, we can simply think of scale values of P as being derived from scale values of S and R. We know that the strongest assumption that we are willing to make is that P numbers are related to M numbers by some unknown order-preserving transformation and that M numbers are related to S and R numbers by some unknown order-preserving transformation. Consequently, the relationship between memory task performance, on the one hand, and storage/retrieval factors, on the other, can be represented as

$$P = f_r(f_c(S,R)), \qquad (4\text{-}1)$$

where f_c and f_r are strictly monotonic functions. f_c is the unknown composition rule, and f_r is the unknown output transformation.

Equation 4-1 encapsulates what, in the absence of a detailed analysis of measurement scales, can justifiably be supposed about the relationships between children's performance on memory tasks, their ability to store information, and their ability to retrieve information. With the aid of some numerical illustrations, it is easy to see that Equation 4-1 does not permit the sorts of inferences that characterize design-based methods of separating storage and retrieval. For the sake of simplicity, it will be assumed in these illustrations that scale values of P, S, and R are always positive real numbers.

First, we reconsider the study-test technique. Remember that this method assumes that storage factors are more important on study trials than on test trials (or, conversely, that retrieval factors are more important on test trials than on study trials) and that manipulations that have different effects on the two types of trials affect storage and retrieval by different amounts. Now, consider the earlier hypothetical study in which the picture-word variable is manipulated across study and test trials in a 2×2 design, with A and B denoting the study and test manipulations, respectively. In this study, let us suppose that the manipulation has a larger effect on storage than on retrieval. In line with this assumption, assume that the scale values for the four conditions of the study are: (a) $S = 4$ and $R = 4$ for A_1B_1 (word-word); (b) $S = 16$ and $R = 6$ for A_2B_1 (picture-word); (c) $S = 6$ and $R = 8$ for A_1B_2 (word-picture); and (d) $S = 16$ and $R = 10$ for A_2B_2 (picture-picture). Note that these values satisfy the constraint that the manipulation affects storage more than retrieval because the average between-condition difference in scale values is 7.67 for S and 3.33 for R. The scale values are also consistent with the study-test method's assumption that storage factors are more important on study trials than on test trials: The average difference in scale values is 6.50 for conditions that have different A treatments but the same B treatment, and the average difference is 2.50 for conditions that have different B treatments but the same A treatment.

Obviously, what the study-test technique anticipates in this situation is that the picture-word variable will have a larger effect on performance when it is manipulated on study trials than when it is manipulated on test trials. With the aid of Table 4-1, however, it can be seen that the magnitude of the study and test effects will actually depend on the nature of the composition rule. As we just saw, the number of possible composition rules and output transformations is indefinitely large. For present purposes, consideration is restricted to two elementary composition rules and two elementary output transformations. The composition rules are the additive rule $M = S + R$ and the log-additive rule $M = \log S + R$. The output transformations are the additive rule $P = M$ and the logarithmic rule $P = \log M$.[2] It is important to observe that all of these rules satisfy the monotonicity constraint discussed earlier. These four rules have been factorially crossed with each other and with the four conditions of the hypothetical picture-word experiment in Table 4-1. The numbers that appear in the cells of the table are values of the memory performance measure, P, that are computed from the S and R scale values of each treatment combination using a given f_c, f_r rule pair. These numbers are empirical values that would constitute the data of a real experiment.

---

[2] The expressions $P = M$ and $M = S + R$ do not look like the standard linear function $Y = a + bX$. But note that P can be expressed as $P = a + bM$, where $a = 0$ and $b = 1$, and note that M can be expressed as $M = a_1 + b_1S + a_2 + b_2R$, where $a_1 = a_2 = 0$ and $b_1 = b_2 = 1$.

Table 4-1. Some Numerical Examples for the Study-Test Method of
Separating Storage and Retrieval

		Condition and Scale Values			
		$A_1B_1: S = 4$ and $R = 4$	$A_2B_1: S = 16$ and $R = 6$	$A_1B_2: S = 6$ and $R = 8$	$A_2B_2: S = 16$ and $R = 10$
f_c:	$M = S + R$ and				
f_r:	$P = M$	8	22	14	26
f_c:	$M = S + R$ and				
f_r:	$P = \log M$	2.08	3.09	2.64	3.26
f_c:	$M = \log S + R$ and				
f_r:	$P = M$	5.39	8.77	9.79	12.77
f_c:	$M = \log S + R$ and				
f_r:	$P = \log M$	1.69	2.17	2.28	2.55

Note: A_1B_1 = word/word, A_2B_1 = picture/word, A_1B_2 = word/picture, and A_2B_2 = picture/picture.

Although the study-test technique anticipates that the picture-word variable
will have a larger effect when manipulated on study trials than on test trials
(because the theoretical locus of its effect is principally at storage), the numbers
in Table 4-1 are not always consistent with this prediction. If one examines the
first two rows of this table, where the composition rule is linear and the output
transformation varies, the observed values of P are consistent with the
prediction. In the first row, the average difference between conditions with
different A treatments is 13 whereas the average difference between conditions
with different B treatments is 9. In the second row, the average difference
between conditions with different A treatments is .82 whereas the average
difference between conditions with different B treatments is .59. But if one
examines the last two rows, the numbers are inconsistent with the prediction.
Indeed, they are in the opposite direction, and would probably lead to the
conclusion that the retrieval effects of the picture-word manipulation are more
pronounced than its storage effects. In the third row, the average difference
between conditions with different A treatments is 3.69 but the average
difference between conditions with different B treatments is 4.20. In the fourth
row, the average difference between conditions with different A treatments is
.43, but the average difference between conditions with different B treatments is
.49.

Thus, depending on one's scaling assumptions, it is quite possible for the
picture-word manipulation to have a smaller effect on study trials than on test
trials. This occurs *even though* (a) the underlying state of affairs is such that this
variable affects storage more than it affects retrieval, (b) this variable has a
larger storage effect when it is manipulated on study trials than when it is

manipulated on test trials, and (c) the composition rules and output transformations all obey the usual monotonicity assumptions.

Next, we reconsider the different-task technique. It will be recalled that this
method attempts to separate storage and retrieval by administering different
memory measures for the same information, where the measures are presumed
to differ in the extent to which memory strength depends on storage difficulty or
retrieval difficulty. For concreteness, let us assume that there are two target
measures such that memory strength on one task (say, recognition) depends
more on storage difficulty than on the other task (say, recall). Further, let us
suppose that the two tasks are factorially crossed with two age levels in a 2×2
design, where the A factor is recall versus recognition and the B factor is
younger versus older. Last, let us assume that between these two age levels,
retrieval ability develops more than storage ability. In line with these
assumptions, let the scale values of S and R for the four conditions of the
experiment be: (a) $S = 4$ and $R = 8$ for A_1B_1 (younger children's recall); (b)
$S = 16$ and $R = 14$ for A_2B_1 (younger children's recognition); (c) $S = 12$ and
$R = 14$ for A_1B_2 (older children's recall); (d) $S = 28$ and $R = 18$ for A_2B_2
(older children's recognition). Observe that these scale values satisfy all of our
assumptions: The values of both S and R are always larger for recognition than
for recall, meaning that memory strength is always greater for recognition; the S
values are always larger than the R values on recognition and the reverse is true
on recall, meaning that storage is more important on recognition and retrieval is
more important on recall; the age change in S values is larger than the age
change in R values on both tasks but this discrepancy is larger with recognition
than with recall, in line with our assumptions about the comparative rates of
storage development and retrieval development.

In this situation, the logic of the different-task approach anticipates more age
change in recognition performance than in recall performance. As before,
however, Table 4-2 shows that confirmation of such a prediction depends
entirely on scaling considerations. In this table, the same two composition rules
and the same two output transformations as in Table 4-1 have been factorially
crossed with the four conditions of our hypothetical different-task experiment.
The numbers that appear in the cells of Table 4-2 are empirical values of
recognition and recall performance that result when a given composition rule
and a given output transformation are applied to the scale values of S and R that
were mentioned in the preceding paragraph.

The numerical examples in Table 4-2 have been arranged so as to produce
roughly the same conclusions as Table 4-1 and to illustrate a point that is not
apparent from Table 4-1, namely, that the composition rule and the output
transformation both affect the pattern of results. In Table 4-1, only the
composition rule was critical. Regardless of the output transformation,
predictions were confirmed in Table 4-1 whenever the composition rule was
additive and were disconfirmed whenever it was log additive. But confirmation
depends on both factors in Table 4-2. In the first row, as predicted, the average
age difference is 16 for recognition, whereas the average age difference is 14 for

Table 4-2. Some Numerical Examples for the Different Task Method of Separating Storage and Retrieval

		Condition and Scale Values			
		A_1B_1: $S=4$ and $R=8$	A_2B_1: $S=16$ and $R=14$	A_1B_2: $S=12$ and $R=14$	A_2B_2: $S=28$ and $R=18$
f_c:	$M=S+R$ and				
f_r:	$P=M$	12	30	26	46
f_c:	$M=S+R$ and				
f_r:	$P=\log M$	2.49	3.40	3.26	3.83
f_c:	$M=\log S+R$				
f_r:	$P=M$	9.39	16.77	16.49	21.33
f_c:	$M=\log S+R$				
f_r:	$P=\log M$	2.24	2.82	2.80	3.06

Note: A_1B_1 = younger children's recall, A_2B_1 = younger children's recognition, A_1B_2 = older children's recall, and A_2B_2 = older children's recognition.

recall. But the developmental trends are just the opposite in the last three rows, where the age differences in recall are always greater than the age differences in recognition. The exact developmental changes are .77 for recall versus .43 for recognition in Row 2, 7.10 for recall versus 4.56 for recognition in Row 3, and .56 for recall versus .24 for recognition in Row 4. By the logic of the different-task method, these latter results show that retrieval develops more than storage during this age range, despite the fact that we know this interpretation to be mistaken.

We see, then, that depending on the nature of the composition rule and the output transformation, it is possible for performance on two tasks that differ in the relative contributions of storage and retrieval factors to memory strength to give an erroneous picture of the comparative rates of storage and retrieval development. As with the study-test illustration, it is important to note that this happens even though the scale values of S and R that were used are entirely consistent with our key assumptions (i.e., that storage factors are more heavily weighted in recognition than in recall and that storage develops more during the target age range than retrieval does).

The bottom line of this section is that scaling considerations, more particularly the issues of composition rules and output transformations, tend to invalidate the designed-based approach to discriminating storage and retrieval effects in memory development. Although this point was drawn out of two instances of the designed-based approach, it applies to any experimental technique that, first, fails to specify the composition rules that map storage difficulty and retrieval difficulty onto memory strength and that, second, fails to specify the output transformations that relate memory strength to performance measures. With the worked examples in Tables 4-1 and 4-2 in hand, it will not be difficult for readers to convince themselves that other instances of the designed-based approach encounter similar difficulties. In each case, the first step is to select scale values of storage and retrieval that satisfy a method's assumptions, and the second step is to find an appropriate "number game" that violates the method's interpretative logic.

Model-Based Separation

In view of what has just been said, it will come as no surprise that the model-based approach attempts to separate process variables by making fine-grained assumptions about underlying measurement scales. Actually, mathematical models of storage and retrieval development do not normally consist of distinct composition rules and output transformations. This is because, as previously mentioned, it is possible to eliminate the notion of memory strength when both types of rules are known, so values of performance measures can be calculated directly from storage and retrieval values by first applying the composition rule and then applying the output transformation to the result. Thus, mathematical models of the sort that we shall be examining in the remainder of this chapter map storage and retrieval values directly onto values of performance measures by means of functions of the form

$$P = f\{(\theta_S),(\theta_R)\}, \tag{4-2}$$

where f is simply an algebraic rule that does the job of both the f_c and f_r rules in earlier examples, and the terms (θ_S) and (θ_R) are sets of one or more parameters that measure storage factors and retrieval factors, respectively.

Although the meaning of this last statement will become clearer as individual models are considered, there is a technical point and a conceptual point about Equation 4-2 that are worth belaboring here. The technical point is that f is some *well-defined* algebraic function, not an unknown rule that is merely assumed to be at least monotonic. It turns out that this feature is responsible for the major advantage conferred by mathematical models in the interpretation of data. The fact that f is well defined means that it delivers measurements of theoretical processes (storage and retrieval variables in our case) *on a common ratio scale*. As we all remember from our first courses in psychology, ratio-scale measurements are essential if one wishes to draw quantitative conclusions about the relative effects of theoretical variables on performance measures (e.g., "Variable X contributes three times as much to performance as Variable Y," "Variable X develops twice as fast as Variable Y," "Group A has three times as much of Variable X as Group B does"). The other point is that from a conceptual standpoint, mathematical models of storage and retrieval development are not very complicated. Frankly, they are much more economical of hypotheses than qualitative theories are. I mention this because it is common for investigators to suppose that since a little mathematics is involved, any model-based theory must have a complex conceptual infrastructure. In fact, just the opposite is true. Because mathematics *is* involved, it is possible to keep theoretical assumptions to a minimum; many hypotheses that must be built into the assumptive bases of qualitative theories can be treated as empirical questions in a model-based theory. Essentially, Equation 4-2 is about all there is to a mathematical model of storage and retrieval development.

There is a final issue that should be raised before taking up the models themselves. We now know that the model-based approach avoids the interpretative pitfalls of the designed-based approach by specifying the pertinent measurement scales. But in so doing, it is necessary to make some assumptions, algebraic assumptions to be precise. It is reasonable to ask, therefore, whether or not there are any empirical controls over such assumptions. Can hypotheses about how the measurement scales associated with theoretical variables interact to produce performance data be disconfirmed empirically? Since the assumptions of qualitative theories are so often resistant to disconfirmation, this is a critical question.

There are two major ways that a model-based theory can be disconfirmed in data, namely, goodness-of-fit tests and validity tests. Goodness-of-fit tests are purely statistical. They derive from the fact that the algebraic assumptions that comprise a model normally constrain the data of performance measures in certain respects; the data must have specific statistical properties if the assumptions are correct.[3] A goodness-of-fit test is simply a mechanical procedure that decides whether or not the necessary properties are present in sample data. When data do not pass such tests, a model-based theory is automatically rejected. Although validity tests are also statistical, they have conceptual aspects that are absent from goodness-of-fit tests. If the parameters that are used to measure certain theoretical processes in a model actually measure what we say they do, these parameters should react in an appropriate manner to experimental treatments that embody these variables. A validity test, therefore, consists of manipulating treatments that should affect theoretical processes and determining whether or not the parameters that are supposed to measure these processes react to the treatments. Such tests are more theoretical than goodness-of-fit analyses because investigators must decide what sorts of manipulations should affect the target processes.

Owing to the availability of goodness-of-fit tests and validity tests, it is much easier, as a rule, to invalidate a model-based theory than it is to invalidate a qualitative theory (Brainerd, 1983; Wilkinson & Koestler, 1983a). Because the precise implications of qualitative theories for data are frequently obscure, often because of scaling problems such as those we have been examining, years of experimentation may be required before a theory is given up as wrong or

---

[3]The major exception to this rule is when the number of parameters in a model exceeds the number of independent empirical probabilities in the data. Even in this admittedly undesirable situation, goodness-of-fit tests are still sometimes possible (cf. Brainerd, Howe, & Desrochers, 1982). If goodness-of-fit tests are not possible, validity tests may still be possible (cf. Chechile & Meyer, 1976).

unproductive. In contrast, a single study may suffice to disconfirm a model-based theory.

A Short-Term Memory Model

In the next three sections, three storage-retrieval models are reviewed, each of which is defined over a memory paradigm that is readily applied in developmental research. The order of presentation is historical: the model considered in this section appeared in the developmental literature before the models considered in the two sections that follow.

Basic Paradigm and Assumptions

The first model was developed by Checile and Meyer (1976). It was originally intended to measure the storage and retrieval components of forgetting from short-term memory, though we shall see that it can be extended to the storage and retrieval components of *acquisition* on long-term memory tasks. This model has been extensively applied by Chechile and his associates to adult short-term memory (Butler & Chechile, 1976; Chechile & Butler, 1975; Gerrein & Chechile, 1977; Skoff & Chechile, 1977) and, more recently, to memory development (Chechile & Richman, 1982; Chechile, Richman, Topinka, & Ehrensbeck, 1981; Roder & Chechile, 1983).

The key feature of most laboratory procedures for studying short-term memory (e.g., span of immediate recall, Sternberg scanning) is that memory performance is measured within several seconds of the time when material is initially encoded (see Dempster's Chapter in this volume). The particular paradigm for which Chechile's model was devised is the Brown-Peterson distractor task (e.g., Peterson & Peterson, 1959). In the Brown-Peterson procedure, subjects are first presented with a subspan set of to-be-remembered items (e.g., three pictures, three nouns, three consonants). Presentation is followed by a brief interval, normally less than 30 s, during which subjects perform a buffer activity that is supposed to prevent rehearsal of the memory set. This task is always irrelevant to the items in the memory set (e.g., counting backwards by threes from some large number designated by the experimenter). Memory is tested immediately after the buffer activity by administering recall or recognition probes.

Chechile and Meyer (1976) began by observing that there is considerable variance of theoretical opinion as to whether forgetting from short-term memory is chiefly a consequence of losing traces from storage (e.g., Norman & Rumelhart, 1970; Reitman, 1970; Wickelgren, 1973) or a consequence of retrieval failures produced by retroactive and proactive inhibition between traces (e.g., Keppel & Underwood, 1962; Melton, 1963). They proceeded to analyze a typical Brown-Peterson situation in which the memory measure was recall with the aim of deciding exactly "what fraction of forgotten information is due to storage failures and what fraction is due to retrieval failures" (Chechile & Meyer, 1976, p. 269). First, Chechile and Meyer assumed that trace storage can be dichotomized as either "adequate" or "inadequate." This assumption does not imply that storage is an all-or-none process, indeed it was assumed that there is continuous variation in trace strength. The adequate-inadequate dichotomy is merely a threshold notion that entails that for any given measure of memory strength (e.g., recall), trace storage either is or is not sufficient to permit retrieval. Chechile and Meyer introduced the parameter θ_S as their measure of storage adequacy, which they defined as the probability across many Brown-Peterson trials that the memory set is adequately stored. In a real experiment, θ_S is the expected proportion of trials on which storage is sufficient to permit retrieval.

Second, Chechile and Meyer assumed that retrieval can also be dichotomized as adequate or inadequate. That is, if the memory set has been adequately stored, subjects either are able to retrieve enough of this information to produce correct recall or they are unable to retrieve enough information to produce correct recall. Note here that the retrieval dichotomy only applies to trials on which storage is adequate. Across a large number of Brown-Peterson trials, the parameter θ_R was defined as the probability that a sufficiently well-stored trace can be adequately retrieved. In a real experiment, θ_R is the expected proportion of trials with adequate storage on which retrieval is adequate enough to produce correct recall.

If the number of different memory sets being administered is large, then the probability of a correct guess on Brown-Peterson recall trials is effectively zero. Hence, the probability that the memory set cannot be recalled on a given trial, θ_F, is the sum of two probabilities: the probability that the memory set is not adequately stored plus the probability that the memory set is adequately stored but is not retrievable or

$$\theta_F = 1 - \theta_S \theta_R. \tag{4-3}$$

It will not have escaped the reader's attention that we now have a complete model in the sense defined earlier (Equation 4-2), where a performance scale from some memory task (i.e., recall probability on Brown-Peterson trials) has been expressed as a simple algebraic function of a storage scale (i.e., probability of adequate storage on Brown-Peterson trials) and of a retrieval scale (i.e., probability of adequate retrieval on Brown-Peterson trials).

Now that a model is available, it would seem that we can proceed to study the relative contributions of storage and retrieval factors to short-term memory performance by estimating the parameters θ_S and θ_R from Brown-Peterson recall data. Unfortunately, Equation 4-3 poses a technical problem that precludes estimation of these parameters without further elaboration of the experimental paradigm. The problem, common in mathematical psychology, is that of parameter nonidentifiability, which refers to situations in which a mathematical model contains more parameters that measure *theoretical* processes than there are parameters that measure *empirical* events in the experimental paradigm (cf. Brainerd, Howe, & Desrochers, 1982; Restle & Greeno, 1970; Wilkinson, 1982). Conceptually, such a model uses up more degrees of freedom (parameters) than are actually available in the data. It is easy to see that Equation 4-3 is just such a model. On the one hand, there are two theoretical processes that we seek to measure, the probability of adequate storage and the probability of adequate retrieval. But if the only data that we have are correct and incorrect recalls on Brown-Peterson trials, there is only one empirical measure that we can compute, namely, the probability of correct recall across trials. For reasons related to the need to estimate storage and retrieval parameters from data, then, Equation 4-3 is not an entirely satisfactory model.

There are basically two methods of dealing with a nonidentifiability problem. One can either simplify the model or one can increase the complexity of the data so that all of the model's parameters can be estimated. As Equation 4-3 has only two theoretical parameters to begin with, both of which are important, the first strategy is obviously not desirable. Hence, Chechile and Meyer (1976) adopted the second strategy. They made three important additions to the usual Brown-Peterson recall procedure. First, the memory test that followed the buffer activity could be *either* a recall task or a recognition task. In designs with large numbers of trials, half the tests are recognition, half the tests are recall, and subjects are unable to predict which type of test will be administered on any given trial. Second, recognition tests could be of two types: (a) "old" recognition tests, where the item that is presented is the same as the memory set, and (b) "distractor" recognition tests, where the item that is presented is not the same as the memory set. On both types of recognition tests, subjects respond "yes" or "no" accordingly as they think the item is or is not the same as the memory set. Third, on both old recognition and distractor recognition, subjects rate their degree of confidence in each yes-no response on a three point scale, where $3 =$ highest confidence, $2 =$ lower confidence, and $1 =$ lowest confidence.

When the Brown-Peterson procedure has been modified in this manner, there are a total of 11 independent, empirical probabilities that can be measured from the data. On trials where a recall test is administered, there is still one empirical probability, the probability of a successful recall (or of an error). On old recognition trials, there are five empirical probabilities. If we let r_o and $\bar{r}_o$ denote a success ("yes") and an error ("no"), respectively, and if we let the numerals 1–3 denote the respective confidence ratings, then the empirical probabilities for old recognition are: $p\,(r_o, 1), p\,(r_o, 2), p\,(r_o, 3), p\,(\bar{r}_o, 1), p\,(\bar{r}_o, 2)$, and $p\,(\bar{r}_o, 3)$. (There are five independent probabilities here, not six, because any one of the parameters can be computed by subtracting the other five from unity.) On distractor recognition trials, there are five more independent probabilities which result from the factorial composition of a success ("no" $= r_d$) or an error ("yes" $= \bar{r}_d$) with the three confidence ratings, namely, $p\,(r_d, 1), p\,(r_d, 2)$, and so on.

Chechile and Meyer (1976) then extended their original assumptions about Brown-Peterson recall to cover the modified procedure. This consisted of providing new expressions that fit the scheme of Equation 4-2 for each of the empirical probabilities associated with old recognition and distractor recognition. Actually, Chechile and Meyer developed four slightly different models for these empirical probabilities. The only model that will be discussed here is the one that gave the best fit to their data and that has been used in subsequent research with children (Chechile & Richman, 1982; Chechile et al., 1981; Roder & Chechile, 1983).

For old recognition items, there were three main assumptions. First, it was assumed that if an item is adequately stored (with probability θ_S), the subject gives both a correct recognition response ("yes") and the highest confidence rating ("3"). Second, it was assumed that if an item is not adequately stored (with probability $1 - \theta_S$), the subject guesses correctly with probability θ_g or guesses incorrectly with probability $1 - \theta_g$. Third, whenever a subject guesses (correctly or incorrectly), there are characteristic choice-response probabilities associated with each alternative on the confidence scale. If a guess is correct (with probability θ_g), the subject selects confidence ratings, 3, 2, or 1 with probabilities θ_1, θ_2, and $1 - \theta_1 - \theta_2$, respectively. If a guess is wrong (with probability $1 - \theta_g$), the subject selects confidence ratings, 3, 2, or 1 with probabilities θ_3, θ_4, and $1 - \theta_3 - \theta_4$, respectively.

It is now possible to express the empirical probabilities for old recognition as functions of the storage parameter θ_S, the guessing parameter θ_g, and the choice-response parameters $\theta_1 - \theta_4$. The relevant expressions appear in the first five rows of Table 4-3. It should be noted here that the four choice-response parameters are noise parameters in Chechile's model and, consequently, they

Table 4-3. Empirical Recognition Probabilities Expressed as Functions of Storage, Retrieval, Guessing, and Noise Parameters in Chechile's Model

Empirical Probability	Theoretical Expression
Old Recognition	
$p(r_o, 3)$	$\theta_s + (1 - \theta_s)\theta_g\theta_1$
$p(r_o, 2)$	$(1 - \theta_s)\theta_g\theta_2$
$p(r_o, 1)$	$(1 - \theta_s)\theta_g(1 - \theta_1 - \theta_2)$
$p(\overline{r}_o, 3)$	$(1 - \theta_s)(1 - \theta_g)\theta_3$
$p(\overline{r}_o, 2)$	$(1 - \theta_s)(1 - \theta_g)\theta_4$
Distractor Recognition	
$p(r_d, 3)$	$\theta_s + (1 - \theta_s)\theta_g'\theta_5$
$p(r_d, 2)$	$(1 - \theta_s)\theta_g'\theta_6$
$p(r_d, 1)$	$(1 - \theta_s)\theta_g'(1 - \theta_5 - \theta_6)$
$p(\overline{r}_d, 3)$	$(1 - \theta_s)(1 - \theta_g')\theta_7$
$p(\overline{r}_d, 2)$	$(1 - \theta_s)(1 - \theta_g')\theta_8$

will not figure in the subsequent discussion. Thus, there are only two important parameters to bear in mind for old recognition, the storage probability θ_S and the guessing probability θ_g.

For distractor recognition items, Chechile and Meyer made the same three assumptions as for old recognition. (In one model, they assumed that in contrast to old recognition, retrieval failures sometimes occur on distractor items. However, estimated values of a distractor retrieval failure parameter proved to be near zero.) The guessing parameter for distractor recognition is $\theta_{g'}$. The choice-response parameters on correct guesses for 3, 2, and 1 are θ_5, θ_6, and $1 - \theta_5 - \theta_6$, respectively. The choice response parameters on incorrect guesses for 3, 2, and 1 are θ_7, θ_8, and $1 - \theta_7 - \theta_8$, respectively. Note that it is not assumed that the guessing parameter and the four noise parameters are the same for distractor recognition as for old recognition. Any such assumpiton would be inconsistent with the well-known fact that distractor recognition performance is better than old recognition performance.

The empirical probabilities for distractor recognition can now be expressed in terms of the storage parameter, the guessing parameter, and the four noise parameters. The relevant expressions appear in the last five rows of Table 4-3.

To sum up, the Chechile and Meyer model is defined over a modified version of the Brown-Peterson paradigm wherein subjects receive three different types of memory tests (recall, old recognition, distractor recognition) and are required to make three-point confidence ratings on two of these tests. The model itself contains a fairly large number of theoretical parameters. There is one parameter each for the measurement of adequate storage, adequate retrieval, correct guessing on old recognition, and correct guessing on distractor recognition. There are also eight parameters that measure choice-response probabilities associated with confidence ratings. But as the latter are all noise parameters, there are only four parameters that are important in the model, namely, θ_S, θ_R, θ_g, and $\theta_{g'}$.

At this point, it remains to estimate the parameters and fit the model to sample data. This requires a statistical procedure for parameter estimation. The specific procedure devised by Chechile and Meyer (1976) is quite unusual because it does not make use of standard methods such as maximum likelihood, least squares, minimum chi square, and so forth. This procedure will be of considerable interest to readers who are concerned with applying the models discussed in this chapter to their own research. But as it seems likely that most readers are more interested in what the models have revealed about memory development than they are in statistical machinery, the issue of how to estimate parameters has been relegated to the Appendix.

The Data Base

I now present some of the main findings about storage and retrieval that the Chechile model has produced. For convenience, these findings are grouped under two headings. First, there is a brief synopsis of data that pertain to goodness of fit and validity. Although these data are of minimal theoretical interest, they are an essential preliminary if the model is to be used to interpret memory data. Second, there is a discussion of data that bear on the relative contributions of storage and retrieval factors to memory development. As principal interest attaches to developmental questions in this chapter, I shall not discuss purely adult findings under this second heading (but see Butler & Chechile, 1976; Chechile & Butler, 1975; Chechile & Meyer, 1976; Gerrein & Chechile, 1977; Skoff & Chechile, 1977).

Goodness of Fit and Validity. For reasons that are connected to the method of parameter estimation (cf. Appendix), traditional goodness-of-fit tests have not been developed for the Chechile model. However, validity tests are possible, and the results have generally been consistent with what the model antici-pates.

Validity tests, it will be recalled, are broadly concerned with whether the values of a model's parameters that one estimates from sample data behave in a manner that agrees with the model's process assumptions. Two types of validity tests have figured in studies reported by Chechile and his associates. The first and more important type of test is focused on the putative independence of the storage parameter, θ_S, and the retrieval parameter, θ_R. If these parameters measure truly distinct aspects of memory, then they ought to be stochastically independent in any subject population. Hence, if it were possible to estimate these parameters separately for each subject in a study, the paired estimates should be uncorrelated across subjects. With the Chechile model, estimates for individual subjects are possible (cf. Appendix). In fact, the method of data analysis that has been used in most studies has been to estimate the parameters for individual subjects and then to perform analyses of variance on these data.

The independence of θ_S and θ_R has been tested in all of the studies reported by Checile and his associates. In both adults and children, estimates of these parameters have been consistently found to be uncorrelated. For example, Chechile and Butler (1975) estimated the parameters for individual under-graduates who participated in a release from proactive interference experiment that involved 33 four-trial blocks of Brown-Peterson trials. Across subjects and blocks, the correlation between θ_S and θ_R was only $-.01$ for Trials 1 and 2 and only $-.06$ for Trials 3 and 4. In a later study with first graders, sixth graders, and undergraduates, the average correlation between the two parameters was .06. It appears, then, that θ_S and θ_R do indeed measure separate aspects of memory.

The other type of validity test is concerned with how the observed values of the four interesting parameters (θ_g, $\theta_{g'}$, θ_s, and θ_R) vary as functions of experimental manipulations. The studies reported by Chechile and his associates contain many findings that are tantamount to validity tests of this sort. The following results are mentioned as illustrations.

1. The parameters θ_g and $\theta_{g'}$ measure the probability of guessing correctly on old recognition items and distractor recognition items, respectively. It has been noted that old recognition performance is normally worse than distractor performance, and the model anticipates that this is a consequence of more accurate guessing on the latter items. Hence, one would expect that $\theta_{g'}$ should be larger than θ_g. This prediction has been confirmed in sample data. Chechile and Meyer (1976, Figure 10), for example, found that the guessing probability for old recognition was in the .5 to .7 range, whereas the guessing probability for distractor recognition was in the .8 to .9 range.

2. Next, consider what the effects of certain temporal manipulations on the storage and retrieval parameters should be in the modified Brown-Peterson paradigm. First, how should these parameters respond to an increase in the retention interval between the termination of the buffer activity and the onset of the recall or recognition test? As this manipulation should increase the chances that a trace is lost from short-term memory (storage failure) or that retrieval plans for stored traces are lost (retrieval failure), the storage and retrieval parameters should both be affected. Consistent with this expectation, Chechile and Meyer (1976, Experiment 1) found that θ_S and θ_R both decreased monotonically as the retention interval was increased from 0 to 12 s. Second, how should these parameters react to changes in the amount of time to respond that is permitted on recall or recognition tests? Since no additional opportunities to study the memory set are involved in this manipulation, its only effect should be on retrieval. The manipulation should allow more opportunities for retrieval operations to locate stored traces, which means that θ_R but not θ_S ought to increase as the amount of time for responding is increased. As predicted, Chechile and Meyer (1976, Experiment 2) observed that the retrieval probability was greater for a 3½- than for a 1½-sec response period, but the storage probability was unaffected.

3. Suppose that the items in a memory set are presented serially rather than simultaneously. Also, suppose that a supraspan number of items (e.g., nine or more) is presented so that the entire list cannot be held in short-term memory. On such tasks, the familiar bowed serial position curve will be obtained on memory tests. How should the storage and retrieval parameters contribute to the primacy and recency effects on serial position curves? Presumably, both effects should be chiefly a consequence of storage difficulty. Concerning primacy, the first few items on a list should be more distinctive and, therefore, their traces should be more likely to be transferred to long-term memory on study trials. Concerning recency, the last few items on a supraspan list may be retained in short-term memory. As predicted, Skoff and Chechile (1977) have found that values of θ_S follow the usual bowed curve when separate estimates are computed for different serial positions, whereas values of θ_R do not change very much as a function of serial position.

Although other validity results from Chechile's research program could be mentioned, these three illustrations are ample to establish the basic point: The signals from validity tests are positive enough to justify applying the model to the study of memory development.

Developmental Data. To date, Chechile and his associates have reported three studies with children (Chechile & Richman, 1982; Chechile et al., 1981; Roder & Chechile, 1983). I briefly summarize the major developmental findings of these studies.

In the initial experiment by Chechile et al. (1981), the subjects were presented with 5-item memory sets (pictures) using the modified Brown-Peterson procedure. A total of 18 such sets were administered to each subject. The age levels studied were first grade, sixth grade, and undergraduate. There were two rehearsal conditions at each age level; half the subjects were instructed to rehearse the picture names during the presentation-test interval and half were not. An important general finding was that storage was easier than retrieval at all age levels. Across the 18 treatment combinations, the mean value of the storage parameter was .80 and the mean value of the retrieval parameter was .50. The main results of developmental interest were: (a) The observed value of the retrieval parameter θ_R increased between first and sixth grade and between sixth grade and college; (b) the observed value of the storage parameter θ_S increased between first and sixth grade but *not* between sixth grade and college; and (c) the old recognition guessing parameter θ_g was completely invariant with age, and there were only very small increases in the distractor recognition guessing parameter $\theta_{g'}$. Further, there was an interesting sex difference. Whereas the two guessing parameters and the storage parameter did not vary between sexes, the estimates of the retrieval parameters were consistently larger for females than for males. The most interesting theoretical conclusions that are suggested by these results are that early age differences in short-term memory performance may be due to improvements in both the capacity of the short-term store (as measured by the storage failure rate) and the efficiency of processing (as measured by the retrieval failure rate), and that later age differences may be due to improvements in processing efficiency but not sheer capacity. Moreover, it may be that the processing efficiency of females' short-term memories, but not their storage capacity, is superior to that of males.

In the experiment by Chechile and Richman (1982), the subjects were presented with supraspan word lists (nine items) in a free recall design that was modified to include recognition tests. There were two age levels, kindergarten and second grade. Half the second graders learned the same list as the kindergarteners. The other half learned a different list that was designed to equate developmental differences in word meaningfulness. Although the model's parameters could be estimated for the second graders, they were not estimated for kindergarteners because certain qualitative findings suggested that the recognition tests were not good measures of memory strength for these children. In particular, accuracy of performance on recognition items depended on their order of presentation, and high-confident recognition was not generally superior to recall. As the model's parameters could not be estimated for the younger children, direct developmental comparisons of parameter values were not possible. However, there was one interesting qualitative finding. While second graders who learned the same list as kindergarteners showed the usual age superiority, second graders who learned a list of age-equivalent meaningfulness did not perform better than kindergarteners, a finding that has also been reported by Richman, Nida, and Pittman (1976). Chechile and Richman explained this result by advancing a "hardware invariance hypothesis," according to which the basic hardware of memory does not change during childhood, and the usual age differences that one observes on memory tasks are consequences of the increasing richness of semantic memory.

The Roder and Chechile (1983) study was concerned with an important applied question about memory development: What are the loci of short-term memory differences between reading-disabled children and nondisabled children? The subjects were three groups of fourth graders who had been classified as poor, average, or superior readers by virtue of reading comprehension tests. All subjects received a total of 16 memory sets to remember via the modified Brown-Peterson procedure. There were six items in each set (words) and the items were presented successively rather than simultaneously. The words in the individual sets were either (a) phonologically similar (rhyming words), (b) orthographically similar, (c) semantically similar (words representing the same concept), or (d) dissimilar on all three dimensions. The first important result was that the storage parameter varied as a function of reading ability, but the retrieval and guessing parameters did not. The mean value of θ_S was .68 for the pooled data of average and superior readers, whereas the mean value of this parameter was .59 for poor readers. A second important finding was that both the storage parameter and the retrieval parameter reacted to the similarity manipulation, but neither guessing parameter was affected (see Bjorklund's Chapter in this volume for possible theoretical explanations). The mean values of the storage parameter were .69 (semantic similarity), .67 (phonetic similarity), .59 (unrelated), and .47 (orthographic similarity). Thus, articulatory and conceptual similarity improved storage, relative to unrelated words, while visual similarity interfered with storage. The mean values of the retrieval parameter were .55 (semantic similarity), .39 (phonetic similarity), .28 (orthographic similarity), and .26 (unrelated). Note the following interesting differences between the storage and retrieval effects: Semantic similarity does not improve storage relative to phonetic similarity, but retrieval is better with semantic similarity than with phonetic similarity; orthographic similarity interferes with storage relative to unrelated words, but retrieval is comparable for unrelated and orthographically similar words; and the retrieval probabilities are lower than the storage probabilities with all four types of lists.

To conclude, applications of the Chechile model to short-term memory situations have produced these main developmental findings. First, subjects at different developmental levels tend to differ both in their ability to retain traces in storage and in their ability to retrieve traces on test trials. Second, storage and retrieval make different contributions to memory development during different age ranges. The suggestion is that storage and retrieval development make roughly equivalent contributions during childhood, but retrieval development predominates thereafter. Third, it is easier to store traces than it is to retrieve them at all age levels. Fourth, sex differences in memory development, which have traditionally been difficult to detect with laboratory memory tasks (Maccoby & Jacklin, 1974), may be confined to retrieval development. Fifth, item similarity manipulations, which are known to have powerful effects on children's memory performance (e.g., Moely, 1977), affect both ease of storage and ease of retrieval.

A Long-Term Memory Model

Strictly speaking, the model to be reviewed now is the oldest of the three models considered in this chapter. However, its use in the study of memory development has been somewhat more recent than the Chechile model.

Assumptions and Paradigm

This model was not originally developed to measure storage and retrieval. It first appeared in the learning literature more than two decades ago in a dissertation study by Theios (1961). It has subsequently been applied to data from many conditioning and learning paradigms, some of them memory tasks. The application of the model to the measurement of storage and retrieval is due to the pioneering work of Greeno and his associates (Greeno, 1968, 1970; Greeno, James, & DaPolito, 1971; Greeno, James, DaPolito, & Polson, 1978; Humphreys & Greeno, 1970).

There is a large group of animal and human learning tasks whose structures make it impossible for a naive subject to respond correctly before the first learning trial (i.e., the "guessing probability" is effectively zero). By and large, these are *production* tasks in that subjects are required to generate correct responses rather than select correct responses from a small number of alternatives made available by the experimenter. Some animal paradigms that fit this description are avoidance conditioning, escape conditioning, and Pavlovian conditioning. Some corresponding human paradigms include the learning of certain types of logical rules by children, the learning of certain types of search strategies by infants, and Pavlovian conditioning. For present purposes, however, the focal class of production paradigms is the list-learning tasks of the memory laboratory, *where the performance measure is recall*. This class includes several paradigms, with some familiar examples being cued recall, free recall, paired-associate learning, serial learning, and *AB-AB$_r$* transfer.

In any production task with the structure $S_1 T_1 S_2 T_2 \ldots$, where S indicates a learning trial and T indicates a test trial (performance measure), three types of error-success protocols are observed for individual subjects and items: (a) a string of successes without any errors; (b) an initial string of errors followed by a criterion run of successes; and (c) an initial string of errors, followed by a string of mixed errors and successes, followed by a criterion run of successes. With most production tasks, Type c protocols predominate, and in fairly difficult production situations (e.g., Pavlovian conditioning, memorizing a moderately long list of nonsense syllables), Type a and Type b protocols do not occur at all.

In the early 1960s, several investigators conjectured that it might be possible to account for the error-success data of such tasks with a very simple model (Bower & Theios, 1964; Crothers, 1964; Kintsch, 1963; Theios, 1961; Theios & Hakes, 1962). This model assumes that learning involves exactly two discrete stages. Specifically, it assumes that learning consists of (a) an initial "unlearned" State U in which only errors can occur, (b) an intermediate "partially learned" State P in which both errors (substate P_E) and successes (substate P_C) can occur, and (c) a terminal "well-learned" State L in which only successes can occur. Most important of all, it is assumed that transitions between these states consist of discrete, all-or-none jumps. From a psychological point of view, this latter assumption means that learning consists of two critical events, escape from the unlearned state and escape from the partially learned state. Taken together, the four assumptions define a general class of three-state Markov processes with no successes in the initial state (Greeno, 1968).

Over the years, models from this class have been successfully applied to the data of several production paradigms (for a review, see Greeno, 1974). Illustrations include rat avoidance conditioning (Theios, 1963), rat escape conditioning (Theios, 1965), Pavlovian conditioning in rabbits (Theios & Brelsford, 1966), children's learning of logical concepts (Brainerd, 1982a), and infant's learning of search strategies (Heth & Cornell, 1983). There have also been many successful applications to recall memorization tasks with both adults (e.g., Brainerd, Howe, & Desrochers, 1980; Brainerd et al., 1981; Greeno, 1968; Greeno et al., 1971; Greeno et al., 1978; Humphreys & Greeno, 1970; Kintsch, 1963; Waugh & Smith, 1962) and children (Brainerd, 1982a; Brainerd & Howe, 1982; Brainerd et al., 1984).

The three-state Markov models that have figured in individual studies have varied considerably in their complexity, as measured by their total numbers of free parameters. The most general of these models that is currently in use is a model with 11 free parameters, and this is the storage-retrieval model that will be examined here. We shall first consider the model as an abstract learning system and then reconsider it under storage-retrieval interpretations. Throughout, it should be borne in mind that the memory paradigm over which the model is defined is just about any list-learning situation where performance is assessed by some sort of recall test.

An Abstract Description of Learning. The model describes learning in production experiments with the standard $S_1 T_1 S_2 T_2 \ldots$ structure as follows. First, consider the effects of the first learning opportunity (i.e., S_1). Before this event, naturally, all protocols are in the initial unlearned State U. As a consequence of S_1, some protocols escape the unlearned state (with probability a'), but others remain there (with probability $1 - a'$). Those protocols that escape the unlearned state either jump directly to the well-learned State L (with probability b') or they enter the intermediate partially learned State P (with probability $1 - b'$). For protocols that enter the partially learned state, the subject may either make an error on T_1 (with probability r) or a success (with probability $1 - r$).

On the first test trial following the first learning opportunity, then, the protocols can occoupy four distinct states: State U (with probability $1 - a'$), State L (with probability $a'b'$), State P_E (with probability $a'(1 - b')r$), and State P_C (with probability $a'(1 - b')(1 - r))$. These learning events and their associated probabilities are summarized in the first four rows of Table 4-4.

Next, consider what may happen between T_1 and the next learning trial (i.e., S_2). If a protocol is in State U, it stays there. If a protocol is in State L, it stays there. But if a protocol is in State P, it can either remain where it is (with probability $1 - f$) or it may drop back to State U (with probability f). Thus, f is a "forgetting" probability.

Now, consider the effects of the second learning opportunity. If a protocol is in State U, it may either escape this state (with probability a) or remain there (with probability $1 - a$). The former protocols may either jump directly to the well-learned State L (with probability b) or enter the intermediate partially learned State P (with probability $1 - b$). For protocols of the latter type, the subject either makes an error on T_2 (with probability e) or makes a success (with probability $1 - e$). If a protocol is in State P_E, it may either stay in this state (with probability $(1 - d)(1 - g)$) or jump to State P_C (with probability $(1 - d)g$) or jump to State L (with probability d). If a protocol is in State P_C, it may either remain in this state (with probability $(1 - c)h$) or jump to State P_E (with probability $(1 - c)(1 - h)$) or jump to State L (with probability c). These learning events and their associated probabilities are summarized in the last ten rows of Table 4-4.

Finally, consider the effects of all subsequent learning oppportunities (i.e., S_2, S_3, ...). It is logically possible for a protocol to be in any one of the four states at the start of any of these learning trials, though the probability that a protocol has not yet entered the terminal well-learned state becomes vanishingly small as the number of previous learning opportunities becomes very large. On all of these subsequent trials, the learning probabilities (i.e., interstate transition probabilities) just described for S_2 are assumed to apply.

Storage-Retrieval Interpretations. Depending on the particular learning paradigm to which it is applied, the 11 parameters of this abstract learning system (a', a, b', b, c, d, e, f, g, h, r) can be assigned psychological interpretations based

Table 4-4. Possible Learning Events on the First and Second Learning Trials in the Two-Stage Model

Learning Event	Probability
Trial 1	
$U \rightarrow U$	$1 - a'$
$U \rightarrow P_E$	$a'(1 - b')r$
$U \rightarrow P_C$	$a'(1 - b')(1 - r)$
$U \rightarrow L$	$a'b'$
Trial 2	
$U \rightarrow U$	$1 - a$
$U \rightarrow P_E$	$a(1 - b)e$
$U \rightarrow P_C$	$a(1 - b)(1 - e)$
$U \rightarrow L$	ab
$P_E \rightarrow P_E$	$(1 - d)(1 - g)$
$P_E \rightarrow P_C$	$(1 - d)g$
$P_E \rightarrow L$	d
$P_C \rightarrow P_E$	$(1 - c)(1 - h)$
$P_C \rightarrow P_C$	$(1 - c)h$
$P_C \rightarrow L$	c

on some theory or theories. In the case of list-learning tasks that involve recall, Greeno and his associates have suggested that storage-retrieval interpretations can be assigned to these parameters, a suggestion that was first made in connection with paired-associate learning (Humphreys & Greeno, 1970). I summarize the basic rationale for this suggestion and then present detailed storage-retrieval interpretations of the 11 parameters.

1. Rationale. In recall memorization experiments, precautions are normally taken to insure that a correct response cannot be made by merely retaining an item in short-term memory. These precautions include such things as inserting several seconds of irrelevant buffer activity between each study and test trial of free and cued recall tasks, and requiring that large numbers of items intervene between successive study and test trials for a given item on paired-associate and serial learning tasks. When such precautions are in place, it would not seem possible for subjects to make a correct recall before a permanent trace of the target item has been deposited in long-term memory. Hence, it is natural to identify the abstract event of escaping State U with the psychological event of storing a trace in long-term memory. Thus, a' becomes the probability of depositing a trace on the first study trial, a becomes the probability of depositing a trace on all subsequent study trials, and f becomes the probability of losing a trace from storage.

After a trace has been stored, the subject may not be able to recall the item infallibly on test trials; successes and errors may both occur. Hence, it has seemed natural to identify the abstract event of escaping State P with the psychological event of learning to retrieve a stored trace. The parameters b', b, c, and d, then, measure the difficulty of acquiring a reliable retrieval operation for a stored trace.

Last, there are the four parameters, e, g, h, and r, that give the probability of errors and successes on various types of trials in State P. According to the interpretations so far, an item in State U has not yet been stored, and an item in State L has been stored with a reliable retrieval operation being available for the trace. Items in State P have been stored and can sometimes be retrieved, but retrieval is not yet infallible. The actual level of retrieval accuracy in State P may vary from only slightly better than zero to only slightly worse than perfect. The parameters e, g, h, and r measure just how accurate State P retrieval is. Halff (1977) introduced the useful terms *heuristic retrieval* and *algorithmic retrieval* to distinguish imperfect retrieval in State P from perfect retrieval in State L.

The essential argument, then, is that because recall would seem to be impossible before a permanent trace has been stored, we can identify storage with the initial unlearned state and retrieval with the intermediate partially learned state. The exact definitions are: State U = trace unstored, State P = trace stored but retrieval fallible, and State L = trace stored and retrieval infallible.

2. Detailed Definitions. Some rather more specific interpretations of the model's 11 parameters have been used in recent research, especially in developmental studies. These interpretations, which I now summarize, are outlined in Table 4-5.

The detailed interpretations of the State U parameters are the same as before—that is, a' is the probability of storing a trace on the first trial, a is the probability of storing a trace on later trials, and f is the probability of losing a previously stored trace. Note, however, that these parameters allow one to investigate whether or not storage becomes easier as trials progress (i.e., a' vs. a) and whether the difficulty of fixing a permanent trace depends more on initial storage difficulty or on the tendency to lose traces (i.e., a' and a vs. f).

The remaining parameters, as we saw, can be partitioned into a subset of four parameters (b', b, c, and d) that measures the difficulty of retrieval *learning* and a subset of four parameters (e, g, h, and r) that measures the accuracy of retrieval *performance* prior to the acquisition of a retrieval algorithm. Taking the learning parameters first, it may be that retrieval learning can occur *before* a trace is stored as well as after it is stored. That is, if storage and retrieval are truly distinct processes, there is no compelling reason to suppose that the processes that constitute learning to retrieve cannot occur simultaneously with the processes that constitute trace storage. Consequently, it would be desirable to have separate measures of the difficulty of retrieval learning *before and after* a trace is stored. This separation is possible with the four retrieval learning parameters. Recall that b' and b give the probability of jumping directly to State

Table 4-5. Theoretical Interpretations of the 11 Parameters of the Two-Stage Model

Parameter	Interpretation
Storage	
a'	Probability of storing a trace on Trial 1
a	Probability of storing a trace on any trial after Trial 1
f	Probability of losing a previously stored trace
Retrieval Learning	
b'	For traces stored on Trial 1, the probability that no further retrieval learning is needed
b	For traces stored after Trial 1, the probability that no further retrieval learning is needed
c	The probability of learning a retrieval algorithm after a success in State P
d	The probability of learning a retrieval algorithm after an error in State P
Retrieval Performance	
$1 - r$	For items entering State P on Trial 1, the probability of a success
$1 - e$	For items entering State P after Trial 1, the probability of a success
g	For two consecutive trials in State P, the probability that a success follows an error
h	For two consecutive trials in State P, the probability that a success follows a success

L upon leaving State U. In storage-retrieval terminology, these parameters give the probability that retrieval learning is already complete (i.e., a retrieval algorithm is already available) at the time that a trace is stored. The parameters c and d, on the other hand, give the probability of jumping to State L when a protocol is in State P. Hence, these parameters give the probability of completing retrieval learning after a trace is stored. The parameters c and d also allow one to distinguish between the relative difficulty of retrieval learning following successful recall (parameter c) and unsuccessful recall (parameter d). This is a useful distinction because some theorists have contended that successes are more important than errors because they act as additional study trials, whereas as other theorists have suggested that errors are more important than successes because they signal subjects that further mnemonic effort is required (see Brainerd et al., 1984; Greeno, 1974; Halff, 1977).

Turning to the remaining four parameters, we have already seen that they measure the overall level of retrieval accuracy between the time a trace is stored and the time a retrieval algorithm is learned. However, they measure retrieval accuracy at different points in State P. The parameter r is the probability that retrieval fails on the first test trial after storage occurs, if storage occurred on the first study trial. The parameter e is the probability that retrieval fails on the first test trial after storage occurs, if storage occurs on some study trial after the first one. The parameter g is the probability that retrieval succeeds on any test trial *after* the first test trial in State P, if an error occurred on the immediately preceding test trial for that item. The parameter h is the probability that retrieval succeeds on any test trial *after* the first test trial in State P, if a success occurred on the immediately preceding test trial for that item. Because of the distinctions between these four retrieval performance parameters, one can examine a variety of questions about the accuracy of retrieval at different points between storage and the acquisition of a retrieval algorithm.

Statistical Methodology

To use this model to interpret data from recall paradigms, statistical procedures are required for estimating the parameters and for evaluating goodness of fit. Because three-state Markov processes have been in use for many years, the associated statistical machinery has reached a high level of refinement (for a review, see Brainerd, Howe, & Desrochers, 1982). As with the other two models, the details of the parameter estimation and goodness-of-fit procedures have been relegated to the Appendix. Here, I discuss only some qualitative features of these procedures that are relevant to the subsequent review of experimental findings.

The parameter estimation and goodness-of-fit methodologies for three-state Markov processes, which rely on the theory of maximum likelihood, date from an important paper by Greeno (1968). It is possible to write a likelihood function for the 11-parameter system just described that expresses the a posteriori probability (likelihood) of the data of recall experiments in terms of the 11 parameters (Brainerd, Howe, & Kingma, 1982, Equations 30–32). The parameters are estimated by using some standard computer optimization algorithm (SIMPLEX, STEPIT, etc.) to minimize this likelihood function.

Following Greeno's (1968) original recommendations, goodness-of-fit tests for three-state Markov models have usually been of two types, namely, *necessity* tests and *sufficiency* tests. Recall that these models assume that learning involves exactly two stages (escaping U and escaping P), no less and no more. Necessity tests ask whether it is really essential to assume two stages or whether one can account for recall data just as well by assuming that learning involves only one stage. The necessity test for the present 11-parameter model can be found in Brainerd, Howe, & Kingma (1982, Equation 38).

Sufficiency tests, on the other hand, ask whether two stages are adequate to account for recall data or whether models that assume three or more stages do a better job. Two types of sufficiency tests have been developed. The first and older variety involves detailed comparisons of the predicted and observed distributions of various statistics of recall data. For the sake of comprehensiveness, separate predicted-observed comparisons are usually made for statistics that are concerned primarily with escape from State U (e.g., total errors before the first success), for statistics that are primarily concerned with escape from State P (e.g., total errors after first success), and for statistics that are concerned with the process as a whole (e.g., the trial number of the last error). The relevant tests for the present 11-parameter model can be found in Brainerd, Howe, and Kingma (1982, Equations 47a–52b). The second and more recent type of sufficiency test involves computing only a single likelihood ratio. This test, which can be found in Brainerd (1984, Equation 8), evaluates the null hypothesis that the likelihood of the data under the present 11-parameter model is not significantly smaller than the likelihood of the data under any model that assumes more than 11 free parameters.

The Data Base

Goodness of Fit and Validity. As would be expected from its longer history, the data on goodness of fit and validity are far more extensive for this model than for the other two models considered in this chapter. An exhaustive review of studies published through 1978 may be found in Greeno et al. (1978), and review of the subsequent literature may be found in Howe (1982).

Taking goodness of fit first, the evidence from both necessity tests and sufficiency tests has been quite consistent. Regarding necessity tests, the two-stage model has almost always passed necessity tests in applications to recall data, regardless of whether the subjects have been undergraduates or children. I know of only two studies in the literature in which necessity tests showed that a one-stage model was adequate to account for recall data: Humphreys and Yuille (1973) obtained this result with undergraduates who memorized short paired-associate lists comprised of very easy words, and Brainerd et al. (1981) obtained this result with undergraduates who were relearning paired-associate lists that had been memorized to a stringent acquisition criterion one week earlier. Some illustrative necessity test results appear in Table 4-6. These data are from an experiment reported by Brainerd, Howe, and Desrochers (1982) in which the subjects were undergraduates, sixth graders, and second graders. The subjects at each age level memorized one of four types of paired-associate lists (picture-picture, picture-word, word-picture, and word-word). The test for one-stage versus two-stage learning in Table 4-6 is a χ^2 statistic with three degrees of freedom, which means that the critical value (.05 level) for concluding that memorization involved more than one stage is 7.81. Note that all 12 tests for this experiment exceeded the critical value by a wide margin; the average value of the test statistic was 222.96.

The results of sufficiency tests have been similarly positive. In most experiments, three-state Markov models have been able to predict fine-grain features of observed statistics of recall data to a remarkably close approximation; there has been strong support for the conclusion that recall memorization involves no more than two stages. As an illustration, I report some necessity

Table 4-6. Illustrative Necessity Tests for Paired-Associate Data

	Statistic		
List	$-2 \log_e \hat{L}_8$	$-2 \log_e \hat{L}_5$	$x^2(3)$
Adult			
Picture-picture	3,107.94	3,426.47	318.53
Picture-word	2,399.92	2,402.11	142.87
Word-picture	3,464.56	3,746.49	280.93
Word-word	3,054.70	3,324.02	269.32
Grade 6			
Picture-picture	1,107.48	1,167.67	60.19
Picture-word	1,225.35	1,256.52	31.17
Word-picture	1,565.52	1,680.18	114.66
Word-word	1,764.59	1,955.22	190.63
Grade 2			
Picture-picture	1,170.21	1,285.87	115.66
Picture-word	1,515.66	1,675.97	160.31
Word-picture	1,558.44	1,998.52	440.08
Word-word	2,277.08	2,828.30	551.22

tests for adult data in Table 4-7 and some necessity tests for child data in Table 4-8. The data in Table 4-7 are from an experiment by Brainerd et al. (1981) in which undergraduates memorized four types of paired-associate lists. For each of these list conditions, Table 4-7 gives the observed distributions of three learning statistics (errors before first success, errors after first success, and the learning curve) along with the corresponding distributions predicted by the two-stage model. Note that the observed-predicted correspondences are virtually exact for all conditions. The data in Table 4-8 are from five experiments with elementary schoolers involving a total of 14 different list conditions (Brainerd, 1983). The children memorized paired-associate lists in some experiments and free recall lists in others. Methodological details about list conditions and the ages of the subjects appear in Table 4-8. This table contains the observed means and variances of four learning statistics (total errors, errors before first success, length of error runs after first success, and length of success runs before the last error) together with the corresponding means and variances predicted by the two-stage model. Note that there is again close correspondence. Of the 56 possible observed-predicted comparisons in Table 4-8, there was only one significant difference.

Turning to validity data, recall that two types of validity evidence have been gathered for the Chechile model, namely, evidence that storage and retrieval parameters measure independent processes and evidence that these parameters respond appropriately to experimental manipulations. Both types of data are

Table 4-7. Observed and Predicted Values of Three Learning Statistics for
Adult Paired-Associate Data

Statistic and List	Probability of k										
	0	1	2	3	4	5	6	7	8	9	$\geqq 10$
Number of Errors Before the First Success											
Picture-picture											
Observed	.25	.23	.19	.14	.09	.04	.02	.02	.01	.01	.01
Predicted	.25	.27	.17	.11	.07	.05	.03	.02	.01	.01	.01
Picture-word											
Observed	.39	.24	.16	.08	.05	.03	.02	.00	.01	.01	.01
Predicted	.39	.24	.15	.09	.06	.03	.01	.01	.01	.01	.01
Word-picture											
Observed	.26	.27	.15	.10	.08	.04	.03	.03	.01	.02	.02
Predicted	.26	.26	.16	.11	.07	.05	.03	.02	.01	.01	.01
Word-word											
Observed	.30	.25	.17	.12	.06	.03	.02	.02	.02	.01	.02
Predicted	.30	.25	.16	.10	.07	.04	.03	.01	.01	.00	.03
Length of Error Runs After the First Success											
Picture-picture											
Observed	.70	.20	.06	.02	.01						
Predicted	.68	.22	.07	.02	.01						
Picture-word											
Observed	.74	.16	.07	.02	.01						
Predicted	.73	.20	.05	.01	.00						
Word-picture											
Observed	.69	.17	.06	.03	.02	.02	.01	.00	.01	.01	
Predicted	.60	.16	.10	.06	.04	.02	.01	.01	.00	.00	
Word-word											
Observed	.68	.17	.10	.02	.03						
Predicted	.67	.15	.08	.05	.03						
Number of Errors on the ith Test Trial											
Picture-picture											
Observed	.74	.55	.40	.27	.21	.17	.11	.07	.06	.03	
Predicted	.74	.52	.39	.24	.21	.15	.11	.07	.05	.03	
Picture-word											
Observed	.60	.40	.25	.17	.11	.10	.06	.05	.05	.02	
Predicted	.60	.41	.29	.21	.14	.10	.07	.05	.03	.02	
Word-picture											
Observed	.74	.51	.40	.32	.23	.18	.14	.10	.08	.06	
Predicted	.74	.53	.42	.31	.24	.18	.14	.11	.08	.06	
Word-word											
Observed	.69	.48	.31	.23	.17	.13	.12	.10	.09	.05	
Predicted	.69	.48	.36	.27	.19	.15	.11	.08	.06	.05	

Table 4-8. Observed and Predicted Values of the Means and Variances of Four Learning Statistics for Child Data

Experiment	T		FC		LE		LC	
	μ	σ^2	μ	σ^2	μ	σ^2	μ	σ^2
Experiment 1								
Pictures								
Observed	2.30	11.67	1.78	8.11	1.77	2.04	1.67	1.39
Predicted	2.27	8.71	1.82	12.59	1.87	1.85	1.67	1.11
Words								
Observed	3.58	16.86	2.84	11.56	1.94	2.40	1.67	2.92
Predicted	2.87	10.27	2.89	10.83	2.08	2.04	1.69	1.19
Experiment 2								
Pictures								
Observed	2.43	10.87	1.85	6.62	2.42	3.11	1.37	.50
Predicted	1.82	5.59	1.80	5.98	2.27	1.35	1.35	.48
Words								
Observed	6.02	28.51	4.06	23.72	2.45	4.77	1.82	1.48
Predicted	7.38	48.29	4.19	20.80	2.90	2.90	1.82	1.48
Picture-word								
Observed	3.00	13.39	2.11	8.15	2.17	4.00	1.54	.76
Predicted	3.45	14.35	2.43	8.24	2.32	2.32	1.54	.83
Word-picture								
Observed	4.56	22.07	3.00	14.26	2.23	3.49	1.46	1.11
Predicted	5.09	27.12	3.10	13.47	2.50	2.52	1.56	.89
Experiment 3								
Pictures								
Observed	1.48	1.61	.97	1.70	1.61	1.53	1.14	1.00
Predicted	1.25	.75	.73	.89	1.50	1.52	1.49	.74
Words								
Observed	2.80	14.86	1.78	8.84	1.84	3.24	1.77	1.64
Predicted	3.03	12.29	1.96	9.45	1.93	1.95	1.87	1.67
Picture-word								
Observed	1.92	8.26	1.20	3.77	1.90	1.83	1.61	1.10
Predicted	2.14	7.19	1.74	5.37	2.02	2.00	1.60	.92
Word-picture								
Observed	2.19	4.66	1.24	3.48	1.74	1.48	1.76	1.50
Predicted	1.65	4.95	.93	1.78	1.88	1.86	1.86	1.58
Experiment 4								
Serial presentation								
Observed	1.73	2.49	1.18	2.04	1.43	1.77	1.67	.85
Predicted	1.91	3.25	.96	1.18	1.34	1.43	1.70	1.26
Random presentation								
Observed	2.40	4.43	1.32	2.73	1.49	1.59	1.94	1.62
Predicted	3.22	10.42	1.74	1.24	1.74	1.75	1.92	1.78

Table 4-8. *(Continued)*

Experiment	T		FC		LE		LC	
	μ	σ^2	μ	σ^2	μ	σ^2	μ	σ^2
Experiment 5								
Serial presentation								
Observed	2.20	2.05	.88	1.22	1.26	.37	1.57	.83
Predicted	1.42	2.01	.67	.63	1.28	1.27	1.59	.93
Random presentation								
Observed	1.46	1.59	.84	1.14	1.44	1.11	1.61	.82
Predicted	1.17	1.43	.71	1.27	1.41	1.41	1.61	.99

Note: T is the total number of errors per item, FC is the total number of errors before the first success, LE is the length of consecutive error runs after the first success, and LC is the length of consecutive success runs before the last error. The first three studies were paired-associate experiments. The last two studies were free recall experiments.

also available for the two-stage model. Concerning the independence question, it is not possible in most experiments to estimate the 11 parameters separately for each subject, so the correlational approach favored by Chechile and his associates has not been used.

Another approach is possible, however. If the three storage parameters and the eight retrieval parameters actually measure independent memorization processes, it will be possible to find experimental manipulations that affect the storage parameters without affecting the retrieval parameters, and conversely. Data of this sort have been reported for both children and adults. Humphreys and Greeno (1970), for example, reported a paired-associate experiment in which they manipulated word difficulty on both the cue and target sides of paired-associate items. They found that whereas the cue manipulation affected both storage and retrieval parameters, the target manipulation only affected retrieval parameters. Similarly, Brainerd et al. (1981) reported a paired-associate experiment in which the picture-word manipulation was executed on the cue and target sides of items. They found that this manipulation affected retrieval parameters but not storage parameters. A final pertinent datum has been discussed by Brainerd et al. (1981, 1984). Variables that have an affect on the storage parameters and on the retrieval *learning* parameters often have no affect at all on the four retrieval *performance* parameters.

As in the research of Chechile and his associates, the second validity strategy has consisted of determining whether the storage and retrieval parameters of the two-stage model do, in fact, react to manipulations that should affect storage difficulty and retrieval difficulty, respectively. A discussion of some relevant findings from the adult literature may be found in Halff (1977). Here, I mention only three illustrative sets of findings, one set with adults and two with children.

    Consider the effects of two manipulatons, perceptual confusability of items
and pronunceability, on recall memorization. If two items are perceptually
confusable (e.g., LLP vs. LLB), it ought to be more difficult to encode a distinct
trace of each (storage difficulty) and to discriminate previously stored traces
(retrieval difficulty) than if the items were not confusable (e.g., LJB vs. CMQ).
Now, consider the pronunceability manipulation. If items are perceptually
distinctive but difficult to pronounce (e.g., consonant-consonant-consonant
trigrams), there is no reason to suppose that they will have a storage advantage
relative to words that are easier to pronounce (e.g., consonant-vowel-consonant
trigrams), assuming other factors have been controlled. But difficult-to-
pronounce items should certainly be harder to decode on recall tests than easy-
to-pronounce items, a retrieval effect. Therefore, if the model's parameters
measure what we say they measure, perceptual confusability should affect both
storage and retrieval parameters, but pronunceability should affect only
retrieval parameters. This is precisely what Humphreys and Greeno (1970)
found.
    Suppose that subjects learn to recall a list of *N* items in one of two ways,
under standard free recall conditions or under standard paired-associate
conditions. In other words, the subjects either receive a series of study-test
cycles in which they memorize *N* separate items (free recall), or the items are
randomly mated in *N*/2 cue-target pairs and the subjects receive an analogous
series of study-test cycles. In this design, it is known that the first list will be
easier to learn than the second. Why? As the same *N* items are being learned in
both conditions and the two-item clusters in the second condition are well below
the chunking capacity of short-term memory, there are no clear grounds for
supposing that presenting items one at a time provides any storage advantages
relative to presenting them two at a time. The obvious difference between the
conditions is that children can rely on their own retrieval cues in the free recall
condition, but they must use retrieval cues provided by the experimenter in the
paired-associate condition (the cue item in each cue-target pair). This suggests
that the performance difference between free recall memorization and paired-
associated memorization should be a pure retrieval effect. If the model is valid,
therefore, the retrieval parameters should differentiate these conditions but the
storage parameters should not. This pattern was obtained for elementary
schoolers by Brainerd et al. (1984, Experiment 3).
    Last, suppose that children are memorizing a categorized list under one of
two conditions, free recall and cued recall—that is, the categories are cued on
test trials in the latter condition but not in the former condition. Consider what
the effects of the manipulation should be on the first test trial and on later test
trials, respectively. If the children in both conditions are not informed of the
categorical nature of the list or of the cuing manipulation, then cuing cannot
possibly affect storage on the *first* test trial (because both groups were treated
identically on the first study trial). Thus, cuing should affect ease of retrieval but
not ease of storage on the first test. After the first test trial, children are aware of
the precise organization of the list, and this should encourage selective encoding

of category-relevant features on subsequent test trials. In short, cuing should affect both ease of storage and ease of retrieval after Trial 1. If the model is valid, therefore, we should find that cuing affects Trial 1 retrieval parameters, that cuing does not affect the Trial 1 storage parameter, that cuing affects the storage parameter for later trials, and that cuing affects the retrieval parameters for later trials. All of these results were obtained in a recent experiment with second and sixth graders by Howe, Brainerd, and Kingma (1984).

Developmental Data. The amount of development evidence on the two-stage model is also greater than it is for the other two models considered in this chapter. This literature includes a paired-associate experiment with second graders, sixth graders, and adults by Brainerd, Howe, and Desrochers (1982), a paired-associate experiment with kindergarteners, second graders, and sixth graders by Brainerd and Howe (1982), a free recall experiment with second graders and sixth graders by Brainerd, Howe, and Kingma (1982), three paired-associate experiments and two free recall experiments with kindergarteners, second graders, and sixth graders by Brainerd (1982a), two free recall experiments and a paired-associate experiment with second and sixth graders by Brainerd et al. (1984), a free recall experiment with second and sixth graders by Howe, Brainerd, and Kingma (in press), and a free recall experiment with normal and learning disabled sixth graders by Howe, Brainerd, and Kingma (1984).

Rather than attempt to review the findings from all these studies, it would be simpler, I think, to present some new data for the reader's inspection that are fairly typical of the sorts of developmental findings that have been obtained. These results are from five studies in which the memorization procedure was free recall. In all of these studies, the subjects memorized lists of 16 items to a criterion of two consecutive errorless test trials. Half the subjects in each study were second graders, half were sixth graders, and there were 30 or more children per age level in all the studies. The only difference between the experiments was in the type of items that were memorized (pictures, categorized lists without cuing, categorized lists with cuing, very familiar nouns, moderately familiar nouns). The estimates of the two-stage model's parameters appear by age level for these experiments in Table 4-9.

Two types of patterns are apparent from Table 4-9, namely, patterns of age change in parameter values and patterns of developmental stability in parameter values. I discuss the two types of findings separately.

The major developmental changes are:

1. Storage and Retrieval. As was the case with the short-term memory model, there is evidence that both the ease of storing a trace and the ease of retrieving it improve during the elementary school years. Concerning retrieval, note that, depending on the experiment, improvement is observed for both retrieval learning and retrieval performance parameters. Concerning retrieval learning, note that, depending on the experiment, improvement is observed for both

Table 4-9. Illustrative Results for Child Recall Experiments

	Storage			Retrieval Learning				Retrieval Performance			
	a'	a	$1-f$	b'	b	c	d	$1-e$	$1-r$	g	h
Experiment 1											
Younger	.39	.46	1.0	.34	.17	.18	.58	.73	.79	.28	.57
Older	.41	.78	1.0	.20	.05	.36	.49	.59	.88	.48	.66
Experiment 2											
Younger	.46	.40	1.0	.07	.06	.27	.56	.85	.82	.21	.63
Older	.57	.67	1.0	.29	.26	.16	.53	.57	.83	.51	.62
Experiment 3											
Younger	.45	.61	1.0	.43	.44	.25	.59	.53	.73	.45	.64
Older	.53	.72	1.0	.38	.47	.47	.69	.81	.77	.69	.81
Experiment 4											
Younger	.51	.73	1.0	.10	0	.32	.50	.63	.86	.31	.73
Older	.59	.74	1.0	.32	.06	.38	.62	.71	.87	.45	.66
Experiment 5											
Younger	.49	.53	1.0	.07	0	.27	.47	.79	.68	.26	.67
Older	.39	.58	1.0	.24	.18	.28	.68	.69	.93	.33	.62

prestorage retrieval learning (parameters b' and b) and for poststorage retrieval learning (c and d).

2. Storage Versus Retrieval Learning. For retrieval in the sense of learning, storage seems to develop at a more rapid rate than retrieval. Over the five experiments, the average value of the three parameters that measure the ease of trace storage (a', a, and $1-f$) is .67, whereas the average value of the four parameters that measure ease of retrieval learning (b', b, c, and d) was .32. Between sixth grade and adulthood, therefore, much more room is left for improvement in the retrieval learning parameters than in the storage parameters. These findings constitute an important point of agreement between developmental results with the two-stage model and the findings of Chechile and his associates.

3. Storage Versus Retrieval Performance. For retrieval in the sense of performance, on the other hand, storage and retrieval seem to develop at roughly the same rate. Across experiments, the average value of the four retrieval performance parameters ($1-e$, g, h, and $1-r$) was .68 and, as noted, the corresponding average for the storage parameters was .69. The former value suggests that, in absolute terms, children's poststorage retrieval performance is reasonably accurate throughout elementary school. Once again, the indication is that developmental change after the early elementary school level is principally localized within the retrieval learning parameters.

4. Prestorage Versus Poststorage Retrieval Learning. We have seen that, logically, retrieval learning can occur both before a trace has been deposited (parameters b' and b) and after storage (parameters c and d). Judging from the estimates in Table 4-9, the latter type of retrieval learning develops more rapidly than the former. The average value for b' and b is .24, but the average value for c and d is .40. From the data of Chechile and his associates and from the data under Item 2, there is support for a "two-stage" view of storage-retrieval development, according to which developmental improvements in storage ability tend to precede developmental improvements in retrieval learning ability. From the data on b'/b versus c/d, there is also support for a "two-stage" hypothesis about the development of retrieval learning, according to which the development of poststorage retrieval learning tends to precede the development of prestorage retrieval learning. This latter hypothesis carries with it the quite reasonable suggestion that younger children may find it more difficult to do two things at once than older children and adults do.

5. Retrieval Performance. Although there is evidence of development in the four retrieval performance parameters ($1 - e$, g, h, and $1 - r$), g is the only parameter that shows reliable age variation in all five experiments: The average value of g was .47 for second graders and .62 for sixth graders. (Note here that g is the probability that a previously stored trace can be retrieved on a test trial if the child *failed* to retrieve it on the immediately preceding test trial.) This tendency of numerical estimates of the retrieval performance parameters to remain relatively constant across changes in subjects' ages and changes in list difficulty has been a fairly consistent outcome in earlier experiments (cf. Brainerd et al., 1981, 1984). When this tendency is combined with the results under Item 4, the following picture of retrieval development emerges. First, although heuristic retrieval, as measured by the four retrieval performance parameters, develops, the changes are much smaller than those in children's ability to learn retrieval algorithms. Second, although prestorage and post-storage retrieval learning both develop, the ability to acquire retrieval algorithms *before* traces are stored seems to develop more than the ability to acquire retrieval algorithms after a trace is stored.

The major invariances in parameter behavior across age levels are these:

1. Storing and Forgetting. The three storage parameters (a', a, and $1 - f$) measure two, complementary aspects of the storage process, namely, the difficulty of depositing a trace in long-term memory (a' and a) and the difficulty of retaining the trace in storage ($1 - f$). Inspection of the estimates of these parameters in Table 4-9 reveals two relationships that hold across ages and list conditions. First, it was always more difficult to store a trace on the first study trial (parameter a') than on later study trials (parameter a). This is not a very surprising result because it suggests that there is some carryover effect from earlier study trials to later study trials. The second result is much more interesting. It was always more difficult to store a trace on the first study trial

retrieval plan, which implies that $c < d$; and (e) there is some advantage from study trials that follow unsuccessful recalls but subjects are more apt to learn if a success has just stamped in the correct retrieval operations, which implies that $c > d$. Inspection of the c and d values in Table 4-9 provides support for the third alternative. While all ten values of c are greater than zero, each value of d is larger than the c estimate for the same condition. In most cases, the d estimate is two or three times the c estimate. Thus, although children do derive some benefit from study trials that follow test trial successes, they are much more likely to learn how to retrieve on test trials that follow errors. This finding is theoretically significant because there has been some disagreement as to whether or not children show the adult tendency to learn primarily on error trials (Brainerd & Howe, 1980).

A Retention Model

The third model has been developed by Wilkinson and his associates (Wilkinson, De Marinis, & Riley, 1983; Wilkinson & Koestler, 1983, 1984). As the initial paper on the model (Wilkinson et al., 1983) was published very recently, data bearing on it are as yet sparse. As we shall see, however, there are already some interesting developmental results. But even if there were no data at all, the model's elegance and its ease of application in research with children would argue for its inclusion in this review.

Assumptions and Paradigm

A familiar procedure in the adult memory literature is one in which subjects receive a series of consecutive test trials on some target lists without intervening study trials. Historically, the best-known illustration is the Estes-type "miniature experiment," wherein subjects are administered a single study cycle on a paired-associate list followed by two complete test cycles without further opportunities to study (Estes, 1960; Estes, Hopkins, & Crothers, 1960). A more recent and widely used example of such paradigms occurs in studies of long-term retention (e.g., Begg & Robertson, 1973; Nelson, 1978; Postman, 1978). In these experiments, subjects first memorize a list to some criterion (e.g., 75% correct, two consecutive errorless test cycles). They return several days after initial memorization and receive a series of retention tests, tests that typically consist of two or more complete test cycles for the list using standard free or cued recall conditions. During the retention phase, the subjects only attempt to recall the list; they are not allowed to study it.

A variation on the long-term retention design involves administering the sequence of nonreinforced test cycles immediately after initial memorization rather than several days later. As performance on such tests would be nearly perfect if memorization were to a strict criterion, opportunities to learn are restricted. As a rule, subjects receive only one study trial before the test cycles begin. Following Wilkinson, I shall refer to this paradigm as *repeated recall*.

Designs such as these have not been very common in the developmental literature. Most work on memory development has involved either short-term memory or list-learning tasks or semantic memory tasks. For example, there seems to be only one series of studies involving Estes-type miniature experiments (Brainerd & Howe, 1978) and three studies involving the long-term retention design (Fajnsztejn-Pollack, 1973; Morrison, Haith, & Kagan, 1980; Rogoff, Newcombe, & Kagan, 1974). Recently, however, repeated recall studies have begun to appear. Bushke (1974a, 1974b) was the first to draw attention to the paradigm as an interesting developmental methodology. Three basic types of repeated recall can be distinguished in the research of Bushke and others: (a) *no reminding*, where a single study trial is followed by several test cycles without any further opportunities to study; (b) *restrictive reminding*, where each item that is not recalled on a given test trial is presented for study before the next test trial; and (c) *selective reminding*, where any item that has not been recalled on at least one previous test trial is presented for study before the next test trial. Experience has shown that these paradigms are useful with poor-memorizer populations such as young children, the aged, brain injury cases, and people who are taking memory impairing drugs (Bushke, 1974a; Bushke & Fuld, 1974; Caine, Ebert, & Weingartner, 1977; Mohs, Davis, & Levery, 1981).

The storage-retrieval model of Wilkinson and his associates is defined over the no-reminding version of repeated recall, though it has lately been extended to the other paradigms (Wilkinson & Koestler, 1984). The earliest and simplest version of this model will be discussed first, followed by a brief synopsis of its recent extensions.

Consider a no-reminding experiment in which children receive a single study trial on some target list and are then administered i complete test cycles on the list. Wilkinson et al. (1983) analyzed performance in such an experiment in terms of three processes, namely, storage, retrieval, and forgetting:

> First, when a word is presented, it is identified and tagged in memory as an associate of the list to be remembered. We call this process "naming-storage." Second, over successive recall trials, the process of "retrieving" a word on a given trial increases the likelihood of that word being retrieved again on a later trial. . . . Third, also over successive trials, a "forgetting" process causes a stored word that was omitted on a given trial to become increasingly likely to be forgotten again on later trials. Together, the retrieving and forgetting processes can be viewed as complementary aspects of list learning. As trials accumulate, there is an increase in the consistency of recall, previously remembered words being ever more likely to be included and previously forgotten words being ever more likely to be excluded. (Wilkinson et al., 1983, p. 905).

Some similiarities and differences between this model and the earlier ones are already evident. First, storage has basically the same meaning as before—that is, depositing a stable trace of a list item. Second, the meaning of retrieval in this model seems to be primarily retrieval *learning*. In contrast, retrieval means forgetting of retrieval operations in the Chechile model, and it means both retrieval learning (acquisition of algorithms) and retrieval performance (heuristic retrieval) in the two-stage model. Third, since forgetting is the complement of retrieval, this notion would appear to connote loss of retrieval operations. In contrast, forgetting means both loss of traces and loss of retrieval operations in the Chechile model, and it means loss of traces in the two-stage model.

Like the two-stage model, this model uses the concepts of storage, retrieval, and forgetting to describe the probability of correct recall on a trial-by-trial basis. Consider the first test trial in a sequence of i repeated recall cycles. Let s be the probability that a given item was stored on the study trial that precedes the first test trial, and let r_0 be the probability that a stored item can be retrieved on the first test trial. If an item was not stored (with probability $1 - s$), then the subject makes an error. If an item was stored (with probability s), then the subject makes a correct response if the trace can be retrieved (with probability r_0) or makes an error if retrieval fails (with probability $1 - r_0$).

The recall probabilities on subsequent trials in the sequence depend on performance on earlier trials. Specifically, these probabilities depend on the cumulative numbers of successful and unsuccessful retrievals:

> First, by a strengthening effect, recalling a word on a given trial increases the probability of that word being recalled on some later trial. More precisely, the probability that a word recalled on trial j will also be recalled on trial $j + 1$ is r_i, where i indexes the cumulative number of recalls for that word over the j completed trials. Second, by a discarding effect, a word omitted on trial j is likely to be omitted on trial $j + 1$ also, because a recall plan is gradually formed by which memory search is limited to an increasingly consistent subset of words over successive trials. More precisely, if a word is omitted or forgotten on trial j, then it is also forgotten on trial $j + 1$ with probability f_i, where i indexes the number of successive (uninterrupted) trials over which the word has been omitted, up to and including trial j. (Wilkinson et al., 1983, p. 905).

Of course, if an item was never stored in the first place (with probability $1 - s$), the subject continues to make recall errors for that item on all subsequent trials.

It is now possible to express the probability of any possible sequence of errors and successes in terms of parameters that mesure the processes of storage, retrieval, and forgetting, respectively. If there are i trials in a particular repeated recall sequence, then the number of possible error-success patterns is 2^i. Thus, there are 8 unique patterns if there are three trials, 16 unique patterns if there are four trials, and so on. In Wilkinson et al.'s (1983) experiment, there were three trials. Let $p(i, j, k)$ denote the probability of a particular response pattern in such an experiment, where the index variables i, j, and k read 0 if a correct recall occurs on a given test trial in a repeated recall experiment and read 1 if an error occurs. The eight possible probabilities for a three-trial sequence can now be expressed in terms of the parameters of Wilkinson's model as follows:

$$p(000) = s r_0 r_1 r_2,$$
$$p(001) = s r_0 r_1 (1 - r_2),$$
$$p(010) = s r_0 (1 - r_1)(1 - f_1),$$
$$p(011) = s r_0 (1 - r_1) f_1, \text{ and}$$

$$p(100) = s(1 - r_0)(1 - f_1) r_1,$$
$$p(101) = s(1 - r_0)(1 - f_1)(1 - r_1),$$
$$p(110) = s(1 - r_0) f_1 (1 - f_1),$$
$$p(111) = 1 - s + s(1 - r_0) f_1 f_2.$$

The meaning of each of these expressions—in terms of storage, retrieval, and forgetting—can easily be seen by translating them into verbal definitions. To illustrate, the probability of three consecutive successes, $p(000)$, is simply the probability that an item was stored (s) times the probability that it is retrievable on Trial 1 (r_0) times the probability that it is retrievable on Trial 2 (r_1) times the probability that it is retrievable on Trial 3 (r_2). Also, the probability of three consecutive errors, $p(111)$, is the probability that an item was not stored ($1 - s$) plus the probability that an item was stored times the probability that it is not retrievable on Trial 1 ($1 - r_0$) times the probability that it is not retrievable on Trial 2 (f_1) times the probability that it is not retrievable on Trial 3 (f_2). The ease with which expressions for response patterns can be translated into verbal definitions greatly facilitates applications of the model to experiments with larger numbers of test cycles. As an illustration, the relevant expressions for four-trial repeated recall designs are provided in Table 4-10.

Wilkinson has extended his conceptual description of repeated recall in two recent papers (Wilkinson & Koestler, 1983, 1984). Because the mathematical models in these subsequent papers are considerably more complicated than the one just considered, they will not be considered here. Instead, discussion will be confined to conceptual issues.

Whereas Wilkinson et al. (1983) proposed that three processes are involved in repeated recall (trace storage, retrieval learning, and retrieval forgetting), Wilkinson and Koestler (1983) have argued for a four-process interpretation. The first process is called *presentation increment*, and is essentially the same as

Table 4-10. Empirical Probabilities Expressed as Functions of Storage, Retrieval and Forgetting Parameters in a Four-Trial Experiment

Empirical Probability	Theoretical Expression
$p(0000)$	$sr_0 r_1 r_2 r_3$
$p(0001)$	$sr_0 r_1 r_2 (1 - r_3)$
$p(0010)$	$sr_0 r_1 (1 - r_2)(1 - f_1)$
$p(0100)$	$sr_0 (1 - r_1)(1 - f_1) r_2$
$p(1000)$	$s(1 - r_0)(1 - f_1) r_1 r_2$
$p(0011)$	$sr_0 r_1 (1 - r_2) f_1$
$p(0101)$	$sr_0 (1 - r_1)(1 - f_1)(1 - r_2)$
$p(1001)$	$s(1 - r_0)(1 - f_1) r_1$
$p(0110)$	$sr_0 (1 - r_1) f_1 (1 - f_2)$
$p(1010)$	$s(1 - r_0)(1 - f_1)(1 - r_1)(1 - f_2)$
$p(1100)$	$s(1 - r_0) f_1 (1 - f_2) r_1$
$p(0111)$	$sr_0 (1 - r_1) f_1 f_2$
$p(1011)$	$s(1 - r_0)(1 - f_1)(1 - r_1) f_2$
$p(1101)$	$s(1 - r_0) f_1 (1 - f_2)(1 - r_1)$
$p(1110)$	$s(1 - r_0) f_1 f_2 (1 - f_3)$
$p(1111)$	$1 - s + s(1 - r_0) f_1 f_2 f_3$

Wilkinson et al.'s storage concept: "A boost in the strength of a trace occurs when new associations are formed that link the trace to cues for retrieving it" (Wilkinson & Koestler, 1984, p. 44). The second concept is *cuing decrement.* This notion resembles Wilkinson et al.'s concept of retrieval forgetting:

> during the period intervening between storage of a word and subsequent attempts to recall it, the associations available for retrieving the word may change. . . . Change in contextual cues tends to diminish the probability of recalling a word, because the context at the time of attempted recall is likely to include some new, irrelevant cues and to exclude some of the cues that were associated with the word at the time of its storage. (Wilkinson & Koestler, 1984, pp. 44 & 45)

The third concept, *recall increment*, is Wilkinson et al.'s (1983) retrieval learning process: "successful recall of a word generates new associations. . . . In effect, successful recall boosts the associative strength of a memory trace" (Wilkinson & Koestler, 1984, p. 45). The fourth concept, the *sampling rule*, is new. It is roughly analogous to the idea of an output transformation in scaling. Wilkinson and Koestler's sampling rule states that the probability of successfully recalling an item is proportional to the total number of associative pathways that include the item:

> in a given context, one of many possible pathways through memory is chosen. How a particular pathway is chosen depends on a process of search and retrieval. . . . We merely assume that one path is sampled from many that are possible and that the probability of recalling a given item is the probability of sampling a path containing that item. (Wilkinson & Koestler, 1984, p. 45) [This statement also resembles some of the ideas about retrieval that are discussed in Ackerman's chapter in this volume.]

In both of the later versions of this model, therefore, three processes (trace storage, retrieval, and forgetting) are involved that are also invoked in the earlier model. Hence, it is possible to investigate some of the same questions that have been studied with the Checile model and the two-stage model by estimating the parameters that measure these processes in repeated recall experiments.

Statistical Methodology

As before, the statistical procedures for estimating parameters and evaluating goodness of fit in connection with Wilkinson's model are confined to the Appendix. Here, we consider these procedures only in broad outline.

The statistical machinery for Wilkinson's model is the simplest of the three models considered in this chapter. Like the two-stage model, the technologies for both parameter estimation and goodness of fit rely on the theory of maximum likelihood. We have seen that a repeated recall experiment with i trials generates 2^i unique patterns of errors and successes. By Bernoulli's theorem, a likelihood function can be written that expresses the a posteriori probability of the data of such an experiment in terms of the probabilities of these patterns. This function has the form

$$L = \prod_1^{2^i} \{p(j,\ k,\ \ldots,n)\},\qquad\qquad (4\text{-}4)$$

where $p(j,\ k,\ \ldots,\ n)$ is the probability of one of the 2^i possible response patterns in the experiment.

Using Wilkinson's model, each $p(j,\ k,\ \ldots,\ n)$ in Equation 4-4 can be replaced by its definition in terms of parameters that measure storage (s), retrieval (r_i), and forgetting (f_i). Maximum likelihood estimates of the storage, retrieval, and forgetting parameters are then obtained in the same manner as with the two-stage model; a standard computer optimization algorithm (SIMPLEX, STEPIT) is used to minimize the revised likelihood function.

Since the parameters are estimated by the method of maximum likelihood, Wilkinson and his associates have used the familiar procedure of *likelihood ratio comparison of submodels* (e.g., Theios, Leonard, & Brelsford, 1977) to test goodness of fit. The general strategy is quite similar to the necessity-sufficiency method that was described for the two-stage model.

The sufficiency tests ask whether or not the data of some experiment can be adequately described by the storage, retrieval, and forgetting parameters. With the exception of repeated recall designs involving only two or three trials, the number of observable empirical probabilities (i.e., the various $p(j,\ k,\ \ldots,\ n)$ terms in Equation 4-4) will be much larger than the number of parameters posited in Wilkinson's model. In Table 4-10, for example, we saw that although there are 15 independent empirical probabilities for repeated recall experiments with four trials, Wilkinson's model assumes that the data can be described by one storage probability (s), four retrieval probabilities (r_0, r_1, r_2, r_3), and three forgetting probabilities (f_1, f_2, f_3). A likelihood ratio statistic is available which tests the null hypothesis that the 8 memory parameters describe the data as well as the 15 empirical probabilities against the alternative hypothesis that the 15 empirical parameters do a better job.

If the data of a repeated recall experiment pass the relevant sufficiency tests, necessity tests ask whether all the storage, retrieval, and forgetting parameters posited in the model are all essential or whether some of them can be eliminated. For example, it might be that the retrieval probability remains constant across trials or it might be that the forgetting probability remains constant across trials. In the former case, there would be only one retrieval parameter, not four, in a four-trial experiment. In the latter case, there would be only one forgetting parameter, not three, in a four-trial experiment. As with sufficiency, likelihood ratio statistics are available to test such necessity hypotheses.

The Data Base

As the data that bear on this model are not extensive, findings on goodness of fit/validity will not be separated from developmental results. Taking goodness of fit first, evidence from repeated recall experiments with children (Wilkinson et al., 1983; Wilkinson & Koestler, 1983), young adults (Wilkinson & Koestler, 1983, 1984), and aged adults (Wilkinson & Koestler, 1983) is favorable with respect to both sufficiency-type and necessity-type tests.

Although validity data on this model are too thin as yet to be considered convincing, there are some interesting supportive results concerned with the behavior of the retrieval and forgetting parameters across trials. It will be remembered that the model assumes that one's ability to retrieve a trace improves as a consequence of previous successful retrievals (retrieval learning) and that retrieval ability declines as a consequence of previous unsuccessful retrievals (retrieval forgetting). One expects, therefore, that the values of parameters that measure retrieval following smaller numbers of successful recalls would be smaller than the values of parameters that measure retrieval following larger numbers of successful recalls. One would also expect that the values of parameters that measure forgetting following smaller numbers of errors would be smaller than the values of parameters that measure forgetting following larger numbers of errors. In Wilkinson et al.'s (1983) notation, one predicts that $r_i \leq r_j$, where $i < j$, and that $f_i \leq f_j$, where $i < j$. Both of these results were obtained in an experiment by Wilkinson et al. (1983) with older children and adolescents. The repeated recall design in this experiment consisted of one study trial on a 12-word list followed by three test trials. The values of the three retrieval learning parameters, averaged across age levels, were $r_0 = .78$, $r_1 = .89$, and $r_2 = .94$. The average values of the two forgetting parameters were $f_1 = .62$ and $f_2 = .76$. (Recall here that the subscripts of the retrieval parameters give the cumulative number of prior successes or errors.) Analogous results were obtained for normal children by Kail, Hale, and Leonard (1983), though language-disabled children in the same study departed somewhat from predictions.

The key developmental finding that has been observed with Wilkinson's model is that trace storage improves with age, but retrieval learning and forgetting are age invariant. The clearest evidence comes from the Wilkinson et al. (1983) experiment. The subjects in this study were 144 children, 24 children apiece from grades 4 through 9. As mentioned, the task was three trials of repeated recall on a 12-word list. The estimates of the storage, retrieval learning, and forgetting parameters appear in Table 4-11 for three age ranges, namely, grades 4 and 5, grades 6 and 7, and grades 8 and 9.

It can be seen that the probability of storing a durable trace of a word following a single study trial increases steadily with age; this probability is .55 for fourth and fifth graders, .64 for sixth and seventh graders, and .70 for eighth and ninth graders. But it can also be seen that the retrieval and forgetting parameters did not develop. There are some slight age changes in certain of these parameters (e.g., $r_2 = .93$ for the youngest subjects and .95 for the two older groups; $f_2 = .69$, .77, and .82 for the youngest, intermediate, and oldest subjects, respectively). However, none of these differences was statistically reliable. In the only other developmental experiment reported by Wilkinson and his associates (Wilkinson & Koestler, 1983, Experiment 2), the storage parameter was also found to vary with age. In this particular study, a five-trial

Table 4-11. Illustrative Values of the Wilkinson Model's Parameters (From an Experiment by Wilkinson, DeMarinis, and Riley, 1983)

Parameter	Age		
	10-year olds	12-year-olds	14-year-olds
Storage			
s	.55	.64	.70
Retrieval Learning			
r_0	.77	.78	.79
r_1	.88	.89	.89
r_2	.93	.95	.95
Retrieval Forgetting			
f_1	.61	.62	.63
f_2	.69	.77	.82

repeated recall task was administered to 30 fifth and sixth graders (median age = 11 years), 30 undergraduates (median age = 19 years), and 30 elderly adults (median age = 67 years). The estimated probability of storing a durable trace following a single study trial was .19 for the children, .30 for the undergraduates, and .18 for the elderly adults. As in the Wilkinson et al. (1983) study, however, parameters that measure retrieval and forgetting did not vary with age.

To conclude, the account of storage-retrieval development in repeated recall that emerges from applications of the Wilkinson model is that subjects' ability to store a trace as a consequence of a single study trial varies with age, but neither the tendency for retrieval to improve as a function of prior successes nor the tendency for retrieval to decline as a function of prior errors develops. Although the data on which this statement is based are by no means extensive, the findings on Wilkinson's model are consistent across two experiments using different subject samples, different lists, and different repeated recall tasks. There are some noteworthy discrepancies between these results and some of those reported earlier for the other two models, a point to which we shall return in the next section.

Storage and Retrieval: The Developmental Picture

In the preceding three sections, my intent was to review the assumptions, procedures, and associated data bases of each model more or less without regard to the other two. To conclude this chapter, some comparative issues will be considered that are concerned with similarities and differences in the patterns of storage-retrieval development revealed by the models.

Obviously, the three agree on some conclusions about development and disagree on others. Before examining these conclusions, however, it is useful to remind ourselves that "storage" and "retrieval" have somewhat different meanings in the three models, a matter of some importance when it comes to resolving empirical discrepancies. In the Chechile model, both concepts refer to forgetting, forgetting from short-term memory to be precise. Because performance on short-term memory tests is normally perfect if the memory set is small enough, it is traditional to assume that storage and retrieval, in the sense of acquisition, are perfect. In the two-stage model and in the Wilkinson model, however, principal emphasis is on the acquisition meanings of storage and retrieval. Storage refers to depositing a stable in long-term memory in both models. Retrieval refers to the acquisition of retrieval operations in both models, though it also refers to the level of accuracy of heuristic retrieval in the two-stage model. Although forgetting is measured in these models, only one aspect of forgetting is assessed in each case. Forgetting in the sense of losing a trace is measured by the two-stage model, and forgetting in the sense of losing retrieval operations is measured by the Wilkinson model. With these caveats in mind, the major points of agreement and disagreement between the models are "storage" and "retrieval."

Storage

The literatures on all three models converge on the conclusion that storage develops. This is true regardless of whether "storage" means losing a trace from short-term memory (Chechile model) or depositing a trace in long-term memory (two-stage and Wilkinson models). When the overall age ranges that have been studied are considered, storage ability appears to improve from early elementary school through young adulthood. Although these models have not yet been applied to preschoolers, there is reason to believe that storage develops during this age and, indeed, that this may be the period when storage improvement is most dramatic.

The models also suggest some limitations on storage development. For storage in the sense of losing traces from short-term memory, results from Chechile and his associates indicate that development is complete by the end of elementary school. The large values of the storage parameter for younger elementary schoolers also imply that storage development in this sense may be largely restricted to the preschool years. For storage in the sense of losing traces from long-term memory, the two-stage model has not generated any evidence of development. In the experiments presented earlier (Table 4-9), the probability of losing a trace from storage was zero for both younger and older children. Although there are some recall paradigms that produce nonzero estimates of this parameter, these same tasks have failed to provide evidence that the tendency to lose a trace from long-term memory changes with age.

When these various results are combined, one is tempted to conclude that storage in the sense of depositing a trace develops more than storage in the sense of losing a trace. However, such conclusions would be subject to the important qualification that very young children have not yet been studied with any of the three models.

Retrieval

The picture of retrieval development is more complicated. According to data from the Chechile model and the two-stage model, retrieval in the senses of losing retrieval operations from short-term memory and of acquiring retrieval algorithms for traces stored in long-term memory both develop. Retrieval in the sense of heuristic retrieval from long-term memory also develops (two-stage model), but the changes are very small in comparison with the other two types of retrieval. Last, retrieval in the sense of forgetting how to retrieve traces from short-term memory seems to develop over a much broader age range than storage in the sense of losing traces from short-term memory, with the same relationship holding for learning to retrieve from long-term memory versus storing traces in long-term memory.

Whereas the Chechile model and the two-stage model suggest pronounced retrieval development, more pronounced even than storage development, developmental applications of the Wilkinson model suggest no retrieval development. Neither the parameters that measure retrieval in the sense of learning to retrieve traces from long-term memory nor in the sense of forgetting how to retrieve such traces were found to vary with age in the Wilkinson et al. (1983) and Wilkinson and Koestler (1983) experiments. The latter result is not necessarily inconsistent with the data on the other two models because neither of them measures this particular form of retrieval forgetting; Chechile's model measures forgetting how to retrieve from short-term memory and the two-stage model does not measure retrieval forgetting. The former result, however, is in direct conflict with data from the two-stage model because this model also measures retrieval in the sense of learning how to retrieve from long-term memory. Indeed, these particular parameters of the two-stage model showed greater age change than any of its other parameters.

Although these discrepancies over whether or not retrieval learning develops remain unsolved, two explanations merit attention. The first concerns ceiling effects in Wilkinson's retrieval learning parameters. Inspection of Table 4-11 reveals that these parameters had near-ceiling values for even the youngest subjects in the Wilkinson et al. (1983) experiment, with the average value of the r parameters being .87. The estimates of the two-stage model's retrieval learning parameters were much smaller (cf. Table 4-9). It could be, therefore, that the retrieval learning parameters for repeated recall would show age change if the task were made more difficult by, for example, administering more difficult lists or studying younger subjects. The other explanation concerns an important difference in the paradigms over which the two models are defined. The data for both models are errors-successes from a sequence of recall trials on a single list. However, the study-trial contingencies are not the same. With the two-stage model, a study trial normally precedes each test trial. But with the repeated recall model, only the first test trial is preceded by a study trial.

Consequently, although both models profess to measure retrieval in the sense of learning how to retrieve traces that have been stored in long-term memory, the measurements are taken under quite different conditions. The essential difference is that whereas the two-stage model measures the retrieval learning that occurs as a consequence of the events on study and test trials, the repeated recall model measures only the retrieval learning that occurs as a consequence of the events on test trials. It is quite possible that retrieval learning on study trials improves with age but that retrieval learning on test trials is age invariant. If so, extant data are not inconsistent with each other.

It would be fairly easy to test the second explanation using the two-stage model, though a relevant study has yet to be reported. For example, consider an experiment in which children from two or more age levels memorize a list under a repeated recall condition of the form $R_1 T_1 T_2 R_2 T_3 T_4 \ldots$ (i.e., each study cycle is followed by two complete test cycles). Suppose that the parameters of the two-stage model were separately estimated for two types of data, namely, the odd-numbered test trials only and the even-numbered test trials only. Now, consider the estimates of the four retrieval learning parameters (b', b, c, d) for the two sets of data. Note that performance on the first and second members of each $T_i T_{i+1}$ pair involves the same number of prior study trials, but performance on the second member of the pair involves one more prior test trial. Thus, if retrieval learning occurs on test trials as well as on study trials, we anticipate that the estimated values of the retrieval learning parameters will generally be larger on even-numbered test trials than on odd-numbered test trials. However, it is the pattern of developmental change on study and test trials in which we are chiefly interested. If, as suggested, retrieval learning on study trials develops but retrieval learning on test trials does not, the age changes observed in parameter estimates for odd-numbered test trials should be of the same magnitude as those for even-numbered test trials. But if retrieval learning develops on both study and test trials, the estimates for even-numbered test trials should show greater age change than the estimates for odd-numbered test trials. It is also logically possible that the age changes for odd-numbered test trials would be greater than those for even-numbered test trials. This could happen if there were no retrieval learning on test trials and, instead, administering additional test trials produces significant forgetting.

Storage Versus Retrieval

A long-standing question about poor-memorizer populations such as children is whether storage difficulty or retrieval difficulty is a more important source of performance errors. The three models provide some answers to this question for their respective paradigms, though the implications are as yet uncertain for memory development as a whole. For storage and retrieval in the sense of forgetting from short-term memory, there is consistent evidence from the Chechile model that it is retrieval, not storage, that is the main cause of errors. Remember, for example, that in the Chechile et al. (1981) study, the average probability that an item was still in storage was .80 for subjects between first grade and young adulthood, while the average probability that a stored item was still retrievable was only .50.

With respect to long-term memory, the two-stage model confirms this finding for short-term memory in one respect and disconfirms it in another respect. When retrieval means learning retrieval algorithms for previously stored traces, then retrieval is more difficult than storage: The average value of the storage parameters in Table 4-9 is .67, and the average value of the retrieval learning parameters is .32. But when retrieval means steady-state, heuristic retrieval from long-term memory, storage and retrieval are equally difficult; the average values of the storage and retrieval learning parameters in Table 4-9 are very similar.

Wilkinson's repeated recall model provides a still different picture. As with the two-stage model, the relative importance of storage and retrieval difficulty depends on the sort of retrieval with which one is concerned. For retrieval in the sense of retrieval learning, storage is more difficult than retrieval, the opposite of what two-stage model shows: The average value of the storage parameter estimates in Table 4-11 is .63, and the average value of the retrieval learning parameter estimates is .87. But for retrieval in the sense of forgetting, retrieval is more difficult than storage: Whereas the average storage probability in Table 4-11 is .63, the average probability of not forgetting how to retrieve is only .31.

In view of these findings, the safest inference is that the relative impact of storage and retrieval factors on performance errors depends rather strongly on the memory paradigm under investigation. This conclusion is consistent with experiments in which the two-stage model has been applied to free recall versus paired-associate learning (Brainerd et al., 1984). Also, it should be stressed again that the discrepancies between the models' respective findings are more apparent than real because of their different conceptions of storage and retrieval. As before, the only clear discrepancy is for the retrieval learning parameters of the two long-term memory models, with the two-stage model showing that retrieval learning is more difficult than storage and the repeated recall model showing the reverse.

Afterword on the Big Question

What of the Big Question about memory development: Are the age changes that we observe in memory performance as functions of chronological age more dependent upon the development of storage processes or upon the development of retrieval processes? Mathematical models of storage-retrieval development, along with the data they have generated, tend to confirm one's hunch that it is forlorn to hope for a simple, clearcut answer to this question.

The reason can be found in the rather precise characterizations of storage and retrieval concepts that form the core of individual models. Storage and retrieval, it now seems, are many-splendored things. In the first place, one may speak of storage and retrieval as occurring in fundamentally different types of memory (parameter a') or on later study trials (parameter a) than it was to retain the trace (parameter $1 - f$). Actually, children had no difficulty whatsoever in retaining previously stored traces; the estimated probability of forgetting was zero in all conditions. This result is theoretically interesting because available theories differ in the extent to which storage difficulty is presumed to depend on the difficulty of depositing traces and maintaining traces, respectively. It is also interesting because it suggests that trace retention is not a major source of memory development, at least not on long-term memory tasks.

2. Heuristic Retrieval. Another finding that seems to hold across ages and conditions concerns the relative difficulty of heuristic retrieval at different points in State P (traces stored but retrieval algorithm not yet available). To begin with, heuristic retrieval clearly is better when an item first enters State P than it is later on. The average value of the parameters $1 - e$ and $1 - r$, which measure the accuracy of heuristic retrieval on the first trial in State P, is .74. The average value of the parameters g and h, which measure the accuracy of heuristic retrieval on later trials in State P, is only .61. In at least one respect, this is a counterintuitive result: One might expect that heuristic retrieval would improve with practice when, in fact, it deteriorates. However, the result might be an item difficulty effect; the parameters $1 - e$ and $1 - r$ are based on all items that enter State P while g and h are based on a subset of items that remain in State P for two or more trials (i.e., more difficult items). There is another invariant relationship among the retrieval performance parameters. The parameter g is always smaller than the parameter h; heuristic retrieval is more difficult if an error occurred on the preceding test trial than if a success occurred. This result is not surprising, and it can be also explained as an item difficulty effect. If the traces of different items vary in their intrinsic retrievability, as seems likely, then in the absence of compensating factors, g will be smaller than h.

3. Algorithmic Retrieval. Last, there is an invariant result for the parameters c and d that is of theoretical significance. Recall that c and d both measure the difficulty of acquiring a retrieval algorithm after a trace has been stored, where c is the probability of this event following successful heuristic retrieval and d is the probability of this event following unsuccessful heuristic retrieval. As Halff (1977) has documented, theories differ widely in their assumptions about the relative importance of successful and unsuccessful recall on subsequent learning. Essentially, there are five theoretical positions: (a) successes are dead weight and subjects only learn when an error signals them to sample a new retrieval plan, which implies that $c = 0$; (b) errors are dead weight and subjects only learn when successful recall stamps in the correct retrieval operations, which implies that $d = 0$; (c) subjects pay no attention to whether preceding attempts at recall were successful or unsuccessful, which implies that $c = d$; (d) there is some advantage from study trials that follow successful recalls but subjects are more apt to learn if an error has just signaled them to change their

systems. Of the three developmental models, one was concerned with storage and retrieval processes in short-term memory, while the other two were concerned with storage and retrieval processes in long-term memory. It is also possible to think of both short-term and long-term memory as being composed of multiple, independent systems. With respect to long-term memory, for example, the distinction between episodic and semantic systems (Tulving, 1972) has become commonplace, though there is disagreement as to whether the data actually favor such a distinction (e.g., Anderson & Ross, 1980). Regarding short-term memory, there is credible evidence that it involves at least two independent systems, one that is specialized for processing traces of recently encoded information and another that is specialized for verbatim retention of recently encoded information (cf. Brainerd & Kingma, in press; Klapp, Marshburn, & Lester, 1983; Surber & Surber, 1983). There is also growing evidence that the latter type of short-term memory may be composed of several independent systems that are specialized for retaining specific types of information (cf. Friedman & Polson, 1981; Klapp & Philipoff, 1983). The bottom line is that the relative contributions of age changes in storage and retrieval to memory development will, in all probability, depend on precisely what sort of memory system one is talking about.

Within a given memory system, the relative contributions of storage development and retrieval development may also depend on the types of storage and retrieval processes under consideration. We saw in connection with the two-stage model that storage can be viewed either as the process whereby traces are deposited or as the complementary process whereby traces decay. Although theoretically these two meanings of storage are opposite sides of the same coin, data reviewed above, as well as some recent findings on adults (Slameka & McElree, 1983), suggest that they obey different laws. We also saw in connection with the two-stage and repeated recall models that retrieval can be thought of as learning how to retrieve on study trials (two-stage model) or as learning how to retrieve on test trials (repeated recall model) or as forgetting how to retrieve on test trials (repeated recall model) or as steady-state retrieval accuracy (two-stage model). Further, learning how to retrieve on study or test trials may refer to learning that occurs before a trace is stored or after storage. As with the different meanings of "storage," there is evidence that these different forms of retrieval may be subject to different laws.

While the developmental literatures on the three models are not as complete as one would wish, the available data do provide strong signals that the type of memory system and the type of storage-retrieval are critical variables when it comes to assessing the contributions of storage and retrieval factors to memory development. Insofar as the type of memory system is concerned, the relative amounts of storage and retrieval development seem to be different for short-term memory and long-term memory. Data from several studies with Chechile's short-term memory model argue for the conclusion that subjects of all ages are much more likely to forget how to retrieve traces than to lose traces and, consequently, age changes in the former ability make larger contributions to short-term memory development than age changes in the latter ability. (The preschool years, where the model has not yet been successfully applied, may be an exception to this rule.) But data from studies with the other two models fail to support a similar conclusion in connection with long-term memory. With the two-stage model, learning how to retrieve on study trials develops more than storage, though this difference is less marked than it is with Chechile's model. But steady-state retrieval accuracy develops *less* than storage. With the repeated recall model, learning how to retrieve on test trials and forgetting how to retrieve on test trials do not develop at all, though storage (in the sense of depositing a trace in long-term memory) is found to develop.

With respect to type of storage-retrieval, the data on the two-stage and repeated recall models indicate that conclusions about development are different for different types of storage and retrieval. For example, storage in the sense of depositing traces is found to develop with both models, but storage in the sense of losing traces is not found to develop with the two-stage model. Similarly, retrieval in the sense of learning how to retrieve on study trials before storage, in the sense of learning how to retrieve on study trials after storage, and in the sense of steady-state retrieval are all found to develop (two-stage model). But retrieval in the sense of learning how to retrieve on test trials after storage and in the sense of forgetting how to retrieve on test trials after storage are found to be age-invariant (repeated recall model).

Acknowledgment. Preparation of this chapter and the research reported herein were supported by Grant No. A0668 from the Natural Sciences and Engineering Research Council. I am indebted to R. A. Chechile, M. L. Howe, and V. F. Reyna for correcting various errors in an earlier draft, and to Johannes Kingma for providing some of the data that are reported in connection with the two-stage model.

References

Anderson, J. R., & Ross, B. H. (1980). Evidence against the semantic-episodic distinction. *Journal of Experimental Psychology: Human Learning and Memory, 6,* 441–446.

Begg, I., & Robertson, R. (1973). Imagery and long-term retention. *Journal of Verbal Learning and Verbal Behavior, 12,* 689–700.

Bower, G. H., & Theios, J. (1964). A learning model for discrete performance levels. In R. C. Atkinson (Ed.), *Studies in mathematical psychology.* Palo Alto, CA: Stanford University Press.

Brainerd, C. J. (1982a). Children's concept learning as rule-sampling systems with Markovian properties. In C. J. Brainerd (Ed.), *Children's logical and mathematical cognition: Progress in cognitive development research.* New York: Springer-Verlag.

Brainerd, C. J. (1982b). Editorial. *Developmental Review, 2,* 209–212.

Brainerd, C. J. (1983). Structural invariance in the developmental analysis of learning. In J. Bisanz, G. Bisanz, & R. V. Kail, Jr. (Eds.), *Learning in children: Progress in cognitive development research.* New York: Springer-Verlag.

Brainerd, C. J. (1984). *The general theory of two-stage learning: An update on statistical methodology.* Research Report, Department of Psychology, University of Alberta.

Brainerd, C. J., Desrochers, A., & Howe, M. L. (1981). Stages-of-learning analysis of developmental interactions in memory. *Journal of Experimental Psychology: Human Learning and Memory, 7*, 1–14.

Brainerd, C. J., & Howe, M. L. (1978). The origins of all-or none learning. *Child Development, 50*, 1028–1034.

Brainerd, C. J., & Howe, M. L. (1980). Developmental invariance in a mathematical of associative learning. *Child Development, 51*, 349–363.

Brainerd, C. J., & Howe, M. L. (1982). Stages-of-learning analysis of developmental interactions in memory, with illustrations from developmental interactions in picture-word effects. *Developmental Review, 2*, 251–273.

Brainerd, C. J., Howe, M. L., & Desrochers, A. (1980). Interpreting associative-learning stages. *Journal of Experimental Psychology: Human Learning and Memory, 6*, 754–765.

Brainerd, C. J., Howe, M. L., & Desrochers, A. (1982). The general theory of two-stage learning: A mathematical review with illustrations from memory development. *Psychological Bulletin, 91*, 634–665.

Brainerd, C. J., Howe, M. L., & Kingma, J. (1982). An identifiable model of two-stage learning. *Journal of Mathematical Psychology, 26*, 263–293.

Brainerd, C. J., Howe, M. L., Kingma, J., & Brainerd, S. H. (1984). On the measurement of storage and retrieval factors in memory development. *Journal of Experimental Child Psychology, 37*, 478–499.

Brainerd, C. J., & Kingma, J. (in press). Do children have to remember to reason? A fuzzy-trace theory of transitivity development. *Developmental Review, 4*, December 1984.

Buschke, H. (1974a). Components of verbal learning in children: Analysis by selective reminding. *Journal of Experimental Child Psychology, 18*, 488–496.

Buschke, H. (1974b). Two stages of learning by children and adults. *Bulletin of the Psychonomic Society, 2*, 392–394.

Buschke, H., & Fuld, P. A. (1974). Evaluating storage, retention, and retrieval in disordered memory and learning. *Neurology, 24*, 1019–1025.

Butler, K., & Chechile, R. A. (1976). "Acid bath" effects on storage and retrieval PI. *Bulletin of the Psychonomic Society, 8*, 349–352.

Caine, E. D., Ebert, M. H., & Weingartner, H. (1977). An outline for the analysis of dementia: The memory disorder of Huntington's disease. *Neurology, 27*, 1087–1092.

Chechile, R. A., & Butler, K. (1975). Storage and retrieval changes that occur in the development and release of PI. *Journal of Verbal Learning and Verbal Behavior, 14*, 430–437.

Chechile, R. A., & Meyer, D. L. (1976). A Bayesian procedure for separately estimating storage and retrieval components of forgetting. *Journal of Mathematical Psychology, 13*, 269–295.

Chechile, R. A., & Richman, C. L. (1982). The interaction of semantic memory with storage and retrieval processes. *Developmental Review, 2*, 237–250.

Chechile, R. A., Richman, C. L., Topinka, C., & Ehrensbeck, K. (1981). A developmental study of the storage and retrieval of information. *Child Development, 52*, 251–259.

Crothers, E. J. (1964). All-or-none paired-associate learning with compound responses.

In R. C. Atkinson (Ed.), *Studies in mathematical psychology*. Palo Alto, CA: Stanford University Press.

Estes, W. K. (1960). Learning theory and the new "mental chemistry." *Psychological Review, 67,* 207–223.

Estes, W. K., & DaPolito, F. (1967). Independent variation of information storage and retrieval processes in paired-associate learning. *Journal of Experimental Psychology, 75,* 18–26.

Estes, W. K., Hopkins, B. L., & Crothers, E. J. (1960). All-or-none and conservation effects in the learning and retention of paired associates. *Journal of Experimental Psychology, 60,* 329–339.

Fajnsztejn-Pollack, G. A developmental study of decay rate in long-term memory. *Journal of Experimental Child Psychology,* 1973, *16,* 225–235.

Friedman, A., & Polson, M. C. (1981). Hemispheres as independent resource systems: Limited-capacity processing and cerebral specialization. *Journal of Experimental Psychology: Human Perception and Performance, 7,* 1031–1058.

Gerrein, J. R., & Chechile, R. A. (1977). Storage and retrieval processes of alcohol-induced amnesia. *Journal of Abnormal Psychology, 86,* 285–294.

Greeno, J. G. (1968). Identifiability and statistical properties of two-stage learning with no successes in the initial stage. *Psychometrika, 33,* 173–216.

Greeno, J. G. (1970). How associations are memorized. In D. A. Norman (Ed.), *Models of human memory*. New York: Academic Press.

Greeno, J. G. (1974). Representation of learning as discrete transition in a finite state space. In D. H. Krantz, R. C. Atkinson, R. D. Luce, & P. Suppes (Eds.), *Contemporary developments in mathematical psychology*. San Francisco, CA: Freeman.

Greeno, J. G., James, C. T., & DaPolito, F. J. (1971). A cognitive interpretation of negative transfer and forgetting. *Journal of Verbal Learning and Verbal Behavior, 10,* 331–345.

Greeno, J. G., James, C. T., DaPolito, F. J., & Polson, P. G. (1978). *Associative learning: A cognitive analysis*. Englewood Cliffs, NJ: Prentice-Hall.

Halff, H. M. (1977). The role of opportunities to recall in learning to retrieve. *American Journal of Psychology, 90,* 383–406.

Heth, C. D., & Cornell, E. H. (1983). A learning analysis of spatial concept development in infancy. In J. Bisanz, G. Bisanz, & R. V. Kail, Jr. (Eds.), *Learning in children: Progress in cognitive development research*. New York: Springer-Verlag.

Howe, M. L. (1982). *The structure of associative traces: A mathematical analysis of learning associative clusters*. Unpublished doctoral dissertation, University of Western Ontario.

Howe, M. L., Brainerd, C. J., & Kingma, J. (in press). Development of Organization in recall: A stages-of-learning analysis. *Journal of Experimental Child Psychology*.

Howe, M. L., Brainerd, C. J., & Kingma, J. (1984). *Storage-retrieval processes of normal and learning-disabled children: A stages-of-learning analysis of picture-word effects* (Research report). University of Victoria.

Humphreys, M. S., & Greeno, J. G. (1970). Interpretation of the two-stage analysis of paired-associate memorizing. *Journal of Mathematical Psychology, 7,* 275–292.

Humphreys, M. A., & Yuille, J. C. (1973). Errors as a function of noun concreteness. *Canadian Journal of Psychology, 27,* 83–94.

Kail, R., Hale, C. A., & Leonard, L. B. (1983). *Lexical storage and retrieval in language-impaired children*. Unpublished manuscript, Purdue University.

Kee, D. W., Bell, T. S., & Davis, B. R. (1981). Developmental changes in the effects of presentation mode on the storage and retrieval of noun pairs in children's recognition memory. *Child Development, 52*, 268–279.

Keppel, G., & Underwood, B. J. (1962). Proactive inhibition in short-term retention of single items. *Journal of Verbal Learning and Verbal Behavior, 1*, 153–161.

Kintsch, W. (1963). All-or-none learning and the role of repetition in paired-associate learning. *Science, 140*, 310–312.

Klapp, S. T., Marshburn, E. A., & Lester, P. T. (1983). Short-term memory does not involve the "working memory" of information processing: The demise of a common assumption. *Journal of Experimental Psychology: General, 112*, 240–263.

Klapp, S. T., & Philipoff, A. (1983). *Order and item information in short-term memory: A dual task test of resource independence*. Unpublished manuscript, University of California at Hayward.

Krantz, D. H., Luce, R. D., Suppes, P., & Tversky, A. (1971). *Foundations of measurement* (Vol. 1). New York: Academic Press.

Krantz, D. H., & Tversky, A. (1971). Conjoint-measurement analysis of composition rules in psychology. *Psychological Review, 78*, 151–169.

Maccoby, E. E., & Jacklin, C. N. (1974). *The psychology of sex differences*. Palo Alto, CA: Stanford University Press.

Melton, A. (1963). Implications of short-term memory for a general theory of memory. *Journal of Verbal Learning and Verbal Behavior, 2*, 1–21.

Moely, B. E. (1977). Organizational factors in the development of memory. In R. V. Kail, Jr., & J. W. Hagen (Eds.), *Perspectives on the development of memory and cognition*. Hillsdale, NJ: Lawrence Erlbaum Associates.

Mohs, R. C., Davis, K. L., Levery, M. I. (1981). Partial reversal of anicholinergic amnesia by choline chloride. *Life sciences, 29*, 1317–1323.

Morrison, F. J., Haith, M. M., & Kagan, J. Age trends in rognition memory for pictures: The effects of delay and testing procedure. *Bulletin of the Psychonomic Society*, 1980, *16*, 480–483.

Nelson, T. O. (1978). Detecting small amounts of information in memory: Savings for nonrecognized items. *Journal of Experimental Psychology: Human Learning and Memory, 4*, 453–468.

Norman, D., & Rumelhart, D. (1970). A system for perception and memory. In D. Norman (Ed.), *Models of human memory*. New York: Academic Press.

Paivio, A. (1971). *Imagery and verbal processes*. New York: Holt, Rinehart, & Winston.

Peterson, L., & Peterson, J. (1959). Short-term retention of individual verbal items. *Journal of Experimental Psychology, 58*, 193–198.

Postman, L. (1978). Picture-word differences in the acquisition and retention of paired associates. *Journal of Experimental Psychology: Human Learning and Memory, 4*, 146–157.

Reitman, J. (1970). Computer simulation of an information producing model of short-term memory. In D. Norman (Ed.), *Models of human memory*. New York: Academic Press.

Restle, F., & Greeno, J. G. (1970). *Introduction to mathematical psychology*. Reading, MA: Addison-Wesley.

Richman, C. L., Nida, S., & Pittman, L. (1976). Effects of meaningfulness on child free-recall learning. *Developmental Psychology, 12*, 46–465.

Roder, B., & Chechile, R. A. (1983). *Encoding flexibility and developmental dyslexia*. Unpublished manuscript, Tufts University.

Rogoff, B., Newcombe, N., & Kagan, J. (1974). Planfulness and recognition memory. *Child Development, 45*, 972–977.

Skoff, B., & Chechile, R. A. (1977). Storage and retrieval processes in the serial position effect. *Bulletin of the Psychonomic Society, 9*, 265–268.

Slamecka, N. J., & McElree, B. (1983). Normal forgetting of verbal lists as a function of their degree of learning. *Journal of Experimental Psychology: Learning, Memory, and Cognition, 9*, 384–397.

Surber, J. R., & Surber, C. F. (1983). Effects of inference on memory for prose. *Merrill-Palmer Quarterly, 29*, 197–207.

Theios, J. (1961). *A three-state Markov model for learning* (Technical Report No. 40). Institute for Mathematical Studies in the Social Sciences, Stanford University.

Theios, J. (1963). Simple conditioning as two-stage all-or-none learning. *Psychological Review, 70*, 403–417.

Theios, J. (1965). The mathematical structure of reversal learning in a shock-escape T maze: Overtraining and successive reversals. *Journal of Mathematical Psychology, 2*, 26–52.

Theios, J., & Brelsford, J. W., Jr. (1966). A Markov model for classicial conditioning: Application to eye-blink conditioning in rabbits. *Psychological Review, 73*, 393–408.

Theios, J., & Hakes, D. T. (1962, May). *Paired-associate response shifts in two-stage all-or-none learning*. Paper presented at Midwestern Psychological Association, Chicago, IL.

Theios, J., Leonard, D. W., & Brelsford, J. W., Jr. (1977). Hierarchies of learning models that permit likelihood ratio comparisons. *Journal of Experimental Psychology: General, 106*, 213–225.

Tulving, E. (1972). Episodic and semantic memory. In E. Tulving & W. Donaldson (Eds.), *Organization of memory*. New York: Academic Press.

Waugh, N. C., & Smith, J. E. (1962). A stochastic model for free recall. *Psychometrika, 27*, 141–145.

Wickelgren, W. (1973). The long and the short of memory. *Psychological Bulletin, 80*, 425–438.

Wilkinson, A. C. (1982). Theoretical and methodological analysis of partial knowledge. *Developmental Review, 2*, 274–304.

Wilkinson, A. C., DeMarinis, M., & Riley, S. J. (1983). Developmental and individual differences in rapid remembering. *Child Development, 54*, 898–911.

Wilkinson, A. C., & Koestler, R. (1983). Repeated Recall: A new model and tests of its generality from childhood to old age. *Journal of Experimental Psychology: General, 112*, 423–451.

Wilkinson, A. C., & Koestler, R. (1984). Generality of a Markov model for repeated recall. *Journal of Mathematical Psychology, 28*, 43–72.

Appendix

The Short-Term Memory Model

A detailed development of the parameter estimation scheme for this model appears in Chechile and Meyer (1976, pp. 275–282). This summarizes only those features of the development that are necessary to estimate the model's parameters for modified Brown-Peterson data. Let n_1 be the number of correct recalls in such data, and let n_2 be the number of incorrect recalls. On old recognition trials, let n_{11}, n_{12}, n_{13}, n_{14}, n_{15}, and n_{16} be the numbers of yes 1, yes 2, yes 3, no 1, no 2, and no 3 responses, respectively. On distractor recognition trials, let n_{21}, n_{22}, n_{23}, n_{24}, n_{25}, and n_{26} be the numbers of yes 1, yes 2, yes 3, no 1, no 2, and no 3 responses, respectively. The sampling distributions given the data (a posteriori distributions) of the four parameters of theoretical interest, plus a fifth parameter (θ_{dr}) that measures retrieval forgetting on distractor recognition are

$$P(\theta_s \mid \{n_i\}, \{n_{ij}\}) = K_1 \int_1^0 IP_2 d\theta_{dr}, \tag{4-A-1}$$

$$P(\theta_{dr} \mid \{n_i\}, \{n_{ij}\}) = K_2 \int_0^1 IP_1 P_2 d\theta_s, \tag{4-A-2}$$

$$P(\theta_{rr} \mid \{n_i\}, \{n_{ij}\}) = K_3 \int_0^1 \int_0^1 (\theta_s \theta_{dr} \theta_{rr})^n 1(1 - \theta_s \theta_{dr} \theta_{rr})^n 2 P_1 P_2 d\theta_{dr} \theta_s, \tag{4-A-3}$$

$$P(\theta_g \mid \{n_i\}, \{n_{ij}\}) = K_4 \int_0^1 \int_0^1 IP_2 G_1 d\theta_{dr} d\theta_s, \tag{4-A-4}$$

and

$$P(\theta_{g'} \mid \{n_i\}, \{n_{ij}\}) = K_5 \int_0^1 \int_0^1 IP_1 G_2 d\theta_{dr} d\theta_s, \tag{4-A-5}$$

where $\theta_r = \theta_{dr} \theta_{rr}$ and the $K_1 - K_5$ are constants of integration.

The other terms in these expressions have the following definitions in terms of the theoretical parameters

$$I = (\theta_s \theta_{dr})^{-1} \int_0^{\theta_s \theta_{dr}} x^{n_1} (1 - x)^{n_2} dx, \tag{4-A-6}$$

$$P_1 = (1 - \theta_s)^{n_0 - n_{13}} \theta_s^{n_{13}} \sum_{i=0}^{n_{13}} (C(n_0 + 1, n_{13} - i)(1 - \theta_s/\theta_s)^i) \div$$

$$(C(n_{11} + n_{12} + i + 2, 2), \tag{4-A-7}$$

$$P_2 = (1 - \theta_s \theta_{dr})^{n_d - n_{26}} (\theta_s \theta_{dr})^{n_{26}} \sum_{j=0}^{n_{26}} (C(n_d + 1, n_{26} - j)$$

$$\times (1 - \theta_s\theta_{dr}/\theta_s\theta_{dr})^j) \div (C(n_{24} + n_{25} + j + 2, 2)), \qquad \text{(4-A-8)}$$

$$G_1 = \theta_s^{n_{13}}(1 - \theta_s)^{n_0 - n_{13}} \sum_{i=0}^{n_{13}} ((1 - \theta_s)/\theta_s)^i \theta_g^{n_{11} + n_{12} + i}$$

$$\times (1 - \theta_g)^{n_{14} + n_{15} + n_{16}}) \div ((n_{13} - i)!(n_{11} + n_{12} + i + 2)!),$$

$$\text{(4-A-9)}$$

and

$$G_2 = (\theta_s\theta_{dr})^{n_{26}}(1 - \theta_s\theta_{dr})^{n_d - n_{26}}$$

$$\times \sum_{j=0}^{n_{26}} (((1 - \theta_s\theta_{dr})/\theta_s\theta_{dr})^j \theta_g^{n_{24} + n_{25} + j}$$

$$\times (1 - \theta_{\gamma\supset})^{n_{21} + n_{22} + n_{23}}) \div ((n_{26} - j)!(n_{24} + n_{25} + j + 2)!).$$

$$\text{(4-A-10)}$$

In Equations 4-A-1 to 4-A-5, the observed mode of the a posteriori distribution of each parameter is used as its estimate for modified Brown-Peterson data.

The Two-Stage Model

The parameter estimation procedure for the two-stage model involves, first, the construction of an observable-states Markov model. Because this model has states that correspond to observable features of the data of recall experiments, it is trivially easy to write a likelihood function from which maximum likelihood estimates of all the parameters can be obtained. However, it is also possible to express the probabilities of observable features of the data in terms of the theoretical parameters of the two-stage model (cf. Table 4-4). When these expressions are substituted in the observable model's likelihood function, the two-stage model's parameters can also be estimated. This new likelihod function also serves as the basis for necessity and sufficiency tests.

Consider some recall memorization experiment that has the following structure: $S_1T_1T_2S_2T_2S_3T_3$. . . . In other words, the first study trial is followed by two consecutive test trials, and each subsequent study trial is followed by one test trial. The observable Markov process for such an experiment has the following states:

$Q =$ the state on all trials in protocols with no errors and the state on all trials after the last error in protocols with one or more errors;

$R =$ the state on all error trials that follow the first correct response;

$S =$ the state on all correct response trials that precede the last error;

$E_1 =$ the event of an error on Trial 1;

E_2 = the event of an error on Trial 2 if an error also occurred on Trial 1;
E_3 = the event of an error on Trial 3 if an error occurred on both Trial 1 and Trial 2;

$\vdots$

E_j = the event of an error on Trial j if errors also occurred on Trials 1 to $j - 1$.

The likelihood function for this observable process is

$$L = (\pi_1)^{N(Q_1 Q_2)}(\pi_2)^{N(S_1 R_2)}(\pi_3)^{N(S_1 S_2)}(\pi_4)^{N(E_1 Q_2)}(\pi_5)^{N(E_1 S_2)}$$
$$\times (1 - \pi_1 - \pi_2 - \pi_3 - \pi_4 - \pi_5)^{N(E_1 E_2)} \times (u)^{N(R_i Q_{i+1})}(1 - u)^{N(R_i R_{i+1})}$$
$$+ \, ^{N(R_i S_{i+1})}(v)^{N(R_i R_{i+1})}(1 - v)^{N(R_i S_{i+1})}(w)^{N(S_i R_{i+1})}$$

$$\times \prod_{i=3}^{j} \{(\alpha_i)^{N(E_i Q_{i+1})}(\beta_i)^{N(E_i S_{i+1})}(1 - \alpha_i - \beta_i)^{N(E_i E_{i+1})}\}, \qquad (4\text{-}A\text{-}11)$$

where i is always an integer greater than 2 and j is the maximum length of the initial error run. The variables inside the parentheses are the parameters of the observable model. The exponents are emprical numbers obtained from an experiment. Specifically, each exponent of the form $N(X_k Y_{k+1})$ is simply the number total number of times that protocols were observed to be in observable State X on Trial k and in observable State Y on Trial $k + 1$.

Maximum likelihood estimates of the 11 parameters of the two-stage model can now be found by substituting the definition, in terms of these 11 parameters, for each of the observable parameters in Equation 4-A-11. Equation 4-A-11 or some logarithmic transformation of it is then minimized using any standard computer optimization algorithm. The definitions that are substituted for the observable parameters are these:

$$\pi_1 = a'b' + a'(1 - b')(1 - r)(1 - f)ch/(1 - (1 - c)h), \qquad (4\text{-}A\text{-}12)$$
$$\pi_2 = a'(1 - b')1 - r)(f + (1 - f)(1 - h)), \qquad (4\text{-}A\text{-}13)$$
$$\pi_3 = a'(1 - b')1 - r)(1 - f)(1 - c)(1 - h)h/(1 - (1 - c)h),$$
$$\qquad (4\text{-}A\text{-}14)$$
$$\pi_4 = a'(1 - b')r(1 - f)cg/(1 - (1 - c)h), \qquad (4\text{-}A\text{-}15)$$
$$\pi_5 = a'(1 - b')r(1 - f)(1 - c)(1 - h)g/(1 - (1 - c)h), \qquad (4\text{-}A\text{-}16)$$
$$u = d + (1 - d)gc/(1 - (1 - c)h), \qquad (4\text{-}A\text{-}17)$$
$$v = (1 - g)(1 - (1 - c)h)/((a - g)(1 - (1 - c)h) + (1 - c)(1 - h)g),$$
$$\qquad (4\text{-}A\text{-}18)$$
$$z = 1 - (1 - c)h, \qquad (4\text{-}A\text{-}19)$$

$$
\begin{aligned}
\alpha_i = \Big\{ &(1-a)^{i-2}(1-a'+a'(1-b')rf)(ab+a(1-b) \\
&\times (1-e)c/(1-c)h)) + (a(1-b)e(1-a'+a'(1-b')rf) \\
&\times \Big(\sum_{k=0}^{i-3} (1-a)^k((1-d)(1-g))^{i-3-k,} + a'(1-b')r(1-f) \\
&\times (1-g)((1-d)(1-g))^{i-2} \Big)(d+(1-d)cg/(1-(1-c)h))\} \\
\div \Big\{ &(1-a)^{i-2}(1-a'+a'(1-b')rf) \\
&+ (a(1-b)e(1-a'+a'(1-b)rf) \times \sum_{k=0}^{i-3} (1-a)^k((1-d) \\
&\times (1-g)^{i-3-k}) + a'(1-b')r(1-f)(1-g)((1-d)(1-g))^{i-2}) \Big\},
\end{aligned}
$$

$$(4\text{-A-}20)$$

and

$$
\begin{aligned}
\beta_i = \Big\{ &(1-a)^{i-1}(1-a'+a'(1-b')rf)(a(1-b)(1-e)(1-c) \\
&\times (1-h)/(1-(1-c)h) + (a(1-b)e(1-a'(1-b')rf) \\
&\times \Big(\sum_{k=0}^{i-3} (1-a)^k((1-d)(1-g)^{i-3-k}) + a'(1-b')r(1-f) \\
&\times (1-g)((1-d)(1-g))^{i-2} \Big)((1-d)(1-c) \\
&(1-h)g/(1-(1-c)h)) \Big\} \div \Big\{ (1-a)^{i-2}(1-a'+a'(1-b'rf) \\
&+ (a(1-b)e(1-a'+a'(1-b')fr) \times \Big(\sum_{k=0}^{i-3} (1-a)^k((1-d) \\
&\times (1-g))^{i-3-k} \Big) + a'(1-b')r(1-f)(1-g) \times ((1-d) \\
&\times (1-g))^{i-2}) \Big\}.
\end{aligned}
$$

$$(4\text{-A-}21)$$

When the definitions in Equations 4-A-12 to 4-A-21 are substituted for the variables in Equation 4-A-11 and the revised likelihod function is minimized for some set of data, the calculated values of the 11 parameters at the global minimum of the function are their maximum likelihood estimates for those data. The calculated value of the function itself, $\hat{L}'$, then serves as the basis for necessity and sufficiency tests.

Necessity Test. Since this model assumes that learning involves exactly two stages, the necessity test asks whether a model which assumes that learning involves only one stage will do as good a job of accounting for the data as the two-stage model does. If so, then the two-stage model fails on grounds of parsimony.

The simpler model to which the two-stage model is compared is the general one-stage Markov model (e.g., Greeno, 1968). This model assumes that learning consists of an initial "unlearned" State U in which both errors (substate U_E) and successes (substate U_C) occur followed by a terminal "learned" State L in which only successes occur. The necessity test involves three steps. First, the likelihood of the data under the two-stage model is calculated using the revised version of Equation 4-A-11 (i.e., with the two-stage model's parameters substituted in the function). Call this value $\hat{L}'$. Second, the likelihood of the data under the one-stage model is calculated. Call this value $\hat{L}''$. This second value is calculated from the likelihood function for the one-stage model, which is

$$
\begin{aligned}
L'' = {}& (m + (1 - m)(1 - n)pc'/(1 - (1 - c')p))^{N(Q_1 Q_2)} \\
& \times ((1 - m)ns/(1 - (1 - c')p))^{N(R_1 Q_2)}((1 - m)n(1 - s))^{N(R_1 R)} \\
& \times ((1 - m)(1 - c')(1 - p)ns/(1 - (1 - c')p))^{N(R_1 S_1)} \\
& \times ((1 - m)(1 - n)(1 - p))^{N(S_1 R_1)} \\
& \times ((1 - m)(1 - n)(1 - c')(1 - p)p/(1 - (1 - c')p))^{N(S_1 S_1)} \\
& \times (d' + (1 - d')sc'/(1 - (1 - c')p))^{N(R_i Q_{i+1})} \\
& \times (1 - d' - (1 - d')sc'/(1 - (1 - c')p))^{N(R_i R_{i+1}) + N(R_i S_{i+1})} \\
& \times ((1 - s)(1 - (1 - c')p)/((1 - s) \\
& \times (1 - (1 - c')p) + (1 - c')(1 - p)s))^{N(R_i R_{i+1})} \\
& \times (1 - (1 - s)(1 - (1 - c')p)/((1 - s) \\
& \times (1 - (1 - c')p) + 1 - c')(1 - p)s))^{N(R_i S_{i+1})} \\
& \times (1 - (1 - c')p)^{N(S_i R_{i+1})}((1 - c')p)^{N(S_i S_{i+1})}, \qquad \text{(4-A-22)}
\end{aligned}
$$

where $i > 2$ and the exponents of the last six terms are summed across all values of i.

The variables inside the parentheses are the six parameters of the one-stage model (c', d', m, n, p, s) whose values are to be calculated by minimizing Equation 4-A-22. The exponents, like those of Equation 4-A-11, are observed states in the data. This model has three observable states, namely, Q, R, and S.

The Q and S states have the same definitions as in the two-stage model. However, R is defined as the state on any error trial—that is, it is the combination of the E and R states of the two-stage model. Each exponent in Equation 4-A-22 refers to the total number of times that the process was observed to be in the indicated states on consecutive trials.

The final step is to compute a χ^2 statistic using the calculated likelihoods for the one- and two-stage models. The statistic is

$$\chi^2(5) = -2\log_e(\hat{L}''/\hat{L}'), \qquad (4\text{-}A\text{-}23)$$

where $\hat{L}'$ is the calculated likelihood of the data under the two-stage model and $\hat{L}''$ is the calculated likelihood of the data under the one-stage model. This statistic tests the null hypothesis that the two likelihods are not reliably different against the alternative hypothesis that $\hat{L}'$ is larger. The two-stage model passes the necessity test in those instances where this null hypothesis is rejected.

Sufficiency Test. The rationale for the sufficiency test is given in Brainerd (1984). Conceptually, we wish to test the null hyothesis that learning does not involve more than two stages against the alternative hypothesis that it involves more two stages. The actual test takes advantage of the fact that since the two-stage model has 11 parameters, a model with more stages would have to have more than 11 parameters. Statistically, therefore, one compares the null hypothesis that a model with 11 parameters accounts for the data as well as models with more than 11 parameters against the alternative hypothesis that these other models do a better job. Here, note that the original version of the likelihood function in Equation 4-A-11 is a model of the latter sort. If the maximum length of the initial error run (i.e., the maximum number of trials before the first correct response) is j, it can be seen that this function has a total of $2j + 3$ parameters, a number which is normally much larger than the 11 parameters of the revised function.

The sufficiency test consists of single χ^2 statistic. Let $\hat{L}$ be the likelihood of the data when the original version of Equation 4-A-11 is minimized, and let $\hat{L}$ be the likelihood of the same data when the revised version is minimized. The test statistic is

$$\chi^2(2j - 8) = -2\log_e(\hat{L}'/\hat{L}), \qquad (4\text{-}A\text{-}24)$$

which tests the null hypothesis that the two likelihoods do not differ against the alternative hypothesis that $\hat{L}$ is greater. The two-stage model passes the necessity test if this null hypothesis cannot be rejected, and it fails for completeness otherwise.

Retention Model

It was shown earlier (Table 4-10) that the probabilities of the various error-success patterns in repeated recall experiments can be expressed as functions of the parameters in the Wilkinson model. There are 2^i such patterns in any experiment with i repeated recall cycles. In such an experiment, let $p_k(a, b, \ldots, i)$ denote the probabilities of the various patterns, where each of the index variables $a, b, \ldots, n$ reads 0 (correct recall) or 1 (error). By Bernoulli's theorem, we may express the likelihood of the data of such an experiment as

$$L = \prod_{k=1}^{2^i} (p_k(a, b, \ldots, i)^{N_k}, \qquad (4\text{-}A\text{-}25)$$

where N_k is simply the total number of times that the kth pattern is observed in the data. Since there are 2^i probabilities in Equation 4-A-25, there are $2^i - 1$ parameters.

We have seen that each of the $p_k(a, b, \ldots, i)$ can be expressed as functions of the storage, retrieval, and forgetting parameters of the Wilkinson model. Let $p_k(a, b, \ldots, i)$ be the probability of the kth pattern when it has been expressed in terms of these parameters. We now write the revised likelihood function

$$L' = \prod_{k=1}^{2^i} (p'_k(a, b, \ldots, i)^{N_k}, \qquad (4\text{-}A\text{-}26)$$

where the N_k are the same as in Equation 4-A-25. The Wilkinson model has one storage parameter (s), i retrieval parameters $(r_0 - r_{i-1})$, and $i - 1$ forgetting parameters $(f_1 - f_{i-1})$, for a total of $2i$ parameters. Since $2i$ is always smaller than 2^i whenever $i > 3$, the number of free parameters in Equation 4-A-25 is greater than the number in Equation 4-A-26 in any experiment where there are four or more repeated recall cycles.

A sufficiency test for such an experiment is

$$\chi^2(2^i - i - 1) = -2\log_e(\hat{L}'/\hat{L}), \qquad (4\text{-}A\text{-}27)$$

where $\hat{L}$ is the estimated likelihood of the data when all parameters are free to vary and $\hat{L}'$ the estimated likelihood of the data with the revised likelihood function. This χ^2 statistic tests the null hypothesis that the two likelihoods do not differ against the alternative hypothesis that the likelihood for the original function is greater.

5. Short-Term Memory Development in Childhood and Adolescence

Frank N. Dempster

This chapter is organized into three main sections. The first focuses on current theoretical issues and controversies concerning short-term memory. Here, among other topics, I include an introduction to leading theoretical models of short-term memory and a discussion of the relationship between traditional measures of short-term memory and more complex measures of intellectual ability. Also, I outline a framework for viewing short-term memory entirely in mechanistic or structural terms (see Chapter 3 by Bjorklund for some analogous perspectives on organizational factors in memory). Although some of these topics have little to do with developmental issues per se, they are concerned with matters that I believe have important implications for the study of short-term memory development. The second main section focuses on possible sources of short-term memory development, while the third contains a summary, along with some concluding remarks.

Theoretical Issues and Controversies

The concept of short-term memory is currently a very controversial one, and thus a review seems especially timely now. One controversy is fueled by doubts about the need for a separate short-term memory system. While the existence of a system for storing information on a long-term basis is taken for granted, the existence of a short-term system is a source of debate, with some researchers favoring a single, unitary memory system. A second area of disagreement is definitional; those who assume a distinct short-term system disagree considerably over its nature. A third controversy pertains to the relationship between measures of short-term memory and other measures of intellectual ability, including reading, while a fourth focuses on the relationship between short-term memory performance and age. Each of these issues will be addressed separately.

The Short- and Long-Term Memory Distinction

The distinction between a short- and long-term memory system is by no means recent. In the late 19th century, James (1890) argued that some memories were readily available and even conscious, while others that had been absent from consciousness for some time were often difficult to recall. These two memories he labeled primary and secondary, respectively. But, even these ideas were not new. They were clearly anticipated by a host of English philosophers.

What these arguments largely lacked, the mid-20th century provided, namely, experimental procedures for studying and attempting to verify the existence of short-term memory. A wider acceptance of short-term memory as a separate system was prompted by the Brown-Peterson paradigm, which showed rapid retention loss when rehearsal was prevented by a distractor activity such as counting backwards. Other observations, such as the sharp discontinuity between immediate memory for 6 or 7 items (the typical adult memory span) and information in amounts that exceeded span, as well as the recency effect in free recall, also seemed to argue for a distinct short-term system. But, it is primarily the fact of rapid retention loss of just presented information that led to the widespread belief in short-term memory. In effect, forgetting in short-term memory seemed to follow laws quite different from those directing the forgetting of old, established memories (Broadbent, 1958, 1963; Waugh & Norman, 1965). The particular conception that was to dominate much of the early research was, of course, the Atkinson and Shiffrin (1968) model. In their view, information is read into a limited capacity, short-term store, in which it may be maintained by rehearsal; otherwise it is quickly displaced by other units.

As might be expected, the very popularity of this dual-process view soon drew some influential critics, including Craik and Lockhart (1972) and Postman (1975). In general, these writers questioned the empirical basis of short-term memory and concluded that the construct of short-term memory and theoretically separate memory stores was unnecessary. Among these reactions, the most visible is the proposal by Craik and Lockhart (1972), who reinterpreted many findings in terms of "levels of processing," rather than in terms of different memory systems. Basically, Craik and Lockhart suggested that information may be processed at different levels, ranging from the processing of sensory attributes to the processing of deeper semantic attributes, depending on the time available for processing and the total processing load. Moreover, retention was directly related to degree of processing. In the Brown-Peterson task, for example, it was assumed that rapid forgetting occurred because the conditions only permit a shallow level of processing. However, in some sense, even this framework seems congruent with the separate stores view. Craik and Lockhart themselves commented on this point.

More recent criticisms stem largely from the fact that the concept of short-term memory has not been used consistently (e.g., Crowder, 1983). Indeed, there are now numerous models of short-term memory, and new findings have often been accommodated by the postulation of new memory systems and the fragmentation of short-term memory into distinct components having different specializations. This development raises questions about the usefulness of short-term memory and has resulted in the charge that it has little theoretical value. According to one critic, "since short-term memory includes practically everything, it means practically nothing" (Crowder, 1983).

Despite these criticisms, most researchers do distinguish between short- and long-term memory. In fact, research on, and models of, short-term memory have grown at a phenomenal rate during the last 15 years. It seems to me that the concept of short-term memory is most vulnerable to criticism when it is viewed in terms of the original Atkinson and Shiffrin (1968) model—that is, as a rather passive rehearsal buffer in which the sheer number of rehearsals or length of occupancy in short-term memory is the sole determinant of transfer to long-term memory. There are converging lines of evidence indicating that mere rehearsal, repeating an item in order to keep it in short-term memory, does not lead to long-term storage (e.g, Weist, 1972). However, while this conception of short-term memory as a simple storage "container" or "box" in which information is deposited still persists, it is not as common as it once was. A more dynamic conception of the memory system has evolved with emphasis on differential processes rather than separate stores (see also Brainerd's discussion in Chapter 4 of mathematical models of short-term memory). When conceived in this way, models of short-term memory have proved to be useful in interpreting vast amounts of data.

Another factor that has led to the proliferation of short-term memory models is some recent findings that are difficult to reconcile with a single-system conception. For example, some studies have shown that amnesia patients have scores well below the normal range on tests of word recognition, but have normal immediate memory span scores. The inference is that a system exits that is damaged in these patients and is critically involved in the recognition of words learned years ago but not in the reproduction of a just-presented series. While these sorts of data were known to Atkinson and Shiffrin (1968) and were cited by them, newer neurophysiological data have served to make single-system models even less plausible (see Shallice, 1979, for a review).

But the case against single-system conceptions does not rest on experimental work with atypical populations alone. Recently, Geiselman, Woodward, and Beatty (1982) estimated short- and long-term memory recall from various performance measures representing traditional theoretical distinctions between the two systems. In one experiment, a single-system model was rejected because of inferior statistical fit while a dual-process model, predicated largely on the notion that qualitatively different types of processing should affect short-and long-term recall differentially, was supported. In another it was found that processing intensity (task-induced activation) enhanced recall from long-term memory, but not short-term memory. Further evidence has been reported by Wickens, Moody, and Dow (1981) and Weingartner and Murphy (1977). In the former study, interference effects were found following a distractor task but not in an immediate memory situation, while in the latter study alcohol-impaired recall following a 20-min retention interval, but it had no effect on immediate memory.

In summary, the concept of short-term memory has a long tradition, dating back to the 19th century. Despite numerous criticisms, the concept has achieved widespread acceptance due to its ability to accommodate various findings, including the limitations of immediate recall, rapid retention loss in the absence of rehearsal, and the differential effects of certain variables on short-and long-term recall [Indeed, as noted in Chapter 4 by Brainerd, there are mathematical models that permit one to measure the contributions of process variables to short-term and long-term memory, respectively.] Nevertheless, there is considerable disagreement over the exact nature of short-term memory, a topic to which I now turn.

The Nature of Short-Term Memory

Dissatisfaction with the container metaphor of short-term memory has resulted in a variety of current conceptions of short-term memory, each of which says something different about the nature of short-term memory. For most investigators, including most developmental psychologists, it appears that the term "short-term memory" has simply been replaced by the term "working memory," in order to convey the idea that short-term memory plays an important role in a vast variety of information processing tasks (Anderson, 1976, 1983; Brainerd, 1981; Brainerd & Kingma, 1984; Daneman & Carpenter, 1980; Halford, 1982; Pascual-Leone, 1969; Schneider & Shiffrin, 1977; Shiffrin & Schneider, 1977). An important assumption here is that short-term memory has both storage and processing functions, though it is usually the processing function that is highlighted (see the discussion of Chechile's mathematical model in Chapter 4 by Brainerd). To me, this position does not represent a fundamental change from the predominant earlier conceptions of short-term memory, but rather a shift in emphasis.

A quite different and much more revolutionary approach to short-term memory is exemplified in the work of Baddeley and his colleagues begun in the early 1970s. Essentially, their original undifferentiated view of short-term memory was upset by the observation that when subjects were asked to retain near span digit loads (i.e., six digits) at the same time as they performed reasoning tasks, performance was not impaired as much as they believed it should have been if the demands of the two tasks competed for a single supply of resources (Baddeley & Hitch, 1974). On the basis of this and other observations, Baddeley and his colleagues abandoned the concept of short-term memory and replaced it with a fragmented conception of working memory (see Baddeley, 1981, for a review). In their model, working memory is subdivided into three components: a Central Executive, which is a control center that selects and operates various processes; an Articulatory Loop, which maintains verbal material by subvocal rehearsal; and a Visuospatial Scratchpad, a system that graphically displays propositionally coded information from long-term memory. An important assumption of this model is that there are two separate though related capacity pools, one for the Executive System and one for the storage and display components. Provided that storage demands can be met by the latter, the controller could use its capacity for reasoning and control activities. However, when storage demands exceed storage capacity, some Central Executive capacity will be devoted to storage, with the result that fewer resources will be available for its activities. With this assumption, Baddeley and his colleagues are able to account for the fact that strings of up to three digits do not impair reasoning performance. Other researchers, however, have pointed out weaknesses in this line of reasoning and have suggested that such results can be also accommodated by more conventional models (Dempster, 1981; Halford, 1982).

Another, growing, view of short-term memory assumes that short-term memory and working memory are separate, functionally distinct, systems. In several models of this type, short-term memory is conceived of in much the same way as it was in earlier box models—as a rather passive storage or representational system (Brainerd & Kingma, 1984; Case, 1978; Case, Kurland, & Goldberg, 1982; Greeno, 1973). For Case and his colleagues, short-term memory is distinguished from a working memory that acts as a kind of central computing space where information is transformed. Tests of short-term memory simply require the storage and reproduction of information, whereas tests of working memory require some transformation of the stored information prior to output. Greeno's model (developed to model problem solving) assumes that short-term memory is a system that registers information from external sources and holds it, whereas working memory is seen as a system that mixes and processes information from both external sources and long-term memory. Similarly, Brainerd and Kingma have suggested that short-term memory is specialized for storing and retrieving traces of recently presented information, while working memory is specialized for processing information and for storing traces of processed information. These three models can be contrasted with those in which short-term memory is seen as the active conscious portion of long-term memory, whereas working or intermediate memory is seen as a system that maintains contextual information (Bower, 1975) or serves as a contextual scratchpad, on which certain operations can be performed (Mayer, 1981). Finally, each of these models may be contrasted to one offered by Klapp, Marshburn, & Lester (1983). In their view, short-term memory is specialized for ordered recall, while working memory is specialized for tasks in which order is not critical.

In sum, there is considerable controversy concerning the nature of short-term memory, but the trend has been toward increasing fractionation of short-term memory, including the articulation of separate capacity pools. While empirical evaluation of alternative models of short-term memory has failed to keep pace with these developments, there are some recent signs that efforts of this sort will become more plentiful. One indicator is experiments designed to assess the proposition that short-term memory and information processing are governed by the same limited capacity system (Brainerd & Kingma, 1984; Klapp et al., 1983). One of the strategies featured in this effort makes use of the concurrent memory load technique adopted by Baddeley and Hitch (1974). Using this strategy, Klapp et al. found that requiring subjects to perform a simple numerical discrimination or a letter-matching task did not affect digit span performance, a finding that they interpreted as inconsistent with the single short-term system hypothesis. However, in view of the simplicity of the processing tasks, I see no reason why interference should have occurred, and thus I see no reason to reject the common resource hypothesis. Besides, other research has provided hard evidence for short-term memory involvement in reasoning tasks, even when the reasoning task made either no obvious storage demands (Baddeley and Hitch, 1974) or minimal storage demands (Wanner & Shiner, 1976). Although the effects observed by Baddeley and Hitch were small, their reasoning task was one that should have made only minor capacity demands (see Halford, 1982, pp. 321–322 for further discussion).

A second favored strategy is to determine whether or not memory and processing activities react differently to selected experimental manipulations (Brainerd & Kingma, 1984; Klapp et al., 1983). Klapp et al. found that certain manipulations, including rhythmic grouping, that normally affect digit span did not affect performance in a task in which subjects were asked to name the digit that was missing in a string of eight digits. Since this task did not require ordered recall, they concluded that a separate working memory system exists for tasks in which order is not critical. But here again the results are not decisive. Their manipulations may have more to do with response production factors or an output buffer specializing in the conversion of cognitive units to speech units (see Baddeley, Thomson, & Buchanan, 1975; Klapp, 1976) than with memory per se. If so, then one would not expect these same manipulations to affect performance on tasks in which a series of items need not be recalled.

In the Brainerd and Kingma (1984) study it was found that manipulations that affected the difficulty of performance in various childhood reasoning tasks had no affect on memory for background facts and vice versa. Moreover, a series of experiments showed that memory performance and reasoning were almost completely independent. They concluded that these data were inconsistent with the common resource hypothesis. However, in their study memory for background facts was tested following an interval during which the child's reasoning was probed with a set of questions. Accordingly, there is no way of knowing what the child remembered at the time his or her reasoning was probed or what affect these probes had on the child's memory performance. In short, I am not sure how to interpret these data.

Taken together, these data as well as the sheer number of alternative conceptions of short-term memory make it difficult to write a chapter on short-term memory, but I have decided to be guided by parsimony and my intuition that working memories are really short-term memories (i.e., the activated portion of long-term memory) in the process of decay. Further assumptions are spelled out in a later section.

Short-Term Memory and Intelligence

Some early investigators saw that short-term memory might have some important intellectual implications. William James (1890) was one, but the classic example is Binet and Simon (1905), who included the digit span test on the first widely used intelligence test. They did this even though they considered "memory" tests less useful than tests of judgment. However, we can assume that Binet and Simon thought that digit span would do a good job of identifying individuals unable to profit from ordinary schooling. It is likely that they were aware of the work of Jacobs (1887), who found a strong relationship between a pupil's rank in class and his or her span, and of Galton's (1887) observation that mentally defective individuals rarely had spans of more than two. Perhaps they were even aware of Oliver Wendell Holmes' (1871) characterization of the span as "a very simple mental dynamometer which may yet find its place in education" (p. 33). Not all characterizations of the relation between short-term memory and intellectual ability were so global, however. Huey (1908) in his classical work on reading, for example, stressed the importance of primary memory for the comprehension of text. In order to read with reasonable comprehension, it seemed to him that at any given moment a portion of what has been read must be "suspended" briefly in memory.

Nevertheless, there is still some question as to whether short-term memory functioning plays an important role in ecologically valid tasks or whether its value is restricted mainly to traditional laboratory settings (see for example, Neisser, 1982). Why should we invest so much time and energy studying short-term memory, when to the typical layperson, the interesting phenomena of memory would include such things as "the limitations of his memory for early childhood, his inability to remember appointments, (and) his aunt who could recite poems from memory by the hour" (Neisser, 1982, p. 5)? Even educators often give the impression that short-term memory is equivalent to "rote learning" and regard short-term memory proficiency as antithetical to academic excellence (see Rohwer & Dempster, 1977, for a discussion). If these examples are not persuasive, particularly of the attitude of many educators, consider the response one would get were one to seek the approval of school administrators to do a study of, say, memory span.

To some extent, of course, this attitude reflects a misconception of what most students of memory mean when they use the term short-term memory. But, in some cases, a casual reading of the memory literature might well reinforce the belief that short-term memory is largely irrelevant to real-world matters. For example, the correlations of digit span with other subtests of the Wechsler Adult Intelligence Test (WAIS) are lower, on average, than those of the other subtests with themselves. For subjects aged 20–34, the average correlation is only .38 (Wechsler, 1958). Similarly, low correlations appear when the criterion measures are the subtests of the Wechsler Intelligence Scale for Children (WISC) (Jensen & Osborne, 1979). Even more compelling are the results of a study by Chiang and Atkinson (1976), who found near zero correlations between digit span and Scholastic Aptitude Test (SAT) scores, both verbal and mathematical. In two more recent studies of university students, correlations between span and SAT scores, while significant, were only in the .30s and .40s (Daneman & Carpenter, 1980; Standing, Bond, Smith, & Isley, 1980). Moreover, while retarded individuals have much smaller spans than normal (Spitz, 1972), no significant differences have been found in spans among gifted children (Jackson & Myers, 1982) nor between gifted children and normals (Globerson, 1983). These results suggest that short-term memory has few intellectual consequences, except when the level of functioning is well below normal.

At first glance, it does not appear that span differences are related to less global measures such as specific indices of reading ability either. Guyer and Friedman (1975) found no significant differences in span performance between normally reading children and children who were 2 years behind in reading achievement. More recently, DeSoto and DeSoto (1983) measured auditory span for unrelated words, visual span for object pictures, and visual span for related syllables in a large sample of 9- and 10-year-olds. Although each of the span measures was correlated with reading achievement, none accounted for more than 11% of the variance after the effects of intelligence were removed.

Low correlations have also been found between span and specific indices of reading ability in adults. Daneman and Carpenter (1980) assessed reading comprehension with a test that required subjects to answer questions about facts given in narrative passages and a test that required readers to identify referent pronouns appearing earlier in the passage. Correlatons between scores on these tests and word span were not significant. Similar findings were reported more recently by Masson and Miller (1983). Equally striking are results of a study by Crawford and Stankov (1983), who found very weak correlations between both forward and backward digit span and a composite measure of several comprehension tasks. Finally, in a study of older adults (mean age = 71), Cornelius, Willis, Nesselroade, and Baltes (1983) found that whereas visual number span accounted for about 25% of the variance in various comprehension measures, including a test of vocabulary and word meanings, auditory number span showed relatively low correlations (in the .30s). Thus, for children and adults, memory span scores, the most widely used estimate of short-term memory functioning, are in many cases either uncorrelated with or only weakly correlated with school-related ability measures.

For a number of reasons, however, it would be premature to conclude that short-term memory does not have important cognitive consequences. One reason is that span is one of the least reliable subtests on psychometric measures of cognitive ability; including the WAIS, where for most age ranges the reliabilities are in the .60s. Spans are quite unstable, as is evident when individual span scores are plotted across trials (Torgeson & Houck, 1980) or when spans are tested 2 years apart (Lachman, 1983). This suggests that low correlations may be due to low reliabilities, an interpretation that is consistent with the fact that correlations with span often increase considerably after being corrected for attenuation. For example, the corrected correlations between digit span and full-scale WAIS (minus digit span) are in the .70s for most age ranges (Jensen, 1964). Moreover, when the reliability of measurement is increased by calculating an individual's span on the basis of mean performance across many different trials, span accounts for about 50% of the variance in a variety of aptitude/achievement test scores, including SAT scores (Dempster & Cooney, 1982).

It is also possible that low correlations could have resulted from a restricted range of ability scores (see Crawford & Stankov, 1983, p. 249, and Standing et al., 1980, p. 537), or from a preponderance of relatively high ability scores, as was the case in studies by Chiang and Atkinson, 1976 (mean SAT verbal score = 600), Daneman and Carpenter, 1980 (mean SAT score = 570), and studies with gifted children (Globerson, 1983; Jackson & Myers, 1982). This last hypothesis has at least two sources of support. First, the higher correlations reported by Dempster and Cooney (1982) were obtained using a sample of undergraduates with substantially lower SAT scores (mean SAT score = 485 verbal and 547 mathematical). Second, while De Soto and De Soto (1983) found that span was only weakly associated with the entire range of reading achievement sampled, span was a good predictor when underachieving readers were considered separately.

In short, span differences appear to have important real-world consequences, except at the upper range of abilities. However, this does not imply that span is irrelevant at higher ability levels. It is more likely that all subjects in this range have at least the average span and that this is a necessary but not a sufficient condition for high ability. Wechsler (1958) argued that only very low spans have predictive utility, since they are invariably associated with mental retardation. It now appears that this argument is only partly true; spans in the low and middle ranges are also good predictors of more general intellectual abilities.

A final interpretation of the low correlations between span and other ability measures is that span is a poor measure of short-term memory. Some researchers have argued that the span task is an undesirable measure of short-term memory because it is subject to output interference and other production factors (Cohen & Sandberg, 1977; Merkle & Hall, 1982). There is evidence to support this claim, because the act of recalling stored information does seem to interfere with the retention of information still awaiting recall (Anderson, 1960; Sperling, 1963). One way in which output interference could be reduced is to measure partial recall by probing only a few serial positions. Cohen and his associates developed a procedure whereby subjects are presented with 9-digit lists and are cued after each list to recall the first 3, the second 3, or the final 3 digits in serial order.   With this procedure, studies with children have consistently found that IQ and achievement test scores are highly correlated with recall of middle and late items, but not early items (Cohen & Lavin, 1978; Cohen & Sandberg, 1977; Merkle & Hall, 1982). With college students, the results were mixed . One study (Crawford & Stankov, 1983) produced the same pattern as with children, but another produced near-zero correlations for all serial positions (Merkle & Hall, 1982).

A similar argument has been given for using a running memory span task in which the subject is presented with supraspan lists of varying lengths and is usually asked to respond with the last few digits in serial order. Given the close correspondence between these task requirements and those of the probed serial recall task, it is not surprising that running memory span scores correlate with ability test scores in children (Cohen & Lavin, 1978; Cohen & Sandberg, 1977; Merkle & Hall, 1982). With adults, near-zero correlations were found (Merkle & Hall, 1982), but procedural variations render the results indecisive.

Many other researchers have argued that span is not an optimal measure of short-term memory because it fails to tap its processing function (Case, 1978; Daneman & Carpenter, 1980; Pascual-Leone, 1969). This argument is supported by the fact that backward digit span, which requires a reordering of the input, is often, though not necessarily (see Crawford & Stankov, 1983; Jensen & Osborne, 1979), more highly correlated with other IQ measures than forward span. Furthermore, backward span shows greater age change than forward span (e.g., Jensen & Osborne, 1979). Accordingly, some researchers have sought more "complex" measures of short-term memory designed to reflect a wider range of short-term memory functions.

One such measure, continuous paired associates, requires the subject to keep track of the current association between each of a small set of stimuli (usually letters) and one of a large set of responses (usually numbers) while the association is changed repeatedly. On test trials, one of the stimuli is presented alone and the subject is asked to state the response most recently paired with it. When the lag, defined as the number of pairings intervening beween the study trial and the test trial, is varied, the data from this task can be used to estimate four parameters, which have been shown to fit the results of a number of experiments very accurately: α, the probability of entry of an item into short-term memory; γ, the number of items that can be held in short-term memory at one time; θ, the rate of transfer of information into long term memory; and τ, the rate at which information becomes unavailable.

Hunt, Frost, & Lunneborg (1973) administered this task to a sample of undergraduates who had taken a battery of tests, including measures of vocabulary, reading, mathematics, and spatial ability. The most striking difference was that τ was reliably lower for subjects who scored high on the composite quantitative tests than for those who scored low. Presumably, the high group was distracted less than the low group by incoming information after an item had been fixed in memory. In addition, subjects with high quantitative scores had considerably higher α scores than subjects with low quantitative scores and subjects with high verbal scores had considerably higher γ scores than subjects with low verbal scores, though neither of these differences was significant. In a later study with older adults, moderately strong correlations emerged between simple recall scores and a number of verbal ability test scores, as well as Raven's Progressive Matrices Test (r's in the .50s and .60s, Cornelius et al., 1983). Moreover, these correlations were higher than those between these same ability measures and number span scores.

Another short-term memory measure that has been found to correlate well with verbal ability is the reading span measure (Daneman & Carpenter, 1980). In this task, subjects read aloud or listen to a series of sentences and then recall the final word of each sentence. Compared to word span, which was weakly correlated with three reading comprehension measures (see preceding), the correlations between these measures and reading span were considerably higher (r's = .40s to .80s) in studies with university students (Daneman & Carpenter, 1980; Masson & Miller, 1983). These correlations were attributed to the heavier processing demands of the reading span task as compared to the memory span task. In addition, subjects with shorter sentence spans made qualitatively different types of errors on fact retrieval and pronoun referent questions. These tended to be more serious, such as confusions reflecting a fundamental misunderstanding of a passage, than those made by other subjects. These results suggest that a relatively slight short-term memory deficiency can have important intellectual consequences.

Finally, the imposition of a short delay between presentation and responding can result in stronger relationships between short-term memory performance and ability measures. In a study of older adults, Cornelius et al. (1983) found that delayed number span scores were more highly correlated (r's = .40s) with most of their ability measures than were number span scores with immediate recall. Using a task in which children made same/different judgments for two series of abstract objects, Cummings and Faw (1976) found that poor readers performed more poorly than normal readers (matched on IQ) only when the comparison series was presented 1 to 6 s following presentation of the standard series. No reading ability differences emerged when the two series were presented simultaneously and, thus, when the subject could give his or her response immediately. Note that this task also minimized response requirements.

In sum, weak correlations between memory span and ability measures can often be attributed to low reliabilities resulting from too few span trials, a restricted range of ability scores, or to ability levels with which span differences are not associated. Under more ideal conditions, span differences are associated with various ability test differences in the normal and subnormal ranges of ability. Nevertheless, there is substantial evidence that other measures of short-term memory, including some that are less complicated by response requirements, some that require the subject to keep track of changing terms, some that have more active processing requirements, and some that require delayed responding, are more strongly correlated with ability differences than is the traditional memory span measure. In short, research as a whole is consistent with the view that short-term memory plays an important role in intellectual functioning.

Short-Term Memory Performance and Age

What is the relationship between short-term memory performance and age? Most researchers seem to believe that short-term memory is critical and that it improves considerably from infancy to adulthood. However, I still encounter the view that changes in short-term memory performance in the developing child are minor and that changes in long-term memory are much more important (but see Chapter 6 by Kail for some possible invariants in long-term memory development). I think the primary basis for this view is that some short-term memory measures show little age change or little change in certain age ranges. Those that come to mind are digit span, immediate recognition memory, and the recency effect in free recall.

There are two aspects of digit span development that promote the idea that short-term memory improvements are rather small compared to changes in other areas of intellectual functioning. First, between the ages of 2½ and young adulthood there is roughly a threefold increase in span, with most studies of adults using college students (e.g., Dempster, 1981, p. 66). Presumably, if nonselected groups of adults were used, the change would be even less. This increase is not large in view of the remarkable improvements in intellectual functioning that occur during this period. Second, while digit span increases rapidly during early childhood, the rate of increase is much slower thereafter. In fact, the improvements in digit span from age 7 to 13, a period of marked increases in general cognitive ability, is little more than 1½ digits. The increase from age 13 to adulthood is less than a digit (Dempster, 1981; Jensen & Osborne, 1979).

However, as I indicated in the previous section, digit span may be a rather insensitive measure of short-term memory. Tasks that use supraspan length lists such as serial recall, tend to yield larger age differences (e.g., Frank & Rabinovitch, 1974; Ornstein & Naus, 1978; Siegel & Allik, 1973). Moreover, age differences tend to be greatest on tasks that require some kind of transformation of information. For example, there is more than a fivefold increase in backward digit span between the ages of 6 and 13, and in the 7 to 13 age range the increase is about 3 digits (Jensen & Osborne, 1979). Compared with other short-term memory tasks, therefore, digit span may be a relatively insensitive measure of short-term memory, and the less than spectacular increases in span should be viewed in this light (see the discussion of age changes in selected short-term memory parameters in Chapter 4 by Brainerd).

Another reason for the view that short-term memory has little developmental significance is that short-term recognition memory may show little, if any, increase with age (e.g., Brown 1975; Perlmutter & Lange, 1978). In fact, young children may exhibit high levels of recognition memory performance equal to or nearly equal to those of adults. This has often been interpreted to mean that at least some components of short-term memory are developmentally invariant (e.g., Brown, 1975). However, some researchers have questioned this conclusion by noting that ceiling effects, which often accompany recognition performance, may conceal age differences (Mandler & Robinson, 1978). Recently, in fact, significant age differences in recognition memory have been obtained using other measures (Sophian & Stigler, 1981; Stoneman & Brady, 1983).

Finally, many studies of free recall have yielded large age differences in prerecency recall, differences usually attributed to long-term memory storage and retrieval processes, but little or no age differences in the recall of recency items. Since it is assumed that the final items on a list are maintained in short-term memory during the interval between presentation and recall (e.g., Moely, 1977), these results have also led to the conclusion that at least some short-term memory processes are independent of age (Belmont & Butterfield, 1969; Moely, 1977; Ornstein, 1978). However, recency performance, like recognition performance, is often contaminated by ceiling effects, especially for the final item (Dempster & Rohwer, 1983). When the recency effect is expanded to include other items in addition to the final one, or when ceiling effects are not present, age differences in recency are nearly as large as those in primacy (Dempster & Rohwer, 1983).

In conclusion, standard short-term memory measures all reveal significant age improvements, although the magnitude of these differences varies depending on specific task demands. The question that I now turn to concerns the source of these improvements.

The Development of Short-Term Memory

The position taken in this chapter is that short-term memory is the *active* portion of long-term memory. Accordingly, the search for sources of improvement in short-term memory should, strictly speaking, be limited to aspects of the activation cycle. Three dimensions of activation seem especially important: (a) activation energy (or capacity)—the maximum number, or amount, of long-term memory representations that can be activated, or reactivated, simultaneously or in near simultaneous fashion; (b) speed of activation (in a more general sense, speed of information processing)—the speed with which an inactive representation can be activated or a recently activated representation can be reactivated; and, (c) rate of deactivation (decay)—the rate at which an activated representation deactivates or subsides to its preactivation long-term memory state.

Viewed in this way, potential sources of short-term memory improvement are structural, nonstrategic, and mechanistic in nature (on the basis of different data, Bjorklund makes a similar argument about organization in Chapter 3). In contrast to long-term memory, therefore, short-term memory is content-free, and improvements in short-term memory can occur only as a normal consequence of biological development. Each of these possible sources of short-term memory improvement will be considered separately.

Capacity (Activation Energy)

Currently, one of the more pervasive theories in the field of cognitive development is that capacity increases throughout childhood and adolescence and that this increase is a major source of age-related changes in intellectual proficiency (e.g., Brainerd, 1981; Biggs, 1971; Case, 1972, 1974; Fischer, 1980; Halford, 1982; Halford & Wilson, 1980; McLaughlin, 1963; Pascual-Leone, 1970, 1973). The appeal of the capacity increase hypothesis is obvious, since age-correlated limitations in capacity would have considerable explanatory power. Indeed, a "shifting upper limit" of such a fundamental nature (Fischer & Bullock, 1981) would seem to predict the kind of stagelike changes that some investigators believe characterize intellectual development, e.g., Flavell, 1982.

Most proponents of the capacity increase hypothesis cite age-related increases in digit span. This is probably due to the fact that digit span norms are widely available, whereas norms for other short-term memory measures are lacking. In addition, span is a measure of maximum performance and the task is easily understood even by young children. However, critics have pointed out that span differences might reflect various long-term memory factors, such as chunking (a process of organizing or grouping stimuli into capacity-conserving chunks [Miller, 1956]) and rehearsal strategies, which can affect the timing and the content of the reactivation process.

The chunking hypothesis is based on the observation that digits tend to occur frequently in various sequential combinations, so that some combinations become more and more familiar with experience. Thus, many sequences are assumed to be chunkable, with the degree of chunking being a function of knowledge of specific combinations and the tendency to employ a chunking strategy (Bachelder & Denny, 1977; Chi, 1976; Dempster, 1978).

Though the fast presentation rates on span tests and the fact that familiar combinations are usually avoided may seem to render this hypothesis implausible (Halford, 1982, p. 345; Huttenlocker & Burke, 1976), certain findings provide it with a measure of credibility. Some of these data are fairly well known, including the way that different kinds of materials yield different span values, and the fact that while practice increases digit span, the increase does not generalize to other material (Ericsson, Chase, & Faloon, 1980; Gates & Taylor, 1925). But, there are other, less well-known observations that are also consistent with this hypothesis. One observation, rarely documented, is that some digit span series are easier than others of the same length. Especially easy are those containing a pair of numbers descending by 1 (e.g., 7, 6), several even numbers in succession (e.g., 6, 2, 8), and many small digits (e.g., 3, 1, 4, 2) (Mefferd, Wieland, & James, 1966). Another observation is that these and other combinations, such as repetitions and rule-defined runs (2, 5, 8) can be found in conventionally constructed series as well as on standardized span tests, including the Wechsler (Dempster & Zinkgraf, 1982) and the Illinois Test of Psycholinguistic Abilities. Finally, in a study using a fast-paced serial recall task, the subjects (who were all college students) performed best with a list that contained very obvious patterns, next best with one that included the sort of combinations referred to above, and poorest with unfamiliar combinations of any kind (Dempster & Zinkgraf, 1982). Thus, the hypothesis that some of the age-related increase in digit span is due to differential familarity with digits does not appear to be entirely implausible, and cannot be dismissed simply on that basis.

For the most part, the chunking hypothesis has been examined by comparing performance on unfamiliar and familiar sequences. The results of these studies have been somewhat mixed. On the one hand, Burtis (1982) found that sequences consisting of consonant pairs designed to be difficult to chunk at any age (e.g., Z, M) revealed age differences of the same size as sequences consisting of two identical consonants designed to be easy to chunk. In addition, the age effect was fairly large considering the age range of his sample (10- to 14-year-olds). Burtis concluded that his results provided no support for the chunking hypothesis and that the age differences were due to underlying growth in capacity. On the other hand, several studies using subjects from broader age ranges found little age difference in span using difficult to chunk material (Dempster, 1978; Hess & Radtke, 1981; Ross, 1969). These increases were extremely small when contrasted with digit span increases of about 40% in this same age range (7- to 15-year-olds). These results, in my opinion, are very difficult to reconcile with the view that the digit span increases reflect some underlying growth in capacity, at least in this age range. Below this range, the chunking hypothesis has not been subjected to similar experimentation. However, extant data suggest that there are significant differences in span that are not attributable to chunking (e.g., Case et al., 1982; Yussen & Levy, 1975), though this is not to say that there is any evidence that these differences are due to a capacity increase.

While chunking differences have been inferred simply by comparing performance under different conditions of familiarity, which may be seen as a dubious procedure (e.g., Halford, 1982), a variety of more direct measures have been used to study rehearsal (see Dempster, 1981, for a review). What is more, these measures have yielded similar results and provide firm support for the following conclusions. (a) Very young children either do not rehearse at all or rehearse very little (e.g., Garrity, 1975). (b) Between the ages of about 6 and 9, children tend to rehearse the item currently being presented either alone or in combination with just one or two other items, whereas older children tend to rehearse more items together (Belmont & Butterfield, 1969; Ornstein, Naus, & Liberty, 1975). (c) Rehearsal activity, in the sense of sheer amount in 4- and 5-year-olds (Garrity, 1975) and in the sense of the number of unique items rehearsed together in older children (Belmont & Butterfield, 1969; Naus, Ornstein & Aivano, 1977; Ornstein, Naus, & Stone, 1977) is positively correlated with recall.

Taken at face value, these findings might imply that rehearsal is an important source of span growth. However, in all of the studies above, supraspan lists were presented at rates considerably slower than traditional span rates, characteristics that clearly provide greater opportunity for rehearsal and which favor its use. In addition, the relationship between rehearsal activity and recall is probably due to enhanced retrieval of rehearsed items from long-term memory (Ornstein et al., 1977). Thus, these findings do not implicate rehearsal differences in span growth.

Another task that has been used to draw inferences about rehearsal processes and that is more comparable to the digit span task is the running span task described earlier. This is predicated on the assumption, which has some support (e.g., Crowder, 1969; Hockey, 1973), that it affords little or no advantage to rehearsing items in combination. In a study by Frank and Rabinovitch (1974), children from three age levels (8, 10, and 12) were administered this task and a fixed span task. Age differences in the fixed span task were typical for this age range, but in the memory span task they were about two-thirds less. In addition, the performance of the 8-year-olds was scarcely affected by the task manipulation. These results may be interpreted to mean that "active" rehearsal is an important source of age differences in conventional span tasks during this age range, but more important from the present perspective, they raise further doubts about the capacity increase hypothesis.

In short, there is really no evidence that increased capacity is a source of age differences in digit span or other traditional short-term memory tasks. Moreover, other kinds of "span" measures have also yielded results contrary to the capacity increase hypothesis. In the apprehension span task, for example, which requires subjects to quantify a variable number of dots as quickly as possible, the results suggests that young children and adults can quantify about the same number of dots (three or four) without counting (Chi & Klahr, 1975). Another span that does not increase with age is the span of the recency effect in free recall (the sudden increase in recall probability associated with the final items in a free recall series). In one study with children aged, 9, 12, and 15, this span was about three items for each age group (Dempster & Rohwer, 1983).

While most proponents of capacity increase have not attempted to quantify the increase nor link it in a precise way to general cognitive development, several theories have been proposed which do. A seminal theory of this type was offered by McLaughlin (1963) who suggested that capacity limitations constrain the child's ability to consider binary concepts simultaneously. McLaughlin proposed that each measurable increase in capacity corresponds with one of Piaget's developmental stages. For example, the capacity to distinguish between 2^0 concepts simultaneously corresponds to the sensori-motor stage while the capacity to distinguish 2^3 concepts simultaneously corresponds to the period of logical operations. Thus, the child's capacity is assumed to increase from a level at which he or she is able to maintain one concept in mind at a time to a level at which he or she is able to maintain eight concepts in mind at a time.

There are several criticisms of this theory. The first is that the relationship between levels and the number of concepts that could be kept in mind were never worked out in detail, and, perhaps as a result, the theory was never subjected to empirical study. Second, concept values were derived directly from digit span norms. However, the evidence reviewed earlier is inconsistent with the view that digit span norms reflect increased capacity. Moreover, as I suggested earlier, digit span is probably a poor estimate of capacity. Super-ficially at least, one nice fit between these norms and developmental stages occurs at the formal operational stage: many people fail to ever reach this stage (Niemark, 1975), and spans of 8, even among adults, are not that common.

A more detailed, and much more complex, formulation was provided by Pascual-Leone.[1] To begin with, the theory uses as its basic construct the Piagetian notion of a scheme, but goes further than Piaget by classifying schemes into three main categories: (a) figuratives, which are analogous to chunks; (b) operatives, which are rules and strategies; and, (c) executives, which include task procedures, task goals, and solution plans. Executive schemes are often responsible for determining just which operative and figurative schemes will be activated in a given problem situation.

Pascual-Leone proposed that whether or not a particular individual succeeds in a given task depends on two principal factors. The first is the repertoire of schemes the individual has available, and the second is the maximum number of schemes the child is capable of coordinating, under executive control, simultaneously. This quantity is referred to as M-space or M-energy. In most respects, it is functionally equivalent to short-term memory, although Pascual-Leone uses this term in the more active sense rather than in the more passive storage sense (Pascual-Leone, 1973).

The most important assumption made about M-space is that it increases steadily about one scheme every 2 years, from one unit at age 3 to seven units at age 16. But while the number of figurative and operative schemes capable of being activated and maintained under the direction of the executive scheme increases with age, the capacity needed to activate and maintain an executive scheme does not. Another point of particular relevance is that an individual's

---

[1]A few of the more accessible accounts of Pascual-Leone's theory may be found in Pascual-Leone (1970, 1980), Ammon (1977), and Case (1974), with Ammon's account perhaps the most concrete, readable, and informative of the lot.

attention is not always focused on task-relevant, goal-directed aspects of the situation. This is especially so for younger children, who have less mental energy for activating and maintaining task-relevant schemes. Pascual-Leone proposed that schemes associated with certain feelings and schemes activated by sensory inputs (which I shall call field schemes) can also play an important role in performance. The relation between M-space and field schemes suggests an explanation for the fact that individuals become increasingly field-independent between infancy and adulthood, and it suggests that relatively field-dependent people (of whatever age) exposed to misleading perceptual cues, will perform as if their M-space is lower than it actually is.

These various features of the theory dictate the minimum requirements for a "pure" measure of M-space. First, the task must be preceded by a familiarization session, to ensure that the appropriate executive scheme is available. Second, the task must be free of misleading perceptual cues. Third, the task must require some kind of mental transformation to ensure that a wide range of short-term memory functioning is taxed. Finally, if each figurative scheme is to function as a separate unit, the task should not permit the use of sophisticated strategies, such as chunking, which are likely to vary with age. For this reason, digit span and backward digit span, which may be subject to chunking strategies, do not qualify as measures of M-space. However, backward digit span, which does require a transformation, would be expected to be a better measure of M-space than digit span. In fact, the age norms for the former are more comparable with M-space values than norms for the latter (Case & Globerson, 1974).

Pascual-Leone's model has been the subject of a fairly extensive research program and the overall theory has received some measure of support. I will not attempt to summarize this research here, since summaries exist that are widely available (see Ammon, 1977; Case, 1978; Halford, 1982). Instead, I will focus upon tests of M-space, the results of which are relevant to age-related increases in short-term memory capacity.

The first task devised to measure M-space is the Compound Visual Stimulus Information (CVSI) task (Pascual-Leone, 1970). On this task, children aged, 5, 7, 9, and 11 were taught a different novel response (e.g., raise hand, clap hands) to each of several different visual cues (e.g., square shape, red color). After learning the entire set to criterion, they were presented with several compound stimuli (e.g., red square) which varied in terms of the number of cues each contained. Each compound was exposed for 5 s and the child's task was to "decode the message" by producing every response that was appropriate. The results show that the number of correct responses produced increased linearly from roughly two at age 5 to five at age 11, as predicted by the model. According to Pascual-Leone's analysis, a child ceases to output responses when the number of previously made responses that he must keep in mind exceeds his capacity. Hence, the failure of younger children to produce as many correct responses as older children was attributed to their more limited capacity.

Since then, a number of other measures of M-space have been developed and used (e.g., Case, 1972; Case, Kurland, & Goldberg, 1982; Globerson, 1983;

Parkinson, 1976). While I have not read all the reports that are cited (e.g., dissertations that are not readily available), I am not as impressed as many writers are with the overall degree of correspondence between the theory and the data. For one thing, different measures have yielded different age norms (e.g., Globerson, 1983) and one measure produced sharply different estimates in two independent studies (Case, 1972; Globerson, 1983). Further, not all tasks that seem to meet the requirements of an M-space measure show the predicted increments of one unit per 2 years (Foellinger & Trabasso, 1977). Finally, there is not always a close degree of correspondence between M-space estimates and the number of figurative schemes required to solve conservation tasks (Lawson, 1976).

But, while measures of M-space have not consistently yielded the growth pattern claimed by Pascual-Leone, they all have yielded increased performance with age. Since these measures were designed to test the limits of short-term memory, this raises the more general question of whether these increases reflect a capacity increase. My response is that they probably do not. Consider, for example, the learning phase of the CVSI task. Although every child was taught to respond to the entire set without error, it cannot be assumed that there were equivalent degrees of learning. Ordinarily, rate of learning is correlated with retention (Underwood, 1964). It seems likely that the older children, who learned more quickly, mastered the novel units more thoroughly than the younger ones. Simply on this basis, older children should have been able to produce more responses. One bit of evidence that is more consistent with this interpretation than with capacity increase is that there were large discrepancies in findings on different cue-response combinations, with age effects apparent on some, but not on others (Pascual-Leone, 1970, Figure 1). Thus, the predicted age effect depended on the specific items used. This difficulty is compounded by the fact that the total number of responses requested were confounded with the age of the children, so that the observed data were likely, a priori, to resemble those predicted by the model (Trabasso & Foellinger, 1978).

In studies using another M-space measure, the digit placement task (Case, 1972; Globerson, 1983) children were exposed to a series of numbers presented one at a time and, except for the last, always in ascending order of magnitude (e.g., 3, 9, 18, 11). The object, then, was to place the final number in its correct ordinal position with respect to the remainder of the series. Although the children received practice trials, it may be questioned whether they all were able to execute the task with equal ease. Quite possibly, the older children, who would have had more experience ordering numbers, were able to order using less capacity than the younger children. If so, then the age effect observed with this measure may be more readily explained in terms of the older children having more of their capacity free for storing the individual numbers than to their having more capacity per se.

Finally, Case et al. (1982) have provided hard evidence that the results of the counting span measure of M-space are attributable to increased operational efficiency or speed of processing. In this task, subjects are presented with a set of arrays to count, and as soon as they are finished counting they are asked to recall the number of objects in each array. The number of arrays varies and, according to Pascaul-Leone's model, the number of arrays counted with perfect recall would provide an estimate of capacity. However, the fact that increases in counting span seem to be caused by increases in counting speed (Case et al., 1982) makes a strong case against the capacity increase explanation.

In sum, observed age increases on M-space measures are open to a number of interpretations, and probably are not indicative of increases in capacity. Much of the variance, in fact, seems attributable to an age-related decrease in the amount of capacity needed to execute basic encoding and retrieval operations (for further discussion see Dempster, 1976, 1978; Rohwer & Dempster, 1977).

The final theory to be considered was inspired by McLaughlin (1963), but it contains some significant points of departure from both that theory and Pascual-Leone's (see Halford, 1982, for a review). Its most distinctive feature is the degree of emphasis given to symbolic representation. These representations may take a number of different forms, but from the present perspective the most important point is that they must be matched to the problem as presented if a solution is to occur. When the internal representation mirrors the structure of the problem, the problem is understood. For example, the symbol elements $a > b$, $b > c$ would probably be assigned to Johnny, Jason, and William, respectively, if in a transitivity problem the premises were Johnny > Jason, Jason > William. In this case the solution to the question "Who is taller, Johnny or William?" is straightforward. The symbol elements simply generate $a > c$ from $a > b$, $b > c$. But if the symbol elements were assigned in an inconsistent manner (e.g., $a > b$, $c > b$), the proper conclusion could not be drawn.

The complexity of the entire symbol system depends on the number of elements (in the example above the relation, $a > b$ is one element) needed to generate that system. At the lowest level (1), which roughly corresponds to the preoperational level, a symbol system is generated by just one element. At the highest level (3), which roughly corresponds to the formal-operational level, symbol systems are generated by three elements (for a more technical description of these levels see Halford & Wilson, 1980). As a consequence, more information is needed to determine whether or not elements are consistent at higher levels than at lower levels. At Level 1, two units must be considered for consistency; that is, the symbol element and the problem element to which it is assigned must be considered. At Level 2, four units must be considered, and at Level 3, six units. Whenever there is insufficient short-term memory capacity for considering the required number of units, the matching process cannot proceed. Like McLaughlin, Halford uses digit span norms to predict the age at which new competencies will emerge. Since spans of 2, 4, and 6 are associated with ages 2, 5, and 10, respectively, the theory predicts that these are the earliest ages at which Level 1, Level 2, and Level 3 abilities will emerge.

The theory, then, has at least one characteristic in common with McLaughlin's, so the same reservation about using digit span as an estimate of capacity is applicable. However, differences between this theory and the others are more striking (see Halford, 1982, p. 359–362 for a discussion). The most important difference, from the present perspective, concerns the way an information-processing load is imposed. In the other theories the short-term memory load is imposed by the mental representations themselves. In Pascual-Leone's theory, these are the schemes activated and maintained by the executive scheme, which is also held in short-term memory. In Halford's theory, however, cognitive structures (e.g., the elements in the example above) do not impose a load on short-term memory. The load is imposed by the requirement of matching the symbol system to the problem elements in a consistent way. Demands on short-term memory capacity then only occur when making consistency checks. Thus, although Halford uses the traditional digit span norms very much like McLaughlin, his view of a short-term memory load is quite novel.

The theory's predictions have been tested in several different paradigms, and the expected correspondence between level and age have been reasonably well confirmed (Halford & Wilson, 1980). In my opinion, though, the data are open to a number of different interpretations. For example, the tasks required the learning of novel relationships, and so one interpretation would be essentially the same as that I proposed to explain the CVSI results. However, the theory has not been subjected to the same number of investigations as Pascual-Leone's, and much more testing is needed before a meaningful evaluation can be undertaken.

In sum, there is no compelling empirical support for the capacity increase hypothesis. In fact, certain data are very difficult to reconcile with this view. These include the severe attenuation of age effects under conditions of low familiarity or under conditions that minimize the contribution of rehearsal in span tasks, the fact that storage parameters of mathematical models of short-term memory do not increase with age (see Chapter 4 by Brainerd) and the relationship between counting speed and counting span, presumably a measure of M-space. Moreover, I am not sure what kind of data would ever verify this hypothesis, at least as it is currently conceptualized. There are simply too many difficulties with this hypothesis which, in its present form, render it essentially untestable.

One problem is that at the present time there is no satisfactory method of measuring capacity. How are we to decide, in a consistent fashion, what constitutes an "item" for any given task? This question has been raised previously (Dempster, 1981, p. 88; Flavell, 1978), and I believe it has to be considered the number one issue confronting the capacity increase hypothesis. In addition to the obvious problem of deciding whether "items" have been chunked, there is the possibility, strongly supported by recent work on memory span (Drewnowski, 1980; Drewnowski & Murdock, 1980), that what is stored is not unitary items but collections of attributes, with the recall process depending on generating the items from the stored information. One implication of this finding for the capacity increase hypothesis is that the particular attributes to which one is sensitive may vary with age (see Foreit, 1977, for data that is consistent with this hypothesis). A related difficulty is that intentionally or unintentionally, the number of attributes activated may vary with age. For example, Brainerd and Kingma (in press) suggest that individuals do not always encode "vivid" traces; instead they may encode "fuzzy" traces (i.e., activate only a portion of the relevant information) under conditions of high memory load. While the fuzzy traces will be subject to more retrieval errors, they should make fewer demands on capacity.

Another related problem is task selection. While memory span is generally considered the best estimate of capacity, the data reported in previous sections suggest that it is a relatively insensitive measure of short-term memory, and one that is contaminated by production factors. In addition, memory span tends to be quite unreliable unless repeated measurements are taken. But when this is done, another problem, namely, practice effects, arises. Dempster (1978) evaluated practice effects by contrasting performance in the first part of a testing session with performance in the second part. Under ordinary conditions of presentation, he found that the performance of older children improved considerably from the first to the second session, but the performance of younger children improved very little. Age differences in memory span were affected by the stage of practice. Moreover, it is unlikely that the use of some other serial recall measure will solve this problem. For example, in serial recall, the performance of young children tends to decline with practice (Rosner, 1972), while the performance of older children tends to improve (Baumeister, 1974).

A third potential problem is preconscious representations, often referred to as sensory memory representations. My concern here derives from the results of a developmental study of the suffix effect, which is assumed to be an estimate of the capacity of the sensory memory (or echoic buffer) which stores aurally presented input for no longer than a few seconds (Foreit, 1977). While both children and adults exhibited approximately equal suffix effects for lists of digits, only adults exhibited an effect for lists of consonants and vowels. These results suggest that adults may have more preconsicous information available with which to augment word and letter spans than do children.

Another problem has to do with just how to decide whether a subject is using all of the capacity he or she has available. There is some evidence, reviewed earlier, that suggests this will not happen in the presence of misleading cues. Hence, researchers attempting to estimate capacity, especially of children who are more field-dependent than adults, will have to try to avoid misleading cues. It seems to me, however, that one can never be sure if such cues are present. In addition, there is the ever present possiblity that older subjects, as a result of certain metacognitive sophistication, will have a tendency to use more of their available capacity than will younger subjects. This possibility seems quite consistent with the finding that more intelligent subjects exhibit smaller task-evoked pupillary responses than do less intellectual subjects under ordinary load conditions, but larger pupillary responses under very high load conditions (Ahern & Beatty, 1981). One interpretation of this finding is that the more intelligent subjects are able to draw upon more of their available capacity when conditions warrant than can their less intelligent counterparts.

Finally, a recent development in information-processing theory is the postulation of more than one pool of capacity. Moreover, there are some data that are at least consistent with this view (Baddeley, 1981; Brainerd & Kingma, 1984; Klapp et al., 1983; Navon & Gopher, 1979; Wickens, 1980). This development parallels the recent fragmentation of short-term memory, and in some cases these data have been used to justify this fragmentation (Baddeley, 1981; Brainerd & Kingma, 1984; Klapp et al., 1983). While it is still too early to estimate the potential impact of this development, it does raise some further questions about the testability of the capacity increase hypothesis. Given the difficulties associated with the measurement of a unitary pool of capacity, imagine the difficulties that would be associated with the measurement of separate, independent pools of capacity.

Speed of Information Processing (Activation and Reactivation Speed)

During the past century, there has been much conjecture about the relationship between "mental speed" and individual differences in intelligence (e.g. Spearman, 1923). Although related experimental work got off to a poor start, due largely to inadequate techniques and measurements, this conjecture now rests upon a fairly firm empirical base. Fairly consistent correlations have been observed between a variety of measures of mental speed and general ability tests (see reviews by Brand, 1981; Cooper & Regan, 1982; Jensen, 1981). Further, this relationship is often stronger over the lower ranges of intelligence than over the higher ranges. This suggests that speed might be crucial up to some level of intelligence beyond which other factors play a more important role (see Brand, 1981), a suggestion also raised by span data (see Chapter 6 by Kail for another perspective on speed of processing data).

More recently, the conjecture has been applied to developmental differences, although here it has been more common to use the term processing efficiency rather than mental speed. This term captures the idea that speed is a variable quantity that depends solely or mainly on specific experiential factors, such as practice and familiarity (e.g., Chi & Gallagher, 1982). Viewed in this way, increased speed of information processing stems from additions to the knowledge base and from changes in the accessibility of information in long-term memory. This position is an appealing one because there is little question that processing speed can be affected by factors such as familiarity and practice. What is not clear is whether such factors can account for all or most of the age-related variance in processing speed and the conditions that affect both the appearance and magnitude of speed differences. In this section, I will review selected data that are relevant to these issues and to the issue of whether age differences in memory performance are attributable to speed differences. I focus on only two types of tasks: namely tasks that require a subject to activate a long-term memory representation and tasks that require a subject to reactivate a short-term memory representation.

Many investigators have proposed that differences in the speed with which presented information is identified or named is an important source of age differences in short-term memory performance (e.g., Case, 1978; Case et al., 1982; Dempster, 1981; Huttenlocher & Burke, 1976; Nicolson, 1981; Spring & Capps, 1974). Several measures of identification/naming speed have been developed, but the most widely used have been vocalization rate and word-recognition rate. In both cases, an item or a series of items is presented which the subject is asked to vocalize as quickly as possible. Recent reviews of research using these procedures are available (e.g., Dempster, 1981). On the whole, they reveal considerable decreases in latency from early childhood to adulthood (but see Chapter 6 by Kail for possible developmental invariants). Moreover, these decreases are related to short-term memory task performance, and account for most, if not all, within-age variance in span (Case et al., 1982; Nicolson, 1981). In Nicolson's study with children aged 8–12, it was found that memory span for a given set of words was equal to the number of words that could be read in 2 s, and that span was independent of age for a given reading rate. These results led Nicolson to conclude that increased information processing speed is a sufficient explanation of span increase. In Case's study, the results were not quite as dramatic. However, his word-recognition task was a purer measure of activation time, since the time to produce and articulate a response was not recorded. Thus, it appears that item-activation processes rather than response-execution processes, are responsible for a large portion of the association between span and information-processing speed. Finally, in this same experiment, Case and his colleagues found that by eliminating speed of recognition differences between adults and children, span differences were reduced also. This suggests that speed causes span differences rather than vice versa.

Another technique that has been widely used to assess the speed with which information in long-term memory can be activated is the Posner letter-identification task (Posner, Bois, Eichelman, & Taylor, 1969). In the standard version of this task, subjects are instructed to indicate whether the second of two presented letters is the same as the first. Under physical identity (PI) instructions, letter pairs are to be identified as "same" only if the letters are exact physical duplicates of each other (e.g., *A, A*). Under name identity (NI) instructions, letter pairs are to be identified as "same" if they are exact duplicates of each other or if they are different ways of refering to the same letter (e.g., *A, a*). In a variation on this procedure, subjects respond by sorting decks of cards containing letter pairs into "same" or "different" piles. In both cases, principal interest attaches to differences between the time taken to respond "same" under NI instructions and the time taken to respond "same" under PI instructions. This difference (i.e., NI − PI) is assumed to be a measure of the additional time needed to access the name of a letter code in long-term memory. This technique has not been frequently used to study age differences, but the few studies that have been conducted reveal large age differences, with activation speed increasing between the age of 9 and adulthood (Hunt, 1978, p. 114; Keating & Bobbit, 1978) and decreasing from young adulthood to old age (Hunt, 1978, p. 114).

In sum, research has revealed (a) substantial age differences in speed of activation and (b) a substantial association (strongly suggestive of a causal relationship) between activation speed and span growth. Unfortunately, research has provided no clear answer to questions about the sources of these differences. One difficulty is that the effects of practice on activation speed have been equivocal. On the one hand, Goldman-Eisler (1961) reported that naming latencies of adults were reduced following simple repetition of words. But only one age group was used. On the other hand, Case (personal communication, October 22, 1979) reported a study in which 6-year-olds were given hundreds of trials of practice per day in counting speed. Yet, the gains in speed were modest and not of the magnitude that would be expected if specific experience makes an important contribution to speed differences. Moreover, age differences in most of the studies cited above were obtained by averaging across many trials. In some studies, experimental trials were preceded by unscored practice trials. In the Keating and Bobbit (1978) study, for example, there were two unscored practice runs, and only the last four of six card sortings were scored.

A similar discrepancy exists in the effects of practice on simple and choice reaction time, tasks that require a subject to respond as quickly as possible to the onset of one or more nonverbal stimuli. Several studies have shown that simple and choice reaction times decrease with practice (e.g., Wickens, 1974) while others have produced no evidence of a practice effect despite many trials (Jensen, 1979; Vernon, 1983). However, it is questionable whether this task requires activation of a representation stored in long-term memory. In short, available data, though hardly conclusive, leave open the possibility that age-related differences in speed of activation are, in part, due to structural factors.

The most commonly used estimate of reactivation speed is search rate, a parameter of the memory-scanning task developed by Sternberg (1966). In this task, the subject is presented with a subspan number of items, called the memory set, and is asked to hold them in short-term memory. The subject is then presented with another item called the probe, which is either a member (positive) or not a member (negative) of the memory set. The subject's task is to decide as quickly as possible whether the probe is positive or negative. Reaction time typically increases linearly with the number of items in the set. The slope of this function is assumed to reflect the amount of time it takes to compare or assess (i.e., reactivate) a single item in short-term memory.

That search rate might be an important source of differences in short-term memory performance became apparent when Cavanagh (1972) pointed out a remarkable association between memory span and search rate; variations in material had very similar effects on span and search rates. Since then, it has been found that this relationship is not quite so strong when compared on an individual basis (Brown & Kirsner, 1980). Nevertheless, Brown and Kirsner's data are still supportive of a connection between search rate and short-term memory performance. The most straightforward explanation of this connection is that items that take longer to reactivate in the memory scanning task also take longer to reactivate (i.e., rehearse) in immediate recall tasks.

Unfortunately, developmental studies of search rate have yielded conflicting results. On the one hand, several studies have failed to obtain significant age differences (Harris & Fleer 1974; Hoving, Morin, & Konick, 1970; Keating & Bobbit, 1978). Two others reported small differences, but in opposite directions (Maisto & Baumeister, 1975; Naus & Ornstein, 1977). Several more have obtained marked increases in search rate from childhood to adulthood (Herrmann & Landis, 1977; Hess & Radtke, 1981; Keating, Keniston, Manis, & Bobbit, 1980). Dempster (1981) speculated that the variable most likely to have been responsible for the conflicting results was practice. In studies that failed to obtain age differences, subjects had received relatively large amounts of practice, either in unanalyzed pretest trials or as a result of receiving many test trials. In contrast, studies that did report age differences based their analyses on relatively unpracticed subjects. But this discrepancy cannot be the entire answer, because at least two studies have subsequently obtained large age-related increases in search rate despite liberal numbers of practice trials (Hess & Radtke, 1981; Keating et al., 1980). These latter findings severely complicate the picture. For a further discussion of developmental data from Sternberg-type tasks, see Chapter 6 by Kail.

In sum, the data reviewed in this section do not clearly rule out the possibility that age differences in activation and reactivation speed are due, in part, to underlying structural differences. Accordingly, increased speed of information processing can be viewed, partly, as a biological consequence of normal development. At this time, one can only speculate about the underlying bases of speed differences. One possibility is increased myelinization, since myelin is known to affect the rate of neural transmission. This possibility is lessened, however, by the fact that with development, progressive myelinization is accompanied by an increase in the length of neurons, which might be expected to offset any gain in rate of transmision. Other possible neural factors include oscillation rate (Jensen, 1982) and neural noise (Salthouse, 1982).

Whatever aspects of the nervous system are involved, this hypothesis has some important implications for cognitive performance. One implication is that with children there is a greater likelihood that previously activated representations will be lost, by decay or interference, before later activations can occur. Assuming that a particular sequence of representations must be activated in order to be successful, this would lead us to expect that young children might perform adequately when only a few representations are required, but much more poorly when many representations must be activated (see Salthouse, 1982, for a similar discussion in relation to cognitive deficits that accompany aging). Another implication is expressed nicely by Jensen (1980):

> The layman is puzzled by the fact that such seemingly small differences in an absolute sense should be related to quite conspicious differences in scholastic attainments, vocabulary, tests of reasoning ability, and the like. But even very small individual differences in rates of information processing, when multiplied by days, weeks, months, or years of interaction with the myriad opportunities for learning afforded by common experience, can result in easily noticeable differences in the amounts of acquired knowledge and developed intellectual skills. At a moment's glance there is scarcely a noticeable difference between a car averaging 50 and another averaging 51 miles per hour, but after a few hours on the road they are completely out of sight of one another. (p. 105).

While Jensen was referring to individual differences, with a few changes in wording his comments also are applicable to age differences. The central point is that a slightly slower rate of processing would slow down considerably the rate at which new representations are learned.

Decay (Deactivation Rate)

It appears that forgetting in short-term memory stems from two sources: namely, decay, which refers to a loss of strength as a result of the passage of time, and interference, which is a function of previously presented or subsequently presented information (e.g., Reitman, 1974; Shiffrin & Cook, 1978). For example, Chechile's mathematical model of short-term memory factors these two variables (see Chapter 4 by Brainerd). But just how much is attributable to each is probably impossible to determine because the two processes are confounded. As one increases, so does the other. Nevertheless, decay seems to progress for at least 30 s following activation, and probably more. On the basis of Shiffrin and Cook's (1978) results it can be crudely estimated that losses attributable to decay increase by about 10%–15% from the beginning of a retention interval to 30 s later. This may seem like a small amount, but the subjects used were university students, not children.

Accordingly, one source of performance differences may be the rate at which short-term memory representations deactivate. This hypothesis was offered by Ellis (1963) to account for certain differences in short-term memory per-formance between retarded and normals of the same chronological age. Although this hypothesis has received a reasonable amount of study, there is no strong evidence to support it. Actually, Ellis has since advanced a different position (Ellis, 1970). To my knowledge, no one has argued that decay is a source of age differences. This may be because of the difficulties of estimating decay independently of interference and of controlling for potential differences in learning strategies. However, there must be other reasons, too, as similar difficulties have not deterred researchers from hypothesizing that capacity is a major source of age differences.

In order to gather meaningful estimates of decay rates for different age groups, several minimum requirements will have to be met. First, it is necessary that the different age groups exhibit the same level of learning, so that any differences in short-term retention are not due to age differences in the amount activated (Postman, 1976). This requirement has not been met in some of the research in which the mentally retarded were compared with normals (Belmont, 1972). A test-retest procedure must be used if retention scores are to have any meaning.

Second, the material must be presented to avoid differences in degree of learning as a result of differences in the use of strategies. Differences in degree of learning exist in most short-term memory research, but they can be reduced by the use of only unrelated items and a short presentation/study interval. Also, the amount of material presented should be well within the most conservative estimates of capacity, so that if there are age differences in capacity, they would not affect the outcome.

A third requirement, and probably the trickiest to meet, is to ensure that the subjects are prevented from reactivating presented material during the retention interval. This is not always done in developmental studies (e.g., Salatas & Flavell, 1976), but in most studies of short-term forgetting, it is accomplished by using a distractor task, such as counting backwards rapidly, or tone detection. In one study, subjects were even instructed to forget, in addition to having to engage in a tone-detection task (Shiffrin & Cook, 1978). Of course, the distractor activity should be as unrelated to the presented material as possible, since similarity increases the potential for interference. A related requirement is that the distractor activity should be equally difficult for all age groups, as distractor difficulty is inversely related to short-term retention (e.g., Posner & Rossman, 1965).

A study that comes close to meeting these requirements was conducted by Kail & Levine (1976), who investigated release from proactive interference in 7- and 11-year-olds using the Brown-Peterson distractor task. On each trial, subjects were presented with two words and repeated them aloud. After a 15-s retention interval filled with distractor activity, subjects attempted recall. Apparently, subjects performed only once in each of five trials. Thus, the results of the first trial, which should have been relatively free of interference, provide an estimate of retention loss. For 7- and 11-year-olds, I estimate the loss to be about 35% and 25%, respectively. Thus, this datum is suggestive of age differences in decay. However, other interpretations are plausible. The presentation/study interval was fairly lengthy, providing sufficient time for differential learning, and the distractor material was also words, so that even first trial results could have been due to differential susceptibility to inter-ference.

Nevertheless, these results suggest that developmental investigations of decay rate might prove worthwhile. Furthermore, associations between short-term memory performance and ability measures are increased when a short retention interval intervenes between presentation and recall (Cornelius et al., 1983; Cummings & Faw, 1976). In addition, the finding that the parameter τ was reliably lower for high verbals than for low verbals (Hunt, Frost, & Lunnebors, 1973) may also be interpreted to mean that superior intellectual functioning may be tied, in some way, to a relatively slow decay rate. Of course, these findings are only suggestive, but the payoff for studying decay processes may be great. As with any structural parameter, a minor difference is of such a general nature that it can be used to predict a large number of more specific differences.

Summary and Conclusions

In this chapter, I began by tracing the history of the concept of short-term memory since the 19th century, and examining its current status. Clearly, the concept of short-term memory has undergone a number of critical developments, including some strong criticisms. Nevertheless, the concept is very much a part of current day cognitive psychology, having survived in a form that James (1890) would understand even though he would not recognize some of the newer labels, such as intermediate memory and working memory. Three indications of its current state are the recent proliferation of models of short-term memory, the frequent use of short-term memory measures in developmental studies and in studies of mental ability, and its increasing use as a theoretical tool in the analysis of complex performance, such as transitive reasoning (Brainerd, 1981; Brainerd & Kingma, in press), conservation (Brainerd & Kingma, 1984; Case, 1978; Halford, 1982), text processing (Baddeley, 1979; Daneman & Carpenter, 1980; Fletcher, 1981; Glanzer, 1981; Hess & Radtke, 1981; Kieras, 1981; Perfetti & Lesgold, 1977), and arithmetic (e.g., Hitch, 1978).

Despite the widespread use of the concept of short-term memory, its future is uncertain. For the most part, this uncertainty is due to the current trend toward model proliferation, a trend that could contribute to the already overcompartmentalized nature of cognitive psychology. I am reminded of the analogy between cognitive researchers and islands in the sea. Although the researchers make frantic efforts to communicate with one another, their models have become so idiosyncratic that they are almost totally unable to understand what their colleagues are saying. If this trend continues unchecked, the concept of short-term memory will surely become meaningless.

But while we should be aware of the dangers of unbridled model proliferation, we should also maintain an open mind toward new developments, especially if they have been subjected to hard experimental scrutiny and have not been embarrassed in the process. One such development is the speech-based articulatory loop espoused by Baddeley (1981). Although the exact nature of this system is unclear, certain data presented in this chapter seem to implicate speech-based processes in many short-term memory tasks. These include the relationship between articulation rate and span (e.g., Case et al., 1982; Nicolson, 1981), and output interference effects (Anderson, 1960; Sperling, 1963). In addition, a speech-based system of this kind or like the one proposed by Klapp (1976) seems necessary for the smooth production of multiple verbal units (Baddeley et al., 1975; Sperling, 1963), especially when these units have to be ordered sequentially. What is much less clear is whether such a system requires the postulation of more than one capacity pool as Baddeley (1981) claims, or whether it draws upon a single common reservoir of capacity, specializing in the activation and reactivation of linguistic programs. The resolution of this and other related issues, including the elucidation of the potential developmental implications of speech-based processes for short-term memory, would be an appropriate goal of future research.

Whether or not future research of this sort is successful will depend greatly upon the ability of researchers to construct convincing tests of the multiple capacity hypothesis. In an earlier section, I argued that empirical evaluation of models that have this feature (Brainerd & Kingma, 1984; Klapp et al., 1983) has failed to provide decisive results. A more decisive test, in my opinion, would be one in which subjects are required to hold a span or near-span number of items, as determined by individual pretesting, while performing a complex reasoning task that makes obvious demands on capacity. In addition, the reasoning task should be of short duration, so that comparisons with control subjects who do not receive the task will not be confounded with differences in the retention interval.

In this chapter, I proposed viewing short-term memory as the *active* portion of long-term memory, as many researchers have. What may be unique about my proposal is that short-term memory is viewed entirely in structural, or content-free mechanistic terms. By contrast, long-term memory is the knowledge base. Certainly, the latter can affect the role played by mechanistic processes. For example, the use of strategies such as rehearsal can obviously determine whether items are reactivated, and of course rehearsal can interrupt the deactivation process. But while strategies can affect short-term memory performance, according to this model they would not be considered properties of short-term memory per se.

To be consistent with this view of short-term memory I have considered three possible sources of short-term memory development, each of which is an aspect of the activation cycle: (a) information-processing capacity or activation energy, (b) information-processing speed or activation and reactivation speed, and (c) decay or deactivation rate. On the basis of existing research, I have concluded that the evidence clearly supports only the second possibility, though Kail (Chapter 6) proposes certain invariances in this variable. However, before this possibility can be fully evaluated, additional research will be necessary to assess the effects of practice and familiarity on speed measurements. Studies are needed in which long-term memory factors, such as strategies and degree of knowledge, are assessed independently of the speed measure and even manipulated, perhaps in the same way that Case et al. (1982) manipulated familiarity. But, in view of the fact that the only studies reviewed in this chapter that did not reveal speed differences used the memory scanning task, I would not be surprised if activation speed and reactivation speed react differently to the same experimental variables. It is my guess that reactivation rate differences can be reduced substantially and even eliminated when long-term memory factors are controlled, but that activation rate differences are due largely to structural differences.

By contrast, research provides no compelling evidence of age-related differences in activation energy, even though it is becoming an increasingly accepted source of age differences. In fact, certain data are very difficult to reconcile with the capacity increase hypothesis. On the basis of these data and other considerations, I suggested that the practice of explaining age differences in terms of capacity differences is totally unproductive. As far as I am concerned, an explanation of this kind, since it cannot be confirmed or disconfirmed, is little more than an act of faith.

Finally, deactivation rate has not been the subject of developmental research, and thus it cannot be evaluated as a possible source of short-term memory development. Nevertheless, I argued that meaningful estimates of decay rate differences can be obtained, and that future efforts of this kind might be worthwhile. Certainly decay rate differences, even small differences, would have important intellectual consequences.

In closing, I wish to point out that there may be other, less obvious, sources of short-term memory development that are consistent with the present model. One possibility is interference, if interference is conceived as a structurally determined tendency for activation energy to flow automatically to task-irrelevant cognitive units. While there are few references to interference in the memory development literature, there are a number of reasons why changes in susceptibility to interference might be a source of memory development. First, children become increasingly field-independent from infancy to adulthood (Witkin, Goodenough, & Karp, 1967). That is, they become increasingly less dependent on and distracted by misleading cues. In an earlier section I noted that Pascual-Leone attributed this tendency to increasing capacity. However, in view of the lack of support for the capacity increase hypothesis, there is no reason not to assume that susceptibility to inteference is an independent source of variability. Moreover, this same source of variability may be responsible for other attentional problems, such as distractibility and the tendency to attend to incidental information, both of which show a similar age trend (see Hale & Lewis, 1979, for a review). Though these phenomena are often classed as perceptual rather than memorial, there is little question that they can play an important role in memory performance.

Another kind of interference, one that has received much attention by memory researchers, is proactive interference. In contrast to the externally generated interference described previously, this type appears to be largely internally generated, occurring after attention has been diverted from the to-be-remembered information (Wickens et al., 1981) but within 2 min of trace activation (Hopkins, Edwards, & Cook, 1972; Loess & Waugh, 1967). As with deactivation rate, proactive interference has been all but ignored by developmental psychologists. Nevertheless, the results of studies linking individual differences in susceptibility to proactive interference to intelligence (Borkowski, 1965; Dempster & Cooney, 1982; Hunt et al., 1973), and the results of the Kail and Levine (1976) study, described earlier, suggest that this kind of interference may also play a role in memory development.

Acknowledgments. Preparation of this chapter was supported in part by a grant from the Barrick Research Fund, University of Nevada, Las Vegas, and a grant from the Dean's Fund, College of Education, University of Nevada, Las Vegas. I thank my colleague, John A. Bates, for his valuable comments on a previous version of this chapter.

References

Ahern, S., & Beatty, J. (1981). Physiological evidence that demand for processing capacity varies with intelligence. In M. P. Friedman, J. P. Das, & N. O'Connor (Eds.), *Intelligence and learning*. New York: Plenum Press.

Ammon, P. (1977). Cognitive development and early childhood education: Piagetian and neo-Piagetian theories. In H. L. Hom & P. A. Robinson (Eds.). *Psychological processes in early education*. New York: Academic Press.

Anderson, J. R. (1976). *Language, memory, and thought*. Hillsdale, NJ: Lawrence Erlbaum Associates.

Anderson, J. R. (1983). A spreading activation theory of memory. *Journal of Verbal Learning and Verbal Behavior, 22*, 261–295.

Anderson, N. S. (1960). Poststimulus cueing in immediate memory. *Journal of Experimental Psychology, 60*, 216–221.

Atkinson, R. C., & Shiffrin, R. M. (1968). Human memory: A proposed system and its control processes. In K. W. Spence & J. T. Spence (Eds.), *The psychology of learning and motivation: Advances in research and theory* (Vol. 2). New York: Academic Press.

Bachelder, B. L., & Denny, M. R. (1977). A theory of intelligence: II. The role of span in a variety of intellectual tasks. *Intelligence, 1*, 237–256.

Baddeley, A. D. (1979). Working memory and reading. In P. A. Kolers, M. E. Wrolstad, & H. Bouma (Eds.), *Processing of visible language* (Vol. 1). New York: Plenum Press.

Baddeley, A. (1981). The concept of working memory: A view of its current state and probable future development. *Cognition, 10*, 17–23.

Baddeley, A. D., & Hitch, G. (1974). Working memory. In G. A. Bower (Ed.), *The psychology of learning and motivation* (Vol. 8). New York: Academic Press.

Baddeley, A. D., Thomson, N., & Buchanan, M. (1975). Word length and the structure of short-term memory. *Journal of Verbal Learning and Verbal behavior, 14*, 575–589.

Baumeister, A. A. (1974). Serial memory span threshold of normal and mentally retarded children. *Journal of Educational Psychology, 66*, 889–894.

Belmont, J. M. (1972). Relation of age and intelligence to short-term color memory. *Child Development, 43*, 19–29.

Belmont, J. M., & Butterfield, E. C. (1969). The relations of short-term memory to development and intelligence. In L. P. Lipsitt & H. W. Reese (Eds.), *Advances in child development and behavior* (Vol. 4). New York: Academic Press.

Biggs, J. B. (1971). *Information and human learning*. Glenview, IL: Scott, Foresman.

Binet, A., & Simon, T. (1905). Methodes nouvelles pour le diagnostic du niveau intellectual des anormaux. *L'Anne e Psychologique, 11*, 191–244.

Bower, G. (1975). Cognitive psychology: An introduction. In W. K. Estes (Ed.), *Handbook of Learning and Cognitive Processes* (Vol. 1). Hillsdale, NJ: Lawrence Erlbaum Associates.

Brainerd, C. J. (1981). Working memory and the developmental analysis of probability judgment. *Psychological Review, 88*, 463–502.

Brainerd, C. J., & Kingma, J. (1984). *Memory and cognitive development: Are short-term memory and working memory separate systems?* Research Report, Department of Psychology, University of Alberta.

Brainerd, C. J., & Kingma, J. (in press). Do children have to remember to reason? A fuzzy trace theory of transitivity development. *Developmental Review, 4*, December 1984.

Brand, C. (1981). General intelligence and mental speed: Their relationship and development. In M. P. Friedman, J. P. Das, & N. O'Connor (Ed.), *Intelligence and Learning*. New York: Plenum Press.

Broadbent, D. E. (1958). *Perception and communication*. London: Pergamon Press.

Broadbent, D. E. (1963). Flow of information within the organism. *Journal of Verbal Learning and Verbal Behavior, 2*, 34–39.

Brown, A. L. (1975). The development of memory: knowing, knowing about knowing and knowing how to know. In H. W. Reese (Ed.), *Advances in child development and behavior* (Vol. 10). New York: Academic Press.

Brown, H. L., & Kirsner, K. (1980). A within-subjects analysis of the relationship between memory span and processing rate in short-term memory. *Cognitive Psychology, 12*, 117–187.

Borkowski, J. G. (1965). Interference effects in short-term memory as a function of level of intelligence. *American Journal of Mental Deficiency, 70*, 458–465.

Burtis, P. J. (1982). Capacity increase and chunking in the development of short-term memory. *Journal of Experimental Child Psychology 34*, 387–413.

Case, R. (1972). Validation of a neo-Piagetian mental capacity construct. *Journal of Experimental Child Psychology, 14*, 287–302.

Case, R. (1974). Structures and strictures: Some functional limitations on the course of cognitive growth. *Cognitive Psychology, 6*, 544–573.

Case, R. (1978). Intellectual development from birth to adulthood: A neo-Piagetian interpretation. In R. S. Siegler (Ed.), *Children's thinking: What develops?* Hillsdale, NJ: Lawrence Erlbaum Associates.

Case, R., & Globerson, T. (1974). Field independence and central computing space. *Child Development, 45*, 772–778.

Case, R., Kurland, D. M., & Goldberg, J. (1982). Operational efficiency and the growth of short-term memory span. *Journal of Experimental Child Psychology, 33*, 386–404.

Cavanagh, J. P. (1972). Relation between the immediate memory span and the memory search rate. *Psychological Review, 79*, 525–530.

Chi, M. T. H. (1976). Short-term memory limitations in children: Capacity or processing deficits? *Memory & Cognition, 4*, 559–572.

Chi, M. T. H., & Gallagher, J. D. (1982). Speed of processing: A developmental source of limitation. *Topics in Learning and Learning Disabilities, 2*, 23–32.

Chi, M. T. H., & Klahr, D. (1975). Span and rate of apprehension in children and adults. *Journal of Experimental Child Psychology, 19*, 434–439.

Chiang, A., & Atkinson, R. C. (1976). Individual differences and interrelations among a select set of cognitive skills. *Memory and Cognition, 4*, 661–672.

Cohen, R. L., & Lavin, K. (1978). The effect of demarcating the target set on IQ-related individual differences in the probed serial recall of very recent items. In M. M. Gruneberg, P. E. Morris, & R. N. Sykes (Eds.), *Practical aspects of memory*. London: Academic Press.

Cohen, R. L., & Sandberg, T. (1977). The relation between intelligence and short-term memory. *Cognitive Psychology, 9*, 534–554.

Cooper, L. A., & Regan, D. T. (1982). Attention, perception, and intelligence. In R. J. Sternberg (Ed.), *Handbook of human intelligence*. Cambridge: Cambridge University Press.

Cornelius, S. W., Willis, S. L., Nesselroade, J. R., & Baltes, P. B. (1983). Convergence between attention variables and factors of psychometric intelligence in older adults. *Intelligence, 7*, 253–269.

Craik, F. I. M., & Lockhart, R. S. (1972). Levels of processing: A framework for memory research. *Journal of Verbal Learning and Verbal Behavior, 11*, 671–684.

Crawford, J., & Stankov, L. (1983). Fluid and crystallized intelligence and primary/recency components of short-term memory. *Intelligence, 7*, 227–252.

Crowder, R. J. (1969). Behavioral strategies in immediate memory. *Journal of Verbal Learning and Verbal Behavior, 8*, 524–528.

Crowder, R. J. (1983). Proliferation, fragmentation, and demise of short-term memory. Paper presented at the annual meeting of the American Psychological Association, Anaheim, Ca.

Cummings, E. M., & Faw, T. T. (1976). Short-term memory and equivalence judgments in normal and retarded readers. *Child Development, 47*, 286–289.

Daneman, M., & Carpenter, P. A. (1980). Individual differences in working memory and reading. *Journal of Verbal Learning and Verbal Behavior, 19*, 450–466.

Dempster, F. N. (1976). *Short-term storage capacity and chunking: A developmental study*. (Unpublished doctoral dissertation, University of California, Berkeley. University Microfilms No. 77-15, 661).

Dempster, F. N. (1978). Memory span and short-term memory capacity: A developmental study. *Journal of Experimental Child Psychology, 26*, 419–431.

Dempster, F. N. (1981). Memory span: Sources of individual and developmental differences. *Psychological Bulletin, 89*, 63–100.

Dempster, F. N., & Cooney, J. B. (1982). Individual differences in digit span, susceptibility to proactive interference, and aptitude/achievement test scores. *Intelligence, 6*, 399–416.

Dempster, F. N., & Rohwer, W. D., Jr. (1983). Age differences and modality effects in immediate and final free recall. *Child Development, 54*, 30–41.

Dempster, F. N., & Zinkgraf, S. A. (1982). Individual differences in digit span and chunking. *Intelligence, 6*, 201–213.

DeSoto, J. L., & DeSoto, C. B. (1983). Relationship of reading achievement to verbal processing abilities. *Journal of Educational Psychology, 75*, 116–127.

Drewnowski, A. (1980). Attributes and priorities in short-term recall: A new model of memory span. *Journal of Experimental Psychology: General, 109*, 208–250.

Drewnowski, A., & Murdock, B. B., Jr. (1980). The role of auditory features in memory span for words. *Journal of Experimental Psychology: Human Learning and Memory, 6*, 319–332.

Ellis, N. R. (1963). The stimulus trace and behavioral inadequacy. In N. R. Ellis (Ed.), *Handbook of mental deficiency*. New York: McGraw-Hill.

Ellis, N. R. (1970). Memory processes in retardates and normals. In N. R. Ellis (Ed.), *International review of research in mental retardation* (Vol. 4). New York: Academic Press.

Ericsson, K. A., Chase, W. G., & Faloon, S. (1980). Acquisition of a memory skill. *Science, 208*, 1181–1182.

Fischer, K. W. (1980). A theory of cognitive development: The control and construction of hierarchies of skills. *Psychological Review, 87*, 477–531.

Fischer, K. W., & Bullock, D. (1981). Patterns of data: Sequence, synchrony, and constraint in cognitive development. In K. W. Fischer (Ed.), *Cognitive development*. San Francisco: Jossey-Bass.

Flavell, J. H. (1978). Comments. In R. S. Siegler (Ed.), *Children's thinking; What develops?* Hillsdale, NJ: Lawrence Erlbaum Associates.

Flavell, J. H. (1982). On cognitive development. *Child Development, 53*, 1–16.

Fletcher, C. R. (1981). Short-term memory processes in text comprehension. *Journal of Verbal Learning and Verbal Behavior, 20*, 564–574.

Foellinger, D., & Trabasso, T. (1977). Seeing, hearing and doing: A developmental study of memory for actions. *Child Development, 48*, 1482–1489.

Foreit, K. G. (1977). Developmental differences in short-lived auditory memory for various classes of speech sounds. *Journal of Experimental Child Psychology, 24*, 461–475.

Frank, H. S., & Rabinovitch, M. S. (1974). Auditory short-term memory: Developmental changes in rehearsal. *Child Development, 45*, 397–407.

Galton, F. (1887). Notes on prehension in idiots. *Mind, 12*, 79–82.

Garrity, L. I. (1975). An electromyographical study of subvocal speech and recall in preschool children. *Developmental Psychology, 11*, 274–281.

Gates, A. I., & Taylor, G. A. (1925). An experimental study of the nature of improvement resulting from practice in a mental function. *Journal of Educational Psychology, 16*, 583–592.

Geiselman, R. E., Woodward, J. A., & Beatty, J. (1982). Individual differences in verbal memory performance: A test of alternative information-processing models. *Journal of Experimental Psychology: General, 111*, 109–134.

Glanzer, M., Dorfman, D., & Kaplan, B. (1981). Short-term storage in the processing of text. *Journal of Verbal Learning and Verbal Behavior, 20*, 656–670.

Globerson, T. (1983). Mental capacity and cognitive functioning: Developmental and social class differences. *Developmental Psychology, 2*, 225–230.

Goldman-Eisler, F. (1961). The significance of changes in rate of articulation. *Language and Speech, 4*, 171–174.

Greeno, J. G. (1973). The structure of memory and the process of solving problems. In R. C. Solso (Ed.), *Contemporary issues in cognitive psychology*. Washington, DC: Winston.

Guyer, B. L., & Friedman, M. P. (1975). Hemispheric processing and cognitive styles in learning-disabled and normal children. *Child Development, 46*, 658–668.

Hale, G. A., & Lewis, M. (1979). *Attention and cognitive development*. New York: Plenum.

Halford, G. S. (1982). *The development of thought*. Hillsdale, NJ: Lawrence Erlbaum Associates.

Halford, G. S., & Wilson, W. H. (1980). A category theory approach to cognitive development. *Cognitive Psychology, 12*, 356–411.

Harris, G. J., & Fleer, R. W. (1974). High speed memory scanning in mental retardates. *Journal of Experimental Child Psychology, 17*, 452–459.

Herrmann, D. J., & Landis, T. Y. (1977). Differences in the search rate of children and adults in short-term memory. *Journal of Experimental Child Psychology, 23*, 151–161.

Hess, T. M., & Radtke, R. C. (1981). Processing and memory factors in children's reading comprehension skill. *Child Development, 52*, 479–488.

Hitch, G. J. (1978). The role of short-term working memory in mental arithmetic. *Cognitive Psychology, 10*, 302–323.

Hockey, R. (1973). Rate of presentation in running memory and direct manipulation of in-put processing strategies. *Quarterly Journal of Psychology, 25*, 104–111.

Holmes, O. W. (1871). *Mechanism in thought and morals*. Boston: Osgood.

Hopkins, R. H., Edwards, R. E., & Cook, C. L. (1972). The dissipation and release of proactive interference in a short-term memory task. *Psychonomic Science, 27*, 65–67.

Hoving, K. W., Morin, R. E., & Konick, D. S. (1970). Recognition reaction time and size of the memory set: A developmental study. *Psychonomic Science, 21*, 247–248.

Huey, E. B. (1908). *The psychology and pedagogy of reading*. New York: Macmillan.

Hunt, E. (1978). Mechanics of verbal ability. *Psychological Review, 85*, 109–130.

Hunt, E., Frost, N., & Lunneborg, C. (1973). Individual differences in cognition: A new approach to intelligence. In G. H. Bower (Ed.), *The psychology of learning and motivation* (Vol. 7). New York: Academic Press.

Huttenlocher, J., & Burke, D. (1976). Why does memory span increase with age? *Cognitive Psychology, 8*, 1–31.

Jackson, N. E., & Myers, M. G. (1982). Letter naming time, digit span, and precocious reading achievement. *Intelligence, 6*, 311–329.

Jacobs, J. (1887). Experiments in prehension. *Mind, 12*, 75–79.

James, W. (1890). *Principles of psychology* (Vol. 1). New York: Holt, Rinehart & Winston.

Jensen, A. R. (1964). Individual differences in learning: Interference factor. (Final Report, Cooperative Research Project No. 1897). Washington, D.C.: U.S. Department of Health, Education, and Welfare, Office of Education.

Jensen, A. R. (1979). G: Outmoded theory or unconquered frontier? *Creative Science and Technology, 2*, 16–29.

Jensen, A. R. (1980). Chronometric analysis of mental ability. *Journal of Social and Biological Structures, 3*, 103–122.

Jensen, A. R. (1981). Reaction time and intelligence. In M. P. Friedman, J. P. Das, & N. O'Connor (Eds.), *Intelligence and learning*. New York: Plenum Press.

Jensen, A. R., & Osborne, R. T. (1979). Forward and backward digit span interaction with race and IQ: A longitudinal developmental comparison. *Indian Journal of Psychology, 54*, 75–87.

Kail, R. V., Jr., & Levine, L. E. (1976). Encoding processes and sex-role preferences. *Journal of Experimental Child Psychology, 21*, 256–263.

Keating, D. P., & Bobbit, B. L. (1978). Individual and developmental differences in cognitive-processing components of mental ability. *Child Development, 49*, 155–167.

Keating, D. P., Keniston, A. H., Manis, F. R., & Bobbit, B. L. (1980). Development of the search processing parameter. *Child Development, 51*, 39–44.

Kieras, D. E. (1981). Component processes in the comprehension of simple prose. *Journal of Verbal Learning and Verbal Behavior, 20*, 1–23.

Klapp, S. T. (1976). Short-term memory as a response preparation state. *Memory & Cognition, 4*, 721–729.

Klapp, S. T., Marshburn, E. A., & Lester, P. T. (1983). Short-term memory does not involve the "working memory" of intellectual processing: The demise of a common assumption. *Journal of Experimental Psychology: General, 112*, 240–264.

Lachman, M. E. (1983). Perceptions of intellectual aging: Antecedent or consequence of intellectual functioning? *Developmental Psychology, 19*, 482–498.

Lawson, A. E. (1976). M-Space: Is it a constraint on conservation reasoning ability? *Journal of Experimental Child Psychology, 22*, 40–49.

Loess, H., & Waugh, N. C. (1967). Short-term memory and inter-trial interval. *Journal of Verbal Learning and Verbal Behavior, 6*, 455–460.

Maisto, A. A., & Baumeister, A. A. (1975). A Development study of choice reaction time: The effect of two forms of stimulus degradation on encoding. *Journal of Experimental Child Psychology, 20*, 456–464.

Mandler, J. A., & Robinson, C. A. (1978). Developmental changes in picture recognition. *Journal of Experimental Child Psychology, 26*, 122–136.

Masson, M. E. J., & Miller, J. A. (1983). Working memory and individual differences in comprehension and memory of text. *Journal of Educational Psychology, 75*, 314–418.

Mayer, R. E. (1981). *The promise of cognitive psychology*. San Francisco: Freeman.

Merkle, S. P., & Hall, V. C. (1982). the Relationship between memory for order and other cognitive tasks. *Intelligence, 6*, 427–441.

McLaughlin, G. H. (1963). Psycho-logic: A possible alternative to Piaget's formulation. *British Journal of Educational Psychology, 33*, 61–67.

Mefferd, R. G., Jr., Wieland, B. A., & James, W. E. (1966). Repetitive psychometric measures: Digit span. *Psychological Reports, 18*, 3–10.

Miller, G. A. (1956). The magical number seven, plus or minus two: Some limits on our capacity for processing information. *Psychological Review, 63*, 81–87.

Moely, B. E. (1977). Organizational factors in the development of memory. In R. V. Kail, Jr., & J. W. Hagen (Eds.), *Perspectives on the development of memory and cognition*. Hillsdale, NJ: Lawrence Erlbaum Associates.

Naus, M. J., & Ornstein, P. A. (1977). Developmental differences in the memory search of categorized lists. *Developmental Psychology, 13*, 60–68.

Naus, M. J., Ornstein, P. A., & Aivano, S. (1977). Developmental changes in memory. The effects of processing time and rehearsal instructions. *Journal of Experimental Child Psychology, 23*, 237–251.

Navon, D., & Gopher, D. (1979). On the economy of the human-processing system. *Psychological Review, 86*, 214–255.

Neisser, U. (1982). *Memory observed: Remembering in natural contexts*. San Francisco: Freeman.

Nicholson, R. (1981). The relationship between memory span and processing speed. In M. P. Friedman, J. P. Das, & N. O'Connor (Eds.), *Intelligence and Learning*. New York: Plenum.

Niemark, E. D. (1975). Intellectual development during adolescence. In F. D. Horowitz (Ed.), *Review of child development research*. (Vol. 4). Chicago: University of Chicago Press.

Ornstein, P. A. (1978). *Memory development in children*. New York: John Wiley & Sons.

Ornstein, P. A. & Naus, M. J. (1978). Rehearsal processes in children's memory. In P. A. Ornstein (Ed.), *Memory development in children*. Hillsdale, NJ: Lawrence Erlbaum Associates.

Ornstein, P. A., Naus, M. J., & Liberty, C. (1975). Rehearsal and organizational processes in children's memory. *Child Development, 46*, 818–830.

Ornstein, P. A., Naus, M. J., & Stone, B. P. (1977). Rehearsal training and developmental differences in memory. *Developmental Psychology, 13*, 15–24.

Parkinson, G. M. (1976). *The limits on learning*. Unpublished doctoral dissertation, York University.

Pascual-Leone, J. (1969). *Cognitive development and cognitive style: A general psychological interpretation*. Unpublished doctoral dissertation, University of Geneva.

Pascual-Leone, J. (1970). A mathematical model for the transition rule in Piaget's developmental stages. *Acta Psychologia, 63*, 301–345.

Pascual-Leone, J. (1973). *A theory of constructive operators, a neo-Piagetian model of conservation, and the problem of horizontal decalages*. Unpublished manuscript, York University.

Pascual-Leone, J. (1980). Constructive problems for constructive theories: the current relevance of Piaget's work and a critique of information-processing simulation psychology. In R. J. Kluwe & H. Speda (Eds.), *Developmental models of thinking*. NY: Academic Press.

Perfetti, C. A., & Lesgold, A. M. (1977). Discourse comprehension and sources of individual differences. In M. A. Just & P. A. Carpenter (Eds.) *Cognitive processes in comprehension*. New York: John Wiley & Sons.

Perlmutter, M., & Lange, G. (1978). A developmental analysis of recall-recognition distinctions. In P. A. Ornstein (Ed..), *Memory development in children*. New York: John Wiley & Sons.

Posner, M., Boies, S., Eichelman, W., & Taylor, R. (1969). Retention of visual and name codes of single letters. *Journal of Experimental Psychology Monographs, 79*, (1, Pt. 2).

Posner, M., & Rossman, E. (1965). Effect of size and location of information transforms upon short-term retention. *Journal of Experimental Psychology, 70*, 496–505.

Postman, L. (1975). Verbal learning and memory. *Annual Review of Psychology, 26*, 291–335.

Postman, L. (1976). Methodology of human learning. In W. K. Estes (Ed.), *Handbook of learning and cognitive processes* (Vol. 3). Hillsdale, NJ: Lawrence Erlbaum Associates.

Reitman, J. S. (1974). Without surreptitious rehearsal, information in short-term memory decays. *Journal of Verbal Learning and Verbal Behavior, 13*, 365–377.

Rohwer, W. D., Jr., & Dempster, F. N. (1977). Memory development and educational processes. In R. V. Kail, Jr., & J. W. Hagen (Eds.), *Perspectives on the development of memory and cognition*. Hillsdale, NJ: Lawrence Erlbaum Associates.

Rosner, S. R. (1972). Primacy in preschooler's short-term memory: The effects of repeated tests and shift-trails. *Journal of Experimental Child Psychology, 13*, 220–230.

Ross, B. M. (1969). Sequential visual memory and the limited magic of the number seven. *Journal of Experimental Psychology, 80*, 339–347.

Salatas, H., & Flavell, J. H. (1976). Retrieval of recently learned information: Development of strategies and control skills. *Child Development, 47*, 941–948.

Salthouse, T. A. (1982). *Adult cognition: An experimental psychology of human aging*. New York: Springer-Verlag.

Schneider, W., & Shiffrin, R. M. (1977). Controlled and automatic human information processing: I. Detection, search and attention. *Psychological Review, 84*, 1–66.

Shallice, T. (1979). Neuropsychological research and the fractionation of memory systems. In L-G Nilsson (Ed.), *Perspectives on memory research: Essays in honor of Uppsala University's 500th Anniversary*. Hillsdale, NJ: Lawrence Erlbaum Associates.

Shiffrin, R. M., & Cook, J. R. (1978). Short-term forgetting of item and order information. *Journal of Verbal Learning and Verbal Behavior, 17*, 189–218.

Shiffrin, R. M., & Schneider, W. (1977). Controlled and automatic human information processing: II. Perceptual learning, automatic attending, and a general theory. *Psychological Review, 84*, 127–190.

Siegel, A. W., & Allik, J. P. (1973). A developmental study of visual and auditory short-term memory. *Journal of Verbal Learning and Verbal Behavior, 12*, 409–418.

Sophian, C., & Stigler, J. W. (1981). Does recognition memory improve with age? *Journal of Experimental Child Psychology, 32*, 343–353.

Spearman, C. (1923). *The nature of "intelligence" and the principles of cognition*. London: Macmillan.

Sperling, G. (1963). A model for visual memory tasks. *Human Factors, 5*, 19–31.

Spitz, H. H. (1972). Note on immediate memory for digits: Invariance over the years. *Psychological Bulletin, 78*, 183–185.

Spring, C., & Capps, C. (1974). Encoding speed, rehearsal, and probed recall of dyslexic boys. *Journal of Educational Psychology, 66*, 780–786.

Standing, L., Bond, B., Smith, P., & Isley, C. (1980). Is the immediate memory span determined by subvocalization? *British Journal of Psychology, 71*, 525–539.

Sternberg, S. (1966). High-speed memory scanning in human memory. *Science, 153*, 652–654.

Stoneman, Z., & Brady, G. H. (1983). Immediate and long-term recognition and generalization of advertised products as a function of age and presentation mode. *Developmental Psychology, 19*, 56–62.

Torgesen, J., & Houck, D. (1980). Processing deficiencies in children who perform poorly on the Digit Span Test. *Journal of Educational Psychology, 72*, 141–160.

Trabasso, T., & Foellinger, D. B. (1978). Information processing capacity in children: A test of Pascual-Leone's model. *Journal of Experimental Child Psychology, 26*, 1–17.

Underwood, B. J. (1964). Degree of learning and the measurement of forgetting. *Journal of Verbal Learning and Verbal Behavior, 3*, 112–129.

Vernon, P. A. (1983). Speed of information processing and general intelligence. *Intelligence, 7*, 53–70.

Wanner, E., & Shiner, S. (1976). Measuring transient memory load. *Journal of Verbal Learning and Verbal Behavior, 15*, 159–167.

Waugh, N.C., & Norman, D. A. (1965). Primary memory. *Psychological Review, 72*, 89–104.

Wechsler, D. (1958). *The measurement and appraisal of adult intelligence* (4th ed.). Baltimore: Williams & Wilkins.

Weingartner, H., & Murphy, D. L. (1977). State-dependent storage and retrieval of experience while intoxicated. In I. M. Birnbaum & E. S. Parker (Eds.), *Alcohol and Human Memory*. Hillsdale, NJ: Lawrence Erlbaum Associates.

Weist, R. M. (1972). The role of rehearsal: Recopy or reconstruct. *Journal of Verbal Learning and Verbal Behavior, 11*, 440–450.

Wickens, C. D. (1974). Temporal limits of human information processing: A developmental study. *Psychological Bulletin, 81*, 739–755.

Wickens, C. D. (1980). The structure of attentional resources. In R. Nickerson (Ed.), *Attention and Performances, VIII*. Hillsdale, NJ: Lawrence Erlbaum Associates.

Wickens, D. D., Moody, M. J., & Dow, R. (1981). The nature and timing of the retrieval process and of interference effects. *Journal of Experimental Psychology: General, 110*, 1–20.

Witkin, H. A., Goodenough, D. R., & Karp, S. A. (1967). Stability of cognitive style from childhood to young adulthood. *Journal of Personality and Social Psychology, 7*, 291–300.

Yussen, S. R., & Levy, V. M., Jr. (1975). Developmental changes in predicting one's own span of short-term memory. *Journal of Experimental Child Psychology, 19*, 502–508.

6. Interpretation of Response Time in Research on the Development of Memory and Cognition

Robert Kail

> Human memory has traditionally been studied by examining how and when it fails—by considering the frequency and pattern of errors in recall or recognition. These errors may result from failures of learning, retention, or retrieval, and one difficulty in the traditional approach is the disentangling of these alternative sources of error.
>
> During the past decade a complementary approach to the study of memory has become increasingly popular. Here memory is examined under conditions in which it functions successfully and produces performance that is virtually errorless. By applying time pressure to the subject under these conditions, the experimenter can induce some of the mechanisms at work to reveal themselves . . . by how much time they need in order to succeed. (Sternberg, 1975, pp. 1–2)

Saul Sternberg's assessment of memory research in experimental psychology is equally appropriate for studies of memory development. Throughout the past two decades, most investigators have used patterns of errors to elucidate the nature of developmental change in memory (Kail, 1984). Beginning in the mid-1970s, a number of developmental psychologists turned to time as a dependent variable in studies of memory. One explanation for this is that success is the norm for many memory operations; errors are atypical. Among the operations that fit this description would be: (1) retrieval of the name of an object shown in a picture, (2) retrieval of exemplars following presentation of a category name, (3) deciding if two objects are members of the same category, (4) deciding if a stimulus is a member of a set presented immediately beforehand, (5) deciding the truth of well-known facts, and (6) deciding if a stimulus is a word in one's native tongue. In each instance, successful performances far outnumber failures. Hence, to study such processes using traditional memory measures means that an investigator may have to collect large quantities of data in order to ensure sufficient numbers of errors. Another possibility is that investigators create conditions so that the likelihood of an error is much higher than would be the case normally.

Neither of these approaches is entirely satisfactory. The first method is inefficient and the second raises the specter that findings are specific to experimental conditions contrived to increase errors. Response speed eliminates both of these problems. Because successes are abundant, sufficiently large amounts of data can be collected without resorting to procedures that artificially increase error rates (developmental findings on certain response speed tasks are also reviewed in Chapter 5 by Dempster).

Interest in time as a dependent variable can also be linked to the dominance of multifactor experiments in research on memory and cognition. The essence of multifactor experimentation is that the presence (or absence) of interactions between independent variables provides the basis for inferences about psychological processes. Specifically, if two (or more) variables affect different memory processes, then they should not interact. As an example, consider a free recall experiment in which the variables are the (1) rate of presentation of stimuli to the subject, and (2) the types of cues that are available to the subject during recall. If we believe that the first variable influences storage but the second influences retrieval, then the prediction is that these variables should have additive rather than interactive effects.

The logic behind this approach is, regrettably, far from airtight (see Loftus, 1978, and Chapter 4 by Brainerd). One of the problems stems from the well-known fact that transforming dependent variables can create or eliminate the very interactions that are the heart of the multifactor methodology. In our hypothetical experiment, the interaction might be statistically significant with percentage correct as the dependent variable, but not with the arcsin transformation of percentage correct. One outcome is consistent with our beliefs about the operation of the independent variables, the other is not. Unfortunately, there is no way to distinguish the "real" outcome. The root of the problem is that the "real" variable of interest is "amount retained"—percentage correct and arcsin percentage correct both represent reasonable but *arbitrarily defined* ordinal measures of this underlying variable. Log percentage correct or the square root of percentage correct would be just as suitable (Pachella, 1974). It is the problem of response scaling, discussed in Chapter 4 by Brainerd, that is responsible for such ambiguities.

An important advantage of time as a dependent variable in this context is that there are procedures for developing (and evaluating) formal models of cognitive processes in which duration of mental events is the property of interest per se; it is not an arbitrary measure of some other "real" variable. Hence, time is not subject to the scaling problems that occur with more traditional variables. Given that two variables produce interactive effects on time, it might be possible to remove the interaction by analyzing some transformation of time (e.g., log time) but this would be an inappropriate transformation because it would substitute an arbitrary dependent variable for a nonarbitrary one (Pachella, 1974).

The power of time as a dependent variable means that there are many potential pitfalls to trap the novice. My aim in this chapter is to stake out some of the important technical issues that must be considered in any study in which time is used to make inferences about the development of cognitive processes. This chapter includes illustrative research from studies of memory development per se as well as studies of "nonmnemonic" cognitive development. In particular, I will frequently illustrate some of the issues with my research on spatial aptitude. This is because many of the technical issues concerning time as a dependent variable are the same regardless of the specific phenomenon that is being investigated. Also, oftentimes there are simply no developmental studies of memory to illustrate the point at hand. (The Appendix provides background information on the rationale for this work and the evolution of the paradigm that has been used most frequently.)

The remainder of this chapter consists of four sections. The first concerns methods for decomposing total response time to derive estimates of the duration of individual cognitive processes. The second section concerns the manner in which age-related changes in processing speed are expressed: The nearly universal finding is that older individuals process information more rapidly than younger ones, which is a finding that also figures in Chapter 5 by Dempster on short-term memory development. I discuss ways in which these age changes might be expressed more precisely. In the next section, the focus is the impact of practice, which is often considerable on tasks in which responses are speeded. I present some useful ways to describe these effects mathematically. The final section is devoted to the relationship between the speed and accuracy of responses. I discuss why the interpretation of age differences in processing speed can be complicated by age differences in error rates and present ways to circumvent these complications.

Decomposing Reaction Times

For most developmentalists, response times are of interest only to the extent that they represent "central" processes as opposed to "noncentral" processes such as the sensory detection of a stimulus or the motoric execution of a response. Because response times always include these latter components, an important technical issue is how to extract the central component of response time. The logic of modern decomposition procedures was first set down by Donders (1868/1969). In a simple reaction time experiment, onset of a stimulus A is always a cue for the subject to make response a (e.g., press a button). Donders elaborated this basic paradigm by adding a second stimulus B with its associated response b (e.g., press a second button). Stimuli A and B

were presented randomly on successive trials. These *choice reaction times* were ordinarily larger than simple reaction times. Donders argued that these choice reaction times involve a decision phase that is unnecessary in simple reaction time tasks. By subtracting the simple reaction time from choice reaction time, one could estimate the duration of the decision phase.

Donders' method (1868/1969) was elaborated by Sternberg (1966) into the *subtraction method*, and his work has since become the cornerstone of much contemporary research in cognitive psychology. The underlying assumptions are that cognitive processes operate in real time and that such times are additive. Total response time can therefore be decomposed to discover the duration and organization of processes. In essence, what is created in this approach are nested versions of tasks; that is, the aim is to create a task A that includes all of the processes of task B plus one additional process; the difference in response time between the two tasks is, putatively, a measure of the duration of the single process that differentiates the two tasks.

More generally, the subtraction method involves the following series of steps: (1) analyze a task to arrive at a set of processes that plausibly could underlie performance on a task; (2) construct experimental conditions that require slightly different processes or different frequencies of a given process, as specified in the task analysis; (3) write equations to express the latency of each condition as a function of the processes involved; (4) measure response latencies in each condition; and (5) use latencies from various conditions to determine the duration of each process, either by subtracting one latency from another or, for cases involving many variables and conditions, by multiple regression.

Sternberg (1966, 1975) developed these procedures in the course of his now well-known work on rapid retrieval processes. Specifically, the task was one in which subjects briefly studied a subspan set of digits. Then a test digit was shown, and subjects judged if the test digit was a member of the immediately preceding set. The subtraction logic entered this experiment because Sternberg varied the number of digits in the study set. That is, he presumed that subjects solve this task in the following sequence: (1) the test digit is encoded in memory, (2) it is compared with each of the digits from the study set, and (3) a subject responds, positively if the test digit matches a digit in the study set and negatively if there is no match.

Some of the processes reflected in response time on the test digit should be of constant duration, regardless of the number of digits studied. Included here would be the time to encode the test digit, e, as well as the time to execute a response once a decision has been reached, r. However, the number of comparisons involved should be exactly equal to the number of digits studied. Thus, the total time for such comparisons would be nc where n is the number of digits in the study set and c is the time to make one such comparison. The result is that total response time on this task should conform to a linear equation of the form

$$RT = (e + r) + (nc). \tag{1}$$

The intercept of this equation represents the combined times for encoding and executing a response, and the slope represents the time to compare the test digit with a digit from the study set.

Keating, Keniston, Manis, and Bobbitt (1980) used these procedures to study memory search in children and adolescents. At all ages, response times increased linearly as a function of the number of digits in the study set, indicating that the task analysis underlying decomposition of response times is plausible and equally so for all age groups. The parameter values decreased systematically with age, reaching asymptotic values in adolescence. The mean slopes for 8-, 10-, 12-, and 14-year-olds were 85, 62, 55, and 52 ms, respectively. Corresponding values for the intercept parameter were 946, 739, 569, and 503 ms, respectively.

In the Keating et al. experiment a model of the processes governing task solution was used to decompose response time into its constituent parts. Obviously, such decomposition is useful only to the extent that the underlying model is accurate. The correspondence between observed response times and those derived from the task analysis is typically indexed by the percentage of variance accounted for (R^2), the root mean squared deviation (RMSD), or some similar measure. Evaluating the "goodness" of a model involves a number of potential problems that sometimes go unnoticed by investigators, problems that are considered at length in Chapter 4 by Brainerd. Values of R^2 may appear to be *less* impressive than they should be, because the reliability of the data imposes an upper limit on goodness of fit, a point that is also stressed in Chapter 5 by Dempster. Procedures for identifying systematic variance that is not accounted for by a model are useful in deciding if any model could have accounted for a greater proportion of variance for a given set of data. For example, determining the reliability of latency data through traditional psychometric methods (e.g., determining coefficient α) provides a standard against which to evaluate the fit of the model to the data.

Another approach is to look for systematicity in the variance that is *not accounted for* by the model under scrutiny. Sternberg and Rifkin (1979) used these procedures in determining how children and adults solve analogy problems. One model of analogical reasoning accounted for 90% or more of the variance in solution times for 10-, 12-, and 19-year-olds. The fact that R^2 values are less than 1 could simply reflect less than perfect reliability in the data, or it may reflect ways in which the data deviate from the model in a small but systematic fashion. To distinguish these possibilities, Sternberg and Rifkin (1979) divided individuals at each age into two arbitrarily defined subsamples, then fitted the model to the data for each subsample. The residuals—the difference between each observed response time and that predicted by the model—were then correlated for the two subsamples. Only if the data deviate systematically from the model's predictions should these residuals be correlated significantly. In fact, the correlation between residuals was significantly greater than 0 at each age, indicating systematic properties of the data that were not captured by the model.

More often, however, R^2 values will appear to be *more* impressive than they really are. One way in which this can occur is that multiple regression tends to capitalize on error in the data, especially when the number of parameters is large relative to the degrees of freedom in the data. Calculating a "shrunken" version of R^2, denoted $\bar{R}^2$, adjusts R^2 values to eliminate this bias (see Cohen & Cohen, 1975, pp. 106–107, for computational details).

Another source of inflated R^2 values is that procedures for estimating parameters can capitalize on variance in the data that is psychologically uninteresting. For example, choice reaction times with many stimuli (and corresponding responses) will be greater than reaction times with few stimuli. This result is hardly surprising, and *any* model predicting this outcome would account for a large portion of the total variance in reaction times, even if the model were completely inaccurate otherwise. Consequently, when reaction times vary considerably across conditions, or when only a single model is being tested, investigators must consider the possibility of spuriously high R^2 values.

These considerations help to define an optimal state for the goodness of fit of the model to the data. Specifically, decomposition of response times can be done with greatest confidence only when both of the following conditions have been met: (1) R^2 is not significantly less than 1 (subject to correction due to unreliability of the data); and (2) the best-fitting model is shown to fit the data significantly better than other theoretically plausible models. Only in this situation can we be confident that the processes included in the model represent an accurate description of a subject's mental activities. To the extent that these criteria are not met, models are inaccurate, and these inaccuracies probably lead to systematic errors in the estimation of processing rate.

Another complication that is unique to developmental research is that the fit of models may vary with age. A frequent event in the developmental literature is that of criteria (1) and (2) described previously, criterion (2) is met but in varying degrees at different ages. For example, in the Sternberg and Rifkin (1979, Experiment 1) study described earlier, the best-fitting model accounted for 91%, 95%, 90%, and 94% of the variance at ages 8, 10, 12, and 19 years, respectively. These differences may seem so small they could be dismissed. Nevertheless, they indicate differences in the goodness of fit of the model that may mean that certain parameter estimates are biased differently by age. Similarly, Carter, Pazak, and Kail (1983, Experiment 2) reported r^2 values for the fit of latency data to the model of mental rotation described in the Appendix. The r^2 values were .87, .94, and .86 for 9-, 13-, and 24-year-olds, respectively. As in the case of the Sternberg and Rifkin (1979) experiment, age comparisons in the parameters of the model of mental rotation may be distorted because of age changes in the adequacy of the model as an account of the latency data.

The logical extreme of this problem is that the best-fitting model changes with age. In many cases this does not represent a methodological puzzle but is, instead, a finding of substantive interest, indicating qualitative change with age in the strategies that individuals use to perform a task. Representative cases revealed by latency data would be developmental changes in strategies for analogical reasoning (Sternberg & Rifkin, 1979), mental rotation (Carter et al., 1983), and accessing semantic information (Gitomer, Pellegrino, & Bisanz, 1983). However, frequently the various best-fitting models have parameters in common (e.g., Sternberg & Rifkin, 1979; Carter et al., 1983; Gitomer et al,. 1983) that invite age comparisons in those parameters. Rarely will the best models for different age groups fit the data exactly the same, so the previous caveats about age comparisons in parameters hold in this case.

Furthermore, nominally identical processes such as encoding or comparison may refer to subtly different processes in different models, so comparisons of their durations may not be meaningful. For example, Carter et al. (1983) described two models of mental rotation, each of which included an encoding component estimated from the data in much the same way. Nevertheless, in one model encoding is presumed to result in a representation of the stimulus that is veridical and long-lasting; in the other, the represention is imprecise and degrades rapidly. Such processes are the same only in name; it would be misleading to make age comparisons between the encoding parameter for children (for whom imprecise encoding was more likely) and the encoding parameter for adults (whose encodings were more likely to be veridical).

The issues just addressed point to a more general problem. Deciding the goodness of a model is more than simply determining the degree of fit between the model and the data. Even when a model meets the twin criteria proposed earlier, this need not imply that it is the "true" model. Two issues are pertinent here. First, labeling an operation that yields an estimable parameter is often a far cry from a full-fledged theory of the psychological processes represented in that operation. For example, encoding is a ubiquitous and time-consuming process in many information-processing models, yet few theorists provide detailed accounts of the actual operation of this component. Such opaque processes need to be clarified before one can hope to conclude that any model gives the definitive account of processing in a particular domain.

The second issue is more complex and concerns the issue of mimicry. Conceivably the current model merely makes the same predictions as some other unthought of model that represents the "true" account of processing on the task. The potential for such mimicry has been worked out in greatest detail for the distinction between serial and parallel models of processing (Townsend, 1971, 1974). As the names imply, processes occur in strict temporal sequence in serial models, but may occur simultaneously in parallel models. Psychologists have traditionally favored serial models over parallel models simply because the former are usually much more tractable. Only recently have methodologies emerged for analyzing parallel models with relative ease (e.g., Schweikert, 1980, 1983). Tradition, however, should not obscure the fact that probably all serial models have parallel analogs that lead to exactly the same predictions (Anderson, 1976, 1978; Townsend, 1974).

To illustrate, a parallel model can lead to the same predictions concerning the linear increase in reaction time that is typical in the Sternberg memory search task. Specifically, suppose that as the test digit is presented, it is simultaneously compared with each of n digits in the study set. At first glance, such a parallel model would appear to predict no increase in latency as a function of set size. However, suppose we assume (1) that each comparison takes effort or mental resources (e.g., Navon & Gopher, 1979); (2) that resources are allocated equally among the n digits to be compared; and (3) that speed of comparison is proportional to the resources allocated for the comparison process. A parallel model of this sort yields exactly the same predictions regarding the shape of the latency function as does the serial model.

This situation has led to proposals for several additional criteria that could be used to evaluate models, including: (1) consistency with known facts regarding the physiology of thought (Simon, 1972); (2) generality, referring to the ability of the model to capture important aspects of performance on more than just a single task (Kail & Bisanz, 1982b); and (3) efficiency and optimality, which simply mean that if human evolution has favored efficient modes of thought over inefficient ones, then models that propose efficient thinking should be favored over those that propose inefficient thinking (Anderson, 1978).

None of these additional criteria is totally sufficient. Some theorists doubt whether many facts concerning the human nervous system would help to distinguish cognitive theories (Anderson, 1978). And, the bias toward efficient models is clearly inappropriate in developmental work, where children frequently use inefficient (as well as insufficient) algorithms.

Because of the problem of mimicry, many cognitive psychologists have argued that efforts to find a "true model" should be deemphasized (Anderson, 1978; Pellegrino & Kail, 1982). After all, a model that predicts the behavior (here, latency data) of many individuals much of the time is not such a bad (or frequent!) thing. Excessive concern over whether such a model is true or merely a surrogate for some model is irrelevant for many purposes (e.g., designing theoretically based instruction) and probably premature given the recency of most of the work in the area. Furthermore, to the extent that there are systematic individual differences in thinking—an idea that, historically, developmental psychologists have embraced much more readily than cognitive psychologists—searching for *the* model of thinking in a particular domain is a seriously misguided endeavor (Kail & Bisanz, 1982a; Pellegrino & Kail, 1982).

Growth Functions

In the modal developmental experiment in which response time is the dependent variable, investigators will typically test individuals from two to four different age groups. Parameters are estimated for each group and then compared to determine if there are age differences. Of course, such differences are the norm, with older individuals generally executing processes faster than younger individuals (see also the review of developmental data on response speed in Chapter 5 by Dempster). Most investigators stop at this point, having detected significant age differences in processing parameters. A plausible next step, however, would be to determine a *growth function* for the parameter. That is, instead of simply declaring the presence of age differences in a processing parameter, one could precisely describe those changes as a function of age.

In fact, although developmental psychologists often use the terms "growth functions" or "developmental functions" metaphorically, there are few instances in the literature where investigators have actually calculated growth curves for cognitive variables. One recent exception would be Kendler's (1979a; Kendler & Ward, 1972) efforts to determine growth functions for components of discrimination learning. Specifically, she has shown that the probability that individuals will make a reversal shift—thereby indicating selective encoding of stimulus dimensions (Kendler, 1979b)—is well described by a simple function of the type $y = a + b \ln x$, where x is age.

I believe there are many explanations for the absence of what many might consider fundamental developmental data. One explanation stems from the arbitrary status of most dependent variables in developmental psychology, a point discussed in the introductory material to this chapter and in Chapter 5 by Dempster. Recall that for such arbitrary dependent variables, any monotonic transformation will yield an equally appropriate dependent variable. Hence, for any given set of data, there is no single growth function, but instead there are as many growth functions as there are plausible monotonic transformations of the dependent variable. These growth functions would certainly differ quantitatively (e.g., the slope and intercept in the case of linear functions) and perhaps qualitatively as well (i.e., the form of the function that best describes the observed age differences, e.g., linear versus logarithmic).[1]

As described in the introductory material, response times are not subject to this arbitrariness under transformation. Time constitutes a ratio scale—it has an absolute zero and units of equal size. Hence, growth curves for time measures are not subject to the criticisms raised earlier regarding arbitrary dependent variables. For any given processing parameter, there is but a single growth function of interest.[2]

Another explanation for the absence of growth functions for cognitive processes is that growth functions are traditionally thought to require longitudinal data because cross-sectional data confound developmental change with cohort change (e.g., Schaie, 1965). Of course, cohort effects do not always

[1] The problem is actually more complicated because the function relating the dependent variable to the underlying construct could change with age.

[2] Deciding the appropriate index for age could complicate matters in some situations. Usually, chronological age in years or months will suffice. However, other indices may be more appropriate when studying infants (e.g., gestational age) or adolescents (e.g., amount of pubic hair).

distort cross-sectional data—they represent a potential confounding effect that may or may not be present in a particular set of data. Their existence has been amply documented in studies of aging (Schaie & Labouvie-Vief, 1974), but I am unaware of comparable evidence for development during childhood and adolescence. To the contrary, at least two sets of evidence imply that cohort effects are negligible for basic information processes of the sort described throughout this chapter. Each involves replications of experiments conducted several years apart. First, Kendler (1979a) described two studies of reversal-shift behavior conducted 8 years apart: in one study, the function describing probability of a reversal shift as a function of age was $-0.39 + 0.21 \ln x$; in the other it was $-0.38 + 0.21 \ln x$. Second, shown in Figure 6-1 are changes in simple reaction time as a function of age. One study is by Goodenough (1935); the other is by Elliott (1970). The developmental changes are remarkably consistent across studies conducted 35 years apart, despite intervening changes in the culture of childhood and in the precision with which reaction time is measured.

These results imply that cohort effects do not pose a serious problem in the interpretation of learning data and reaction time data. This does not mean that cohort effects can be discounted categorically; my claim is simply that they have yet to be demonstrated for basic information processes that are the focus of this chapter. Hence, at this stage, deriving growth functions from cross-sectional data is defensible.

Describing changes in this way seems like a particularly useful approach for studies of processing speed, because many of the studies point to a common

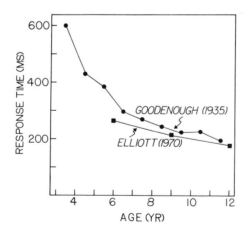

Figure 6-1. Reaction time (in milliseconds) as a function of chronological age (in years). The data from Goodenough (1935) are means calculated from her Table 3. The data from Elliott (1970) are estimated from his Figure 1, from the condition with procedures most like those used by Goodenough (1935): first session, low incentive, with a regulatory preparatory interval of 1 s.

pattern of developmental change. Specifically, in many of these studies, the bulk of the developmental change occurs in childhood and early adolescence, with little change thereafter. For example, Kail, Pellegrino, and Carter (1980) found that rate of mental rotation changed approximately 2 ms/deg between 8 and 11 years of age but after age 11, rate of rotation changed on the order of .5 ms/deg over a span of 8 years. Thus, it seemed as if early adolescence was the point in development when mental rotation reaches mature speed. The picture seems to be much the same for visual search (e.g., Bisanz & Resnick, 1978; Keating et al., 1980) and memory search (e.g., Keating & Bobbitt, 1978; Keating et al., 1980). Here, too, age differences are large in childhood and smaller thereafter. Adolescence seems to mark the onset of functional maturity for these processes, as it also does for categorization processes (see Chapter 3 by Bjorklund).

A limit to our own data and those of other investigators was that a handful of means provides few clues as to the precise shape of the developmental function. One useful source of information was the literature of developmental biology (e.g., Richards, 1969), where scientists have long been interested in precise characterizations of quantitative change. In fact, the three functions listed in Table 6-1 and illustrated in Figure 6-2 have been found to be useful for characterizing quantitative changes in growth, such as the number of cells as a function of time. All three are negatively accelerated functions. They differ only in subtle ways. The monomolecular function is negatively accelerated throughout. The logistic and the Gompertz functions have an initial portion where change is positively accelerated; the logistic and the Gompertz differ in that in the logistic function the initial positively accelerated component is exactly symmetrical to the later negatively accelerated component. The Gompertz does not share this symmetry.

To determine if information-processing parameters could be fitted to these growth curves from developmental biology, I (Kail, 1983) undertook what was essentially a replication of the initial Kail et al. (1980) study. The principal difference was that I sampled age broadly but not very densely. In other words,

Table 6-1. Fit of Growth Functions to Mental Rotation Data

Name	Equation	Parameter Estimates			
		r^2	a	b	c
Monomolecular	$Y = a(1 - be^{-ct})$	.8189	453.75	4.61	0.0187
Logistic	$Y = \dfrac{a}{1 + be^{-ct}}$	.8328	433.73	79.56	0.0367
Gompertz	$Y = ae^{-be^{-ct}}$	.8279	439.98	18.60	0.0277

Note: In all equations, e is the base of natural logarithms, t is age in months. Parameter estimates are expressed in degree of mental rotation per second (i.e., 1000/slope of the mental rotation function).

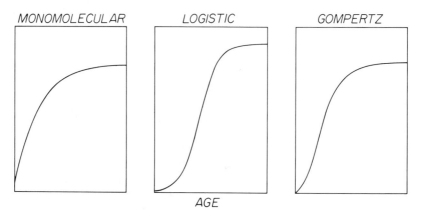

Figure 6-2. Three common growth functions. Equations for these functions are provided in Table 6-1.

I included a large number of groups (twelve: 8-, 9-, 10-, 11-, 12-, 13-, 14-, 15-, 18-, 19-, 20-, and 21-year-olds) but with relatively few subjects per age, only eight. All subjects were tested on procedures akin to those of the earlier study: There were 144 trials in which alphanumeric stimuli were systematically presented at six different orientations.

Figure 6-3 shows the basic reaction time data. In this figure, the data for children are in the left panel, for adolescents in the middle, and, for adults in the right. Age is strongly predictive of response time in the left-hand panel of Figure 6-3, less predictive in the middle panel, and completely unpredictive in the right-hand panel. These data are more meaningful when replotted in terms of rate of mental rotation as a function of age, shown in Figure 6-4. Because slopes

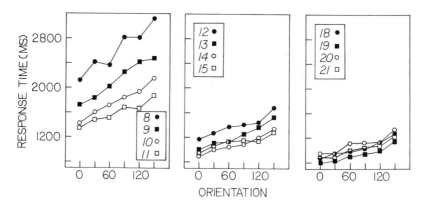

Figure 6-3. Response time as function of orientation, for 12 age groups. From Kail (1983).

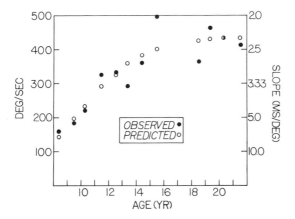

Figure 6-4. Rotation rate derived from data in Figure 6-3, plus predicted rates derived from the best-fitting logistic function. From Kail (1983).

of the latency function decrease with age rather than increase, the data in Figure 6-4 are essentially speed scores, namely, the number of degrees that a stimulus could be rotated mentally in 1 s. As in the first study, rate of rotation reaches adultlike levels in early adolescence.

I fitted these data to a number of different functions. The fit to a simple linear function was statistically significant, and accounted for 78.27% of the variance. Nonetheless, the linear function is unsatisfactory for two related reasons. First, in achieving this fit, the linear function systematically underestimates rotation speed for adolescents and overestimates it for children and adults. Second, the linear function provides unreasonable predicted values for individuals both younger and older than those included in the study.

The three growth functions provide better fits to the data and are not subject to either of the criticisms regarding predictive errors. The percentage of variance accounted for by the three functions, as well as the parameter estimates, are shown in Table 6-1. All account for approximately 10% additional variance over the linear function, a significant increment. The similar fit of the three functions is not surprising. Recall that the functions differ only in their initial portions, which is precisely where we have limited data because of the inability of young children to perform this task with much accuracy.

At this point, I want to consider another reason for the traditional reliance upon longitudinal data for growth curves. Developmental functions derived from cross-sectional data are composites that, conceivably, may not correspond to growth functions for individuals. Put another way, averaging across individuals in a cross-sectional study may result in systematic deviations in the shape of the resulting growth function. As with putative cohort effects, bias is not a necessary consequence of averaging across data for individuals. As Estes (1956) showed years ago, many functions are not distorted at all by such averaging. For example, the slope and intercept of a linear function based on group data is exactly equal to the means of slope and intercept parameters when functions are calculated for individuals. The growth functions used most often to describe growth are *not* like the linear function in this regard: It is possible for group functions to differ from individual functions both in shape and in parameter values. However, the mere possibility of such discrepancies does not mean that we must abandon efforts to derive growth functions from cross-sectional data. Instead, the strategy is to recognize the possibility of these discrepancies, then evaluate them in one's data.

For example, consider the possibility that the growth function for mental rotation is really a step function in which rotation rate is stable for many years, but with the onset of puberty achieves adultlike levels very rapidly. Because puberty begins at different ages, averaging across individuals' step functions would yield a negatively accelerated growth function such as the one depicted in Figure 6-4.

It is possible to evaluate this hypothesis without growth functions for individuals, because the hypothesis leads to two related predictions for cross-sectional data. First, the variance in rate of rotation should be significantly larger during adolescence (when rotation rate is changing) than in either childhood or adulthood (when rotation rate is stable). Second, the distribution of rotation rates during adolescence should be distinctly bimodal: One mode represents individuals who have achieved the postpubertal rotation rate, the other represents the slower prepubertal rotation rate. In fact, in the Kail (1983) study the variance in rotation rate did not vary with age, and the distributions were unimodal at all ages. Hence, it is unlikely that the growth function shown in Figure 6-4 is an artifact of averaging across individuals' step functions. Of course, other functions for individuals might give rise to the average function in Figure 6-4. But these other individual functions would also lead to predictions about the consequences of averaging, consequences that could be evaluated as I have done here for the step function.

The significance of this growth function is twofold. One contribution concerns its descriptive value. Given the ubiquity of age differences in processing rate, one would think that we would have a precise description for them. On the contrary, the most specific description one can cull from the literature is that "older is faster"—at least until 25 to 30 years of age (but see also Chapter 5 by Dempster). Hence, providing an equation that fits these developmental changes well represents a large advance over conventional levels of descriptive precision.

My second point concerns cognitive development during adolescence. The traditional view of adolescent cognition is as the time when formal operational thought emerges; even for non-Piagetians (e.g., Keating, 1979), the sophisticated reasoning and problem-solving skills embodied in formal operations represent the hallmark of adolescent cognition. But why do these more powerful forms of thought emerge during adolescence? One possibility is that in adolescence the elementary information processes are now functionally mature, thus allowing the full commitment of processing resources, mental effort, and the like to the more demanding processing that Piaget described. One way to provide evidence for this hypothesis would be to show that the pattern of results shown here—achievement of functional maturity during adolescence—is not restricted to rate of mental rotation, but instead holds across a wide variety of elementary information processes.

Practice

For both adults and children, reaction times decrease with practice, though some of the data are criticized in Chapter 5 by Dempster. Elliott (1972), for example, found that 7-year-olds' simple reaction time declined from 360 to 220 ms after 1000 trials, a drop of 39%. These changes due to practice pose serious problems for investigators interested in age differences in processing parameters. To illustrate the problem, consider the normal procedures used in developmental research with response time as a dependent variable. First the experimenter gives instructions to the task, which usually include several preliminary trials without emphasis on speed. Several trials follow with speeded responses, trials that are considered practice in the sense that investigators do not report these data. The final phase consists of the test trials, which differ from trials in the middle phase only in that the data *are* reported.

Although the sequence is standard in the developmental and experimental literatures, the amount of time devoted to each step varies enormously. In the developmental literature, some investigators proceed almost directly to the third phase (i.e., test trials); others give considerable practice. Developmental studies of memory scanning using the Sternberg paradigm illustrate the variability: At one extreme, Naus and Ornstein (1977) used 240 practice trials; at the other, Herrmann and Landis (1977) used only 16 practice trials in each of two sessions. Not surprisingly, Naus and Ornstein estimated that 11-year-olds scanned memory at a rate three times faster than that of the 12-year-olds in the Herrmann and Landis (1977) study.

These large effects due to practice can complicate age comparisons of processing parameters, for these improvements due to practice need not occur at the same rate for individuals of different ages. The potential problem is illustrated in Figure 6-5, which depicts hypothetical practice curves for children and adolescents. Because practice effects are not the same for the two groups, estimates of the age difference will vary as a function of the amount of practice.[3]

---

[3] The situation depicted in Figure 6-5 is definitely not unique to response time as a dependent variable; it is a potential problem in any developmental work. Practice is more likely to have impact on response times only because they are so much more labile than most dependent variables in psychology.

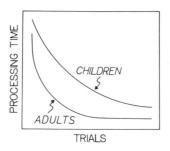

Figure 6-5. Hypothetical functions showing changes in processing speed due to practice, for children and adults.

There are two steps that can help to remedy this situation. The first is to recognize that the usual distinction between practice and test trials has significance only for the experimenter, not for the subject. That is, unless the experimenter goes to great lengths to discount the importance of practice trials—to the extent that subjects use qualitatively different strategies for task-solution, or trade off speed and accuracy in a radically different fashion—the transition in the subject's performance from practice to test trials is continuous, not discontinuous. Hence, there is little rationale for artificially dividing subjects' data into practice and test data, and then reporting only the latter. Data for all speeded responses should be reported, broken down into the smallest number of trials that will yield reliable parameter estimates.[4]

The second procedure is more elaborate. Changes due to practice are regular and usually asymptotic. Hence, a nonarbitrary way to deal with these increases would be to test subjects until they reach asymptotic levels of performance. Then, one can fit the practice data to any of the functions that have been used successfully to describe such effects, including exponential, hyperbolic, and power functions (Mazur & Hastie, 1978; Newell & Rosenbloom, 1981). These functions provide an estimate of a subject's asymptotic processing rate, that is, the rate that would be achieved after infinite practice. These asymptotic values could then be compared for different age groups.

In fact, there is no single study in the developmental literature in which practice functions have been fitted to latency data (primarily because performance sometimes reaches asymptotic levels only after an extraordinarily large number of trials). The closest approximation is a study by Pew and Rupp (1971), who used a tracking task in which subjects used a joy stick to keep a randomly moving cursor centered on a screen. The subjects—boys in grades 4, 7, and 10—were tested on six blocks of trials, with each block consisting of four

---

[4]This distinction should not be confused with the nonarbitrary distinction, often used by cognitive psychologists, between preasymptotic and asymptotic levels of performance. Adults will sometimes be tested on a task until their performance achieves a "steady state" or asymptotic levels of performance, and only these data will be reported.

separate trials each lasting 2 min. One parameter of subjects' performance was τ, a measure of the lag between the movement of the stimulus and subjects' corrective responses. At all grades, τ reached asymptotic values within the 48 min of testing, with values of 209, 198, and 173 ms for grades 4, 7, and 10, respectively. In this study, then, developmental differences remained even after subjects reached maximal processing speeds.

This study illustrates a useful approach for dealing with the practice effects that complicate age comparisons on speeded tasks. Instead of presenting response times for one arbitrarily selected point on the practice function, one collects enough data to generate actual practice functions. The parameters of these practice functions can then be compared for different age groups.

The Speed-Accuracy Trade-Off

In most experiments in which a response is speeded, subjects are encouraged to respond correctly and to do so as rapidly as possible. Typically, subjects are not explicitly instructed as to an appropriate speed of response or level of accuracy. Hence, they must set their own criterion for a speed of response that will lead to acceptably high levels of accuracy. Typically, there is a trade-off between the speed and accuracy with which an individual responds. Encouraged to respond faster, individuals will usually err more often; asked to respond more slowly, they err less frequently.

This state of affairs can make it difficult to interpret response latencies and the parameters derived from those latencies. Suppose that the mean response time for Condition X is 800 ms with a 10% error rate and the mean response time for Condition Y is 900 ms with a 5% error rate. Responses are faster in Condition X but less accurate. That is, subjects sacrificed accuracy for speed in Condition X. Such a situation precludes meaningful comparisons between the response times in Conditions X and Y.

The phenomenon of speed-accuracy trade-off presents additional interpretive problems in a developmental context. Suppose that for both children and adults, faster processing is possible if more errors are tolerated, a situation depicted in Figure 6-6. Notice that very small differences in error rate can lead to apparent similarities in rotation rate. It is plausible, for example, that children would err on 4% of the trials and adults on 1%, a difference most investigators would dismiss as negligible. Yet, as illustrated by points B and C in Figure 6-6, the conclusion of similarity in rate of rotation is a by-product of differences in error rate. The only appropriate comparison for point A in Figure 6-6 is Point C; the appropriate comparison for B is D.[5]

---

[5]In Figure 6-6 the function describing response time as a function of accuracy is linear and identical for the two groups. This is not an essential part of the argument.

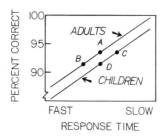

Figure 6-6. Speed-accuracy trade-off functions illustrating a possible interpretive problem in developmental research.

This situation is not simply hypothetical. It is not difficult to find data that may be subject to this interpretive problem.[6] Bisanz, Danner, and Resnick (1979), for example, used a variant of the Posner matching paradigm in which subjects decided if pairs of stimuli were identical physically (i.e., physical match) or in name (i.e., name match). Name matches took more time than did physical matches, reflecting the additional time needed to retrieve the names of the stimuli from semantic memory. These values did not differ significantly for 12- and 19-year-olds (97 and 80 ms, respectively) suggesting that name retrieval reaches adultlike speeds in late childhood. (Possible reasons for age trends in retrieval are considered in Chapter 1 by Ackerman.) However, differences in error rates preclude our reaching this conclusion with confidence: 12-year-olds erred more than twice as often (5.1%) as the 19-year-olds (2.15%). In other words, the Bisanz et al. data may correspond to the situation represented by points *A* and *D* in Figure 6-6.

The most direct escape from this interpretive morass is to generate functions such as those depicted in Figure 6-6. Doing so involves two issues: (1) collecting accuracy data at a number of different latencies, and (2) using these accuracy data to adjust the latency data across groups.

Obtaining Speed-Accuracy Data

Three general procedures have been used to obtain the data necessary to derive speed-accuracy functions. (For details, see Pachella, 1974; Wickelgren, 1977; Woods & Jennings, 1976).

Instructions. Instructions that emphasize response speed will decrease response times and increase errors. Conversely, instructions that emphasize the accuracy of a response will increase response times and decrease errors. The virtue of this approach is that the procedures are simple and readily understood, especially compared to the more complex approaches to be described. Hence, it

---

[6]The problem is complicated by the fact that some investigators simply report error rates in cursory fashion, or dismiss them altogether (e.g., Keating et al, 1980).

may be the most appropriate method to use with young children. Its drawbacks are twofold. First, in this approach, subjects must interpret the instructions and decide the appropriate compromise between speed and accuracy, just as they do in a standard reaction time study. In this situation individuals may elect to vary their accuracy only modestly but let response time fluctuate a great deal. The reverse, of course, could also occur. The result is that the precise points on the speed-accuracy function are primarily under the subject's control, not the experimenter's, and thus cannot be selected a priori.

A related shortcoming is that instructions can generate only a small number of points for speed-accuracy functions. One can readily imagine an experiment with three conditions: speed emphasis, accuracy emphasis, and equal emphasis on speed and accuracy. Adding more conditions, such as extreme speed emphasis or extreme accuracy emphasis, would increase the points only to five and would compound the problems of reliance upon subjects' interpretation of speed-accuracy instructions.

Payoffs. One way to specify instructions for subjects is to associate specific rewards and penalties with particular levels of accuracy and particular response speeds. For example, to encourage accuracy, Banks and Atkinson (1974) provided a 1.5 cent reward for a correct resonse but a 25 cent penalty for an error. To encourage speed, they used a payoff matrix built around the definition of a "fast" response as one that was 90% (or less) of the mean response time during practice trials. For fast and correct responses, subjects were rewarded 5 cents; fast, incorrect responses incurred a penalty of 1 cent; slow responses resulted in a 5-cent penalty regardless of accuracy.

Payoffs offer the virtue of clarifying the intent of general instructions. They share many of the shortcomings of instructions. First, subjects still must decide how to translate payoff matrices into actual emphases on speed and accuracy. Second, the range of speed-accuracy combinations that can be explored is not large. Payoffs would more readily convey to subjects what is meant by extreme emphasis on speed or accuracy, but it is not clear that subtle manipulations in payoff matrices would always accomplish the desired changes in speed and accuracy. Both of these problems are likely to be severe in developmental research, where children would not be expected to translate complicated payoff matrices into the desired performance changes consistently.

There is another important shortcoming common to both instructions and payoffs. In each of these methods, subjects know before a trial (or more often— before an entire block of trials) the desired emphases on speed and accuracy. This raises the possibility that subjects may resort to different processing strategies under the different conditions, which would complicate interpretation of the resulting data as different points along the same underlying speed-accuracy function.

Response to Signals. An approach that deals with many of the objections to instructions and payoffs is to signal the subject to respond at the desired time.

To illustrate, the probe in a recognition memory task could be presented, followed after a variable interval by a tone signaling the subject to respond immediately (e.g., Dosher, 1981). This procedure addresses many of the problems encountered with other methods. First, the speed-accuracy function does not depend on the subject's interpretation of instructions (or payoff matrices)—instead, the timing of the responses is under experimental control, as is the number of points generated for the speed-accuracy function. Second, subjects cannot alter their processing strategies because they do not know, for any given trial, how much time will be alloted for processing.

One difficulty with this method is that the usual response time paradigm has now been turned into what is, in effect, a time-sharing paradigm. That is, during processing of the target stimulus (e.g., the recognition memory probe in the example provided previously), the subject is also monitoring the presence of the cue to respond. Given the frequent finding of developmental differences in performance on time-sharing tasks (e.g., Wickens & Benel, 1982), this characteristic of the response-signal methodology is not attractive. The way to evaluate the extent of this problem is to embed a standard response time experiment within the response-signal paradigm, then compare performance in the two variants in order to determine the disruptive effects of the response signal (e.g., Reed, 1976).

Deriving Adjusted Response Times

When procedures are used to generate a large number of points for a speed-accuracy function, the function typically consists of three components: accuracy does not differ from chance for very brief response times, then increases approximately linearly for intermediate response times, then tapers off at longer response times. This characteristic is illustrated in a recognition memory experiment by Dosher (1981) in which the response-signal paradigm was used. She found that accuracy (measured in d_t units[7]) was a negatively accelerated function of the time alloted for retrieval; d_t values were .19, .85, 1.25, 1.51, 1.61, 1.57, and 1.68 for response cues presented at 300, 700, 100, 1500, 2000, 2500, and 3000 ms, respectively. In other words, accuracy was at chance levels for the 300 ms cue, improved in a linear fashion between 300 and 1500 ms cues, and reached asymptotic values shortly thereafter.

Dosher (1981) showed that data of this sort were well described by the function

$$d(t) = A(1 - e^{-R(T-1)}), \text{ for } T > I \qquad (2)$$
$$d(t) = 0, \text{ for } T \leq I,$$

where A denotes the asymptotic level of accuracy, R is an index of the speed with which the speed-accuracy function achieves asymptotic accuracy, T is time, and I is the intercept, representing minimal processing time.

---

[7]This is a signal-detection measure of recognition accuracy, analogous to d', derived from confidence ratings.

Often the speed-accuracy function will be linear for the majority of the response time-accuracy data. As a consequence, for many purposes a linear function will often provide a suitably precise description of the speed-accuracy relation. Salthouse (1979), for example, found that response time and accuracy on a choice reaction task were well described by linear functions, for each of several different measures of accuracy. In cases like this one, when accuracy is expressed as a function of time, the slope expresses the increase in accuracy achieved for each additional unit of processing time. When time is expressed as a function of accuracy, one can derive the processing time needed to achieve a stated level of accuracy.

There are few developmental studies of speed-accuracy relationships. Salthouse (1979; Salthouse & Somberg, 1982) has conducted some relevant work with young and old adults. (Issues other than the speed-accuracy trade off in research with aged subjects are discussed in Chapter 7 by Salthouse and Kausler.) His work was motivated by the suggestion (e.g., Birren, 1964) that age differences in many speeded tasks could be due to older adults emphasizing accuracy to a greater extent than do younger adults. Salthouse and Somberg (1982), for example, used a procedure in which elaborate instructions were used to derive speed-accuracy functions for a choice reaction task. Specifically, after each trial, the subject's most recent response time was displayed as a "time line" on a computer display, along with the desired region of response times. Subjects were first requested to respond between 375 and 475 ms. On successive blocks of trials this interval was decreased in 50 ms steps until the target interval was 125 to 225 ms; then it was incremented in 50 ms steps to the original interval of 375 to 475 ms.

Salthouse and Somberg (1982) tested young and old adults (mean ages 18 and 69 years, respectively) on this procedure and then fitted linear equations to the speed-accuracy data. The important findings were these. First, the linear equations described the data well, accounting for 96% of the variance for young adults and 92% for old adults. Second, the intercept of the function relating time to accuracy indicated that older adults needed significantly longer processing time to achieve chance accuracy (50%) than did young adults, 222 versus 176 ms, respectively. Most interesting for the purpose of the experiment was the finding concerning the slope of the function relating accuracy to processing time. These slopes were nearly identical for young (.27) and old (.26) adults; for both groups, accuracy increased by approximately ¼% for each additional millisecond of processing time. These comparable slopes, then, discredit the explanation of age differences in terms of differential speed-accuracy trade-off; to the contrary, the young and old adults in the Salthouse and Somberg (1982) study traded speed for accuracy in essentially the same way.

To determine how speed and accuracy trade off in a mental rotation task, I manipulated speed and accuracy of responses experimentally (Kail, in press). Children (11-year-olds), adolescents (14-year-olds), and adults were tested on a variant of the mental rotation paradigm used previously. All subjects were first administered 48 trials using standard instructions in which they were encouraged "to answer as rapidly as you can, but not so rapidly that you make lots of mistakes." The subjects then received one of three forms of feedback, depending on their experimental condition. Individuals in the *control* condition were simply told that they had done well and that they should continue to solve the problems in the same way. Subjects in the *speed-emphasis* condition were told that

> You made *n* mistakes. Most people your age make many more mistakes than you did. So, this time . . . I think you can try to answer a little faster than you did last time, even though you might make a few more mistakes.

Subjects in the *accuracy-emphasis* condition were told that "you made *n* mistakes. This time . . . it would be a good idea if you answered more slowly. That way you'll get more of them correct." (For these latter two groups, the number of errors, *n*, was recorded by the computer and displayed on the computer terminal immediately following the 48th trial.).

For all groups, the manipulations had the intended effects. Mental rotation was fastest in the speed-emphasis group, followed by the control and accuracy-emphasis groups. This order was reversed for errors.

Because the manipulations were effective, it was possible to determine "iso-accuracy contours" (Pachella, 1974). That is, I could derive response time functions in which accuracy is held constant. The first step in this procedure was to determine the relation between accuracy and response time for each of the 18 combinations of age (3) and orientation of the comparison stimulus (6). For each combination, I calculated the correlation between response time and accuracy. These correlations ranged from .52 to .97, with median correlations of .70, .82, and .86 for children, adolescents, and adults, respectively. Given the magnitude of these correlations, the linear function relating response time to accuracy could be used to derive a predicted response time at each orientation for various levels of accuracy. Shown in Figure 6-7 are the predicted response

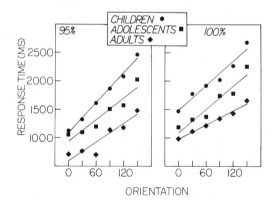

Figure 6-7. Iso-accuracy contours: reaction-time functions in which accuracy has been equated at the different orientations and for the three age groups. Contours in the left panel are for 95% accuracy, those in the right panel are for 100% accuracy.

times for 95% and 100% accuracy levels. For the 95% iso-accuracy contour, the slope of the latency function is significantly steeper for children than for adolescents; slopes for adolescents and adults do not differ significantly. This pattern of age differences, in which adultlike speeds of mental rotation are achieved by adolescents, replicates the earlier findings (Kail et al., 1980; Kail, 1983). A different pattern emerges for the 100% iso-accuracy contour. Here, slopes for children and adolescents do not differ, but both are significantly larger than slopes for adults.

The key finding of this study is that the pattern of developmental change in speed of mental rotation depends upon the accuracy criterion. It is important to determine if this same phenomenon occurs for other cognitive tasks in which response times have been used to infer patterns of developmental change (e.g., reasoning, memory search, visual search).

Concluding Remarks

Decomposition of response time has become a powerful analytic tool for both experimental and developmental psychologists since it was rediscovered by Saul Sternberg in 1966. Like many powerful tools, analysis of response time must be used with proper care. Used carelessly, it can easily lead to erroneous conclusions about cognitive processes and developmental changes therein.

In this chapter, I have discussed four topics concerning the proper use of response times to reveal developmental change in memory and cognition. The first topic concerned the descriptive power of the model underlying decomposition of response time. Inadequacies in models can preclude meaningful developmental comparisons. Second, age differences in processing parameters are traditionally expressed only in ordinal terms (e.g., older individuals process information more rapidly than younger ones) when, in fact, these age differences can be expressed more precisely using growth functions. Third, response times typically decrease with even small amounts of practice. Hence, the recommended procedure would be to derive practice functions for a cognitive process and make age comparisons in terms of the parameters of the practice function for that process. Fourth, response times cannot be interpreted independently of the accuracy of responses. Studies of the speed-accuracy trade-off indicate that even small differences in accuracy can result in large differences in the speed of cognitive processing. One solution to this problem is to vary speed and accuracy experimentally, thereby allowing one to derive processing parameters for which accuracy is equated statistically.

Based on these considerations, the ideal study would be one in which individuals are tested on the task of interest until they achieve asymptotic levels of performance for all parameters. Throughout the test trials, traditional response time trials would be supplemented with instructions designed to manipulate speed and accuracy of responses. Ideally, in all cases (i.e., all combinations of Age × Amount of Practice × Speed-Accuracy manipulations) the model underlying decomposition of response times would account for all of the reliable variance in those response times. If these conditions were met, one could derive the growth curve for the asymptotic level of each parameter, for each of several levels of accuracy.

No study in the developmental literature approximates this ideal. Nor is it reasonable to expect many studies to do so in the forseeable future, for including all of these components in a single project results in an enormous undertaking. A more reasonable approach is to address some of the issues raised throughout this chapter individually, determining (for example), the extent to which the pattern of age differences is modified by the speed-accuracy trade-off. After work of this sort establishes the boundary conditions for practice effects, the extent of speed-accuracy trade-offs, and the descriptive power of models, then one would be better prepared to tackle the ideal study in which all of these issues were addressed. In the interim, the ideal study should remind us of the need to be cautious in claims based on studies that are less than ideal.

References

Anderson, J. R. (1976). *Language, memory, and thought*. Hillsdale, NJ: Lawrence Erlbaum Associates.

Anderson, J. R. (1978). Arguments concerning representations for mental imagery. *Psychological Review, 85*, 249–277.

Banks, W. P., & Atkinson, R. C. (1974). Accuracy and speed strategies in scanning active memory. *Memory & Cognition, 2*, 629–636.

Birren, J. E. (1964). *The psychology of aging*. Englewood Cliffs, NJ: Prentice-Hall.

Bisanz, J., Danner, F., & Resnick, L. B. (1979). Changes with age in measures of processing efficiency. *Child Development, 50*, 132–141.

Bisanz, J., & Resnick, L. B. (1978). Changes with age in two components of visual search speed. *Journal of Experimental Child Psychology*, *25*, 129–142.

Carter, P., Pazak, B., & Kail, R. (1983). Algorithms for processing spatial information. *Journal of Experimental Child Psychology, 36*, 284–304.

Cattell, R. B. (1971). *Abilities: Their structure, growth, and action*. Boston: Houghton-Mifflin.

Cohen, J., & Cohen, P. (1975). *Applied multiple regression/correlation analysis for the behavioral sciences*. Hillsdale, NJ: Lawrence Erlbaum Associates.

Cooper, L. A. (1975). Mental transformation of random two-dimensional shapes. *Cognitive Psychology, 7*, 20–43.

Cooper, L. A., & Shepard, R. N. (1973). Chronometric studies of the rotation of mental images. In W. G. Chase (Ed.), *Visual information processing*. New York: Academic Press.

Donders, F. C. (1969). On the speed of mental processes. *Acta Psychologica, 30*, 412–431. [Translated from the original by W. G. Koster from *Onderzoekingen gedaan in het Physiologisch Laboratorium der Utrechtsche Hoogeschool*, 1868, *Tweede reeks, II*, 92–120.]

Dosher, B. A. (1981). The effects of delay and interference: A speed-accuracy study. *Cognitive Psychology, 13*, 551–582.

Elliott, R. (1970). Simple reaction time: Effects associated with age, preparatory interval, incentive-shift, and mode of presentation. *Journal of Experimental Child Psychology, 9*, 86–107.

Elliott, R. (1972). Simple reaction time in children: Effects of incentive, incentive-shift and other training variables. *Journal of Experimental Child Psychology, 13*, 540–557.

Estes, W. K. (1956). The problem of inference from curves based on group data. *Psychological Bulletin, 53*, 134–140.

Gitomer, D. H., Pellegrino, J. W., & Bisanz, J. (1983). Developmental change and invariance in semantic processing. *Journal of Experimental Child Psychology, 35*, 56–80.

Goodenough, F. L. (1935). The development of the reactive process from early childhood to maturity. *Journal of Experimental Psychology, 18*, 431–450.

Herrmann, D. J., & Landis, T. Y. (1977). Differences in the search rate of children and adults in short-term memory. *Journal of Experimental Child Psychology, 23*, 151–161.

Kail, R. (1983). *Growth functions for information-processing parameters.* Presented at the annual meeting of the Psychonomic Society, San Diego, CA.

Kail, R. (1984). *The development of memory in children* (2nd ed.). New York: W. H. Freeman.

Kail, R. (in press). Development of mental rotation: A speed-accuracy study. *Journal of Experimental Child Psychology*.

Kail, R., & Bisanz, J. (1982a). Cognitive strategies. In C. R. Puff (Ed.), *Handbook of research methods in human memory and cognition*. New York: Academic Press.

Kail, R., & Bisanz, J. (1982b). Cognitive development: An information-processing perspective. In R. Vasta (Ed.), *Strategies and techniques of child study*. New York: Academic Press.

Kail, R., Pellegrino, J., & Carter, P. (1980). Developmental change in mental rotation. *Journal of Experimental Child Psychology, 29*, 102–116.

Keating, D. P. (1979). Adolescent thinking. In J. Adelson (Ed.), *Handbook of adolescence*. New York: Wiley.

Keating, D. P., & Bobbitt, B. L. (1978). Individual and developmental differences in cognitive processing components of mental ability. *Child Development, 49*, 155–169.

Keating, D. P., Keniston, A. H., Manis, F. R., & Bobbitt, B. L. (1980). Development of the search-processing parameter. *Child Development, 51*, 39–44.

Kendler, T. S. (1979a). Cross-sectional research, longitudinal theory, and a discriminative transfer ontogeny. *Human Development, 22*, 235–249.

Kendler, T. S. (1979b). The development of discrimination learning: A levels-of-functioning explanation. In H. W. Reese & L. P. Lipsitt (Eds.), *Advances in child development and behavior* (Vol. 13). New York: Academic Press.

Kendler, T. S., & Ward, J. W. (1972). Optional reversal probability is a linear function of the log of age. *Developmental Psychology, 7*, 337–348.

Loftus, G. R. (1978). On interpretation of interactions. *Memory & Cognition, 6*, 312–319.

Lohman, D. (1979). *Spatial abilities: Individual differences and information processing.* (Technical Report #8, Aptitude Research Project, School of Education.) Palo Alto, CA: Stanford University.

Mazur, J., & Hastie, R. (1978). Learning as accumulation: A reexamination of the learning curve. *Psychological Bulletin, 85*, 1256–1274.

Naus, M. J., & Ornstein, P. A. (1977). Developmental differences in the memory search of categorized lists. *Developmental Psychology, 13*, 60–68.

Navon, D., & Gopher, D. (1979). On the economy of the human processing system. *Psychological Review, 86*, 214–225.

Newell, A., & Rosenbloom, P. S. (1981). Mechanisms of skill acquisition and the law of practice. In J. R. Anderson (Ed.), *Cognitive skills and their acquisition*. Hillsdale, NJ: Lawrence Erlbaum Associates.

Pachella, R. G. (1974). The interpretation of reaction time in information-processing research. In B. H. Kantowitz (Ed.), *Human information processing: Tutorials in performance and cognition*. Hillsdale, NJ: Lawrence Erlbaum Associates.

Pellegrino, J. W., & Kail, R. (1982). Process analyses of spatial aptitude. In R. J. Sternberg (Ed.), *Advances in the psychology of human intelligence* (Vol. 1). Hillsdale, NJ: Lawrence Erlbaum Associates.

Pew, R. W., & Rupp, G. L. (1971). Two quantitative measures of skill development. *Journal of Experimental Psychology, 90*, 1–7.

Reed, A. V. (1976). List length and the time course of recognition in immediate memory. *Memory & Cognition, 4*, 16–30.

Richards, F. J. (1969). The quantitative analysis of growth. In F. C. Steward (Ed.), *Plant physiology* (Vol. 5A). New York: Academic Press.

Salthouse, T. A. (1979). Adult age and the speed-accuracy trade-off. *Ergonomics, 22*, 811–821.

Salthouse, T. A., & Somberg, B. L. (1982). Time-accuracy relationships in young and old adults. *Journal of Gerontology, 37*, 349–353.

Schaie, K. W. (1965). A general model for the study of developmental problems. *Psychological Bulletin, 64*, 92–107.

Schaie, K. W., & Labouvie-Vief, G. (1974). Generational versus ontogenetic components of change in adult cognitive behavior: A fourteen-year cross-sequential study. *Developmental Psychology, 10*, 305–320.

Schweikert, R. (1980). Critical path scheduling of mental processes in a dual task. *Science, 209*, 704–706.

Schweikert, R. (1983). Latent network theory: Scheduling of processes in sentence verification and the Stroop effect. *Journal of Experimental Psychology: Learning, Memory, and Cognition, 9*, 353–379.

Simon, H. A. (1972). On the development of the processor. In S. Farnham-Diggory (Ed.), *Information processing in children*. New York: Academic Press.

Sternberg, R. J., & Rifkin, B. (1979). The development of analogical reasoning processes. *Journal of Experimental Child Psychology, 27*, 195–232.

Sternberg, S. (1966). High speed scanning in human memory. *Science, 153*, 652–654.

Sternberg, S. (1975). Memory scanning: New findings and current controversies. *Quarterly Journal of Experimental Psychology, 27*, 1–32.

Thurstone, L. L. (1938). Primary mental abilities. *Psychometric Monographs* (No. 1). Chicago: University of Chicago Press.

Thurstone, L. L., & Thurstone, T. G. (1949). *Manual for the SRA primary mental abilities*. Chicago: Science Research Associates.

Townsend, J. T. (1971). A note on the identifiability of parallel and serial processes. *Perception & Psychophysics, 10*, 161–163.

Townsend, J. T. (1974). Issues and models concerning the processing of a finite number of inputs. In B. H. Kantowitz (Ed.), *Human information processing: Tutorials in performance and cognition*. Hillsdale, NJ: Lawrence Erlbaum Associates.

Vernon, P. E. (1961). *The structure of human abilities* (2nd ed.). London: Methuen.

Wickelgren, W. A. (1977). Speed-accuracy tradeoff and information processing dynamics. *Acta Psychologica, 41*, 67–85.

Wickens, C. D., & Benel, D. C. R. (1982). The development of time-sharing skills. In J. A. S. Kelso & J. E. Clark (Eds.), *The development of movement control and co-ordination*. London: Wiley.

Wood, C. C., & Jennings, C. R. (1976). Speed-accuracy tradeoff function in choice reaction time: experimental designs and computation procedures. *Perception & Psychophysics, 19*, 92–102.

Appendix

Hierarchical theories of aptitude, such as those developed by Cattell (1971) and Vernon (1961), typically distinguish among verbal, general reasoning, and spatial-mechanical aptitude factors. The latter factor is then divided further into a number of subfactors, including *spatial relations* (Lohman, 1979). On tasks that define this factor, individuals must rotate stimuli mentally in order to determine if they are identical (see Figure 6-A-1). My research has focused on a single task from this domain—the Spatial Relations subtest of the Primary Mental Abilities (PMA) battery (Thurstone & Thurstone, 1949). This task was chosen for several reasons. First, it is typical of many measures of spatial aptitude in which an individual must "mentally rotate" a stimulus in the picture plane in order to differentiate it from other similar stimuli and match it against some standard. Second, the PMA loads heavily on the spatial-relations factor in factor analysis studies (e.g., Cattell, 1971; Lohman, 1979; Thurstone, 1938). Third, the PMA is appropriate across a relatively broad developmental range, beginning at 10 or 11 years of age and continuing through adulthood (Thurstone & Thurstone, 1949).

Performance on simple spatial-relations problems such as those found on the PMA can be related to a model of the processes required for mental rotation problems proposed by Cooper and Shepard (1973), shown in Figure 6-A-2. The model was based upon data obtained in a paradigm in which individuals decided, as rapidly as possible, if two stimuli presented in different visual orientations were the same. This single-trial comparison of a stimulus pair closely resembles the individual comparisons that must be made to solve PMA

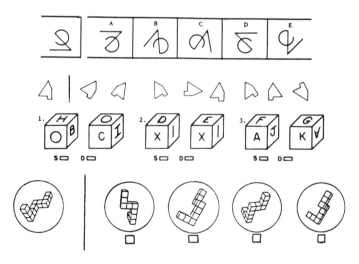

Figure 6-A-1. Illustrative examples of spatial-relations tasks. From Pellegrino & Kail (1982).

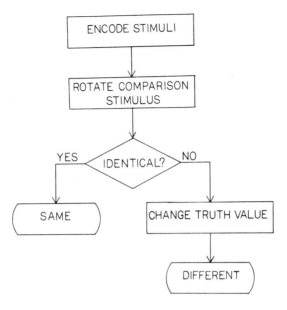

Figure 6-A-2. The Cooper and Shepard (1973) model of mental rotation.

problems. The first stage of processing requires encoding the orientation and identity of the stimuli. The second phase involves rotating the mental representation of the nonvertical stimulus to bring it into congruence with the vertical stimulus. This phase is followed by a comparison of the stimulus representations to determine if they are identical. The outcome of this comparison leads to a positive or negative response.

As shown in Figure 6-A-2, only the mental rotation component is affected by the orientation of the stimulus; encoding, comparison, and response take the same amount of time regardless of the orientation of the stimuli. Consistent with these claims, cuing individuals as to the orientation or identity of a stimulus reduces response time by the same amount, regardless of the orientation of the stimulus. Also, when encoding and rotation are separated experimentally by having subjects first view a stimulus briefly and then rotate it to a specified orientation, rotation rates are quite similar to those found in other studies in which encoding and rotation are measured simultaneously (e.g., Cooper, 1975). Consequently, total response time (RT) on these problems is given by the equation

$$RT = xr + (e + c + m),$$

where x represents the difference in orientation between the two stimuli, and r, e, c, and m represent the times for rotation, encoding, comparison, and response, respectively. Thus, the slope of the function relating response time to stimulus orientation is used to estimate the rate of mental rotation, whereas the intercept provides an estimate of the total time necessary for the remaining processes.

An example of the application of this model is a study by Cooper (1975), in which she presented two nonsense shapes that differed in orientation from 0° to 300°. Subjects judged whether the shapes were identical. As predicted, response latencies in this tasks increased linearly as a function of the difference in orientation between the two shapes. Such a result was interpreted as indicating that subjects mentally rotate the stimuli in a manner analogous to the actual physical rotation of the object. The greater the "mental distance" to be traveled, the longer it takes to solve the problem.

7. Memory Methodology in Maturity

Timothy A. Salthouse and Donald H. Kausler

Several years ago a chapter appeared with the intriguing title of "Are We Overloading Memory?" (Underwood, 1972). The author was dismayed to discover that at least seven different kinds of memory, along with numerous attributes, durations, modalities, and so forth, had been investigated. Moreover, because the article appeared nearly 13 years ago, it is reasonable to expect that the number is considerably greater now. The dramatic increase since the time of Ebbinghaus in the number of phenomena considered to fall within the realm of memory can be considered a sign of progress, but the profusion of concepts also creates problems for authors attempting to discuss issues related to memory. Indeed, it is now nearly a prerequisite in writing about memory to present an overview of one's theoretical perspective before proceeding with the specific discussion of interest (e.g., see Chapters 1, 3, 5, and 6).

While this trend of briefly describing one's current theoretical bias contributes to a lamentable sameness of organization, it is apparently necessary in light of the extremely large number of phenomena currently considered to involve memory in one form or another. Without some sort of classification scheme that can define and limit the scope of coverage, it is nearly impossible to present a meaningful discussion of any topic related to memory. The classification scheme we adopt here is based on three memory distinctions that are currently popular, or being developed, and which appear to provide a reasonable organization of many of the available research findings from adults of varying ages. After a brief discussion of our system of memory classification, we devote two sections to selected issues in the broad areas of internal and external validity in research on memory and aging. The chapter concludes with a section on the problem of controlling or identifying characteristics of one's subject samples. Throughout the chapter, we emphasize issues that transcend specific paradigms or theoretical perspectives in an attempt to increase the generality of our arguments and proposed solutions. Readers interested in a more paradigm-based approach to methodological issues in memory research are referred to a recent volume edited by Puff (1982).

It is not our intention to provide a how-to guide to methodology in research on memory during maturity, nor to attempt a comprehensive analysis of methodological issues. Instead, we propose to describe what we feel are some potential problems in contemporary research on memory processes and aging, and to indicate possible consequences if these problems continue to go unrecognized. At the outset, we wish to make it clear that the following remarks are not intended as criticisms of past work (some of which is our own), but rather are designed to serve as constructive suggestions for the design and interpretation of future research. In keeping with this intent, we will not cite specific studies but instead will rely upon anonymous or hypothetical examples to illustrate our points.

Memory Classification Scheme

A growing body of literature suggests that a useful distinction can be made between memory processes and phenomena that are or are not dependent upon overt, conscious effort on the part of the subject, a theme that also figures prominently in Chapter 3 by Bjorklund. Memory that results only after some intent to remember is said to be effortful, while that which occurs without any discernible intent by the subject is considered to be automatic (e.g., Craik & Byrd, 1982; Hasher & Zacks, 1979). Effortful memory is assumed to be dependent upon the available store of "cognitive resources," "attentional capacity," or "mental energy." Adult age differences in performance on tasks presumed to involve effortful memory are therefore postulated to occur because of an hypothesized age-related reduction in the amount of resources, capacity, or energy. Automatic memory is considered to be independent of these types of processing limitations and thus some theorists (e.g., Hasher & Zacks, 1979) claim that there should be little or no age difference in the efficiency of automatic memory processes. The empirical evidence for this effortful-automatic distinction is currently equivocal with respect to the presence or absence of age differences in measures of memory functioning, but the distinction is nevertheless very popular in contemporary gerontological research.

Another important distinction at the current time is between episodic memory on the one hand, and semantic or generic memory on the other hand (Tulving, 1972). Episodic memory is concerned with the retention of specific, personally experienced, episodes or events such as the items of a to-be-remembered list of words in a psychology experiment. Semantic or generic memory refers to the storehouse of world knowledge possessed by an individual, including such information as the meaning of words, the skills associated with driving an automobile, and the cumulative impact of one's schooling and life experiences (e.g., the organizational aspects of memory discussed in Chapter 3 by Bjorklund). Because the term "semantic" usually has a linguistic connotation, we will use the term "generic" to indicate the form of memory concerned with world (and not just word) knowledge. It is currently assumed, although the evidence is still rather limited, that adult age differences in proficiency are much greater for the episodic form of memory than for the generic type.

A third distinction that we consider important in classifying types of memory is between retrospective memory, the remembrance of things or events from the past, and prospective memory, the intent to perform some action in the future (e.g., Kreutzer, Leonard, & Flavell, 1982; Meacham & Leiman, 1982; Wilkins & Baddeley, 1978). In common usage, memory failure is assumed to be responsible both for failing to remember the name of an acquaintance one recently met, and for forgetting to stop at the grocery store on the way home from work. Although similar processes may be involved in these two types of memory, a distinction is possible. The latter, prospective memory, seems to require unconscious activation of the information by internal time cues, as when one remembers to perform a previously planned activity at an appropriate time. However, the former, retrospective memory, is considered effective if the information is available only upon conscious demand and usually in the presence of external cues, as when one attempts to recall information acquired at an earlier time such as a person's name in the presence of that person. We therefore suspect the retrospective-prospective distinction is an important one, although there is currently little experimental evidence on the attributes of prospective memory, or its susceptibility to the effects of aging.

The three dimensions that we have described (i.e., effortful-automatic, episodic-generic, and retrospective-prospective) are probably not completely orthogonal, and they clearly do not exhaust important memory dimensions. For example, working memory (which is discussed in Chapter 5 by Dempster) and metamemory, both important processes of memory, are not easily classifiable within these dimensions. Nevertheless, the present system is sufficient to illustrate two points we wish to make. The first is that these various types of memory, if truly distinct, will require somewhat different investigative procedures, and, therefore, are likely to raise somewhat different methodological issues. It certainly requires different procedures to investigate prospective as opposed to retrospective memory, and, to a lesser extent, different procedures to investigate effortful compared to automatic memory. Moreover, the methodological prescriptions will tend to vary with the type of memory being investigated as different aspects of the situation, material, or task are emphasized. To illustrate, it would be prudent to match age groups on a variable such as vocabulary ability in investigations of semantic or generic memory, but such matching may be relatively unimportant in studies of episodic memory.

The second, more important point is that regardless of the ultimate validity of these distinctions as applied to aging, some types of memory have been subjected to much more investigation by gerontological researchers than others. Until recently, for example, the great majority of research has focused on effortful, episodic, and retrospective forms of memory. Lately, a number of studies have appeared on automatic memory and generic memory, but we are aware of only one published study on prospective memory with adults of varying ages (Moscovitch, 1982). This disproportionate emphasis has important implications for the evaluation of overall memory functioning during adulthood, particularly if it is eventually discovered that the kinds of memory involved in normal, extralaboratory activities are not the same as those studied in the laboratory.

Establishing Phenomena—Internal Validity

All textbooks on research methodology devote considerable attention to the topic of internal validity for the simple reason that a study is likely to be worthless unless one is confident that the results are attributable to the variable of primary interest and not due either to an extraneous variable, to chance, or to unsuspected artifacts of measurement. In light of the importance of high internal validity, it is somewhat surprising that examples of questionable internal validity can be so easily found in the literature on memory and aging. Actually, however, many of the concerns are quite subtle, and are just beginning to be recognized in the research community. In this section, we will discuss three fairly fundamental aspects of internal validity as they relate to research on memory during maturity (i.e., failure to control extraneous variables, failure to conduct relevant statistical analyses, and inappropriate interpretation of Age × Treatment interactions), and also suggest tentative remedies to the problems we identify.

Each of these threats to internal validity presents obstacles to answering the central question of research on aging and memory—What are the nature and causes of age differences in memory? Precise localization of the specific factors responsible for age differences in memory is hampered by each of the problems we discuss, and until the age differences are well-described one can expect little progress in discovering the causes of those differences. There are undoubtedly other methodological issues that could be raised, but the ones discussed seem to represent the greatest problems in the contemporary literature, both in terms of their frequency in published articles and with respect to the potential for misleading interpretations.

Control of Extraneous Variables

Probably the most fundamental methodological guideline for good research is to ensure that experimental and control groups are equivalent in all respects except for the treatment manipulation. Although seemingly inviolate, many researchers have come to believe that this is an unattainable requirement in gerontological investigations because people of varying ages differ on many variables besides age itself, and it is virtually impossible to equate individuals of different ages on all those other variables. For instance, increased age is inevitably correlated with greater cumulative exposure to the physical and social environment. If that environment is undergoing change, then older adults will have experiences that are not only quantitatively, but also qualitatively, distinct from those of young and middle-aged adults. We will discuss the problem of attempting to match individuals from different age groups in greater detail in a subsequent section, but for the present we can simply state that no satisfactory means of eliminating this confound have yet been devised. However, acceptance of the fact that the age variable includes more than mere years since birth does not mean that one should abandon attempts at ensuring methodological rigor. In fact, we argue that the vagueness and imprecision associated with the primary variable of age dictates an even greater concern with control of potential confounding variables than in other areas of research. Only by pursuing, controlling, and examining variables suspected to be associated with age will definitive conclusions on the true causes of adult age differences in memory become possible.

Of greater and more immediate concern to many researchers are the design flaws in which some age groups receive treatments that differ in important respects from those received by other groups. These differences may include variation among age groups in amount of personal attention and conversation before and during the experimental session, in the age and sex of the experimenter, in the number of activities performed in the session, in the monetary compensation received for participation, and even in the number of items presented for remembering. Unfortunately, while there are often defensible reasons for these practices, they are all potential threats to internal validity.

As an example, a frequently cited study on the effects of age upon imaginal mediation involved the presentation of lists of 20 word pairs to young adults, but lists of only 10 word pairs to older adults. The rationale for this methodological decision, one that introduces a confounding of age and list length, was to minimize frustration and discouragement among the older subjects and yet still have room for performance variation among the young subjects. Viewed in this context, one's judgment of the severity of the error is somewhat tempered, although it is unlikely that the procedure would ever be considered methodologically sound.

Another, more recent example of differential treatment is evident in a study designed to compare the susceptibility of young and old adults to various kinds of interference. A primary manipulation in the study was to have participants count backward during the interval between the presentation and the test of the items. The backward counting was either by threes (fairly difficult) or by twos (somewhat easier), based on the difficulty experienced in a pretest. However, the fact that all of the younger group and only about half of the older group counted backward by threes means that the age comparison is confounded with differential treatment. One simply cannot ignore the basic principle that valid comparisons of the performance of different groups require that the groups receive exactly the same treatment; otherwise, it is impossible to rule out the possibility that differential treatment, and not group membership, was responsible for the observed results.

A preferable strategy in the study just described might have been to use an independent indicator of the effectiveness of the manipulation as the basis for assigning a given level of treatment to an individual. In other words, if the counting backward procedure is intended to prevent rehearsal of the to-be-remembered items, it would be desirable to have a measure other than memory performance per se reflecting the extent to which surreptitious rehearsal was in fact prevented. Subjects in each age group could then receive treatment levels (i.e., magnitude of the subtrahend) individually determined to produce the same degree of rehearsal inhibition. A procedure introduced by Reitman (1974) in which the performance of the distractor activity is compared with and without the primary memory task is one means by which the degree of surreptitious rehearsal could be assessed.

Occasionally an investigator might defend the mixed-treatment procedure by conducting an analysis of the data from the two subgroups receiving different treatments. If a nonsignificant difference were observed, one might conclude that the groups are equivalent and that the differential treatment was of little or no consequence. For example, the investigator in the study described earlier could have conducted an analysis of the difference in memory performance between older adults who counted backward by threes and those who counted backward by twos. The difficulty in this case is that there might be an interaction between the specific treatment (e.g., counting backward) and the other manipulations of interest (e.g., retention interval). Since that interaction could only exist for the older age group which received two different treatments, a confounding of group and treatment still exists.

It is often desirable, either because of theoretical assumptions or for reasons related to measurement (to be elaborated later), that all individuals perform within the same relatively narrow range of the dependent variable, but one must be quite careful that the equivalence in performance was not achieved by altering other potentially important characteristics of the task. A conservative strategy might be to include tasks or conditions designed to be "favorable" to each age group, and then to present one's arguments for why a particular comparison is to be emphasized. In this manner, the reader can judge the reasonableness of the arguments, and if they are not compelling, the remaining results could still be of some value.

It is also worth mentioning that sometimes there can be too much control of variables, with somewhat less control leading to more valid inferences. This paradoxical situation can occur when a design calls for balancing of task sequence, stimulus materials, or some other experimental variable across, rather than within, subjects, and then making detailed examinations of the data from individual subjects. For example, consider what would happen if the sequence of subtests in an intelligence battery was not the same for each subject. Altering the sequence across subjects is a useful control technique to minimize practice and fatigue effects in comparisons across specific subtests, but it is not good practice in individual difference analyses. The problem with this procedure is that the various individuals would differ not only in their intrinsic attributes, but also in the specific type of treatment they received. Strictly speaking, then, the differential treatment, even if only in the form of a different order of the tasks, is confounded with preexperimental individual characteristics. It would therefore be inappropriate to make comparisons across individuals receiving different balancing conditions, different sets of materials, and so on.

The possibility of Subject × Treatment interaction effects is a serious problem only when the focus is on variations across individuals within the same age group, and not in comparisons across groups of different ages (assuming, of course, that the same percentage of individuals in the various age groups received each balancing procedure). However, it can be a serious problem when one is interested in the differential use of strategies to perform a task, or in the relationship between performance on two or more tasks. The solution, fortunately, is quite simple, and merely involves preserving the treatment distinctions in all analyses of the data; that is, examining the frequency of various strategies, computing correlation coefficients, and so on, separately for each subgroup. Of course, since these separate analyses will generally be accompanied by much reduced statistical power, it would be prudent to increase one's sample sizes accordingly in the design phase of the experiment.

Consider a hypothetical experiment in which the memory performance of young and old adults is to be compared in two presentation conditions, either successive displays of each item or a single simultaneous array of all items. In order to avoid confounding sequence with presentation condition, one-half of the subjects in each age group might receive the conditions in the order successive-simultaneous and one-half in the order simultaneous-successive. Potentially misleading inferences might result if one were to conduct overall analyses of the percentage of subjects exhibiting evidence of organization in the recall of successively presented items, for example, since it is likely that these percentages would be higher among the simultaneous-successive subjects than the successive-simultaneous subjects. Notice that it is not the interpretation of the main effects of age that is threatened by this procedure of ignoring subgroup distinctions in the analyses of data, but instead the more subtle interactions are missed (e.g., the possibility that young adults exhibit greater increases in organization than old adults after exposure to the simultaneous presentation but are equivalent without that exposure).

Some investigators conduct an initial analysis to determine if there are any performance differences across subgroups, and if not, then proceed to collapse the subgroups in subsequent analyses. A potential problem with this procedure is that equivalent overall performance could be achieved with different combinations of processes, and it is usually the specific processes that are of primary interest in the analyses of data from individuals rather than groups. Also, as mentioned earlier, there is the possibility that the specific balancing treatment may interact in an important and interesting way with the other manipulations in the study and yet one would be unable to detect this if the subjects in the various subgroupings were collapsed after a preliminary analysis.

Statistical Confirmation

Assuming that a well-designed experiment has been conducted, that is, one in which nearly all extraneous variables have been controlled, the next step in most studies is to determine the statistical reliability of the results. While this is an obvious step, there are a surprising number of studies in which the contribution of chance in producing the results cannot be dismissed on the basis of the evidence presented. A major problem is that age groups are often compared to some chance value, but are not directly compared to one another. This trend is not only evident in studies employing a design that would call for an interaction test in an analysis of variance (e.g., comparing the differences between two conditions in various age groups against chance rather than against each other) but also in correlational designs (e..g, determining whether correlation coefficients obtained in various age groups are significantly different from zero rather than from each other). In view of the frequency with which these procedures are followed, it is worth iterating that one should always assess the statistical significance of the result of primary interest, which in developmental research is most often a comparison across age groups. Unless the significance of the age difference itself is determined, one cannot rule out the hypothesis that the various age groups are not truly different from one another.

As an example, in a recent study it was reported that there was a strong negative relationship between level of recall and an index of the uniformity of retrieval modes (i.e., recalling words by topical theme or by taxonomic category), across successive attempts at retrieval. That is, ability to shift one's recall according to topical theme or taxonomic category was associated with better recall than strict reliance on a single mode of retrieval. It was further reported that the relationship, while still statistically significant, was weaker among older adults than among young adults. However, there was apparently no test of the significance of the difference between the correlations obtained in the two age groups. The primary issue here concerns the specific null hypothesis of interest. If, as these investigators apparently assumed, the null hypothesis was that there was no relationship between the retrieval-consistency and level-of-recall variables, that is, $H_0: r = 0$, then the comparison of the obtained correlations against the chance value was appropriate. In many studies of aging, however, a more relevant null hypothesis is that there is no age difference. This latter hypothesis requires a direct contrast of the two correlations, even if one or both of them is not significantly different from 0. Only if the difference between the correlations is found to be significant is one justified in concluding that there is an age difference in the relationship between the variables of interest.

Another tendency prevalent in much of the contemporary research on memory in adulthood concerns the failure to document the reliability of one's measures, a problem that also arises in developmental research on short-term memory (see Chapter 5 by Dempster). This is particularly troublesome when the pattern of results leads one to accept the null hypothesis of equality in performance between young and elderly adults, because it is possible that the lack of significance was at least partially attributable to low measurement reliability. If two repetitions of the procedure yield widely varying results, it is unlikely that many systematic effects could be detected regardless of the strength of the experimental manipulation.

In general, it is desirable, and perhaps even essential, to provide some indication of the reliability of one's measures whenever one is attempting to make inferences from the lack of a statistically significant difference. Because of the importance of null results in the areas of automatic and generic memory processes during adulthood, an immediate priority should be to report information about the reliability of the relevant variables. This is necessary to rule out the possibility that the absence of age differences is simply caused by low reliability. If the reliability is low, some improvement might be possible by increasing the number of relevant observations, utilizing the principle of aggregation (Rushton, Brainerd, & Pressley, 1983).

Evidence that at least some reliable variance exists can be provided by finding a statistically significant effect of some other manipulation. For example, in a study investigating age differences in spatial memory accuracy there might not be a significant age effect, but the presence of a significant effect of spatial array size could indicate that enough systematic variance is available to allow some meaningful partitioning. There is still a question of differential statistical power for detecting a treatment effect of a given size, however, particularly if the variable yielding a significant effect is a within-subjects manipulation as is likely the case with the size of the spatial array, and the other variable yielding a null effect is a between-subjects manipulation, as is the case with the age variable. It is therefore still optimal to have direct, rather than indirect, assessments of reliability whenever possible.

Lack of reliability may also be contributing to some of the inconsistencies in results evident across studies employing very similar tasks, materials, and population samples. An example of this phenomenon is apparent in the data from several studies of age differences in the accuracy of frequency judgments, which are thought to be mediated by an automatic memory process. Reliability coefficients for frequency judgments were calculated from the data obtained by Kausler and Puckett (1980). The young and elderly subjects in this study performed two consecutive frequency judgment tasks, the first under incidental memory instructions, the second under intentional memory instructions. (The instructional variation had no effect on accuracy of frequency judgments.) The intertask correlation, which can serve as an estimate of the reliability coefficient under these circumstances, was .64 for the young subjects and only .39 for the elderly subjects. The low consistency of the scores, particularly for the older adults, probably accounts for the differences in the age-performance relationship reported in several studies dealing with adult age differences in frequency judgment accuracy. Kausler and Puckett (1980) found a null effect of age in their study, while both Kausler, Wright, and Hakami (1981), and Kausler, Lichty, and Hakami (1984) found significantly higher scores for young subjects than for elderly subjects, despite similar procedures and identical list materials across all three studies. Examination of the group means indicated that the disparities in outcomes resulted primarily from across-study variation in the mean performance of the older adults, as one would expect on the basis of their lower reliability.

If the scores on two repetitions (or two equivalent forms, or separate halves) of a task by the same individual are not highly related to one another, it is unreasonable to expect the results of different individuals to exhibit any closer agreement. It should also be noted that, as suggested by the previous example, the lack of reliability can be present in only one of several age groups and the replicability of the age trends can still be jeopardized. Actually, the examination of reliability separately for each age group should be encouraged for two reasons. The first is that if there is an age difference in the mean level of the dependent variable, then the range of variation, and consequently the correlation coefficient reflecting reliability, will be inflated relative to that from a more homogeneous group. In other words, the correlation will incorporate the age effect in addition to the effect of measurement reliability. The second reason for separate examination of reliability in each age group is to determine whether interesting age differences occur. Reliability might be greater in older adults, which would be expected if they exhibit a greater range of variation than young adults, or it might be lower in older adults, implying that they exhibit less consistency than young adults.

Some data are available on the reliabilities of selected memory variables in samples of young adults (e.g., Anastasi, 1930; Garrett, 1928; Lemmon, 1927; Underwood, Boruch, & Malmi, 1978). For example, reliabilities for digit-span tasks have been reported to range from .68 to .87, those for free-recall tasks from .61 to .70, and those for paired-associates tasks from .63 to .95. It is therefore possible to compare one's results to those of earlier studies to determine the comparability of various population samples.

Interpretation of Interactions

One of the most powerful tools of the gerontological psychologist is the Age × Treatment interaction test in an analysis of variance. (See Kausler, 1982, pp. 177–231, for a thorough discussion of this topic.). We will use the term "treatment" in the present context to refer interchangeably to experimental tasks, conditions, procedural variations, or alternative dependent measures. The reasoning behind the interaction procedure is that the comparison of several age groups across two or more treatments is presumed to indicate whether some age groups are differentially affected by particular treatments, in which case the unique components of that treatment are presumed to be age sensitive.

To illustrate, several investigators have found that age differences are greater in recall tests of memory than in recognition tests, and in a number of these studies it has been reported that the interaction between age and type of memory test was significant (see also the discussion of these data in Chapter 4 by Brainerd). On the basis of such results, it has been inferred that a component present in the recall procedure but not in the recognition procedure, perhaps the requirement to retrieve information from memory, is particularly sensitive to the effects of age. A conclusion that the component was not age sensitive would have been reached had the interaction of age and the relevant manipulation failed to reach significance with adequate statistical power.

We will now outline two classes of problems that must be considered when interpreting Age $\times$ Treatment interactions in gerontological research. While still a useful technique for exploring the nature of age differences in memory and other cognitive processes, these interactions do have some limitations that should be recognized. Because the problems to be outlined can distort the interpretation of the relationship between independent and dependent variables, they are considered issues of internal validity.

One class of problem can be broadly categorized as those concerning one's measurement assumptions, a problem that is also examined in Chapter 4 by Brainerd and Chapter 6 by Kail. These include fairly obvious factors such as floor and ceiling effects in which the dependent variable is completely insensitive to variations in the underlying psychological process, quite subtle and difficult-to-detect nonlinearities in the functional relationship between the psychological process and the value of the dependent variable, and differential discriminating power in the dependent variable (e.g., see Tables 1 and 2 in Chapter 4 by Brainerd). Actually, even floor and ceiling effects can be rather subtle in that these terms need not refer only to the theoretical lower and upper limits of the measurement scale, respectively. If there are characteristics of the subject populations, the stimulus materials, or the experimental procedures that serve to constrain performance within a fixed region of the measurement scale, then the effective or functional range of performance variation is less than that which is theoretically possible. In other words, the functional floor of measurement may be greater than 0% or chance, and the functional ceiling may be less than 100% or perfect performance.

The functional ceiling concept can be illustrated by considering an experiment in which the rate of stimulus presentation is varied in an attempt to investigate the effects of time available for stimulus encoding on memory of young and old adults. At fast rates of presentation the time per stimulus is likely to exert substantial effects on the accuracy of subsequent recall, but after a certain value performance will be independent of presentation rate. However, this asymptotic level of performance will depend upon a variety of other factors such as number of items to be remembered, memory abilities of the subjects, and so forth, and could easily be less than 100%. For the sake of argument, we will assume that the asymptotic level is 80% for both young and old adults. We will also assume that a reduction in the rate of presentation from 2 items/s to 1/s results in a shift from 75% to 80% accuracy for young adults, but a shift from 60% to 80% accuracy for old adults. Such an interaction pattern would probably be interpreted as evidence that encoding time was a major source of the age difference in memory. However, if performance had not been limited by other factors it is possible that both age groups would have exhibited the same increase with a slower rate of presentation, for example, from 75% to 95% for young adults and from 60% to 80% for old adults. The mere fact that performance is not at the theoretical maximum is therefore no guarantee that distortions of measurement are not influencing one's results.

Although no method is fail-safe, the presence of a functional floor or ceiling can often be detected by examining the distribution of the obtained scores. Range restrictions will tend to reduce the variance of the scores. Differences in the spread of scores across conditions or groups can therefore be an indication that an effective floor or ceiling may be operating in the data.

The consequences of curtailment of the range of the dependent variable are to distort the nature of the age differences in the psychological processes of interest. Poorer-performing individuals might experience a smaller deterioration when confronted with a more difficult condition because their scores were initially closer to the effective floor. Or, conversely, poorer-performing individuals might experience a greater improvement under a facilitating condition because their subsequent scores were not restricted by the effective ceiling. This point is evident in the earlier hypothetical example in which the improvement of the young adults with a slower rate of presentation was limited by a functional ceiling imposed by factors other than those manipulated in the study.

Few techniques are truly suitable for dealing with floor and ceiling effects in the data and thus these measurement artifacts should be avoided by careful pilot testing whenever possible. Transformations are often applied to the scores, but this procedure is admittedly post hoc and justified only if the variable and its underlying processes are well understood (see Chapter 6 by Kail). Another questionable procedure is to attempt to eliminate the problem by discarding the data from individuals suspected to be near the floor or ceiling. To illustrate, a recent study claimed that

> though recognition rates were high, this lack of an age effect did not appear to be due to ceiling effects . . . [because] . . . [w]hen those participants with over 90% correct recognitions were eliminated . . . the same pattern of results was obtained.

However, by reducing the sample size in this fashion, statistical power was also diminished. It is therefore not surprising that one should then find a non-significant difference, even had the initial difference achieved conventional levels of significance.

Much more pernicious difficulties arise when there are no obvious floor or ceiling effects in the data, but there are suspected nonlinear or nonmonotonic trends in the functional relationship between the theoretical process or component under investigation and the dependent variable being measured. Loftus (1978) presented an excellent discussion of this topic and consequently we will mention this issue only briefly to alert readers to the nature of the problem. Assume that the relationship between the relevant psychological process and the dependent variable used as an index of the operation of that process is logarithmic in that it takes geometric increments to the psychological process to result in arithmetic increments to the dependent variable. Under these conditions one would often obtain statistical interactions, that is, significantly greater change in the dependent variable within the task or group with the initially lower performance, even when the effect on the psychological component was identical in all groups and tasks. Moreover, no interaction might be obtained when there was actually a greater effect of the manipulation on the component in the group or task with the higher initial performance. The permutations of permissible inferences under alternative outcomes with varying assumptions about the process-variable relationship become quite complicated, and the interested reader is referred to the Loftus (1978) article for further discussion.

Figure 7-1 illustrates the preceding argument with a nonlinear relationship between the psychological process and the dependent variable. Of course this relationship is merely hypothetical since it is not yet possible to obtain direct measures of the magnitude of psychological processes. Nonetheless, it is certainly possible to speculate about the manner in which dependent variables are related to the psychological processes from which they derive. For example, assume that young and old adults participate in two experimental conditions, A and B, and that not only are there measures of memory performance available for both young (A_y' and B_y') and old (A_o' and B_o') adults, but that some unspecified techniques are available to also assess the strength of memory traces in young (A_y and B_y) and old (A_o and B_o) adults. The figure illustrates that if trace strength is not linearly related to memory performance, misleading interactions would often occur. That is, even if the condition manipulations have the same effect on the trace strength in young (B_y vs. A_y) and old (B_o vs. A_o) adults, the nonlinear relationship could result in greater dependent variable differences in the old adults (B_o' vs. A_o') than in the young adults (B_y' vs. A_y'). This type of spurious interaction can occur with any manipulation, but it is particularly likely with those suspected to have nonlinear effects such as depth of encoding, amount of cognitive effort, stimulus pacing, and material familiarity.

The reason for this concern with the process-variable relationship is that there is no law that says that all psychological processes relate in a simple, linear fashion to the measurable aspects of behavior. As long as there is a possibility that the measurement scale is not equally sensitive in all regions to the effects of variations in the underlying psychological process, one runs the risk of reaching inappropriate conclusions from tests of statistical interactions. Moreover, the

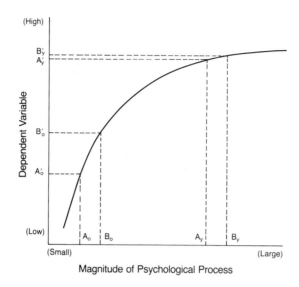

Figure 7-1. Consequences of a nonlinear relationship between the psychological process and the dependent variable used as an index of that process. The differences between A_o and B_o and between A_y and B_y are equal on the psychological process axis, but the differences between A'_o and B'_o are much greater than those between A'_y and B'_y on the dependent variable axis.

imposition of transformations upon the data is also inadequate unless one knows the true process-variable relationship in the first place.

Another concern within the class of measurement assumptions is the discriminating power of the measures employed in various tasks (cf. Baron & Treiman, 1980; Chapman & Chapman, 1973). It has been demonstrated that the distinguishability of the performance of individuals of varying ability levels depends upon both the difficulty of the task and the reliability of the dependent measures. In general, performance differences will be most detectable in the middle of a variable's range, and thus manipulations that alter the average level of performance will also tend to affect the performance differences between groups. If initial performance is fairly low and is increased to a moderate level, group differences will tend to increase. If the initial level is moderate and the new level of performance is fairly high, group differences will tend to decrease.

Figure 7-2 illustrates these points in an abstract representation. The argument can be made more concrete by attempting to place various memory tasks at plausible positions along the difficulty continuum. For example, most standard recall tasks would probably fall in the middle of the continuum, while recognition and cued-recall tasks would be located toward the left end of the continuum. These respective positions lead to the expectation that age differences would be smaller with the latter two tasks than with standard recall

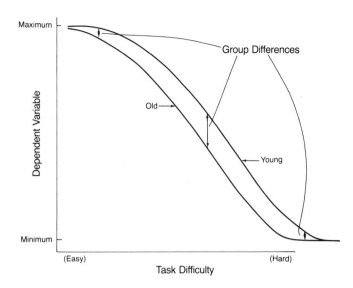

Figure 7-2. Relationship between task difficulty and performance distinguishability. The absolute magnitude of the performance differences is greatest in the middle of the variable's range, and necessarily diminishes at the extremes where performance is insensitive to task difficulty for all individuals.

tasks, a prediction generally confirmed in the research literature. It is interesting to note that this interpretation is independent of the specific manipulation employed to alter task difficulty. As long as the average level of performance is affected, the possibility exists that statistical interactions result simply from a shift in discriminating power.

Discriminability is also directly related to reliability. The task or condition in which the measures are the least reliable will tend to yield smaller differences between groups because the variability is greater when the measurement consistency is lowest.

Both reliability and relative level of performance can therefore contribute to spurious interactions because the variables in different tasks or conditions are not equally sensitive to alterations in the underlying psychological processes. These are serious concerns in much contemporary gerontological research because, as noted earlier, estimates of measurement reliability are seldom reported and there has been little attempt to ensure that the various treatments yield equivalent levels of performance. Indeed, the existence of treatment main effects in many studies indicates that the treatments clearly do not produce equivalent levels of performance and thus the interaction is not easily interpreted.

Although researchers are sometimes advised to eliminate the problem of differential discriminating power by matching the treatments (tasks, conditions, measures) on difficulty and reliability (e.g., Chapman & Chapman, 1973), this should be done quite judiciously. The risk is that in adjusting the difficulty of a task one may introduce an irrelevant factor whose effects could be confused with those of the process of interest. As an example, comparisons of recognition and recall tasks generally reveal that recognition accuracy is higher than recall accuracy. Hence, target-distractor similarity is sometimes increased to reduce the level of performance. However, the specific dimension of the distractor similarity is very important in that few researchers would be comfortable accepting conclusions about retrieval processes in memory if the distractors differed from the target only in slight perceptual characteristics such as the spacing of the letters in the word, or in the darkness of the ink used to print the letters. The point, of course, is that while matching on measurement properties is desirable, one must be very careful that in so doing the fundamental nature of the task is not also altered.

A second class of problems affecting the interpretation of statistical interactions can be labeled level-of-attribution problems in that the focus is on the specificity of the mechanism presumed responsible for the observed interaction. At least two further distinctions can be made within this general class: cases of overattribution, in which an inference is made about a mechanism that is more general than that actually responsible for the results; and cases of underattribution, in which a specific mechanism is postulated to be responsible for the results that are actually caused by a more general mechanism. In both cases, the problem is at the inference stage, in which one attempts to interpret the results in terms of psychological processes.

As an example of an overattribution error of inference, consider a (hopefully fictitious) experiment in which two conditions are administered to samples of young and old adults. Both conditions involve the presentation of 20 words to be remembered in a free recall paradigm, but in one condition the physical size of the words is twice as large as in the other condition. Also, assume that a significant interaction is obtained such that the older adults improved their recall performance more than the young adults in switching from the small to the large stimuli, but that significant age differences were still present in both conditions. A possible error of overattribution might occur if one were to conclude that stimulus encoding was responsible for all (or most, or some) of the age differences in memory. A possible implication of this interpretation is that the age deficit may have disappeared if still larger words had been used. The problem is that the manipulation may have only compensated for aspects of age-related visual acuity decline, which while of undeniable importance, probably have little to do with the psychological processes of stimulus registration or trace formation that are usually implied by the concept of encoding.

A similar objection can be raised concerning several studies in which the familiarity of the stimulus material has been manipulated in samples of young and old adults. In several of these studies the familiarity manipulation interacted significantly with age, indicating that the participants in each age group were more effective with the material most familiar to their generation. For example, young adults might be superior with words such as cassette and freon, while older adults might be better with words such as settee and poultice. A potential overattribution error is to conclude that the efficiency of memory processes was age invariant, and that age differences were simply an artifact of differential familiarity of stimulus materials. Before such a conclusion would be warranted one should demonstrate that the familiarity manipulation affected the same psychological processes (e.g., effectiveness of encoding, degree of elaborative rehearsal, etc.) as the age variable. Without such evidence, one might hypothesize that familiarity affected some processes, that age affected other processes, and that tasks involving suitable combinations of these processes yield an assortment of performances. Note that the finding that there are situations in which the performance of older adults is equivalent or superior to that of young adults would still be of considerable interest, but the inference that the age variable is functionally equivalent to the familiarity variable would not be justified.

The solution to the problem of overattribution of inference is simply to carry out more investigations of the proposed interpretation. If several different manipulations assumed to affect the same psychological process all yield comparable results, one could be confident that the inferences are appropriate. On the other hand, if various manipulations thought to influence a common psychological process produce discrepant results, it is likely that the inferences are broader or more general than is appropriate. In the familiarity example discussed earlier, one could contrast the results with the population- or generation-defined manipulation of familiarity with analyses of exposure frequencies of specific words within individuals, or with experimentally induced frequency within the laboratory. It would also be desirable to conduct studies that allow more precise localization of the age and manipulation effects within specific memory processes such as encoding, rehearsal, and so forth. Many readers will recognize that our proposed solution is merely a restatement of the Garner, Hake, and Eriksen (1956) argument for the use of converging operations in the establishment of psychological concepts. In our opinion, multiple demonstrations of a phenomenon are as necessary in ensuring that one does not make inferences from interactions that exceed the available evidence as in selecting the appropriate level to which conceptual terms apply.

Underattribution errors of inference exist when an investigator concludes that a specific deficit is responsible for an interaction that was actually caused by a general difference between age groups. Because most researchers assume that an Age $\times$ Treatment interaction signifies a specific deficit, the idea that an Age $\times$ Treatment interaction could occur in the presence of a general difference between age groups requires some explanation. Actually, an interaction with a general rather than specific difference between age groups could arise for several of the reasons mentioned earlier. That is, a nonlinear or nonmonotonic relationship between the psychological process and the dependent variable will frequently result in differential effects across the poorer- and better-performing individuals because they are operating in different regions of the measurement scale (cf. Figure 7-1). In this case the interaction occurs as a consequence of the individuals differing in initial ability such that their psychological processes, which may or may not be equally susceptible to the effects of the treatment, are at levels where they do not produce comparable quantitative effects of the treatments.

Another manner in which an Age × Treatment interaction might arise from a general rather than specific deficit is when the treatment manipulation is associated with a change in the overall level of task difficulty. There are both psychometric and theoretical reasons for expecting shifts in task difficulty to affect the likelihood of a statistical interaction in the absence of a specific deficit. The psychometric reasons were mentioned earlier (and illustrated in Figure 7-2) and concern the fact that the greatest discriminating power of a test lies in the middle of the variable's effective range, with progressively less differentiation between groups possible as one reaches the limits of the variable at either end of the scale. Shifts away from the middle of a variable's effective range will therefore tend to alter the absolute difference between groups even if no specific mechanism were involved.

The theoretical basis for predicting task difficulty to influence interaction visibility rests on the assumption that a general deficit will tend to affect most psychological processes by roughly the same proportional amount. Manipulations of task difficulty that are accompanied by changes in the number or complexity of psychological processes will therefore tend to yield progressively larger absolute performance differences between groups. As long as different age groups exhibit a proportional relationship to one another with respect to the efficiency of the relevant psychological processes, and differ in the absolute level of their initial performance, different effect magnitudes will result even if the same manipulations are employed and there is a simple linear relationship between the psychological process and the dependent variable (Arenberg, 1982; Bogartz, 1976).

To illustrate this point, assume that a group of young adults achieves 80% correct recall on an immediate recall of a list of 20 unrelated words, and that a group of older adults performs at a 60% level under those same conditions. We will also assume that in different conditions of the experiment an interfering activity is performed prior to the recall attempt, and that its effect is to attenuate the residual trace strength at a rate of 10% every 3 s. In other words, after 3 s of interfering activity the performance of the two groups would be: $16 - 1.6 = 14.4$ for the young, and $12 - 1.2 = 10.8$ for the old. Under these assumptions the performance with intervals of 6, 9, and 12 s of interfering activity would be: 12.96, 11.66, and 10.50 for the young, but 9.72, 8.75, and 7.87 for the old. An analysis of variance might well reveal a significant interaction since the age difference was $16 - 12 = 4$ with a 0-s interval, but only $10.50 - 7.87 = 2.63$ with a 12-s interval. However, the interaction pattern in this example was produced by a process that exerted exactly the same effect (10% attenuation every 3 s) in the two age groups, and thus the interpretation of the interaction would likely be misleading.

It is worth mentioning that the proportional process need not only operate in the direction of reducing the absolute magnitude of the performance differences between groups but could actually increase the difference. For example, instead of postulating that the interfering activity attenuates trace strength, one could assume that it functions to increase the level of "confusability" or "noise" in the system by a proportional amount. Taking incorrect responses as a reflection of confusability or noise, and assuming an increase in confusability of 10% every 3 s, the performance levels of young adults would be $20 - 4 = 16$ at 0 s; $20 - (4 + (4 \times .1)) = 15.60$ at 3 s; $20 - (4.4 + (4.4 \times .1)) = 20 - 4.84 = 15.16$ at 6 s; $20 - (4.84 + (4.84 \times .1)) = 20 - 5.32 = 14.68$ at 9 s; and $20 - (5.32 + (5.32 \times .1)) = 20 - 5.86 = 14.14$ at 12 s. Comparable values for the older adults would be 12, 11.2, 10.32, 9.35, and 8.29, respectively. Under these circumstances, the age differences increase from $16 - 12 = 4$ with a 0-s interval, to $14.14 - 8.29 = 5.85$ with a 12-s interval.

Without further information it is unclear whether the proportional effects are more likely to operate by reducing the signal (memory trace) or by increasing the noise (confusability), but in either case interaction patterns could be produced by a process that was identical in the two age groups. Very little is yet known about proportional mechanisms in psychology, but the potential for their existence necessitates extreme caution in interpreting results within an interaction framework.

The net effect of the preceding considerations is that a statistically significant interaction can easily be erroneously attributed to a more specific mechanism than actually exists if the tasks or conditions being compared differ in their relative levels of difficulty. At the very least one should be extremely cautious in making inferences about specific deficits when there is evidence that differences in difficulty are present, as would be the case when the treatment manipulation yields significant main effects in an analysis of variance.

We will not discuss difficulties in interpreting interactions associated with specific theoretical perspectives, but it is important to be cognizant that one's theoretical assumptions have implications for the meaning of interactions. For example, Bogartz (1976) has argued that some manipulations can be reasonably argued on theoretical grounds to yield multiplicative rather than additive effects as in the interference example described above. In cases such as this, a statistically significant interaction might actually indicate equivalent effects of the treatment in groups that differed in initial level of performance. Also, Brainerd and Howe (1982) have demonstrated that interpretations are exceedingly complex if the learning process occurs in a series of stages, and members of some age groups are more likely to complete the entire stage sequence than members of other age groups.

In view of the large number of potentially serious complications associated with the interpretation of Age $\times$ Treatment interactions, it is worth examining an alternative that appears to be growing in popularity. This is the use of a single task accompanied by a model containing several distinguishable parameters, each presumed to reflect a different theoretical process (e.g., Brainerd & Howe, 1982; Wilkinson & Koestler, 1983). In the Wilkinson and Koestler study the task was free recall with distraction activity performed between the presentation of the items and their attempted recall. Subjects performed the task five times with the same material, and the primary data consisted of the recall performance for specific items across the five successive trials. A five-parameter model was developed to characterize performance on the task, with one parameter reflecting the efficiency of initial storage or encoding of information and four assessing the dynamics of other memory processes. The results indicated that adult age differences were primarily localized in the encoding process, which is similar to a conclusion reached in a review of the traditional literature on age differences in memory (Salthouse, 1982, pp. 133–144).

The model-based procedure may be more efficient than the interaction approach because only a single task or experimental condition is involved and sets of independent parameter estimates are available for each age group. This theoretical approach has been resisted by many researchers in the past because of the large number of assumptions that are necessary. However, the growing recognition of interpretation problems inherent in more conventional procedures, such as those discussed previously with respect to interactions, may lead to a modification of this attitude. At any rate, the technique could be extremely valuable if a number of alternative studies, each employing models with differing assumptions, all converged on the same conclusion about the presence or absence of adult age differences in specific memory processes (cf. Chapter 4 by Brainerd).

The Question of Generalizability—External Validity

Researchers investigating the effects of aging on memory are often confronted with the criticism that the tasks, conditions, and measures employed in the laboratory are not representative of the daily activities of most adults. Or, alternatively, these characteristics might be claimed to be more representative of the activities of some age groups than of other age groups. If these criticisms are correct, results obtained from such procedures are necessarily of low external validity. One of the motivations for this protest against what are said to be sterile and esoteric laboratory procedures arises from a contrast between the results of many laboratory studies and one's informal judgments about the memorial competence of older adults. As Schaie and Zelinski (1979) state:

> [despite] the average older person . . . [appearing] . . . to show memory deficit in laboratory situations . . . older people seem to remember to arrive in time for the experiment, to retrieve information about income, education, number of grandchildren, and other demographic data requested in our questionnaires, and to acquire information correctly about how to perform the experimental tasks (p. 140).

There are, of course, several reasons why a discrepancy might exist between laboratory findings and one's observations in the "real world" (e.g., see Salthouse, 1982, pp. 202–204). Nonetheless, the suggestion that much contemporary research is of little or no value in understanding naturally occurring behavior is an important and often repeated criticism that merits careful consideration. If it is truly the case that most laboratory-based research on memory is too trivial and artificial to allow any statements about everyday memory, including adult age differences in the efficiency of such memory functioning, then this fact should be recognized and accepted.

In this section we address three issues related to the external validity of laboratory-based memory research in adults of varying ages. The first concerns the limitations of subjective judgments about face validity, the second deals with the problem of identifying a suitable criterion for the assessment of criterion validity, and the third is a reevaluation of the concept of external validity.

Limitations of Current Assessments of External Validity

In examining many writings that contain criticisms of the external validity of laboratory memory tasks, we have been struck by the near unanimity of opinion that certain tasks are unlike those of everyday life, accompanied by considerable lack of consensus about which specific tasks these are. Some writers object to paired-associate tasks as esoteric tortures devised by sadists portraying themselves as psychologists, while others defend such tasks as being similar to remembering the names attached to faces or learning the foreign-language equivalents of familiar words. Tasks designed to assess the accuracy of judgments about the relative frequency of various kinds of events can be criticized as unlike anything done in the real world, and yet teachers are often asked about the approximate ratios of boys to girls in their classrooms, salesmen are sometimes requested to estimate the popularity of different product models based on the relative number of sales of each model, and so on. The variation in the specific tasks singled out as particularly unrepresentative of everyday life is so large that we suspect that one's opinion about the representativeness of a task is directly related to the individual's degree of involvement with that task; it is judged low in external validity if it has never been used in one's own research or was abandoned some time ago, and it is judged high if it is currently being used or planned to be used.

As we see it, past criticisms of the lack of external validity of laboratory investigations of memory have been flawed by a reliance on a notoriously unreliable assessment of validity–subjective opinions of face validity. One cannot expect substantial scientific progress in an area if there is no way to resolve a conflict between different assessments. This currently seems to be the situation with respect to the issue of external validity in gerontological research on memory. Proclamations of the presence or absence of external or ecological validity in particular tasks have been based almost entirely on the writer's subjective opinion and not upon empirical data (cf. Bahrick & Karis, 1982).

Much more desirable forms of validity assessment would involve either content validity or criterion validity. Content validity is defined by Kerlinger (1973, p. 458) as "the representativeness or sampling adequacy of the content—the substance, the matter, the topics—of a measuring instrument." In the present context, it refers to the extent to which tasks are representative of the universe of activities normally performed by the individual. Criterion validity for our purposes concerns the degree to which performance on a laboratory task predicts performance on some criterion activity carried out beyond the confines of the laboratory.

Unfortunately, neither of these more objective indicants of validity is currently feasible in gerontological research, although the reasons for their impracticality are important to note. The primary limitation on content validity is that it ideally requires complete specification of the universe of activities to which one wishes to generalize. In other words, to judge the representativeness of a laboratory task to everyday activities one must have a detailed inventory of activities and the average frequency of occurrence of each. This is a formidable requirement that currently shows little signs of being met. In practice, assessments of content validity are often based on the judgment of experts (e.g., teachers select examination questions based on their content validity opinions), but it is doubtful that there are any true experts in the classification and distribution of the activities of daily life. There certainly has not yet been any consensus about the relative importance of different kinds of memory in the average day of the average adult, and until there are, judgments about representativeness are primarily speculation. The comments of Hartley, Harker, & Walsh (1980) are especially pertinent in this connection:

> We do not know how relevant or how ecologically valid various experimental tasks are to adult life. There has been no systematic examination of the kinds of learning required in the typical adult's daily life. What cognitive demands are actually made on adults? What kinds of learning behaviors do adults engage in? What changes in cognitive demands and learning behaviors occur at different stages of adulthood? Are different cognitive demands made on persons in different occupations, and do these demands ultimately affect their pattern of cognitive development? When a few of these questions are answered we will have some notion of ecological validity based on fact rather than the beliefs or hopes of researchers (p. 244).

The principal difficulty with obtaining assessments of criterion validity is the absence of suitable measures of the effectiveness of everyday memory activity. Without a well-accepted criterion against which one's laboratory measures can be validated there is obviously no hope of demonstrating a relationship between performance in the laboratory and performance in the real world.

Identification of a Suitable Validation Criterion

Some investigators have proposed the use of self-reported memory effectiveness as the criterion for establishing the validity of laboratory variables. However, there appear to be at least four objections that must be overcome before this procedure could be considered useful. First, very little data are available on the reliability of personal assessments of memory effectiveness used in studies of aging (but see Herrmann, 1982, for a review), although it is clear that the correlation between two variables will be limited by the reliability with which each variable can be measured. For the results from self-assessments to serve as a suitable criterion, it must be demonstrated that they are consistent across repetitions. This is a particularly important consideration when dealing with self-reports because of the possibility that they simply reflect fleeting, and possibly irrelevant, subjective impressions.

A second objection concerns the global, omnibus character of most self-report inventories of memory functioning. Herrmann's (1982) review of research on memory questionnaires indicated that the items vary in types of information requested (e.g., concerning frequency of forgetting, clarity of remembering, awareness of lifespan changes, and attitudes toward memory), response criteria (e.g., frequency in absolute time, frequency per specified number of occurrences, or frequency relative to one's peers), and in the detail expected (e.g., general or specific). Table 7-1 contains a sample of the types of questions contained in three recent everyday memory inventories, along with a gross classification of each type of memory according to the three theoretical dimensions discussed in the introductory material. Notice that the questions sample widely from several aspects of memory postulated to be distinct on theoretical grounds, for example, effortful versus automatic, episodic versus generic, and retrospective versus prospective. However, because a single composite score is derived from the entire pool of items, these potentially important distinctions are ignored. A seemingly more effective procedure would be to segregate the inventory items according to the type of memory involved, and then to compute a separate score for each class of memory (e.g. an effortful memory scale, an automatic memory scale). This finer differentiation could not only help improve the quantitative relationship with various laboratory tasks, but might also contribute to further validation of the theoretical distinctions. Dixon and Hultsch (1983) have provided a useful beginning of this type of effort by describing their results from a metamemory inventory in terms of eight separately scored dimensions.

The third objection that can be raised concerning the use of self-report memory inventories is also related to the specific types of questions contained in the inventory. This objection has to do with the representativeness of the events or scenarios in the respondent's daily life. As mentioned previously, we have almost no information on the frequency distribution of daily activities with various kinds of memory components for adults of any age. It would be very misleading if items addressing events of quite different frequencies were assigned equal weighting in scoring the inventory responses. Moreover, such a practice would lead to drastic distortion if the distribution of memory activities varied across age groups. It is sometimes claimed that older adults live in a different cognitive world than young adults, either because of the demand upon their memories, the importance of their decisions, or numerous other factors.

Table 7-1. Representative Questions or Tasks Included in Three Different Everyday Memory Inventories

Herrmann & Neisser (1978)	Zelinski, Gilewski, & Thompson (1980)	Sunderland, Harris, & Baddeley (1983)
Think of the times someone has given directions to get to some unfamiliar place. How often do you forget the directions before you get there? (retrospective, episodic memory)	How is your memory compared to the way it was when you were 18? (metamemory)	Repeating a story you have already told. (retrospective, automatic, episodic memory)
How often do you find, at the end of a conversation, that you forgot to bring up some point or some question that you had intended to mention? (prospective, effortful memory)	How often do these present a memory problem to you? names (retrospective, effortful, episodic memory) things people tell you (retrospective, automatic, episodic memory) phone numbers you've just checked (short-term effortful, episodic memory)	Unable to remember the name of someone you met for the first time recently. (retrospective, effortful, episodic memory)
When someone says he has told you something already (at some earlier time), how often do you find that you have no recollection of his telling you any such thing? (retrospective, automatic episodic memory)		Finding that a word is "on the tip of your tongue." You know what it is but can't quite find it. (generic memory, internal lexicon)

Note: Each question is categorized in terms of the hypothesized type of memory evaluated by that question.

There is apparently no empirical evidence that can yet substantiate this assertion, but the potential for a biased sampling of memory-related activities both within and across age groups certainly exists and should not be ignored.

The final objection to self-report memory inventories has to do with the possibility that memory deficiencies will lead to a systematic underestimation of the severity of one's memory problems (Sunderland et al., 1983). That is, if an individual is truly prone to memory problems, then he or she may also be likely to forget many failures of memory when completing the questionnaire and thus give an unjustifiably optimistic report of memory competence. It is also possible that there are individual or group differences in the willingness to report memory deficiencies that occur and are remembered. One or both of these biases might be involved in many studies of aging based on the findings that increased age is often associated with poorer performance on laboratory tests of memory (e.g., Kausler, 1982; Salthouse, 1982), and with a greater reluctance to respond in the face of uncertainty (Botwinick, 1978).

It is worth noting that additional steps can be taken to verify the accuracy of self-reports. For example, Sunderland et al. (1983) employed, in addition to the subjects' self-reports, a week-long diary of specific memory failures kept by the subject, and both questionnaire and diary reports by a close relative of the subject. The results from these various assessments were not in complete agreement, but the attempt to obtain converging evidence of the validity of everyday memory is admirable and should be pursued.

In view of these criticisms of the assessments of everyday memory, it is not surprising that the results from studies employing such instruments have been unimpressive and often contradictory. In some studies moderate correlations hae been reported between one or more laboratory measures of memory and a score derived from a self-report inventory (e.g., Bennett-Levy & Powell, 1980; Hulicka, 1982; Schmeck, Ribich, & Ramanaiah, 1977; Sunderland et al., 1983; and Zelinski, Gilewski, & Thompson, 1980), but in others there has been a near-zero correlation (e.g., Broadbent, Cooper, Fitzgerald & Parkes, 1982; Kahn, Zarit, Hilbert, & Niederehe, 1975; Zarit, Cole & Guider, 1981). Moreover, there is not yet any consistency with respect to which particular laboratory variables are related to which types of self-reports.

We have devoted substantial discussion to perceived weaknesses in one potential candidate for a criterion against which the results of laboratory studies could be validated in order to outline some of the characteristics that a suitable criterion must possess. It is obvious that considerable research is necessary on the description of the types of memory involved in everyday activities, and reliable techniques for its accurate assessment need to be developed. In sum, we fully agree with Hulicka's (1982) statement:

> Greater effort should be directed toward relating laboratory findings to behavior in naturalistic settings, and similarly observation of behavior in naturalistic settings should be used as a guide to hypotheses to be investigated in the laboratory (p. 339).

Reexamination of the External Validity Concept

The issue of the nature of external validity has recently been reexamined by Mook (1983). Because many of his remarks are pertinent to the present discussion we have excerpted several of them as follows:

> External validity is not an automatic desideratum; it *asks a question*. It invites us to think about the prior questions: To what populations, settings, and so on, do we want the effect to be generalized? (p. 379)

> The distinction between generality of findings and generality of theoretical conclusions underscores what seems to me the most important source of confusion in all this, which is the assumption that the purpose of collecting data in the laboratory is to *predict real-life behavior in the real world*. Of course, there are times when that is what we are trying to do, and there are times when it is not. When it is, the problem of EV [external validity] confronts us full force. When it is not, then the problem of EV is either meaningless or trivial, and a misplaced preoccupation with it can seriously distort our evaluation of the research. (p. 381)

Mook goes on to suggest that the most important aspect of generalization may not be specific task characteristics or even particular research findings, but rather an understanding derived from an analysis of basic mechanisms. In this respect, it is the equivalence of common processes, and a similar susceptibility of those processes to an assortment of variables, that leads to the greatest prediction of behavior, irrespective of whether the behavior occurs spontaneously in naturalistic situations or is deliberately elicited in a laboratory.

In practice, it is not literal generalizability that is, or should be, the objective of studies of adult age differences in memory. As Mook points out, what is at stake in laboratory research is the generalizability to the real world of the conclusions arrived at by that research. Laboratory tasks represent simulations of real-world activities, not copies. To be useful, a simulation must involve the same processes that enter into the real-world activities the simulation mimics. Of course, it may be difficult to demonstrate isomorphism at the process level, but one should not automatically reject the possibility of common processes merely because of superficial differences in type of material, location of the testing environment, procedural characteristics, and so on.

Acceptance of the view that laboratory tasks are designed to simulate selected behaviors rather than provide a high-fidelity representation of everyday activities leads to a different conclusion about the usefulness of laboratory investigations than that suggested by critics of contemporary research. The most important criterion for generalizability may not be the resemblance of specific characteristics of the test environment to the everyday environment, but the degree to which there are similar relationships between various manipulations and levels of performance in the laboratory and in everyday activities. For example, the specific details of the laboratory situation may not matter if one is interested in investigating the effects of number and distribution of material repetitions, length and meaningfulness of material, duration of retention interval, level of subject's motivation and effort, and so on. To the extent that a laboratory task is sensitive to variations found to be meaningful in everyday memory, the task is likely to have substantial external validity regardless of how artificial it may appear. Furthermore, if adult age differences are found in such a laboratory task, one is likely to find similar differences in selected everyday activities after one has considered the effects of vastly different amounts of experience in the respective activities.

Sampling Considerations—Subject Selection

Because the problem of assuring equivalence of samples across age groups affects both internal and external validity, it is considered separately in the present section. Internal validity is jeopardized if there are factors other than age that systematically differ across the age groups being compared, and external validity is threatened if the samples from each group are not representative, and to an equivalent extent, of the larger populations to which one wishes to generalize.

The currently accepted practice in many gerontological studies is to obtain samples of convenience from two or more age segments in the population, and then to report the values of selected psychometric tests and demographic characteristics along with the measures derived from the experimental memory tasks. For example, the scores on a standardized test of vocabulary and the number of years of formal education are often reported as a means of demonstrating the equivalence of the various age groups on certain relevant characteristics. Because many aspects of verbal intelligence appear to remain stable across most of the adult life span (e.g., Kausler, 1982; Salthouse, 1982), using a variable of this type to assess the initial comparability of the samples has seemed justified.

Unfortunately, this procedure is hampered by two limitations: first, in practice the groups are often found not to be equivalent on the available measures; second, there is little or no evidence that the measures are indeed relevant to performance on the experimental tasks. With respect to non-equivalence, it is frequently found that older individuals have higher scores on a vocabulary test or on other measures of verbal intelligence than do younger adults, and they often also have a higher mean level of education, particularly when contrasted with young adults still attending college. The investigator obtaining such a result must then decide whether to abandon the study, increase the sample sizes in an attempt to obtain greater equivalence, or report the results despite clear evidence that the groups are different in at least one potentially important variable besides age. Many times the results are reported, and if increased age is found to be associated with poorer performance on the experimental task, the investigator is tempted to conclude that the observed age differences are actually underestimates of the true differences because of the positive sampling bias of the older group.

However, even the inference that the age differences have been underestimated may not be justified since there is little evidence available to indicate that, at least within normal ranges, performance on the experimental task is related to either the psychometric or the demographic characteristics. That is, the equivalence or nonequivalence of the groups on these attributes could be completely irrelevant to the experimental task and there is seldom any evidence, correlational or otherwise, to indicate that the variables are in fact related to performance on the experimental task. It is therefore quite possible that two studies, each employing samples of young and old adults found to be comparable on an assortment of demographic and psychometric characteristics, could yield strikingly different age trends in the dependent variable. Should the experimental tasks be different in the two studies one might be tempted to conclude that the tasks varied in one or more age-sensitive processes. Such a conclusion could be erroneous if the samples differed on the efficiency of relevant memory processes that were not detected by the available psychometric or demographic variables. This problem is much less severe (because it is often detectable) when the same task is involved in the two studies since the differential process efficiency would be reflected in different levels of performance on the dependent variable. However, when studies involve different tasks, there is no means of verifying that the subject samples, rather than the task characteristics, were responsible for the discrepancy in results.

One possible solution to this problem is to administer a standard memory task, or a battery of several standard memory tasks, to all subjects serving in gerontological investigations of memory. Performance on the standard task could then be used as an index of efficiency in memory-relevant processes, and in this way the comparability of subject samples across independent studies could be determined. In order to be useful, the standard task should satisfy the following criteria: (a) be of moderately high reliability; (b) be quick and easy to administer; (c) be amenable to the development of age-specific norms based on measurements of large representative samples; and (d) be intrinsically related to many types of memory.

The first and second criteria are self-explanatory in that these are desirable characteristics of any measurement in psychology, particularly one that is to be used as a supplement to the manipulation of primary interest. The availability of normative data would be quite helpful in identifying atypical samples, which might then be further investigated to attempt to determine the factors responsible for systematic nonrepresentative performance. The fourth criterion deserves somewhat more explanation because, on the one hand, the measure should be more relevant to memory functioning than currently employed psychometric tests, but, on the other hand, it should not be identical to the experimental task. Furthermore, in light of the large number of distinctions that can be made among various types of memory (e.g., the three dimensions discussed in the introductory material), it may be impossible to identify a single measure that is relevant to all types of memory. Nevertheless, tasks could, and should, be selected that load heavily on one of the major memory factors or clusters identified through statistical analyses of many different memory measures.

We propose as an initial candidate for this type of standard task a version of the common paired-associate procedure, perhaps the paired-associates control task implemented by Underwood et al. (1978). Measures of performance on this type of task have been found to yield split-half or test-retest reliabilities with samples of young adults between .63 and .95 (e.g., Anastasi, 1930; Garrett, 1982; Hall, 1936; Lemmon, 1927; Underwood et al., 1978); versions of it can be administered in less than 10 min; it is easily adapted for group administration to allow efficient acquisition of normative data; and it has been found to contribute to a central memory factor in several factor-analytic studies of memory (e.g., Botwinick & Storandt, 1974; Kelley, 1964; Underwood et al., 1978).

In proposing the inclusion of some type of standard task in future studies, it is important to point out that we are not advocating that the traditional psychometric and demographic assessments be abandoned. These measures are often very useful in providing further description of the characteristics of one's samples, and in general, the more complete the description the better (a review of the relationships between such measures and short-term memory can be found in Chapter 5 by Dempster). (Indeed, we view the proposal to include standard task assessments in all studies of memory and aging primarily as a more refined and sensitive means of describing one's sample.) There are also situations in which one would rationally expect a relationship between the psychometric variable and task performance, even if the relevant empirical evidence is not yet available. For example, semantic memory tasks which require the subject to make judgments based on the meaning of words would clearly be expected to be related to level of vocabulary ability, and it would therefore be desirable to have evidence that the age groups did not differ in the same direction on this task as on the variables in the experimental task.

Conclusion

We have been concerned throughout this chapter with potential problems in the research methodology employed to investigate adult age differences in memory. The initial section introduced a theoretical classification scheme to emphasize the need to consider a variety of different kinds of memory, each with its own methodological prescriptions and requirements. Our first major section focused on threats to internal validity posed by common practices in gerontological investigations of memory. Some of these problems are fairly obvious, but others involving measurement assumptions in the interpretation of Age × Treatment interactions are not yet recognized by many researchers in the field. The second major section dealt with the broad issue of external validity, and specifically the generalizability of laboratory findings to real-world situations. Our conclusion here is considerably less pessimistic than that suggested by the critics of contemporary research, in part because we emphasize the generalizability of functional relationships rather than the resemblance of superficial task characteristics. The final section of the chapter contained a specific proposal for increasing the validity of age comparisons in memory. Our suggestion is to administer a standard memory task to all participants in aging studies of memory, which could be used to evaluate the representativeness and comparability of samples in a manner more relevant than is currently the case.

Although our discussion of methodology has been in the context of memory processes in maturity, it is clear that many of the issues we have raised transcend this specific area. The concerns with internal validity, external validity, and comparability of groups are common to nearly all research investigating individual differences in some aspect of behavior. The specific manifestations of the problems may vary across research domains, but many of the same methodological issues are evident across a number of subdisciplines.

It is possible that some readers may feel that at least part of the objections to current practices in memory research in maturity discussed in this chapter are merely nit-picking exercises of no real consequence. We are sensitive to this criticism, but firmly believe that the quality of knowledge in an area is largely dependent upon the methods used to attain that knowledge, and that it is therefore occasionally useful to subject those methods to detailed scrutiny. In this connection we were somewhat surprised to discover that many of our concerns, particularly with the need to document the reliability and validity of one's dependent measures, were also addressed nearly a half-century ago in a classic article by Melton (1936). The emphasis upon empirical rather than intuitive determination was also present in the earlier article:

> When the advantages and disadvantages of various materials and procedures in the study of human learning can be removed from the realm of individual conjecture and either placed on a solid empirical basis or defended in terms of certain clearly stated postulates, we may expect an increase in the validity and reliability of particular experimental results. (p. 308).

Perhaps it is fitting to end the present chapter with this quotation as a reminder that although theories and interpretations tend to come and go, the concern with improving methodology always remains. It is our hope that the issues raised in the preceding pages will contribute to such methodological improvement in research on memory during maturity.

Acknowledgements. We wish to thank Ken Prill for his valuable comments on an early draft of this chapter. T.A.S. was supported during the preparation of this chapter by a Research Career Development Award (1K04 AG00146-01A1) from the National Institute on Aging.

References

Anastasi, A. (1930). A group factor in immediate memory. *Archives of Psychology*, (Whole No. 120).

Arenberg, D. (1982). Learning from our mistakes in aging research. *Experimental Aging Research, 8*, 73–75.

Bahrick, H. P., & Karis, D. (1982). Long-term ecological memory. In C. R. Puff (Ed.), *Handbook of research methods in human memory and cognition* (pp. 427–465). New York: Academic Press.

Baron, J., & Treiman, R. (1980). Some problems in the study of differences in cognitive processes. *Memory & Cognition, 8*, 313–321.

Bennett-Levy, J., & Powell, G. E. (1980). The subjective memory questionnaire (SMQ): An investigation into the self-reporting of "real-life" memory skills. *British Journal of Social Clinical Psychology, 19*, 177–188.

Bogartz, R. S. (1976). On the meaning of statistical interactions. *Journal of Experimental Child Psychology, 22*, 178–183.

Botwinick, J. (1978). *Aging and behavior*. New York: Springer.

Botwinick, J., & Storandt, M. (1974). *Memory, related functions and age*. Springfield, IL: Charles C Thomas

Brainerd, C. J., & Howe, M. L. (1982). Stages-of-learning analysis of developmental interactions in memory, with illustrations from developmental interactions in picture-word effects. *Developmental Review, 2*, 251–273.

Broadbent, D. E., Cooper, P. F., Fitzgerald, P., & Parkes, K. R. (1982). The cognitive failures questionnaire (CFQ) and its correlates. *British Journal of Clinical Psychology, 21*, 1–16.

Chapman, L. J., & Chapman, J. P. (1973). Problems in the measurement of cognitive deficit. *Psychological Bulletin, 79*, 380–385.

Craik, F. I. M., & Byrd, M. (1982). Aging and cognitive deficits: The role of attentional resources. In F. I. M. Craik & S. Trehub (Eds.), *Aging and cognitive processes* (pp. 171–211). New York: Plenum Press.

Dixon, R. A., & Hultsch, D. F. (1983). Structure and development of metamemory in adulthood. *Journal of Gerontology, 38*, 682–688.

Garner, W. R., Hake, H. W., & Eriksen, C. W. (1956). Operationism and the concept of perception. *Psychological Review, 63*, 144–159.

Garrett, H. E. (1928). The relation of tests of memory and learning to each other and to general intelligence in a highly selected adult group. *Journal of Educational Psychology, 19*, 601–613.

Hall, C. S. (1936). Intercorrelations of measures of human learning. *Psychological Review, 43*, 179–196.

Hartley, J. T., Harker, J. O., & Walsh, D. A. (1980). Contemporary issues and new directions in adult development of learning and memory. In L. W. Poon (Ed.), *Aging in the 1980s* (pp. 239–252). Washington, DC: American Psychological Association.

Hasher, L., & Zacks, R. T. (1979). Automatic and effortful processes in memory *Journal of Experimental Psychology: General, 108*, 356–388.

Herrmann, D. J. (1982). Know thy memory: The use of questionnaires to assess and study memory. *Psychological Bulletin, 92*, 434–452.

Herrmann, D. J., & Neisser, U. (1978). An inventory of everyday memory experiences.

In M. M. Gruneberg, P. E. Morris, & R. N. Sykes (Eds.), *Practical aspects of memory* (pp. 35–51). London: Academic Press.

Hulicka, I. M. (1982). Memory functioning in late adulthood. In F. I. M. Craik & S. Trehub (Eds.), *Aging and cognitive processes* (pp. 331–352). New York: Plenum Press.

Kahn, R. L., Zarit, S. H., Hilbert, N. M., & Niederehe, M. A. (1975). Memory complaint and impairment in the aged: The effect of depression and altered brain function. *Archives of General Psychiatry, 32*, 1569–1573.

Kausler, D. H. (1982). *Experimental psychology and human aging*. New York: John Wiley & Sons.

Kausler, D. H., Lichty, W., & Hakami, M. (1984). Frequency judgments for distractor items in a short-term memory task: Instructional variation and adult age differences. *Journal of Verbal Learning and Verbal Behavior, 23*, 660–668.

Kausler, D. H., & Puckett, J. M. (1980). Frequency judgments and correlated cognitive abilities. *Journal of Gerontology, 35*, 376–382.

Kausler, D. H., Wright, R. E., & Hakami, M. (1981). Variation in task complexity and adult age differences in frequency-of-occurrence judgments. *Bulletin of the Psychonomic Society, 18*, 195–197.

Kelley, H. P. (1964). Memory abilities: A factor analysis. *Psychometric Society Monographs*, No. 11.

Kerlinger, F. N. (1973). *Foundations of behavioral research* (2nd ed.). New York: Holt, Rinehart & Winston.

Kreutzer, M. A., Leonard, C., & Flavell, J. H. (1982). Prospective remembering in children. In U. Neisser (Ed.), *Memory observed: Remembering in natural contexts*. San Francisco: W. H. Freeman.

Lemmon, V. W. (1927). The relation of reaction time to measures of intelligence, memory and learning. *Archives of Psychology* (Whole No. 94).

Loftus, G. R. (1978). On interpretation of interactions. *Memory & Cognition, 6*, 312–319.

Meacham, J. A., & Leiman, B. (1982). Remembering to perform future actions. In U. Neisser (Ed.), *Memory observed: Remembering in natural contexts*. San Francisco: W. H. Freeman.

Melton, A. W. (1936). The methodology of experimental studies of human learning and retention: I. The functions of a methodology and the available criteria for evaluating different experimental methods. *Psychological Bulletin, 33*, 305–394.

Mook, D. G. (1983). In defense of external invalidity. *American Psychologist, 38*, 379–387.

Moscovitch, M. (1982). A neuropsychological approach to perception and cognition in normal and pathological aging. In F. I. M. Craik & S. Trehub (Ed.), *Aging and cognitive processes* (pp. 55–78). New York: Plenum Press.

Puff, C. R. (Ed.). (1982). *Handbook of research methods in human memory and cognition*. New York: Academic Press.

Reitman, J. S. (1974). Without surreptitious rehearsal, information in short-term memory decays. *Journal of Verbal Learning and Verbal Behavior, 13*, 365–377.

Rushton, J. P., Brainerd, C. J., & Pressley, M. (1983). Behavioral development and construct validity: The principle of aggregation. *Psychological Bulletin, 94*, 18–38.

Salthouse, T. A. (1982). *Adult cognition: An experimental psychology of human aging*. New York: Springer-Verlag.

Schaie, K. W., & Zelinski, E. (1979). Psychometric assessment of dysfunction in learning and memory. In F. Hoffmeister & C. Muller (Eds.), *Brain function in old age: Evaluation of changes and disorders* (pp. 134–150). New York: Springer-Verlag.

Schmeck, R. R., Ribich, F., & Ramanaiah, N. (1977). Development of a self-report inventory for assessing individual differences in learning processes. *Applied Psychological Measurement, 1*, 413–431.

Sunderland, A., Harris, J. E., & Baddeley, A. D. (1983). Do laboratory tests predict everyday memory? *Journal of Verbal Learning and Verbal Behavior, 22*, 341–357.

Tulving, E. W. (1972). Episodic and semantic memory. In E. Tulving & W. Donaldson (Eds.), *Organization of memory* (pp. 382–403). New York: Academic Press.

Underwood, B. J. (1972). Are we overloading memory? In A. W. Melton & E. Martin (Eds.), *Coding processes in human memory*, (pp.1–23). New York: John Wiley & Sons.

Underwood, B. J., Boruch, R. F., & Malmi, R. A. (1978). Composition of episodic memory. *Journal of Experimental Psychology: General, 107*, 393–419.

Wilkins, A. J., & Baddeley, A. D. (1978). Remembering to recall in everyday life: An approach to absent-mindedness. In M. M. Gruneberg, P. E. Morris, & R. N. Sykes (Eds.), *Practical aspects of memory* (pp. 27–34). London: Academic Press.

Wilkinson, A. C., & Koestler, R. (1983). Repeated recall: A new model and tests of its generality from childhood to old age. *Journal of Experimental Psychology: General, 112*, 423–451.

Zarit, S. H., Cole, K. D., & Guider, R. L. (1981). Memory training strategies and subjective complaints of memory in the aged. *Gerontologist, 21*, 158–164.

Zelinski, E. M., Gilewski, M. J., & Thompson, L. W. (1980). Do laboratory memory tests relate to everyday remembering and forgetting? In L. W. Poon, J. L. Fozard, L. S. Cermak, D. Arenberg, & L. W. Thompson (Eds.), *New directions in memory and aging* (pp. 519–544). Hillsdale, NJ: Lawrence Erlbaum Associates.

Author Index

Subject Index